**THE SPECIALTY
COFFEE BOOK
NEW SOUTH WALES**

WRITTEN BY
Jonette George

DESIGN
Susan Hardjono

PHOTOGRAPHY
Kaitlyn Wilton
Amanda Davenport

ILLUSTRATION
Alexis Winter

MILK & COFFEE TYPOGRAPHY
Bianca Taylor-Andrews

FOR LOVERS OF FOOD, WINE AND COFFEE

@SMUDGE_EATS SMUDGEEATS.COM.AU

Smudge Culinary Travel Publishers

A heartfelt thank you to the crew at the
Grinders Coffee, KeepCup, Bonsoy and La Marzocco
for their ongoing support of our small family business
and for helping to make this book possible.

Single Origin Roasters | Botany

WELCOME

with Jonette George
Smudge Publishing Editor

How do you like your coffee?

Whatever your choice of bean or brew, we have you covered. Colombian, Indonesian, Ethiopian... Cappuccino, Latte, Macchiato, or Ristretto... Espresso, Stove Top, Cold Drip or AeroPress... or any combination of the above! The more you understand your coffee, the better your cup can be.

Cafes spruiking specialty coffee are springing up all over the place, relying solely on their special brew as their point of difference. We have had a lot of fun, and drunk a lot of coffee, exploring the myriad of NSW cafes to find our favourites, those that truly care about your cup of coffee... And understand the long, hard journey from crop to cup.

Take the journey with us. You may be a specialty coffee aficionado or a relative beginner. Regardless, you can't help but be excited to read the stories about our cafes and their baristas who make the coffee we drink so superb. Your first step might be akin to your first taste of wine or whisky... not at all what you were expecting, with unusual flavour tastes popping throughout your mouth, or leaving an aftertaste that is unfamiliar. You may not like your first taste of a specialty coffee, especially after years of drinking bland instant coffee, coffee roasted months ago, or coffee that has had the life roasted out of it.

Be patient and give your taste buds a go. Find a local roaster who holds coffee cupping sessions – get to know your coffee like you know your wine. Understand that, like wine, there are variations that can suit different times of the day and different occasions. And there is no right or wrong, your preferred flavour is what matters. And this will change over time as you discover new and exciting origins, ways of brewing, the addition of milk and sugar, or not, and adventurous baristas who are willing to experiment a bit.

Let the journey begin!

This book gives you our selection of the most amazing coffee in the CBD, urban and regional cafes. The common thread is the quality of their coffee – the quality of the beans, where they were grown, the roasting and the extraction technique. They all come together to produce a symphony of flavours that will satisfy your daily caffeine fix as well as your adventurous spirit that is searching for new tastes.

Walk the journey with us, we have certainly enjoyed it. We have travelled far and wide to discover the origin of coffee from the discovery of the first little bean to its journey across land and sea to Australia. We have looked at the different methods of producing a cup of coffee, and the cafes who are producing the best.

Read our stories and get to know your local barista. Don't be intimidated if she is a nerdy-looking coffee geek, or if he is a beard-trotting punk... Behind the machine is someone full of wonderful experiences and who can offer stories about origins, methods of brewing, different beans to try, and all sorts of information about coffee. Their story might well be in this book – otherwise it is just one question away.

The passion that goes into producing one little cup is enormous. That passion, for some, becomes an addiction. For others, a religion with secret rituals and ingredients. For you, let your passion take you to whatever heights you wish.

Simply – enjoy the passion of coffee.

```
                    GOOD EDDY

COFFEE              TEA                 SHAKES
MILK       4/4.5    BREAKFAST      4    ESPRESSO      5.5
BLACK      3.5      SPRING TONIC   4    BERRY         5.5
FILTER - FROM 3.5   RANCHO RELAXO  4    CHOC          5.5
EXTRAS     .5       BILO CHUN      4    LOLLI REDINI  5.5
HOUSE BLEND - SEVEN SEEDS                SALTED CARAMEL
GUEST ROASTER - SMALL BATCH

TAKE A BAG HOME !  250 G  14             PHONE ORDER
                   1KG    52             02 63 617379

THANKS
SEVEN SEEDS, REUBEN HILLS, LITTLE BIG DAIRY,
MÖRK CHOCOLATE, STORM IN A TEA CUP, THE ØLD CONVENT
```

Good Eddy | Orange

CONTENTS

Welcome by Jonette George	7
What is Specialty Coffee? by Jonette George	11
Coffee From Crop to Cup	12
Coffee Taster Wheel	16
One of Life's Greatest Pleasures – Coffee by Al Ramsay, co-founder of Beanhunter.com	18
History of Coffee Giancarlo Gusti of Giancarlo Coffee reflects on the history of espresso in Australia	20
The Future of Coffee with Shae Macnamara, National Brand Ambassador, Grinders Coffee	22
Talk the Talk	28
How Do You Like Your Espresso?	32
Who Drinks What?	34
Pursuing the Perfect Coffee with Saxon Wright of Pablo & Rusty's Coffee Roasters	36
Getting to Know La Marzocco with Piero Bambi, Honorary President of La Marzocco	41
The World of Coffee with Kent Bakke, CEO of La Marzocco	42
Where Does Coffee Come From?	46
Single Origin Single Country with Cesar Vela CEO of Colombian Connection	48
A Barista's Perspective with Sasa Sestic, World Barista Champion 2015	52
Making the Perfect Espresso by Shae MacNamara, Head Barista Trainer, Grinders Coffee	54
Air Roasting: Roasting the Perfect Bean with Dan Fitzsimmons of Chinook Coffee Roasting Systems	56
Pulling the Strings with Ed Cutcliffe of The Little Marionette	60
Setting Up A Micro Roastery with Marcio Brito of Salvador Coffee, Est. 2010	65
Home Grown Coffee Machine with Craig Hiron, founder of The Little Guy	68
Going Against The Grind with Rob Stewart & Lachie Cairns of DC Specialty Coffee	70
Keeping Coffee Sustainable with Abigail Forsyth, KeepCup CEO	74
The Milk Connection with Bonsoy	76
The Perfect Soy Latte	79
Prana Chai: Give it a Try	80
A Little Latte Art with Jibbi Little, NSW Latte Art Champion	83
Adding Some Flavour with DaVinci Gourmet	84
Methods to Make Coffee	87
AeroPress	88
Chemex	91
Cold Drip	92
Espresso	95
French Press	96
The Little Guy	99
Stovetop	100
Syphon	
V60 Pour Over	104
Australian Specialty Coffee Association by Brent Williams, President of ASCA	106
Venue Categories	108
Sydney CBD	110
North of the City	158
East of the City	244
South & West of the City	326
Regional NSW	414
The Origins of Coffee	459
Ethiopia with Ona Coffee	461
Panama with Toby's Estate	471
Sulawesi with Campos Coffee	479

WHAT IS SPECIALTY COFFEE?

by Jonette George
Smudge Publishing Editor

WE HAVE A VERY ACTIVE ORGANISATION DEDICATED TO PROMOTING AND PROVIDING PROFESSIONAL TRAINING FOR THE DEVELOPMENT OF SPECIALTY COFFEE THROUGHOUT AUSTRALIA, THE AUSTRALIAN SPECIALTY COFFEE ASSOCIATION.

This support has seen our coffee industry go ahead in leaps and bounds, to the point where we can say we are leading the world in specialty coffee. Our Australian representative, Sasa Sestic, has just placed first in the 2015 World Barista Championships, showcasing how far we have progressed in our understanding of what makes quality coffee here in Australia.

Sasa is not only an amazing barista, or a green bean hunter sourcing coffee from overseas, he works hand-in-hand with the farmers to improve the quality of their beans. As a result of one such project, he was able to showcase a Panama coffee to the judges and score extremely highly on the resulting taste.

His presentation displayed a profound interest in the complete process of coffee, from bean to cup. He went above and beyond the typical presentation that captures the part played by baristas in front of the machine. He told a story that was heart felt and full of passion for the farmers that work with him to produce the best of specialty coffee.

What is specialty coffee?

Technically, specialty is a grade given to a bean that is scored by qualified Q-graders at over 80 when cupped. This is a very technical way of testing using specific criteria to try to provide an even playing field, no matter where you are in the world. But this is a very static way of judging coffee and is only one very small part of the coffee process.

It is a great indicator of the quality of the bean, but after this testing, so many things can affect the flavour by the time it arrives in your cup.

Firstly, cupping has a prerequisite set of parameters to compare all beans – but the obvious anomaly for us in Australia, is that the testing is done by pouring hot water directly onto the measured grounds. Given most Australians prefer espresso coffee, you could question whether this is the ideal method of testing for espresso? Perhaps we could say that specialty coffee should only be served using a French Press or an AeroPress – so that the brewing process has the time to capture all the flavours and aromas that the bean can produce.

But we have to start somewhere.

The transport method could affect the taste of the final coffee. If it is not stored well while being shipped to Australia, the beans could become mouldy, dry or even old by the time they come out of the container.

Roasters are then required to ensure the best storing methods for their beans, and make sure they are roasted within the perfect time frame to capture their full flavour before they are too old. And then, the roaster can make or break the flavour of the bean, depending on how he roasts it. Over and under roasting can affect the end result, which may or may not be enjoyed by the end consumer, depending on their taste likes and dislikes.

And then it comes down to the training of the barista. You can go into the same cafe and find different baristas on different days. The taste in your cup can differ dramatically depending on the experience and care given by each individual. Inconsistent care can affect your coffee that may have been "specialty" at some stage – but now just tastes awful.

These variations can affect your experience with what is considered "specialty coffee" – which may have started out great coffee, and scoring over 80% but end up, through no fault of its own, unpleasant.

This is why it is important that every step along the way is given the due diligence required to maintain the bean through its journey. Roasters and baristas are very important in the end result so that the specialty coffee that we drink is still special.

Brighton The Corner | Petersham

Before you are swept up into the morning rush, before your senses are reignited with the burr of the coffee grinder and the whirring sounds of steaming milk, before that first sip of your daily ritual, the humble coffee bean has been on an incredible journey...

PLANTING

A coffee bean, before it is dried, roasted and ground, is actually a seed and can be planted to grow into a coffee tree. The seeds are usually planted in large beds in shaded nurseries. After they have sprouted, the seedlings are taken out of their beds and planted in individual pots. The plants are shaded and watered frequently until they are strong enough to be permanently planted.

Planting will often take place during the wet season, so that the soil around the young trees remains soft while the roots establish themselves.

HARVESTING THE CHERRIES

Once planted, it will take approximately three to four years, depending on the variety of the coffee tree, to start bearing fruit. The fruit or 'cherry' is ripe and ready to be harvested when its colour is a bright, deep red. Because the coffee plant grows in countries of high altitudes and mountainous terrain, most coffee crops are picked by hand.

Once the cherries are at their peak ripeness, pickers will rotate through the crop hand selecting the cherries. The harvest from the coffee farm is then transported to a processing plant.

PROCESSING THE CHERRIES

Once the coffee has been picked, processing begins straight away to avoid wastage. Coffee, depending on its location, is processed in one of two ways.

WET PROCESS

In the wet process, the pulp is removed from the coffee cherry after harvesting by passing them through a pulping machine where the skin and pulp is separated from the bean. The pulp is washed away with water. The beans are then separated by weight and size. Once separated, they are put into water-filled fermentation tanks to remove a thin gooey layer known as the mucilage. The fermentation dissolves this layer. The beans are then rinsed and ready for drying on the drying beds or floors. Machines are then used to remove the parchment layer (outer crust) from the wet processed coffee.

DRY OR NATURAL PROCESS

This is the original method of processing coffee and is favoured in countries where water is limited. The cherries are spread out on raised drying beds or concrete surfaces and allowed to dry in the sun. During the day they are raked and turned. Once the moisture content of the cherries drops to 11%, the dried cherries are then stored in a warehouse.

GRADING AND SORTING

Before being exported, the coffee beans are sorted by size and weight. Beans are looked at for colour flaws or other imperfections and the defective beans are then removed.

EXPORTING THE BEANS

The 'green beans' are packed into large bags or containers, trucked to a shipping dock, and loaded into shipping containers for transport.

ROASTING THE COFFEE

The coffee is then roasted at roasting warehouses or increasingly today in-store at many cafes. The roasting process brings out the aromas and flavours of the coffee. The green beans are put inside the roaster and roasted depending on the flavour profile desired. The beans are kept moving throughout the entire process to keep them from burning.

Once they begin to turn brown and reach a certain temperature, the oil inside the beans begin to emerge. This is where the flavour and aromas come from. The beans are then dropped from the roaster into a cooler where they are kept moving and agitated so they cool evenly.

PACKAGING

Coffee is then packaged and sent to your local cafe. All before you are swept up into the morning rush madness, all before the satisfactory clunk as your coffee hits the table. Before that first drop touches your lips, the humble coffee bean has had many hands helping it along the way, long before it reaches your cup.

GRINDING THE BEANS

Coffee grinders crush the roasted beans into smaller particles. The size of the particles will determine how long hot water will be in contact with the coffee grinds, which will affect the overall end flavour. Therefore finding the right size grind for your brewing method is critical to producing the perfect cup of coffee. Espresso uses pressure to force water through the coffee and needs to be ground very finely so the fast moving water captures all of the flavours. A Pour Over brewing method, on the other hand, is ground more coarsely so the water is in contact for a shorter amount of time.

Next time you take a sip, consider the work from crop to cup. Here's to the pickers, the farmers, the roasters and the baristas!

COFFEE TASTER FLAVOURS WHEEL

This wheel will help you understand the different flavour and body profiles that you might find in a cup of coffee. You will note that there are a lot more than those found in wine!

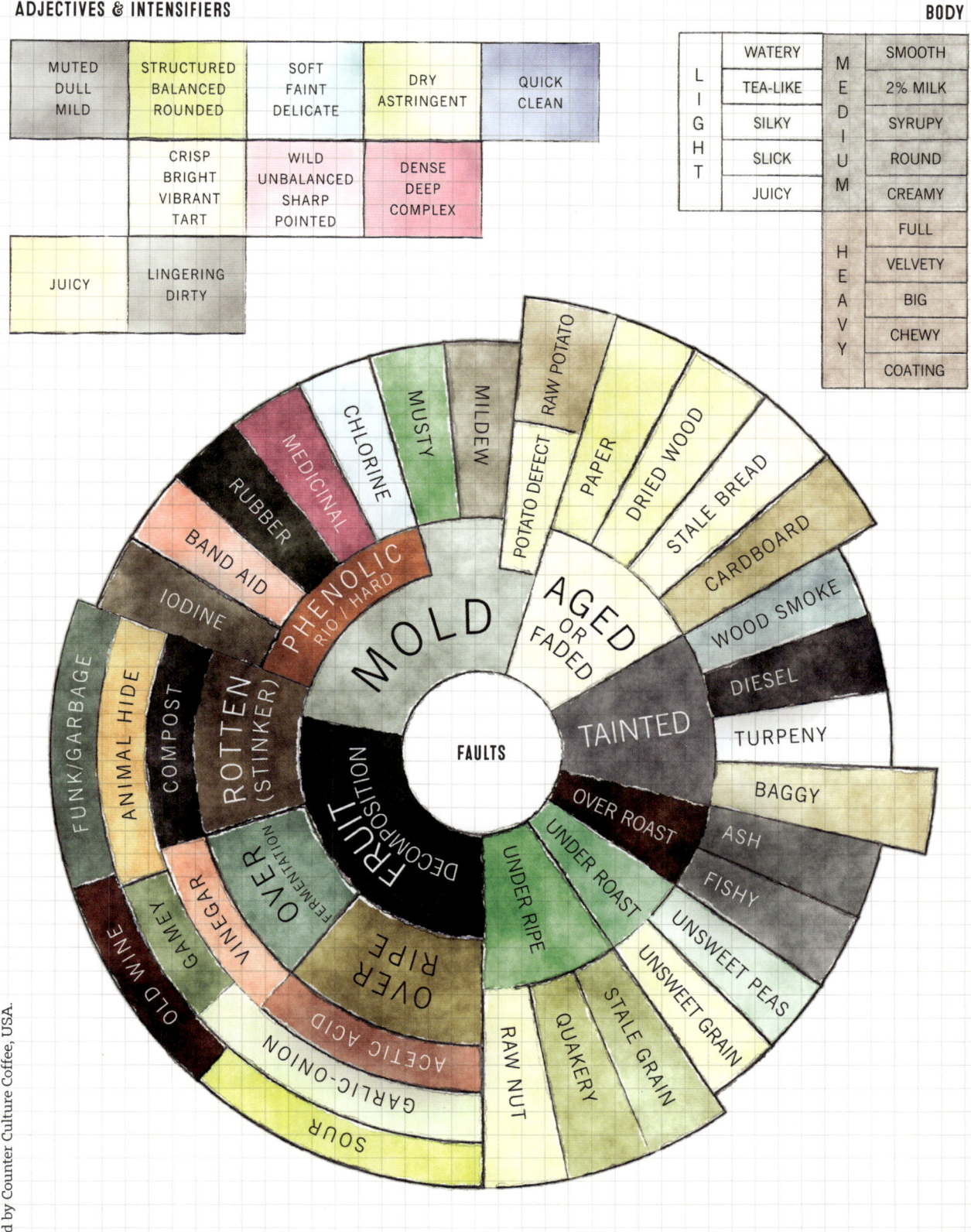

ONE OF LIFE'S GREATEST PLEASURES – COFFEE

with Al Ramsay, co-founder of Beanhunter.com

There is something really special when you sit down in a cafe and taste a well-made coffee, whether that be an espresso, flat white or a pour-over. It can turn a bad day into one filled with optimism and renewed energy. It's a drink that has a following and passionate subculture unlike any other on earth. Finding great coffee is what inspired us to create Beanhunter and we have been very fortunate that our passion is also shared by millions of people around the world.

It all started back in 2008 when I was in London on a work trip. Growing up in Melbourne, my friends and I were spoilt for choice when it came to good coffee. The standards here are pretty high, (some say the best in the world) and you can usually find a good coffee close by. However when travelling to other countries or even other suburbs you are unfamiliar with, it becomes clear very quickly that good coffee is not so easy to find. I had my fair share of average coffee travelling the world, in hotels or mass chain coffee shops. So out of frustration I began to search Google each night trying to find the best place to get a morning coffee. There were some random blogs that pointed me in the right direction and soon enough I had found some world class coffee in most of the cities in my travels. The only issue was this information was not easily accessible in one place and required a lot of searching the web. So on my return home I talked with friends and co-founders, James and Adam, who shared the same love of coffee and we decided to build what is today now known as Beanhunter.

The idea was to have a place where coffee lovers from all over the world could go to find and share great coffee. It became clear pretty quickly that we weren't the only ones wanting to find and share our coffee experiences, and the Beanhunter community quickly grew. Now millions of people can find amazing cafes all over the world due to recommendations from other Beanhunter users. It's a pretty amazing resource to have in your pocket. As founders, myself, James and Adam are active members in the Beanhunter community and add cafes and reviews of amazing places in our travels. It's really cool being in a foreign area, pulling out the Beanhunter app, and finding a new place nearby that serves amazing coffee!

> 'The more you know about this amazing bean, the more you realise you don't actually know.'

It's funny though because of all the great cafes around the world, there's something special about being back in Melbourne and heading to a local regular cafe. I think it's the feeling of community and having a personal relationship with a cafe and it's owners. When you walk into a cafe that knows you by name and starts making your exact coffee preference before you even get to the counter – it feels pretty special. Melbourne and coffee are part of each other. When I think of Melbourne I think of great little cafes bustling with people and pumping out coffee, you can even smell coffee in the air.

Melbourne is a city where the a passion for coffee borders on obsessive. There is a specialty coffee shop in just about every suburb, and then you have suburbs like Collingwood where you're never more than a few hundred metres from

a decent coffee. So we are very lucky in Melbourne. Cafe owners take a lot of pride in their coffee here and it seems that all the competition has only increased the passion, and business owners have just raised the bar higher and higher.

This passion has been passed directly onto the customer who has become very knowledgeable about coffee and probably some of the fussiest coffee drinkers in the world!

So what actually makes a great tasting cup of coffee?

Well there are a lot of elements that go into making our morning 'cup of joe' delicious, but I think having clean coffee equipment is up there with the most important. Dirty coffee machines with old burnt beans on the group head and burnt milk inside the steamer generally produce pretty average coffee.

Because coffee is so complex you really need to get every element correct to bring out the best flavours. Once equipment is clean, then you also need beans roasted correctly and at their prime post-roast date, ideal grind coarseness for the bean, correct water temperature and pressure, correct dosage of ground beans into portafilter, correct tamping pressure and level. The list just goes on and on and that's just for a basic espresso.

They say coffee has more flavour profiles than wine and is more complex. I used to think this was rubbish but after tasting some absolutely amazing coffees with so many amazing flavours punching through from blueberries to chocolate and everything in between, I would have to say this is true.

There has been many a day when I have felt stressed about a big day ahead, have grabbed a strong Flat White (my morning coffee choice) and then everything feels like it will be ok again. It's been an amazing journey learning about the complexities of coffee and meeting some amazing people, be it either talented baristas or passionate coffee enthusiasts.

One thing I have learnt is the more you know about this amazing bean, the more you realise you don't actually know. I think that is the part that makes coffee so exciting. People are still learning different ways to roast and brew beans all the time, to bring out the best flavours in coffee. I guess it's why so many people are so passionate about this humble bean and why the 'specialty coffee' industry is still growing stronger each year.

Melbourne has become a world leader and the evidence is in the cup at so many amazing cafes dotted around this city. There are thousands of independent cafes listed on Beanhunter in Melbourne and there are more opening all the time. As a coffee drinker I feel extremely lucky to have grown up in this city! So have a read through the following pages highlighting some of Melbourne's coffee treasures, download the free Beanhunter app (beanhunter.com/get) and then go out there and explore them for yourself. Enjoy! Coffee soon?

PS: Special thank you goes out to co-founders and friends James Crawford and Adam Lowe, and the rest of the Beanhunter team, Jesse Collis and Pete Hare, who all worked tirelessly on Beanhunter to ensure people from all over the world can find and share great coffee.

HISTORY OF COFFEE

Giancarlo Giusti of Giancarlo Coffee reflects on the history of espresso in Australia

When Grinders' founder, Giancarlo Giusti, first arrived in Australia in 1960, he was excited to discover a lively European community flourishing in both Sydney and Melbourne. There were Europeans relishing that they could find a cafe culture similar to what they had left back home, as well as Australian residents keen to experience what they embraced as exotic.

Giancarlo said Lygon Street in Melbourne and Norton Street in Leichhardt were like walking into an Italian village, with coffee, pasta, salumi and vino all accompanied by good cheer and a welcoming ambience. He said he had arrived in a country that was thirsty for all things European, and he knew he was in a great position to develop that.

He found that the coffee being served was roasted back home and then shipped to Australia, losing its flavour qualities on the way. Together with his business partner and friend, Rino Benassis, he decided to start fresh roasting beans like they did back home.

He knew this would provide a much better cup of coffee than was available at the time, so after buying a large, red grinder for one pound, he started roasting, grinding and selling coffee beans from the back of what became the Grinders Coffee House in Lygon Street, Melbourne. By 1969 he was supplying coffee to other cafes throughout the city.

As they say, the rest is history. Giancarlo has been able to watch the coffee story develop in Australia from the day he arrived. And, true to his roots, the original roaster has been refurbished, ready to start roasting again from Lygon Street.

Finding themselves in the heart of Sydney's Little Italy was no accident. Norton Street, Leichhardt was chosen as Grinders' Sydney operating headquarters. With an extraordinary number of passionate bean hunters, roasters and baristas in Sydney and throughout NSW, Grinders set up a warehouse able to train their many clients.

Giancarlo said that looking back, the coffee bean has had an interesting journey to Australia, and it has its own unique story to tell. When the First Fleet set out for Australia in 1787, it stopped at Rio de Janeiro to replenish supplies. Amongst seeds for cocoa, bananas, figs, quinces and strawberries, they also brought coffee to the shores of Australia.

The first recorded growth of coffee, however, seems to be in 1832 at Brisbane's riverside suburb of Kangaroo Point. By the late 1880s, a vibrant coffee-growing industry had spread along the east coast of Australia, from northern NSW to the tablelands of northern Queensland.

So good was the coffee, it won awards in Paris and Rome, and it was being exported to Europe. Unfortunately by the 1920s, labour and freight costs had become prohibitive and the country's coffee production took a nose dive.

During the 1830s coffee houses, or 'Palaces,' started to take the place of hotels, with a Temperance Movement that encouraged the replacement of lagers and pints for the sober option – coffee. When the Depression hit in the 1890s, many of the coffee houses closed or had to apply for liquor licenses to keep their business alive.

Making improvements on steam driven coffee-making devices, the first patented espresso machine was created by Luigi Bezera in Italy in 1901. During the early part of the century, these machines made their way to Australia and could primarily be found in Italian grocery stores.

> 'Grinders set up their Sydney headquarters near where Bar Italia opened in Leichhardt in 1952, keeping Sydney's history at the core of the business...'

Street coffee stalls could also be found from the 1850s to the 1920s. Strewn across Melbourne's CBD street corners, these small stalls provided cheap snacks throughout the day for the city's working class.

During the Second World War, over a million American servicemen were stationed in Australia, and their 'sophisticated' way of life had a huge influence over the nation which traditionally drank tea. Being huge coffee drinkers, the Americans introduced new ways to enjoy coffee, and during their stay, the consumption of coffee in Australia doubled.

In 1947 the first lever machine was produced by an Italian firm called Gaggia. This system dramatically modified the way coffee was extracted by using a spring activating piston which pressurised water through the coffee, making the most of the flavour of the roasted beans. This transformed the taste of coffee and produced 'crema' which became the standard by which a quality cup is still judged.

After World War II, Australia saw a great influx of Italian migrants who had an infectious, cultural influence that would forever lay the groundwork for our coffee culture. Large pockets of European migrants populated the inner city suburbs of both Sydney and, despite luggage restrictions, they brought bucket loads of their culture, their recipes, and ultimately their way of making coffee.

It was during the 1950s that the older style tea-rooms and tea houses were converted into coffee lounges and the love of espresso-enthusiasts and coffee culture flourished and spread throughout the city.

The first espresso machine to be imported to Sydney was installed in 1952 in the Andronicus brothers' café on George Street. The coffee house was so poplar hundreds of people would enjoy an espresso at lunch-time, standing up at the counter Italian style. The cafe became the benchmark for coffee houses to come.

Other landmark Sydney coffee houses include Bar Italia which opened in Norton Street, Leichhardt in 1952, and Darlinghurst's Bar Caluzzi , set up in 1957. These cafes introduced espresso style coffee to Sydney, winning the hearts of the locals.

During the 1980s, cafes targeted a younger audience with as much focus and detail spent on the décor and music, as was on the coffee and food. When the previously industrial-laden inner-city businesses started moving to cheaper outer suburbs after the 1990's recession, the hospitality industry was given incentive to thrive and propagate through Sydney's inner city.

Grinders Stand at MICE 2015, mural by Elmz Street

THE FUTURE OF COFFEE

by Shae Macnamara,
National Brand Ambassador, Grinders Coffee

With over 53 years of experience roasting coffee in Australia, Grinders Coffee doesn't have to reinvent the wheel. Relying on the experiences of a young Italian immigrant, Giancarlo Giusti, who came to Australia in 1960, Grinders today retains a wealth of experience in coffee roasting and the industry's changing trends. Giancarlo's company was one of the first coffee roasters in Australia and effectively started the espresso culture in Melbourne.

Giancarlo understood that roasted coffee that was imported from Italy was beyond its use-by date by the time it reached our shores, losing most of its flavor and taste, so he started importing green beans and roasting on a Probat roaster that is still in operation in Lygon Street today. In fact, if you visit the Carlton store, you may even find Giancarlo mixing it up with the customers and staff, making sure standards are being maintained.

Giancarlo has inspired three generations of coffee lovers, commencing with fellow Italians who had moved to a new land to make a new life, but didn't want to compromise on cultural habits like their beloved espresso coffee. This in turn influenced my grandparents' generation and taught them a new way to enjoy their morning cuppa.

My parents were brought up being treated to simple sandwiches at "the local milk bar" where they would enjoy the community spirit and novelty when an espresso was served. They also explored alternative methods to brew coffee at home, like French press and others that are making resurgence today alongside retro and industrial-style cafes.

Giancarlo has been roasting coffee all this time, and Grinders has benefited from his understanding of the shifts in consumer requirements over all these years. He must have been doing something right to have been so successful for so many years, and now Grinders is reaping the benefits.

I joined Grinders in 2012 to train our clients and their baristas with the goal of guaranteeing quality, flavour and consistency with our beans. We go to so much trouble sourcing, roasting and delivering our product, we want to make sure that our clients treat the beans with respect and provide the best customer experience possible.

Our beans have won many awards over the years, the most recent at the Sydney Royal Fine Food Show – Coffee Competition where we our Single Origin Ethiopian Yirgacheffe was voted Overall Champion Espresso. It also won a bronze in the Plunger category. On top of that, our Grinders Coffee Rich Espresso won a Silver in the Espresso category, and we won four further Bronze Awards in the Plunger, Decaffeinated and Cappuccino categories.

Recently, Grinders sent me to Costa Rica and the trip confirmed all my expectations about the coffee journey. It gave me a greater appreciation of how much work goes into getting high quality beans into Australia. Grinders is investing in me and my training, so in turn I can train in-house and educate our team so they are armed with the knowledge to pass onto our clients. We aim to keep educating our clients so they can deliver the best possible experience to their customers.

> "We have invested in the past, and now we are investing in the future."

We have invested in the past, and now we are investing in the future.

'What is the future of coffee going to be?' This is a question that I am asked a lot. At Grinders, we are constantly looking at and reevaluating every step of the process and making sure we are flexible enough to move with the industry whichever way it goes. We also understand that small changes can make huge differences, and we are determined to keep improving our coffee, the way we make it and the experience for the customer.

I believe in the future we will need to embrace science, respect the past and control every step of the coffee journey from the farm to the cup. The science behind coffee is helping to improve all aspects. Scientists, technicians and engineers are playing more of an important role in the industry every day. People like Vince Fedele who helped create things such as the mp3 player and finger print scanning technology during his working life, before he became totally engrossed in coffee and started his business VST.

Vince worked out that the output of coffee from coffee filter baskets was inconsistent due to the hole sizes and positions, so he produced a laser cut filter basket with precision and optimal placement of the holes to ensure an even flow, resulting in the maximum extraction and flavour.

Grinders has implemented these baskets and made them the standard for all our clients' cafes to make sure that this small piece of the process is ensuring the best quality in the output.

We are also constantly experimenting with the weight of coffee that goes into the basket and the weight of liquid that comes out through the extraction to improve outputs. We use Refractometers in all states to study TDS (total dissolved solids) and extraction yields to maximize the amount of flavor that is being produced in each cup for each blend of coffee.

And when it comes to coffee machines, we partner with Rancilio. One of the biggest variables in machinery is the temperature of the water. We have looked at water temperatures before but now Rancilio, a company that says it is dedicated to innovation, has released its newest technological innovation, the Rancilio xcelsius. This is the only machine in the market that can change the temperature of the water throughout the extraction.

This allows us to enhance the acidity and taper off the bitterness by starting at higher temperatures and taking it lower or you can enhance the bitterness and lower the acidity by starting low and raising it throughout the shot. You can also keep a flat temperature and adjust between settings with an easy touchscreen adjustment. This allows you to run multiple blends in your venue and have dedicated group heads for each of them.

So for the future we are committed to technology, innovation and science. We will continue building relationships with producers and co-ops as well as continually training our staff and customers to ensure quality from the start to the finish. But saying that, we will always respect our past, our history and our experience in the coffee industry.

TALK THE TALK

ARABICA	The most widely grown variety of coffee. Approximately 75% of the global harvest is Arabica.
BIRD FRIENDLY OR SHADE-GROWN	A designation for coffee that is grown amongst native plants and trees, as opposed to being grown on a plantation of cleared land.
BLOOM	The foam found on top of brewed coffee, formed by escaping carbon dioxide and coffee oils, is known as bloom. Bloom is only found when using freshly roasted coffee.
CERTIFIED ORGANIC	A designation for coffee grown in a 'natural' fashion, with regard to the fertilisers, insect repellents, plant treatments and water used. It should be noted that just because a coffee is not 'certified organic' does not automatically mean that it's not organic. Most coffee from Africa and South America is grown without expensive industrial chemical inputs – just not certified so.
CHERRY	The fruit of the coffee tree, from which the seed or bean is harvested. It is red and looks like the fruit, cherry.

CREMA	The defining characteristic of espresso. A foam created by carbon dioxide contained in emulsified oils, forced out of the bean during extraction. This is part of the anatomy of espresso, and is the sweetest, most flavoursome part of the experience.
DEMITASSE	A French word meaning 'half cup'. A measure of 90ml or 3 oz used for Espresso and Macchiato.
DOPPIO	Italian for 'double'. Two servings of espresso in one cup.
DRIP COFFEE	A brewing method whereby ground coffee is contained in a coffee filter inside a filter basket while hot water is trickled on top of the ground coffee. Gravity pulls the brewed coffee through the filter, and into a carafe.
FAIR TRADE	A concept originated by the American organisation Transfair to pay coffee farmers a fair price for their product in order to support them and enable them to keep doing what they do best. More complex in practice than it sounds in theory due to the bureaucracy and certification involved.
LATTE ART	Patterns and shapes presented on the surface of servings of latte, macchiato, cappuccino etc.
ROBUSTA	A variety of coffee bean that contains on average 4 times as much caffeine as Arabica. Approximately 20% of the global harvest is Robusta.
SUSTAINABLE HARVEST INTERNATIONAL	An organisation which aims to create economically, environmentally and socially sustainable markets for coffee.
VACUUM BREWER	A device used to brew coffee, comprised of various chambers, filters and tubes. Water is heated in the lower part of the machine and then pressured up through a tube into the upper part which contains the ground coffee. When the coffee has brewed long enough, the heat is turned off, allowing the system to cool and depressurise, which then causes the brewed liquid to return to the lower chamber which doubles as a serving carafe.

Suspension Espresso | Islington

ESPRESSO

Also commonly called a 'short black.' The name comes from the process of expressing the coffee extract from the bean. A single shot of pure coffee. For two shots, ask for a double shot espresso or a 'Doppio.'

30ML OF ESPRESSO

DOPPIO

Meaning 'double' in Italian, doppio refers to a double shot of espresso.

60ML OF ESPRESSO

HOW DO YOU LIKE

RISTRETTO

Italian for 'restricted' or 'shortened.' A rich and concentrated espresso drink using less water but the same amount of coffee, making it less bitter than a standard espresso.

20ML OF ESPRESSO

LONG BLACK

Also known as an 'Americano.' One and a half shots of coffee blended with steamed water.

30ML OF ESPRESSO
+ HALF CUP OF HOT WATER

SHORT MACCHIATO

An Italian word meaning 'marked' or 'stained.' A single shot of espresso is stained with just enough steamed milk to change the colour of the coffee.

SINGLE SHOT OF ESPRESSO
STAINED WITH A DASH
OF STEAMED MILK

LONG MACCHIATO

An Italian word meaning 'marked' or 'stained.' A double shot of espresso is stained with just enough steamed milk to change the colour of the coffee.

DOUBLE SHOT OF ESPRESSO
STAINED WITH A DASH
OF STEAMED MILK

PICCOLO

This is a single espresso shot in a macchiato glass that is then filled with a small amount of steamed milk in the same fashion as a latte.

90ML GLASS WITH 30ML OF ESPRESSO
+ STEAMED MILK TOPPED WITH FOAM

LATTE

A little bit of espresso and a lot of milk, with a thin cap of foam. Ideally served in a glass.

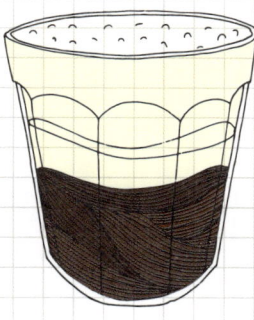

30ML OF ESPRESSO
+ STEAMED MILK TOPPED WITH FOAM

FLAT WHITE

An espresso with steamed milk. Similar to a cappuccino, but with smaller proportions of foam.

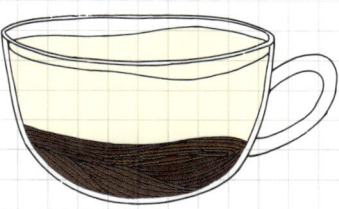

30ML OF ESPRESSO
+ STEAMED MILK

CAPPUCCINO

The world's most popular retail coffee. Steamed and foamed milk over a shot of espresso, topped with foam. Usually topped with chocolate powder.

30ML OF ESPRESSO
+ STEAMED MILK TOPPED WITH FOAM
+ DUST WITH COCOA POWDER

YOUR ESPRESSO?

MOCHA

Named after the port of Mocha. Made with chocolate, espresso, steamed or frothed milk, and topped with whipped cream.

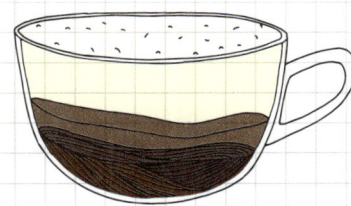

30ML OF ESPRESSO
+ DRINKING CHOCOLATE
+ STEAMED MILK
+ TOPPED WITH FOAM
+ DUST WITH COCOA POWDER

AFFOGATO

Italian for 'drowned.' A shot of espresso poured over the top of a scoop of vanilla ice cream or gelato. A dessert favourite.

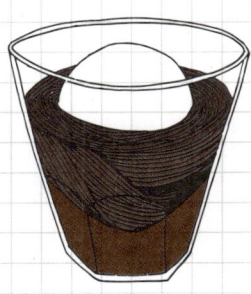

30ML OF ESPRESSO OVER
A SCOOP OF VANILLA ICECREAM

WHO DRINKS WHAT?

In a report that found Australians are consuming 10.8 billion coffees annually, the following caffeinated conclusions have been polled from 1,043 Australian coffee consumers with some interesting statistics to digest

- CAPPUCINO 33%
- LATTE 32%
- FLAT WHITE 23%
- LONG BLACK 6%
- MACHIATO 2%
- RISTRETTO 2%
- OTHER 2%

Brewtown Newtown | Newtown

Panama, Finca Buenos Aires +2000m

PURSUING THE PERFECT COFFEE

with Saxon Wright of Pablo & Rusty's Coffee Roasters

My coffee journey began while I was studying chemistry at university and working in production at a roastery part time. I would observe the roasters work and think about the chemical components of the process. When I'd ask "Why are you doing this or that?" the response would be something to the effect of, "because this is how it's always been done". It was an era when only a few were seeking to understand, and my curiosity was struck right there. Later I began to roast experimentally, studying how processing, transport and other aspects of the chain affected the green product and I immediately saw gaps in the industry. I could see with innovation and research the delivered product could be brought much closer to the farmer's original vision for their green beans.

This curiosity and thirst for knowledge further developed to tasting and judging at the World Barista Championships every year from 2009 and becoming an SCAA Instructor and Examiner. Over the years, I've been fortunate to taste some of the best coffees in the world. There is no doubt that every transition including harvesting, processing, roasting and brewing are critical in determining the best coffee results in a cup.

Coffee is a fascinating product – it changes constantly. From cherry to green (raw); from green to roasted; from dry to brewed; everything involved, as coffee changes its form, is a process of chemistry. As an industry, we are only recently embarking on a more scientific approach. At Pablo & Rusty's, we consider this to be our key strength. This flows into our sourcing, roasting and brew education. Who we are and what we do bridges the gap between these three key stages. Our ongoing research in these areas works together to provide the best possible coffee experience.

Our approach when sourcing is to find beans that are super sweet, clean and expressive. We prefer vibrant coffees that expose the full array of flavour possible in different growing regions. We work directly with farms on harvesting and drying techniques, to enhance both cup quality and longevity. Our direct sourcing model continues to expand with regular visits to farms, ensuring we're buying the best coffees and engaging with development and experiments at a farm level.

In the roasting space, we are taking our research to a new level working with organic chemistry professors at Sydney University studying changes to beans at the atomic level during processing and roasting. The project is covering a range of experiments including: molecular changes from specific heat application throughout the roast; analysis of enzyme and bean acid production from experimental and standard processing methods; and chemical changes of raw coffee in variable storage conditions. Greater understanding not only improves quality, control and consistency but also exposes new flavours and characteristics hidden in what is a highly complex and fragile structure.

'Greater understanding not only improves quality, control and consistency but also exposes new flavours'

Education is key to unlocking knowledge so baristas and cafe owners can transfer value gains at the last point of the supply chain. We are seeing a deeper level of knowledge slowly infiltrating the industry and a higher emphasis on learning challenging the status quo. However, these are early days and adoption of new techniques, technologies and products is still slow. Pursuing concepts that will make significant improvements to the quality of coffee, from one end of the supply chain to the other, will ensure end consumers experience coffee at its best.

The industry is evolving at a rapid rate with the curious leading the way. This expanding knowledge base is opening up new opportunities to develop coffee, making it more sustainable and more delicious. Technology is also having a significant effect with new roast control and management software improving roast consistency. Advanced machinery such as the new Black Eagle Gravimetric, using weight to measure shots, and even the humble tamp is getting a makeover with precision fitting and sharp edges. We are also seeing better green coffee land on our shores than ever before, with major advances in picking, processing and storage techniques moving beyond experimental volumes into larger lots.

Whilst NSW may have had a relatively short history of coffee and cafe culture, we are rapidly making up for it with a forward thinking approach. Capitalising on new technologies and scientific research and applying innovation to our processes, NSW is producing coffees at an exceptional standard.

I think we are aware that there is more to the coffee landscape. We have seen a sharp increase in the value people place on design, with stunning interiors and environments that create desirable social spaces. Combined with knowledgeable and passionate service staff to complete the transaction, successful cafes are excelling in all areas. In this regard, we are moving on from the product that is Specialty Coffee, to a concept we're calling Super-Specialty. Encompassing all this and more, we're taking the very best coffees from around the world and turning them into a powerful and memorable experience.

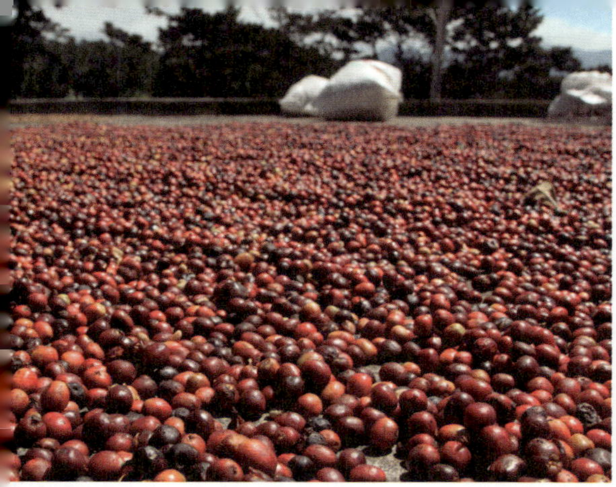

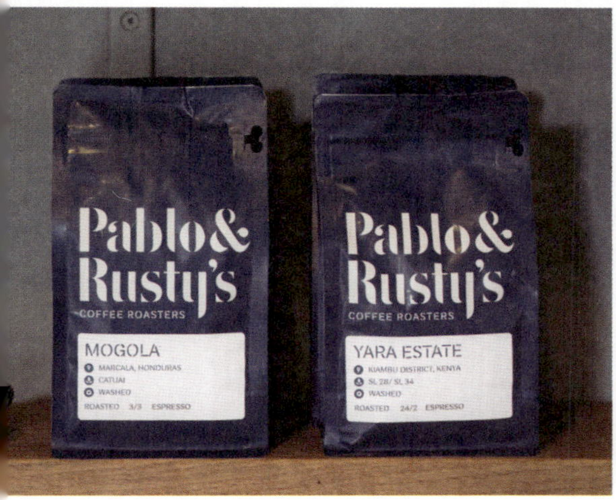
Pablo& Rusty's
COFFEE ROASTERS
MOGOLA
MARCALA, HONDURAS
CATUAI
WASHED
ROASTED 3/3 ESPRESSO
Pablo& Rusty's
COFFEE ROASTERS
YARA ESTATE
KIAMBU DISTRICT, KENYA
SL 28/ SL 34
WASHED
ROASTED 24/2 ESPRESSO

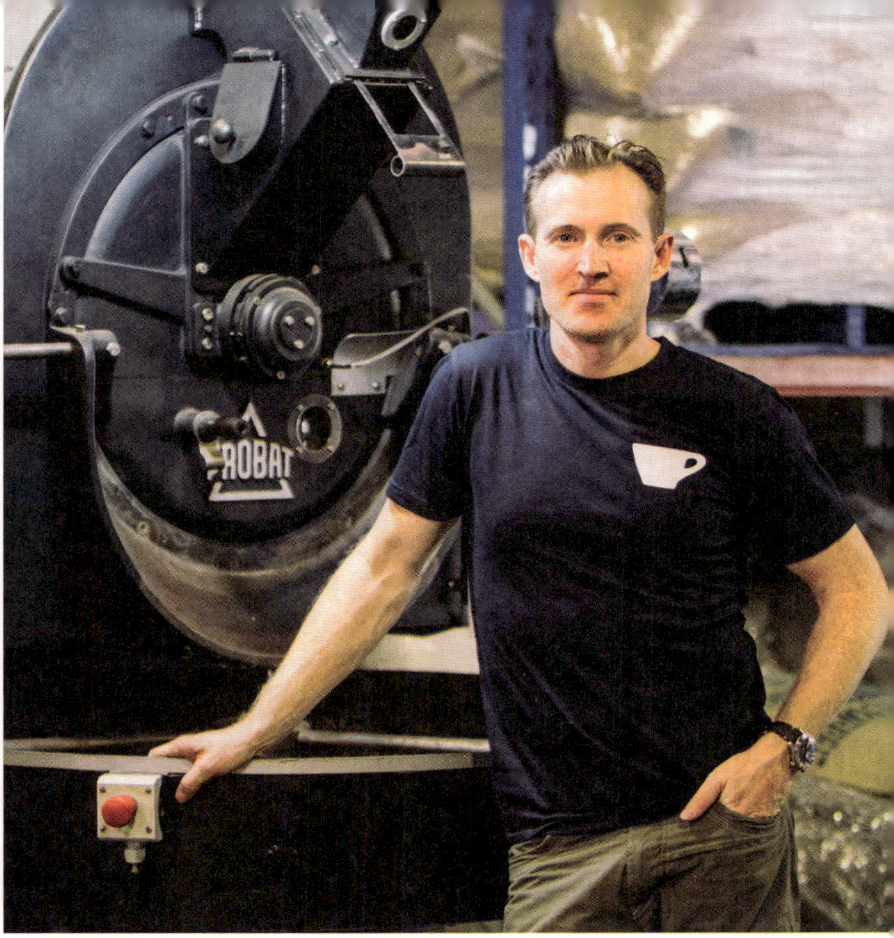
ROBAT

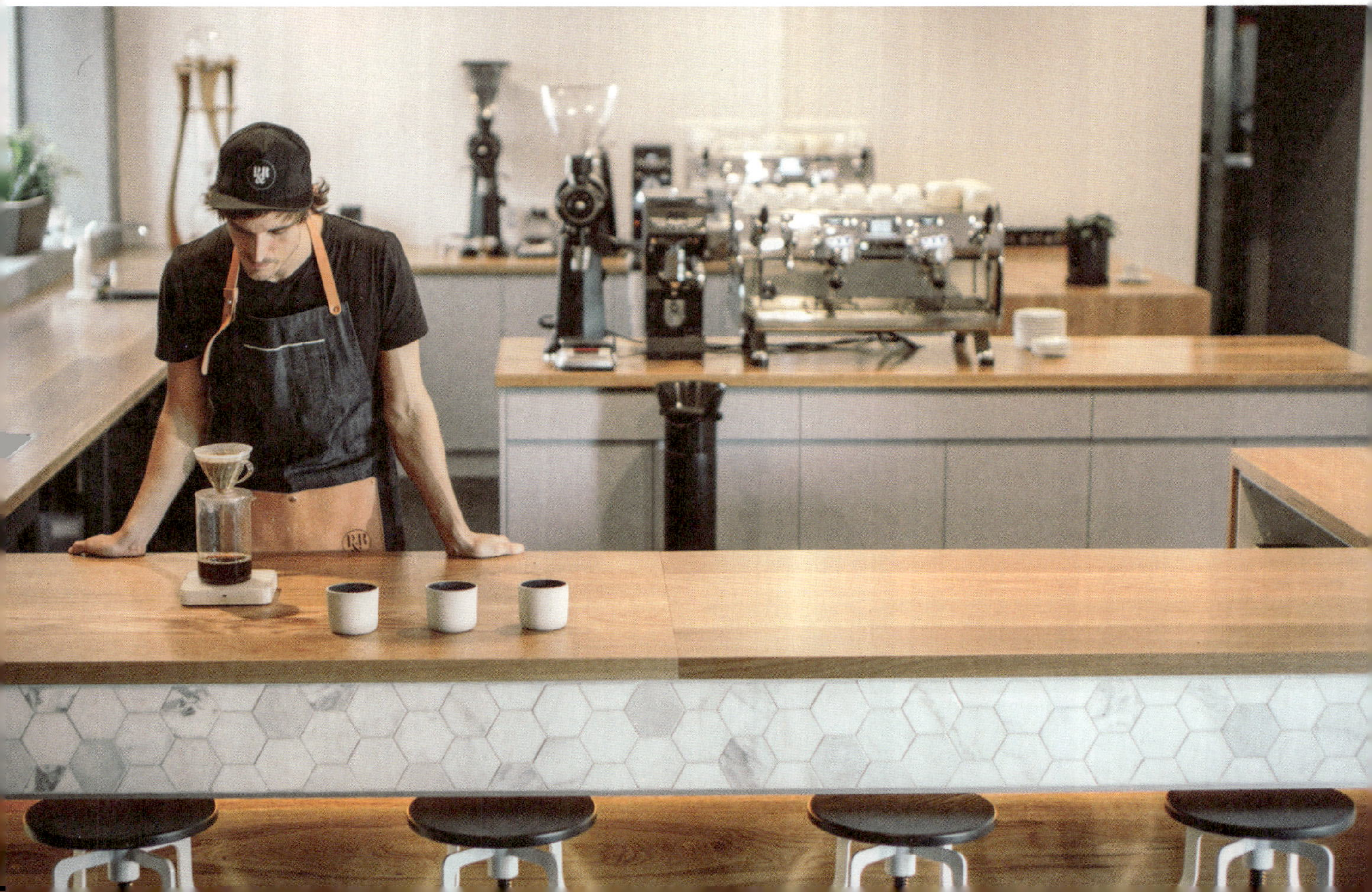

GETTING TO KNOW LA MARZOCCO

with Piero Bambi, Honorary President of La Marzocco

With three generations of passionate artisans building La Marzocco, selling it to an outsider could have been a tragedy. But with no further family to hand the business down to, it was great judgement by Piero Bambi, to impart a majority of the business into the hands of another young artisan, Kent Bakke, some 20 years ago.

My family passed their skills and experience from son to son, but I knew I was going to hit an end in the road. I simply didn't have any children to pass the business down to. My family had built this business over many years of blood, sweat and tears, commencing production before the Second World War.

So when a brash, young man came over from the United States back in the 1970s, and knocked on our door, I took a good look at him. American, Kent Bakke, had set himself up as an espresso machine technician, after working on only a few machines in Seattle at the time.

However, I noticed that he loved to tinker with machines. That was what caught my eye initially.

We agreed to start exporting machines to him, and he started selling them in earnest. He reminded me of the early Bambi boys – my father and my grandfather – keen to get their hands dirty, and elevate the coffee industry while they were at it.

After 15 years working amicably, Kent came to me and asked if we could start producing more machines. He was on the brink of doing a deal with a company called Starbucks who wanted La Marzocco machines to go into new cafes they were building. They had estimated they would be opening 300 cafes a year.

I recognised Kent's ambition, but I was getting too tired to want to work any harder. I lived in Tuscany – who would want to be working harder when living the idyllic life?

I thought long and hard, and felt I could trust this man to take care of the Bambi heritage and ethics of the Italian company. I decided to offer him a licence to manufacture machines in the USA, but this offer came with a catch.

I told Kent he would have to purchase 90% of the company to get his licence. And that's when Kent and a consortium of investors took over the helm. That was twenty years ago, and I couldn't be happier with what Kent has done with La Marzocco machines for over 35 years now.

He may not be my son, but he is certainly family! And I'm still in the business, working as hard as ever keeping the Bambi flame alive.

> "My family built this business over many years of blood, sweat and tears."

THE WORLD OF COFFEE

with Kent Bakke, CEO of La Marzocco

I KIND OF FELL INTO THIS JOB REALLY. I mean, I started out the same as most of my friends, going to college and getting a Business Degree. I thought that was my ticket to the world, and that I could conquer all odds.

My father was an entrepreneur, and I never thought I would end up like him. Both my parents were coffee lovers, and apparently when they would have friends and family over, I would walk around sipping down the remains of anyone's coffee cup I could find.

Perhaps the combination of an early appreciation of coffee and my father's example, led me to the life I enjoy today.

After college, I started working in a burger shop and enjoyed being part of the food service business. Being young and full of ourselves, my partners and I decided, we can do this!

I thought, I'm a college graduate – I'm smart.

In the historic part of Seattle in Pioneer Square, we bought a defunct soup and sandwich shop in 1976 and after refurbishing it, reopened it in 1977. In this café was a tall, brass, shiny thing which I learned was an espresso machine.

I'd never seen one before and I'd never had an espresso.... In fact my earlier years seemed to put me off coffee, and I definitely wasn't a coffee drinker!

However, I became fascinated by this machine. I loved mechanical things and it always needed something. And I was happy to comply.

"I met Piero Bambi and for me, that was a life changing moment."

At the time there were only about 8 espresso machines in the whole of Seattle, and after tinkering with our machine and getting it up and running, I would go about town pretending to be an espresso technician to make a bit of extra money on the side.

There was no-one else in town to debate whether I was or wasn't. So I would open up machines and try to fix them. The machine we had was a Victoria Arduino, and others about town included Rancilio, Gaggia, Caramali, Cimbali, and perhaps some others – but every one of them was different! So as a result of tinkering with them, my partner, who had come from California, said if you can work on these machines we should import them! I said something like, "Far out dude! Let's do it!" These were the 70s after all.

We travelled to Italy and visited a few manufacturers, and ended up visiting some relatives in Florence. We saw these La Marzocco machines everywhere and called up the company to see if we could visit the factory.

We met Piero Bambi and for me, that was a life changing moment. I was hooked. I felt the love and passion that went into every machine, and to hear Piero's family story was inspiring. We went back after that trip with two brand new machines and an agreement to import. However, we had no idea where this would take us.

Some La Marzocco machines had already been imported into the New York area in the 60s, and there were already a few machines in Seattle. So they weren't entirely new to

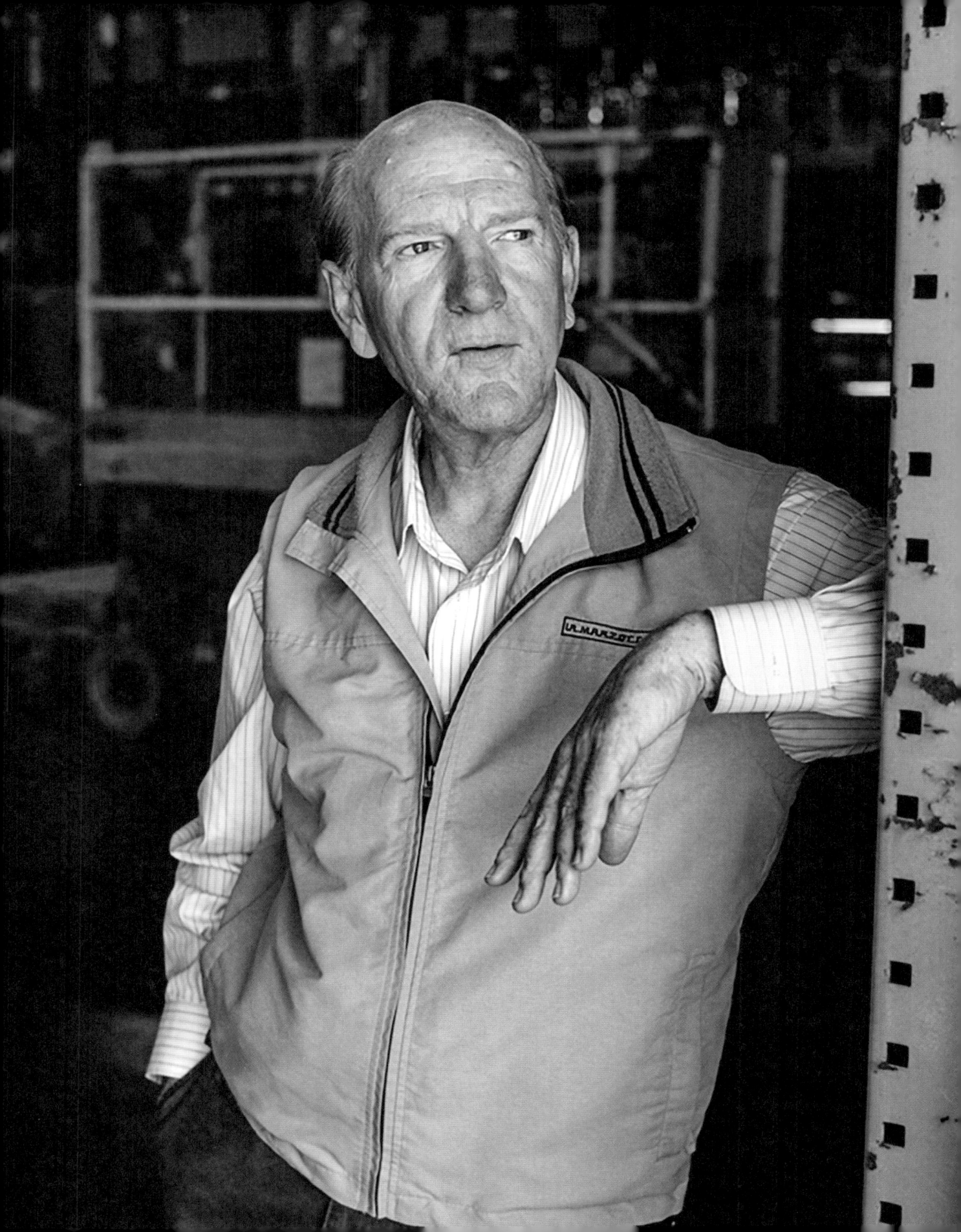

the United States. I decided to make selling these machines my priority, and I have to admit it probably took me a whole year to sell my first one!

I really enjoyed it though and I was learning a lot about coffee on the way. It was also fun having to go to Italy once in a while. This was prior to the internet and prior to cell phones – you really had to learn things on your own. And most of our contacts in Italy didn't speak English, so I was slowly learning some Italian. So after the first machine sold in 1979, this became a full-time venture.

The original Starbucks were importing espresso machines and selling them into the market, so originally they were competitors. Then they decided to focus on roasting and we decided to work with them. So when the original owners sold and the new Starbucks started with their retail expansion – we weren't their first machine but we had a long history with them. So in the late 80s we started providing for them.

When they started vamping up their stores, we sat down with them and they said they were going to open around 300 stores per annum! And we just couldn't believe our luck!

So I called Piero to say I needed a heap of machines, and he said, "Ah, no!" And I said, "What, you don't want to work a bit harder to sell more machines?" And he said, "Ah no!"

I persisted, and he said, "Well you can manufacture machines under our licence, but there's one catch. You have to buy the company.

He told me there was no future generation to go on – and we already had a 15 year history with them. He said he trusted us and he made an offer I couldn't refuse. I put together a group of investors and we bought 90% of the company. That was really for the purpose of setting up a manufacturing plant in Seattle in 1994.

Then we built machines for ten years – 3 and 4 group Linea model espresso machines for Starbucks until 2004. However, in the early 2000s Starbucks started adopting super-automated machines and so, at the time, they stopped buying espresso machines.

There wasn't enough of a world market to keep two manufacturing plants open and our commitment was always to keep the Italian heritage and plant going. So we closed the US plant in 2004 and concentrated on manufacturing in Florence.

I have to say, though, that Starbucks certainly put La Marzocco on the map, and coffee on maps around the

world. They have to be respected for their contribution to the coffee industry.

During all that time we were still buying from Italy for the rest of the US and we had started developing more international distribution for the company. Today we are just going from strength to strength. In fact, La Marzocco has grown so much in the last 4 years, it is even more important than ever to stay close to our ideals and maintain the culture.

Today I travel a lot as CEO and owner of the company. It is now my responsibility to honour the heritage of Piero and his family – it is in the company DNA. It's about preserving what the company is and was, and working on global strategies. We really have to stay focussed on what we do best… partly on what we have created, and partly on what the market has created for us.

We understand that our niche is in high quality, hand-crafted beverages. As I think you know, it's a complete chain from the farmer all the way to the consumer. That's a big picture these days. To help stay in the picture, the farmers need help to support their families, support agriculturally, and with everything in between.

We're proud to be an Italian family yet espresso is taking off all over the world. You may find people in Australia, Japan, or England who think espresso is their own, which is great, but coffee has a fascinating culture around it. It is an honour to be part of that. Every day there are new coffee drinkers, and then they get involved in the cafe, and then each generation brings their own interpretation.

We want to keep our history and culture so coffee, for us, doesn't just become a commodity item. And that's not just keeping the quality of the beverage in the cup, but doing what we can to help people make it their own. To expand their knowledge is what we want to be known for.

We're never going to sell the company, so there has to be a way to maintain the heritage of three generations in the company now. We are looking for a way to hand over the legacy and look after the people in the company – to prepare a continuing story of our family of baristas, family and friends.

It's the espresso and the people culture of our company that's important – preserving, developing and continuing to share that story moving forward.

Where Does Coffee Come From?

As we sip on our morning coffee, it is well worth taking a minute or two to think about the origin of the bean. Where has it come from and how did it make its way here? For many of us the process of what took place at origin is too big to comprehend. But, there is so much to learn about the intricate processes at origin that ensures only the best beans are purchased and delivered to our shores.

We believe that the story of where coffee is grown and how it is processed is just as important as where you can purchase it. We have travelled far and wide to explore the lives of the growers, pickers and the processors who work tirelessly to provide us with the best quality coffee beans.

Go on a first-hand trip to Ethiopia with Sasa Sestic, World Barista Champion 2015, as he continues on his quest for discovering new and exciting flavours. Or make your way to Bita Bonga with him as he seeks out the elusive Geisha bean.

Travel to South America with Toby Smith and continue exploring origins at Panama's high altitude coffee plantation, Finca Santa Teresa. Here we are lucky enough to meet the dedicated, hard working staff that live and work on the farm. We also learn more about the ever-improving working conditions for workers living on the farm.

In Sulawesi, we are able to visit Benteng Alla Utara with Will Young from Campos Coffee and learn more about the mutually beneficial relationship between grower and supplier. This partnership ensures the town and its residents have continued flourishing through a stable income and Campos Coffee benefits from receiving higher quality and quantity beans.

For a quick refresher on the various coffee processing methods from crop to cup, head to page 12 and equip yourself with all of the basic terminology. Head to page 458 to read our origin stories.

WITH CESAR VELA
CEO OF COLOMBIAN CONNECTION

Travelling to Australia in 1999, the owner of Colombian Connection Coffee Roasters, Cesar Vela, had no idea that his past would become so significant and, indeed, shape his future. Cesar came to Australia to study Audio Engineering and Musical Production, as well as looking for adventure and stimulation in the country he had heard so much about from an Aussie neighbour back home in Colombia.

While picking up extra jobs in the hospitality industry to keep himself afloat while he studied, he started to learn about coffee. His first job was in an Italian-owned café where he learnt how to make Italian espresso. He said at the time, most Australian cafes were pumping out Italian-style coffee so it was a great skill to learn.

For Cesar, this is when the love affair began; slowly at first, as his focus was still on audio production, but then he finally decided to put his musical career on hold. Cesar's new dream was to become the best coffee barista possible and one day, own his own cafe. He threw himself all in and started running cafes for owners like Chocolat, learning how to run a shop as well as ongoing improvement of his barista skills.

He opened his first café in Rosebery with an investor who had purchased a whole building. But 12 months later when they received an offer too good to be true for the whole building, Cesar had to walk away. And although it was only opened one year, Cesar said his café had been very popular and constantly busy.

Having an opportunity to reflect on what was next, Cesar started to wonder about other steps of the coffee process: roasting techniques as well as where these beans were coming from. And so, Cesar travelled to Italy to find out more. Surprising himself, he discovered that Italians create great roasting and brewing equipment, but his epiphany was that they don't actually grow coffee.

Around this time, Cesar was given the opportunity to open a stall at the Everleigh Markets where he started using Allpress Beans. At the same time, he met up with an old university friend, Allan Anchislavsky, who had started his own coffee company, Calima Coffee, contract roasting for various companies.

Discovering their shared interest in coffee, the pair discussed opportunities and decided to merge interests. They invested in a 60kg Turkish roaster and a warehouse in Marrickville to house it. Cesar started to learn the art of roasting by doing a few courses back home in Bogota, and by sneaking in the back doors of some of our larger roasters to learn how it was all done.

Through this process, Cesar decided he wanted to start his own brand of specialty coffee with organic beans sourced 100% from Colombian beans. This decision took him back to his home country where he started to appreciate what had been under his nose all his life... some of the best coffee in the world. With his family still in Bogota, it was easy for Cesar to start meeting coffee farmers and researching his home country's coffee industry.

Situated right on the Equator, Colombia grows beans all year round – in both the wet season and the dry season, so Cesar was not only guaranteed a continuous supply of beans, but he could also specify that he wanted organic only. He discovered a very well organised, national Coffee Federation, the FNC, which was full of information and connections, and that was more than willing to assist a fellow Colombian. The Federation was founded in 1927 and is one of the oldest coffee trading, and Fair Trade organisations in the world. Today it represents more than 563,000 coffee growers' families. Through a network of 36 coffee cooperatives with 540 purchase points, the Federation guarantees all Colombian coffee growers the full purchase of their harvest at a fair and transparent price.

Around the same time, Cesar also connected with an International brokerage that was willing to help with all aspects of the logistics to get coffee from Colombia to Australia, including purchasing his selected beans and storing them until he was ready to have them shipped to Australia. Cesar said that he had to pay a premium for this service, but the brokerage not only helped financially, but also stored and, then, freighted his valuable cargo, keeping an eye on important factors like the temperature and humidity, directly to his warehouse in Australia.

"They began supplying us with the best of Colombian beans," Cesar said, "and we were able to control the quantities from month to month. Half of the year we source from Pitalito, and the other half, the beans come from the Cauca Valley. The processing plant is based centrally in Popayan."

Today, Colombian Connection coffee has found its niche in Australian cafes. Cesar is roasting the specialty beans in Marrickville and supplying a number of cafes throughout NSW.

The beautiful Colombian branding, with a mule on the coffee bags and other marketing collateral, stands proud as a symbol of Cesar's pride in his home country and his new home.

Since 1958, the Colombian National Federation has used the fictional character, Juan Valdez, in their advertising to represent Colombian coffee. Juan typically appears with his mule, Conchita, carrying sacks of harvested coffee beans. He is an icon for Colombia as well as for coffee in general.

Part of the National Federation's advertising campaign educates consumers about the merits of Colombian-grown and harvested coffee beans, including how soil components, altitude, varieties and harvesting methods create good flavor.

They didn't need to convince their national aficionado, Cesar. One sip, and Cesar changed the way Australian consumers enjoy single origin – single country. The best from the best!

A BARISTA'S PERSPECTIVE

Sasa Sestic, World Barista Champion 2015

This year saw an Australian win the 2015 World Barista Championship, putting Australia in the spotlight for our cutting-edge coffee standards. And the trophy couldn't have gone to a more deserving coffee personality than Sasa Sestic, owner of Ona Coffee in Canberra.

Sasa and his brother, Dragan, came to Australia and secured their citizenship in time to represent Australia in the men's handball team in the 2000 Olympics. They had moved from war-torn Bosnia and saw Australia as an ideal place to live and raise a family.

Sasa said that he always knew he wanted to work in the hospitality industry after his sporting career ended. And while he was playing handball he completed an Advanced Diploma in hospitality operations and worked his way through various jobs, including functions, fine dining and bars. As soon as he got behind an espresso machine in a bakery he knew that was it. He fell in love and wanted to work with coffee for the rest of his life!

Up until three years ago, Sasa said he was passionate about coffee. But since then, he admits that he has become obsessed.

"For me, it has become a lifestyle," Sasa said. "It's what I love to do."

He said, "Some people find it exciting to go to Niagara Falls. But for me, I go to a farm and taste amazing coffee. And I just can't think of anything better."

Sasa admitted that coffee is a drug and he is addicted. He said, "Coffee means so much to me, it actually gives me goosebumps!"

"Coffee means so much to me, it actually gives me goosebumps!"

Sasa said he was always learning as much as he possibly could but pushed himself to learn and develop more. Finally, in 2008, Sasa and his wife bought their first cafe, providing fresh coffee and sandwiches to Canberra locals. How far he has come from such humble beginnings.

Soon after, he bought his first specialty coffee cafe, and it wasn't long before he started roasting. Sasa got straight into buying direct trade coffee and getting involved in experiments at an Indian coffee farm, Thalanar Estate.

Eager to understand all aspects of the coffee industry, Sasa started competing in barista competitions. The first coffee he fell in love with was a Yemen Mocha, and he received great results in some of his earlier competitions with it. At the time, this coffee was more than six times the cost of any other coffee on the market, and Sasa said that was the indicator he used at the time to know it was better – the price.

How far Sasa has come to achieve his World Championship title this year in Seattle. His whole presentation paid tribute to the years of dedication he has put in to learn every aspect of coffee, from the seed right through to the cup.

Sasa said, "I think my mission in coffee is to keep chasing after that perfect cup, which I don't think I ever will find. But I'll keep striving for better and better."

Sasa said he decided early on that he didn't want to simply visit various countries each year and look for the best coffee. He wanted to establish relationships with farmers, where they both benefited.

He said, "My mission statement is I don't want to go to farms and select the best coffee for the year, and then come back next year and buy from a different producer. I want to come back and maintain the relationship with a farmer who is willing to make some changes. He has to be a humble person and have a passion to work with me for a long time."

Sasa started Project Origin, his bean sourcing company, four years ago in India with the intention of improving the lives of the people living on the farm and in the processing plants.

He said, "As we know, over the last few years Rainforest Alliance, Fair Trade, and UTZ have been very important in developing the coffee world to give a fair deal to workers. And I really respect that – but with Project Origin, I wanted to go the next step. I wanted to do more than just giving a fair deal, so we make it our mission to pay at least 30% more for their coffee."

Sasa wants to provide a better, traceable cup while at the same time, offering a fair deal to the people picking and processing these coffees. Sasa said that the benefit to him is knowing exactly where the coffee is grown, how it has been picked, how it's processed, and exactly where it's been dried and kept. Part of the project is to influence the farmer to improve their product, and in return, they can raise funds back home to actually give back to the communities that they work with.

SHAE MACNAMARA is a passionate coffee enthusiast, barista, barista trainer, and National Brand Ambassador for Grinders Coffee. With more than 15 years industry experience, Shae has travelled extensively throughout Europe, USA and Asia learning the art of coffee, discovering differences within coffee cultures and working in cafes. He has consulted on cafe openings across Sydney and is heavily involved in industry events across the country. He is also on the board of the Australian Speciality Coffee Association (ASCA) and is accredited for sensory and technical judging. Shae holds the position as head judge for the Golden Bean Awards, and has judged at the National and State Barista Championships, as well as many other barista and coffee competitions across Australia.

MAKING THE PERFECT ESPRESSO

with Shae Macnamara,
National Brand Ambassador, Grinders Coffee

There are so many different varieties of coffee, so below is a guide to the 15 key elements you will need to produce the perfect espresso.

---

1. FRESHNESS Always start with freshly roasted coffee, 5-14 days is best. Freshly ground and dosed within 1 minute of grinding.

2. GRIND SIZE A fine grind size makes the best espresso. Just coarser than flour is ideal.

3. DOSING You need to use the correct amount of coffee in the basket. Normally 2-4g more than the basket size, so if you use an 18gram basket try 20-22g.

4. TAMPING Your tamping needs to be flat with even pressure using a small amount of body weight, then polish lightly. Make sure you use a tamp that fits the filter basket tightly.

5. VOLUME OF COFFEE We used to say 25-35ml now we talk in grams due to fresh coffee producing more crema and less liquid. The best espresso is in between 18-35g.

6. EXTRACTION TIME 24-35 seconds.

7. AMOUNT OF GROUND COFFEE The best espresso is made using a double shot. That's two espressos made from the same basket pouring at the same time and using between 18-28g of ground coffee in the basket.

8. FILTER BASKETS Filter baskets that are laser cut, like VST, have close to no variations and will produce a consistency you will not get using standard baskets.

9. TDS (TOTAL DISSOLVED SOLIDS) AND EXTRACTION YIELD % We now look at espresso as a science not just an art from... TDS will vary but the extraction yield needs to be between 18-22%.

10. PUCK Your puck, the wet ground coffee in the filter basket after the coffee has been made, should be firm and consistent in colour. Although there is not as much emphasis put on how firm it is anymore, it does need to be one colour and one texture.

11. LOOK The pour should start as a dark almond, brown colour and gradually change to a lighter caramel colour. You shouldn't see black or yellow.

12. OILS Your espresso will start pouring with lots of oil and will become more watery throughout the extraction.

13. CREMA The crema which is the oils on top of the espresso should be thick and light reddish-brown in colour.

14. FLAVOUR The perfect espresso should be a rounded mix of sour, sweet and bitter. The first third of your espresso will be sour, the second third should be sweet and the final third will be bitter in taste.

15. BODY Your espresso should have good body (not like Elle McPherson but a rounded feeling in your mouth).

AIR ROASTING: ROASTING THE PERFECT BEAN

with Dan Fitzsimmons of Chinook Coffee Roasting Systems

IN THE MID 70S, DAN FITZSIMMONS WAS WORKING AS A SYSTEMS ANALYST FOR A SMALL SEATTLE COMPUTER COMPANY. Out of the blue he received an interesting assignment; it was to write a small inventory application to quickly determine what items were moving most frequently and generating the most profit at the little known Starbucks Coffee Tea & Spices at Pike Street Markets.

It seems the company was changing direction and Starbucks was changing from a laid back enterprise to one more carefully managed. Many items were gathering dust on their shelves and proper management required turnover and profit visibility. Dan's analysis did the trick and, to their surprise, they discovered coffee moved rapidly and was a very significant profit contributor. And, as they say, the rest was history.

A post script to this anecdote is that Dan's software expertise was to play a significant role in his future acquaintance with coffee. But more on that later.

Dan and his wife, JoAnne, chose to migrate to Australia with their daughter, Whitney, in 1983. They pursued their existing careers, in the computer industry and investment field respectively, for several years before boredom caused them to explore more interesting occupations.

Becoming frustrated in their inability to purchase good coffee on a consistent basis, they decided to start a coffee roasting business. The emerging movement to Specialty Coffee was well underway in the rest of the world. So they chose to quit their jobs and travel for a year exploring the world of coffee in all its manifestations preparing to craft their new business.

During the next Northern winter, Dan got a job in Bend Oregon driving a Mount Bachelor Snowcat on the ski fields at night. This left him free all day to ski the back country... er, I mean continue exploring the coffee scene.

And explore he did, discovering Michael Sivetz, one of the world's foremost coffee authorities, in Corvallis Oregon. Michael had published many coffee text books, worked in the coffee industry all his life, was inducted into the Specialty Coffee Association of America (SCAA) Hall of Fame, and more.

He demonstrated his 'Fluidized Bed Hot Air Coffee Roasting System' which he patented in 1976. It was immediately obvious to Dan that this elegantly simple method for roasting coffee would give him much more control over the roasting process than traditional drum roasters. Unfortunately Michael Sivetz passed away in March of 2012.

'... frustrated in their inability to purchase good coffee on a consistent basis, they decided to start a coffee roasting business.'

DAN'S ROASTING NOTES

When we roast coffee we are really roasting each coffee bean. Most roasting methods apply heat simultaneously by three different methods... Conduction, convection and radiation.

These methods make it impossible for all beans to be treated the same. The beans on top are receiving heat from drum (radiation) & exhaust heat (convection). The beans in the middle are receiving a different amount of heat from the adjacent roasting beans (conduction). Finally, the beans

trapped next to the drum are receiving the highest heat from the drum (conduction).

The operator tries to overcome this limitation by rotating the drum which contains the beans at a varying RPM and applying heat in a way that will treat them all differently in the same way. The skill required to do this is somewhat different for each drum roaster and even different models of the same roaster.

This is why roasting operators can justly wax lyrical about their ability to achieve a good outcome with their equipment. And if you are that good at doing something, it is not unexpected that you would want to be called a Roastmaster rather than a roasting operator.

The Fluidized Bed Hot Air Coffee Roasting System levitates each coffee bean on a cushion of heated air. In this way the process applies the same heat to the total surface area of each coffee bean, allowing the operator to easily control the heat applied to the coffee and to achieve the exact degree and type of roast for each coffee bean being roasted.

One of the biggest problems for coffee roasting operators is to compensate during the roasting process for the change in moisture content over weeks and months of a given coffee while it is being used. This complex juggling of the radiation, convection and conduction heat is eliminated with Air Roasting.

All air roasting actions are determined by the actual temperature of the coffee bean which is measured 10 times per second during the roasting process. Hence, the control system automatically compensates for any variation of the green coffee moisture content.

Production air roasting operators do not derive pride from operating our appliances. We do experience two emotions… Firstly, happiness for the extra free time we have because we are not shackled next to a hot roaster telling it what to do with varying degrees of success. Secondly, satisfaction in the results we achieve when we use this free time to develop new coffee blends and single origin roasting methods on our Piccolo Chinook sample roaster.

After all, this is what humans are good at, using our analogue senses to try different things until we achieve our goal. Repeating this process should utilise equipment that requires as little input from the related human as possible. Humans are not good at using our analogue senses to achieve repeat processes with difficult-to-control equipment.

Back in Sydney in 1991 a 4kg Sivetz roaster was put to work in the front room of a terrace house at 113 Arundel Street

Glebe. Complemented by a three group espresso machine, freshly roasted coffee and other beverages were soon on sale.

Close proximity to Sydney Uni meant that, before long, the foot path was covered with upturned milk crates supporting students enjoying coffee. When Theo, the blind man who lived next door, walked to the corner shop, the milk crates would part like the Red Sea then quickly resume their position as Theo passed.

Retail and wholesale popularity quickly exceeded the capacity of the little Sivetz roaster. So a much more sophisticated 15kg Sivetz roaster was commissioned and the roaster moved to Union Square, 100 metres from where Star City Casino would later be located.

The most sophisticated coffee roaster, formerly manufactured by Sivetz, still required much input from the operator. Coming from the computer industry, Dan realised that a properly configured computer control system would improve the process and the roasting results, while reducing the repetitive work of the operator.

As luck would have it, the need to install a roaster in Queensland caused Dan to begin scribbling his own design on a serviette. Soon after, a 15kg Chinook Air Flow Coffee Roaster was installed at The Coffee Roaster QLD. Word got out and, six months later, a second Chinook was installed at Zarraffa's Coffee in a new Harbourtown Shopping Centre location on the Gold Coast.

Meanwhile, back in Sydney, expanded wholesale and retail sales necessitated an upgrade to a 25kg roaster. So Dan set about designing a larger version of the previous two Queensland Chinooks. In 2000, this 25kg roaster was installed at their current Sydney location, 380 Botany Road, Alexandria, NSW.

It was felt that the control system still demanded too much from the operator. Luckily recent emerging advances in computer technology supported the design of the current Chinook Control System. This control system allows the operator to enter the batch size, roasting recipe, and start roasting with six clicks of the computer mouse.

No need to watch the roaster after that. Operators are free to express their Artisan Craftsmanship by developing new blends and roasting recipes in the Piccolo Chinook sample roaster while the production Roaster does all the repetitive work.

A coffee roasting company from Adelaide was waiting for the previous 25kg Chinook to be decommissioned while the new computer controlled Chinook was being installed.

Today that Adelaide company is still using the original 25kg Chinook to roast their coffee. Since then, three more 25kg computer-controlled Chinooks have been installed in various parts of Australia.

Most recently, Chinook Coffee Roasting Systems has adopted a modular approach to fabricating the Chinook System. Each system is built, shipped and commissioned in its own modular unit. The unit is positioned at the installing location, and then gas, water and electricity are simply connected. Operation begins once the exhaust ducting is extended through the roof.

25kg and 50kg Chinook systems have been deployed in Australia and New Zealand using this novel approach. Expeditious transport, easy installation and rapid commissioning are some of the benefits. Moreover, each unit can be easily moved to a new location simply by disconnecting, securing the doors and calling the transport provider. Recommissioning could be accomplished in less than a week.

The 50kg Chinook system consists of four modules containing eight one tonne green coffee silos, automatic weighing system, Chinook roaster, 4 one Tonne roasted coffee silos and transport to a form fill & seal packaging machine through an electronic destoner.

The theme of elegant simplicity extends to the Chinook's ancillary components. Most commonly used coffee transport systems like cable drag systems, bucket elevators and screw conveyors have their Genesis in the agricultural industry. Instead we use vacuum air to move green & roasted coffee through stainless steel pipes at the command of the control computer. These subsystems have very few moving parts, very low maintenance requirements and keep the environment (vacuum) clean during operation.

Dan said, "All of our efforts have been directed to the purpose of roasting coffee well and consistently. We are overjoyed that it works. And we are gratified that this approach frees us from the roaster allowing us to pursue the more enjoyable aspects of coffee selection, blend development and roasting recipe creation.

"Please come and join us for a coffee while we watch the Chinook Air Flow coffee roaster do all the work."

PULLING THE STRINGS

with Ed Cutcliffe of The Little Marionette

From its humble beginnings, The Little Marionette's master puppeteer, Ed Cutcliffe, has been seamlessly pulling all the right strings to bring coffee to life.

Ed's understanding of roasting, which comes from years of experience combined with a passion for his product, can be paralleled to the food world and the role of a chef. A chef transforms raw ingredients into fine dishes by refining flavours and aromas to create the best possible experience for the consumer.

When starting up a coffee roastery, Ed believes the first step should be to establish a distinct flavour profile. Defining what direction to take in the initial stages is essential to finding a place in an extremely competitive market.

Since The Little Marionette's inception, the focus was on both the product as well as finding out what customers want and need, from the flavour of the bean to assistance maintaining equipment.

Instead of concentrating on the direction of a brand, The Little Marionette has honed its combined expertise, hard work and coffee knowledge to deliver the best possible product. This has gained the respect and attention of peers and customers alike.

The Little Marionette team has worked extremely hard to deliver a product they truly believe in. From perfecting the roast and flavour profiles of carefully selected green beans to creating a unique customer experience.

Ed's charm and energy combined with dedication, knowledge and spirited generosity sets The Little Marionette apart as not just another coffee roastery, but as a serious contender in Australia's competitive coffee roasting industry.

'...we're supplying cafes and they are depending on us for product, price point, service, equipment, training and everything thereafter.'

The Little Marionette's emphasis on flavour is tailored towards the best way to please the customer and not by imposing personal preference on the public. Ed expands by saying, "The majority of the population just want a hot cup of coffee with a taste that's smooth. You've got to realise that you are trying to support the cafe you are supplying, by providing a product that their customers will enjoy. It has to be viable for them, and at The Little Marionette we try to give them a product that works best through espresso.

"Understanding the limited time available to extract the flavours on an espresso machine is essential to understanding how to roast beans for this machine. And given that Australia is predominantly an espresso culture, the majority of beans need to be roasted in a way that the machine can extract all the flavours within a timeframe of around 30-34 seconds.

"Of course, this can depend on the machine. Typically a La Marzocco machine will take around 32 seconds, whereas a Synesso will take 42 seconds. You have to be true to the equipment that you have.

"So if you roast lighter, the bean may not be malleable enough to allow the full flavour to be extracted in a short amount of time. That's when you get more acidity and that tart flavour coming through. Some people like that, some people have trained their palate to like that, and others in certain parts of the world love that.

"We are in Australia and we know our customers. The majority of the population drinks espresso or instant coffee, unlike in Norway for instance where the majority drink filtered coffee.

"Understanding the customer helps the roaster produce what people like. At The Little Marionette, we try to be true to the individual bean at the same time as being true to the market we are in. If I were to roast just for our own cafes, I could wear the consequences of my individual taste. But we're supplying cafes and they are depending on The Little Marionette for product, price point, service, equipment, training and everything thereafter. I am obliged to respect the wider audience."

The other issue roasters have, Ed said, is to provide consistency. "There is a fine balance between retaining the flavours of the beans, and providing consistency. If you over-roast, your flavour goes out the door. If you under roast, there is not enough time to extract the flavours through your machine. We like to roast to retain the flavours of the beans, but not take them to a point where they lose their subtleties. We have built our brand on product and built our reputation around a roast that everyone can enjoy. I believe that is what makes our brand successful, and keeps the cafes that we supply to so loyal."

SETTING UP A MICRO ROASTERY

with Marcio Brito of Salvador Coffee, Est. 2010

IN THE BEGINNING, THE SEARCH FOR THE HOLY GRAIL SAW A RELIGIOUS MAN REDUCED TO STEALING, AT THE RISK OF HIS OWN LIFE. Such is the grip of this little thing called coffee.

Today we see devotees of coffee going to all lengths to produce perfection in our cups. Devout, pious and pure. The coffee bug seems to get into their veins and their dedication can only be admired. The various waves of learning and change have brought a whole range of tastes and flavours to the ever-changing world of coffee, similar to the exciting flavours continually evolving in wine.

One pioneer to be smitten by coffee, is Salvador Coffee's Marcio Brito. A self-confessed perfectionist with Brazilian heritage, it has taken him several years of following the roast/taste, roast/taste, roast/taste regime.

Marcio admits his first passion was travelling – discovering exotic places and diverse cultures. It was this journey that saw him start in the hospitality industry to pay for his journeys. He found that he always gravitated towards the espresso machine, and said that he always enjoyed the challenge of a new machine, different coffee and unusual taste profiles to fulfil.

One day he stood back and realised, that it was no longer the travel that he was craving. It was the journey to learn more about this innocuous bean that made itself a necessity in the daily lives of the people in all the cities he visited. He came back to Australia and started working as a barista, and the cafe owner was so impressed, he nominated Marcio to enter the Australian Barista Championships in its second year.

That was nearly 18 years ago, and Marcio hasn't looked back. A judge at that competition happened to be an up-and-coming roaster called Toby Smith, who had just returned from his own travels to Brazil. He asked Marcio to work for him in his mother's garage, and the two starting building the empire of what is today, Toby's Estate.

Marcio said that initially the business was so small the he learnt everything – sourcing, roasting, blending, and cupping. He learnt so much, but his adventurous spirit took hold once more, and Marcio decided he wanted more control of the final product. He bought himself a small roaster and started roasting small batches in his own garage.

'...it has taken several years of following the roast/taste, roast/taste, roast/taste regime.'

This led him to decide to go out on his own, and he went into partnership in a small coffee kiosk in Sydney's CBD to help fund his dream, and he continued his small batch roasting at home.

Today he has a large folder filled with notes from those days of experimentation – roast/taste, roast/taste, roast/taste... And he said that he wouldn't change a thing. In order to become the best roaster you can be, he recommends that you ignore everything that you learn during a roasting course or online.

"The most critical thing is to develop your taste buds," he said, "similar to a great chef, sommelier or wine maker."

He said, "You can learn the formula for creating good coffee, but you cannot produce great coffee until you understand the taste profiles on your tongue."

It took Marcio several years to develop his roasting formulas, all the while developing his taste and developing what he liked. He said what wasted a lot of time was recreating the formulas he thought he was supposed to roast – both light and dark coffees from existing formulas.

It wasn't until he started developing his own idea of what he liked and didn't like, that he started to make headway in his business. He said that today he can go and visit a roaster who is very precise about everything, following the traditions passed down.

"They can be very precise about the way they source, store and roast their beans," he said, "but still pour a very ordinary coffee. And the worst of all is that they don't even know that their coffee is ordinary!"

Marcio recommends anyone wanting to make the leap to become a micro-roaster is that you take your time experimenting with different roasts. He said, "No-one can teach you what you are tasting, and if you don't love what you are producing, it will show in the flavour."

He said he wasted a lot of time trying to perfect the art of coffee roasting – trying for absolute consistency – before realising there is no such thing as perfection with coffee. He said that is when he realised the difference between craftsmanship and coffee from a factory.

In the beginning, it took Marcio 9 months to get permission from local council to roast in his small space in Darlinghurst. Being very determined, he fought battle after battle and won in the end.

In hindsight though, Marcio said that if you wanted to make life easier for yourself, he would recommend not setting up in a residential area, and making sure you could meet all the council criteria before leasing any property. The other consideration he recommended was that wherever you set up, be certain that you will be happy to get out of bed every day and spend time there – day in, day out.

After council approval, it took Marcio another 6 months of trial roasting until he was happy with the result. Until

then, he said he was not prepared to open the doors. He said, "If I was younger, I would have opened straight away without caring – but it took me another 2 years to even start selling wholesale.

"Until I felt my product was excellent and consistent, I couldn't open the doors, I just didn't feel confident in the product."

He said that he was given some wise words during this period. He was told not to rush to the destination – to remember that the journey is what it is all about. He suggests anyone wanting to follow his path to remember this ethos. To remember that success will follow hard work and integrity.

He said he watches others that have caught a wave of success, and it has inspired him to keep pedalling. He said, "I remind myself to keep heart and soul. Eventually I will catch a little wave if I keep doing my job well. If I maintain passion and integrity, success will follow."

He also reminds anyone wanting to go into this business that it is not medicine you are going into. "We are not saving lives," he said.

He said that some in the industry forget that to enjoy a cup of coffee is not curing cancer.

"You can lose perspective of what you really want," he said. "This is a passion and I love getting out of bed. At the end of the day it gives me a business – and the money allows me to continue my passion. I don't specifically want a $100,000 car. What I want is $100,000 to go to India.

"But then, I'm a traveller. I want to be able to make a difference!"

HOME GROWN COFFEE MACHINE

with Craig Hiron, founder of The Little Guy

Having used and admired his own Atomic stovetop machine for ten years, Craig Hiron decided it was time the machine was re-engineered. He had developed a passionate ritual of squeezing the best coffee out of his beloved machine every day, and wanted to create an at-home machine that rivalled commercial espresso machines.

Craig's ultimate goal was to extract espresso and texture milk to the same quality a commercial machine could. "If I could walk down the road and get a better coffee than what this was to become, then I would walk down the road and get a better coffee."

This machine had to meet the requirements to make cafe quality coffee at home.

A roof tiler by trade, Craig was looking for an alternative career when his light bulb moment struck when close friend, Nikki Di Falco, suggested remaking the esteemed atomic coffee machine. He said he wasn't looking to reinvent the wheel, but just to improve it.

Meeting with designer after designer, one of the biggest features Craig wanted was that the machine be seamless. With initial designs mapped out, he was faced with multiple obstacles, and was told his product could not be manufactured. He was told to put his idea on the backburner and move on. Having spent a year on the project, he was bitterly disappointed.

However when he met up with Tiller Design's, the lead designer just sat down and doodled for ten minutes. In that space of time he had developed a concept to have the base of the body completely open so that it could have a separate brewing system bolted inside.

The problem then was to figure out how to make water and coffee behave together in order to produce great coffee. There was no mechanism to control the temperature, which affected the coffee's extraction.

Craig sought the help of Dr. Allan Wallace from Adelaide University, who invented what is the corner stone to The Little Guy's patents. He invented a fluid delay valve, which determined the temperature and pressure of what the water needed to be before the extraction could begin.

To figure out the best size for the valve, Craig called upon Ian Bersten of Belaroma. Through testing and flavour profiling, the last piece of the puzzle had fallen into place, and The Little Guy was born.

"I wanted to create something people will buy once, use it their whole life, and be able to use it numerous times a day, never having to replace or be without it," explained Craig.

Through passion and perseverance Craig developed a machine that has enabled at-home baristas to never forego a quality cup of coffee.

'a machine that has enabled at-home baristas to never forego a quality cup of coffee.'

GOING AGAINST THE GRIND

with Rob Stewart & Lachie Cairns of DC Specialty Coffee

DC'S APPROACH TO SPECIALTY COFFEE IS DIFFERENT. They see beyond coffee culture and see coffee as a part of culture. They continue to explore different mediums that bridge the grower to the consumer to deliver the specialty coffee message.

This unconventional way of doing business starts at the top, with two visionaries taking this team forward, each managing their own divisions with care. This lateral management model combines Rob Stewart and Derek Doyle's expertise and experience to what is traditionally the top role, allowing them to share their knowledge and involvement through the entire organisation.

Since 2002 DC has been committed to roasting specialty coffee. Rob said, "Specialty grade coffee is a given at DC! We don't see this as a point of difference. We see this as a non-negotiable and it's an attitude that is ingrained in all of our staff." With this mantra, DC has since expanded its operations in NSW by setting up camp in Potts Point in an old heritage listed Laundry adequately named The DC Laundry.

"We are a Melbourne coffee roaster, simply because our manufacturing infrastructure is there, but we have been servicing the Sydney and Adelaide markets since day one. We found that in Sydney, we needed a base for our team and a place that we could show off the potential of coffee, so we created the space that is the DC Laundry. This space isn't a cafe, it is part showroom, part cupping room and part disco," Rob said.

"It's a relaxed atmosphere, where our customers and their staff can use their time practically away from the pressures of their own businesses. Whether it's experimenting with alternative brew methods, cupping single origins, barista training or latte art practise, there is always something going on."

At first glance, you will find some of the latest brewing gear and sample some of the freshest crop available. "It's not just a space for us or our customers to engage in our coffee, we have thrown some wild parties here for the industry and suppliers. We have a tendency to include the industry in our space rather than exclude."

DC Culture

DC's celebration of culture rather than the specialty coffee culture is driven by support they have been giving to independent artists in both the music industry and in the visual arts. DC started supporting the music industry at a time where licencing laws were affecting the live music scene in Melbourne and some of the venues and artists suffering from this were DC clients. Rob said, "We found ourselves in a unique position to offer support and create a program that celebrated unsigned artists and take the financial burden off the venues.

"We have since supported over 50 bands, several live music venues, music schools and public radio stations. We assisted in PR campaigns and the recent pressing of an album."

To assist this initiative, DC launched the B-side as a fund raising coffee that supported the program. B-Side's make up comprises of some beautiful origins such as The Nicaraguan Luis Bellatez and the Colombian Santa Rita, maintaining DC's stance on quality.

> "Specialty grade coffee is a given at DC... We see this as non-negotiable!"

The music program snowballed and soon DC's attention turned to the Visual Arts by providing independent artists a giant canvas for them to express their creative flair. DC's packaging became the medium for these artists, and it was kicked off with Sydney artist, Thomas Townend, and his unique tattoo inspired design for the Monsoon blend. This was followed by another Sydney artist, Sindy Sinn, and his street/rock and roll style artwork for the Reale Blend.

Rob said, "We gave the artists a wide berth to create a piece that they felt interpreted the uniqueness of the coffee they were designing for."

Rob said that the exposure given to these artists has had an incredible influence on their work and DC has already two more artists designing more works to be released later this year. This continual push from DC away from the specialty industry and the barrage of noise created from companies spreading the same message, offers DC a unique space to voice their brand culture and have fun doing it.

"The team at DC puts a lot of effort into creating a brand culture that is supportive of independent thinking, challenging and fun, but at the heart of it all is coffee. If we don't get this right then all the peripheral stuff falls over. Our relationships we have built over the years with the farms we support is paramount to DC whether it's with the Mandiri Coop in Sumatra or Boa Esperanca in Brazil, they are an extension of the greater DC family," Rob said. "We invest heavily in our staff and in our customers so they understand the philosophy of specialty coffee and the effort we take from origin to cup, to make sure it's bang on every time."

DC's collaboration with likeminded entities has seen them explore non-traditional styles of marketing and consumer engagement. This is all underpinned by a commitment to specialty coffee and exceptional service which creates a brand culture none like any you will find in the world of coffee.

dc
REALE
COFFEE BEANS 1kg NET

dc
cooxupé

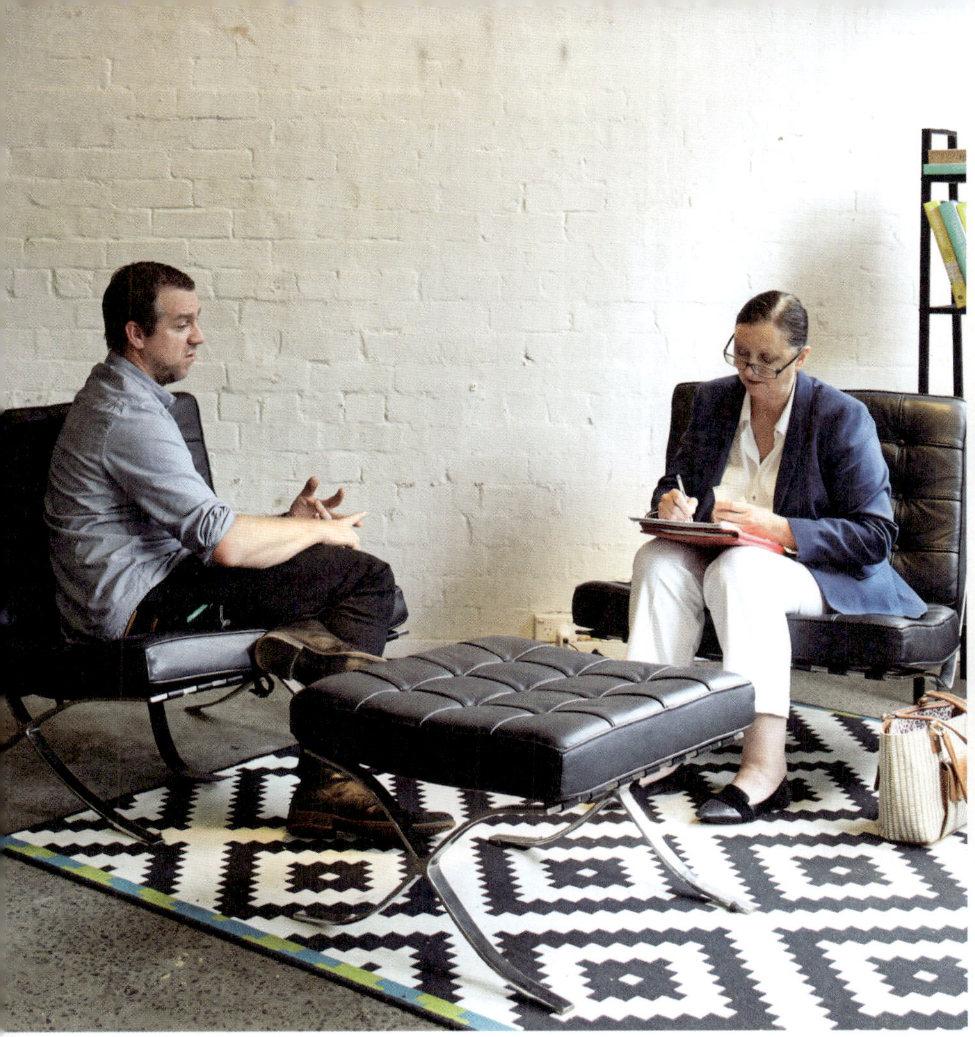

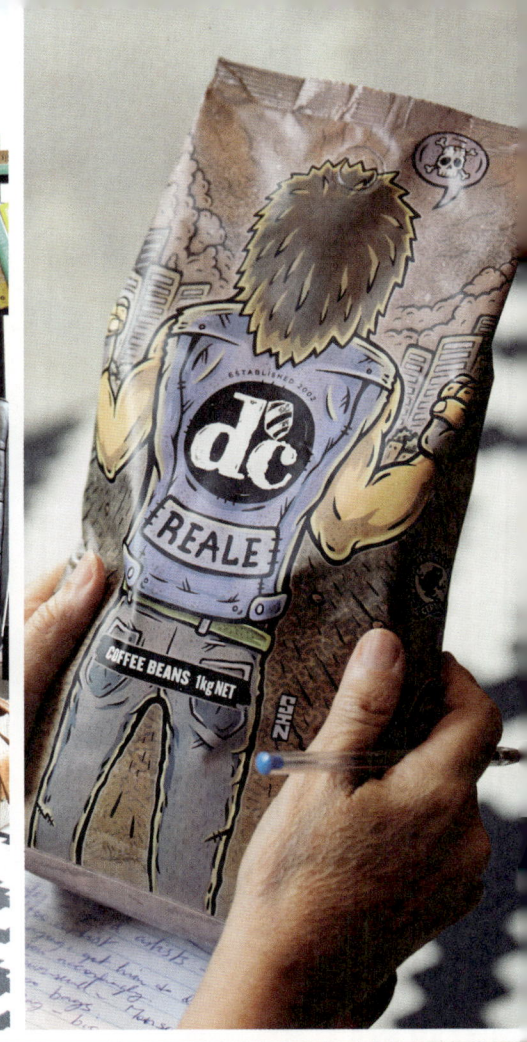

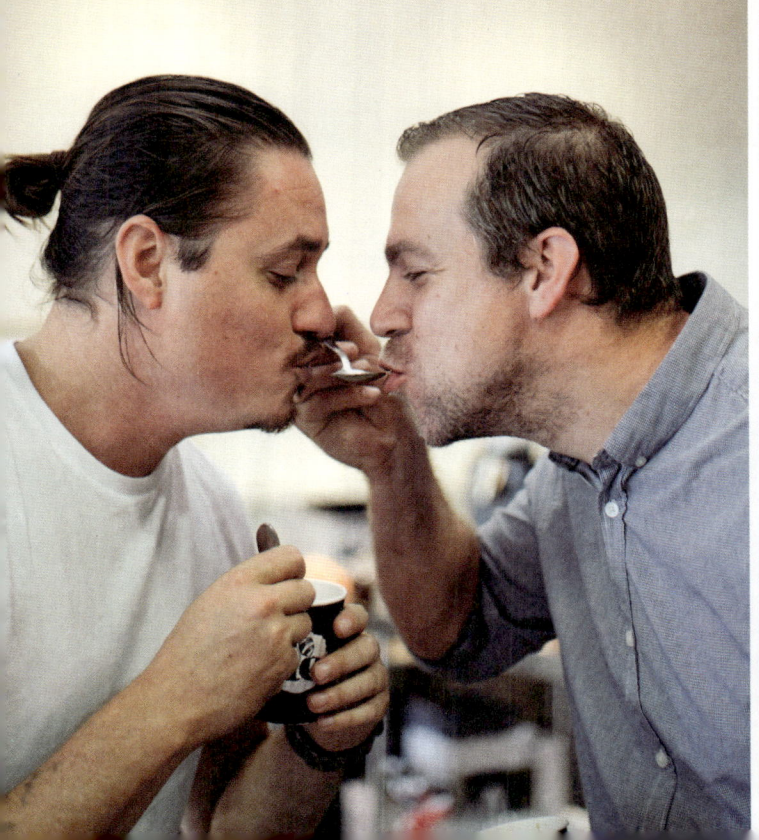

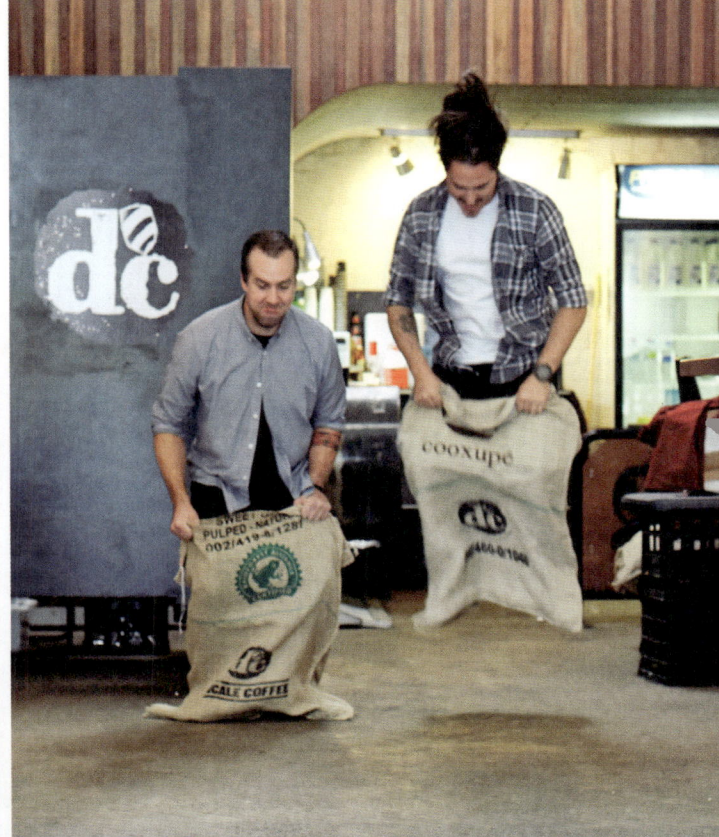

ABIGAIL FORSYTH is the CEO of Keepcup whose mission is to encourage the use of reusable cups. Abigail said, "We do this by delivering sustainably made products that are fit for purpose in the context of a positive global campaign that strives to make a difference to how we think about convenience culture. We want to create a global brand and to be one of the organisations that kick started the demise of the disposable."

KEEPING COFFEE SUSTAINABLE

with Abigail Forsyth, KeepCup CEO

"A movement happens when people talk to one another, when ideas spread within the community, and most of all, when peer support leads people to do what they always knew was the right thing."
– Seth Godin, Tribes

Very few industries in the world illustrate the sustainability loop as the coffee industry. At trade events, a grower might have a stand beside the paper cup company. If you are a multinational chain talking about climate change and poverty at origin and yet disposable cups account for 98% of sales, you are creating the problem you are trying to solve. It is the task of Sisyphus, no one wins.

Due to the altitude required to grow coffee, the second largest traded commodity in the world, it is one of the crops most adversely effected by climate change.

The world over, sustainability is moving from being a department in an organization with no budget, to a bottom line performance evaluation for the whole business. Within the next ten years sustainability will no longer be a marketing platform, it will be a precondition of commercial viability.

The industry can only continue to grow if it looks after the environments it affects. We designed and manufactured KeepCup, the world's first barista standard reusable cup with a mission to reduce the widespread use of disposable cups. Every minute around the world one million disposable cups are discarded to landfill. That's over 500 billion disposable cups a year. So whilst on a global scale it's a small problem, in terms of gain versus cost, it's catastrophic.

In just under five years, our mighty KeepCups, manufactured in Australia, have had an amazing journey from a design market in Melbourne to coffee shops in Reykjavik and design stores in Valparaiso. It is a fantastic example of a business model that has had great commercial outcomes maintaining sustainability and reuse as its core purpose.

Eighty percent of the environmental outcomes of any product are determined in the design phase. Care in product design; choice of materials, shipping, longevity and end of life, take you a long way to deliver sustainable outcomes. But whilst product design is critical, we give equal weight to creating the right circumstances to tip the behaviour change from discard to reuse.

Here are some of the lessons we have learned

Strike a positive note, for most of us, the word 'should' is immediately disengaging. We all need to do better, and we can, it's about giving ourselves and others the space to take positive action.

Find the enablers within your industry and engage them. I've been to many of the cafes in this book with my KeepCup and the barista has said 'good on you' or 'nice KeepCup'. It's a wonderful feeling to have your efforts acknowledged and assists to embed the positive behaviour. Take a bow baristas of the world!

Provide an accessible entry point to the sustainability journey. For many of our customers it has been the beginning of a journey to reduce the consequences of convenience behaviour.

Ultimately what sustainability is about is creating sustainable livelihoods for everyone, so we donate a portion of our profits to Coffee Kids. It is a charity that supports families in coffee growing regions to develop viable sources of income outside the growing season. This year we are supporting a microcredit scheme for women in Honduras. I read once that every time you take a woman out of poverty she brings eight people with her. Now that's a sustainable outcome.

Re-users, we salute you!

> "The industry can only continue to grow if it looks after the environments it affects."

THE MILK CONNECTION

with Bonsoy

As any top barista will tell you, milk is not all made the same; and when it comes to your daily coffee, the quality of the milk is a vital ingredient in creating that perfect cup of coffee. With so many variations available, what should we know about the effect of milk on our daily cup of coffee?

With over 90% of coffee sold in Victoria today containing milk, the combination of coffee and milk is an obvious winner. And although the trend towards single origin, black coffee is increasing, it has by no means caught on as the beverage of choice. Both roasters and baristas test their roasts with various milk types to ensure their flavours cut through well, and the rest is left to you. If you like what they provide, you will keep going back!

The significant factors that can influence milk include the percentage of fat, the seasons, how the milk is processed, and the temperature that it is kept at. If you prefer soy or almond, it is important that your barista has perfected the unique way that milk is treated.

One of the main differences with milk is in the fat level. Full cream milk contains around 3.5g of fat while 'lite' milk is usually around 1.3g and 'extra lite' milk 0.1g of fat. 'Skinny milk' is usually considered harder to work with by baristas. It contains less fat than full cream milk so it is a little harder to bind and to achieve the glossy sheen on top that baristas like to create.

Another variation with milk lies in the seasonal changes. The same cows aren't milked all year round so different types of cows produce different types of milk – and that creates different outcomes in the coffee cup.

How the milk is processed and the temperature it is kept at is also vital to quality. In Australia all cows' milk must be pasteurised. Most milk is also homogenised, to prevent cream floating to the top, whilst UHT milk is treated with ultra high temperatures to improve shelf life. Whatever processing is undertaken, the taste, life and quality of the milk will be affected.

What the farmers are feeding their cows also plays a major role in the flavour outcomes of the milk and, by extension, the coffee. Finally, the type of cow is an important factor.

Which cows make the best milk is speculative but milk from all the main Australian cow types, including Jersey, Guernsey and Holstein is ideal.

So then it is down to your choice of milk and what will cut through the espresso shot or other type of brew, to give you the flavours you are looking for. With roasters going to extensive lengths to ensure their roasted beans get the balance of sweetness, acidity and bitterness spot on, it is logical for them to find milk that is consistent and works with them to improve the flavour profile of the roast.

Then, if you prefer skinny, soy or almond – then it is your choice. However, in Melbourne you may find the odd, precocious barista who refuses to hand over your preferred choice. With so many people intolerant to lactose or trying various diets, these coffee snobs need to take a good, long look at themselves.

More people are choosing soymilk now than ever before. The decision to forgo dairy isn't always taken lightly, especially if it means giving up the comforts of our daily cup of coffee.

In the past, a soy latte would often connote a less-than-pleasant idea of a coffee. Many soy milks have a distinctive taste and its properties make it more complex to work with than its dairy counterpart. What changed it all was the introduction of Australia's first modern soy milk, BONSOY. Regarded now as the industry standard, it's uncommon that you won't find it served at your local cafe. Bonsoy is itself a reflection of the evolution of soy milk, in which taste, texture and premium ingredients take no backseat.

The soybeans are grown in the US by a family of farmers now in their third generation, and it is made from a select variety of whole organic soybeans. More importantly, it's free from genetic modifications, preservatives, harmful pesticides and chemicals, thwarting the myth that often surrounds soymilk. Its packing is also environmentally conscious.

"The beautiful feature of Bonsoy is that it has a flavour profile which is not overbearing, oily or too sweet," said Marwin Shaw, owner of Melbourne's Monk Bodhi Dharma, a specialty coffee and roastery establishment. It stays true to its full-bodied, subtle flavour, which is balanced with an inherent sweetness found in the natural tapioca syrup.

"This coupled with a lighter-roasted, naturally sweet coffee reduces the need for sugar," added Marwin.

What are the other health benefits? Bonsoy is also high in vegetable protein making it a nutritious supplement. Monk Bodhi Dharma is one of many cafes that chooses to serve Bonsoy.

Marwin said, "It's easy to work with as it requires a less-is-more attitude to steaming it, that is, minimal stretching and lower heat. Soy milk has a fine band at which a latte can be 'just ok' to excellent. An overheated soy drink (including any nut milk) can in fact taste quite offensive, like cardboard."

If you're a soy drinker, you're more discerning of the difference between other types of soy milk. From the perspective of a barista, the type of roast and the acidity of the bean will affect the properties of the milk, which impacts both taste and texture.

"As a specialty coffee roaster, we are exposed to at least 150 coffees from different coffee farms from around the world every year. We roast for farm transparency, which results in a lighter roasted coffee with the acid structures intact. For example, a washed Brazilian Yellow Caturra varietal coagulates a lot less than a natural process Ethiopian Heirloom varietal. As such, some coffees, being more acidic, do tend to react more to Bonsoy in the form of a curdled look," explained Marwin.

Fika Swedish Kitchen | Manly

THE PERFECT SOY LATTE

There are various strategies a barista should always carry out when working with soy. We asked baristas, Stewart Clark and Simon Luxton, of Doppio and Nothing Espresso in Port Macquarie, New South Wales on how to make the perfect Bonsoy coffee.

BEFORE YOU BEGIN, IT'S IMPORTANT TO REMEMBER THE FOLLOWING:

- Always start with a clean jug.
- Only fill your jug to the base of the spout. If you need more Bonsoy, upsize your jug – portion control limits wastage.
- Purge your steam wand and make sure it's clean.
- Ensure the steam wand lies just below the surface of your Bonsoy.

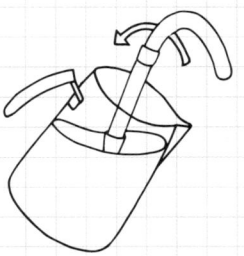 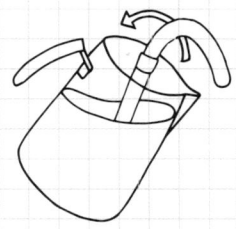 

STEP 1: As the steam enters the Bonsoy, position the jug at an angle that encourages the liquid to spin, creating the whirlpool and a kissing sound. Whilst you are doing this, ensure that you always have your hand resting on the side of the jug to feel the change of temperature.

STEP 2: Once the Bonsoy reaches its warm point (which is 30-35°C body temperature), stop allowing the introduction of air by gently burying the steam tip deeper into the jug. Continue with the whirlpool method until you reach a desired temperature of between 50-60°C.

STEP 3: Turn off the steam wand, wipe and purge, leaving it clean for the next jug.
Tip: If the surface of the Bonsoy has bubbles in it, they can be removed by swirling and gently tapping the jug on the bench top. Leave the jug to settle for around 30 seconds, allowing it to form itself into the perfect texture for pouring.

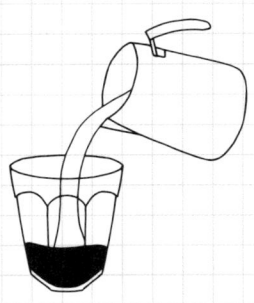  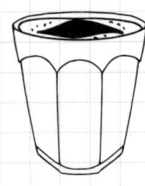

STEP 4: By now you should have a fresh shot of espresso ready. Take the jug of Bonsoy and begin using a swirling motion as to turn the liquid into a consistent texture. This is known as 'turning'. Keep turning your jug right up until you physically begin the pour. Aim the stream of Bonsoy into the centre of the crema on top of your shot, pouring just enough that you don't abruptly break the surface.

STEP 5: Begin pouring in a circular motion as if you are drawing around a 20-cent piece in the crema.
Once you are confident you have enough of a Bonsoy base in your cup, you can begin pouring your favourite latte art design.

STEP 6: Now you're done. Don't forget to deliver your Bonsoy drink with a smile. Since its introduction, Bonsoy has had a loyal following amongst baristas and soy drinkers alike – and rightly so. Made up of organic whole soybeans and natural ingredients, its cultivation ensures its premium, sought-after taste. This is how soymilk was revolutionised in Australia and became an everyday food – something that we've been waiting on for quite some time.

PRANA CHAI GIVE IT A TRY

It was a trip to the sub-continent that inspired Mario Minichilli and Vincent Conti to bring the delicious, mixed spice brew to Australia. The childhood buddies are the brains and brawn behind Prana Chai, the much-loved masala tea that is now brewing throughout Australia, Asia, North America and Europe.

In 2001, the pair took off on a globetrotting adventure, visiting five continents over four years. It was on the sub-continent that they happened upon their first cup of authentic chai. The masala tea we now refer to as "chai" can be traced unmistakably to the Hindu natural healing system called "ayurveda" in which combinations of spices and herbs are used to cure bodily ailments.

The specific blend of spices within a cup of chai include cinnamon, cardamom, star anise, peppercorns, cloves, Ceylon tea and honey. This is added to hot milk to create this warm, milky brew. For many the enjoyment of a cup of chai comes through the warming, soothing feel it delivers.

The pair realised there was a gap in the market in Australia, where you could only buy powders and syrups. Upon their return, they worked tirelessly out of their St Kilda cafe Inkr7, perfecting their blend of tea and spices through experimentation with their regular customers. Soon, the word spread and they found themselves with a demand for distribution.

At an early stage when only a few venues were stocking Prana, Vincent was personally delivering zip lock bags of the herbs and spices each week. A regular Inkr7 customer, Koray Gencel, received a spontaneous invitation from Vincent to join him on a weekly delivery run. Koray has a business and marketing background and upon this first trip with Vincent he witnessed an insight into the enthusiasm for Prana, from both the customer and supplier. He was hooked, and joined the gentlemen in their new venture.

Since then Prana Chai has grown organically within all parts of Australia, especially in Sydney where Prana is now seen on the shelves of quality cafes all over the city, a success that Mario attributes to a large group of health conscious consumers, "It's been received well in Sydney, there are so many quality brunch establishments around town and a lot of people are becoming more conscious about what goes into their bellies. It's a warm, soothing drink made with only natural ingredients, and our customers really enjoy it."

'...Hindu natural healing system called "ayurveda" in which combinations of spices and herbs are used to cure bodily ailments'

The team's success can be in part attributed to staying true to their simple process. Much of the original recipe devised by Vincent remains - changes have come through learning about how to source and judge the best-quality ingredients. They find fresh, whole spices from all over the world, including India, Sri Lanka and Guatemala. Cracking these open, they are crushed, pan roasted and combined with black Ceylon tea, fresh ginger and Australian honey.

They have expanded from mixing up batches of tea in soup pots to an industrial food-grade mixer affectionately named Big Red, but everything is still done by hand and with love. They've also expanded to a Prana Agave range - which substitutes honey for Mexican agave syrup - catering to vegans and those with special dietary requirements."

Mario, Koray and Vincent are definitely living up to the Prana name - meaning 'life force within', it's a concept reflected in their natural ingredients, authentic blending process and approach to getting the customers chatting about chai.

Handcraft Specialty Coffee | Newtown

A LITTLE LATTE ART

with Jibbi Little, NSW Latte Art Champion 2015

Jibbi Little didn't exactly plan to be a barista. She definitely didn't plan to be the current New South Wales Latte Art champion. The 35-year-old coffee connoisseur fell into the industry in 2007 when she travelled to Australia to learn English.

Having worked in advertising in her hometown Bangkok for three years, she arrived in Australia in need of work, any work, and started earning some money at a local cafe.

Jibbi began perfecting her craft with Vittoria coffee, learning first about the coffee and its ability to blend with milk, before moving on to the basic shapes that form the foundation of all latte art – the rosetta or heart shape. Mastering the simple techniques meant that she could start to experiment with more complicated outlines, which were essentially a combination of the basic silhouettes.

Over many years, Jibbi perfected her art, working her way through a series of awards, including wins at Sydney's Preferred Milk Smackdown and La Marzocco's Throw at Single O. In 2014, she placed third at the AASCA National Latte Art competition, as well as taking out the state competition. In 2015, she backed her achievement up, coming first once again at a state level.

Jibbi's formula for the perfect latte art is multi-faceted. The first step is the milk. It is essential to start with fresh milk in a cold pitcher, one that hasn't already been steamed. After reaching 72 degrees, the milk starts to separate, so she recommends you aim for 60 degrees when attempting latte art. If the art isn't the main concern of the coffee, 65 degrees is the ideal temperature for a cup of coffee. If a thermometer isn't on hand, the best test of the temperature is holding the jug for three seconds. If it's too hot, it's ready.

It's not just touch and sight that indicate when the milk is ready. When texturing milk, all that you should be able to hear is a quiet hiss. A squeal demonstrates the wand is too close to the jug and a low gurgle indicates the milk is burnt.

Jibbi believes it's best to use full-cream milk, as the fat upholds the volume of the milk. In saying that, it can be done with any form of milk, including almond or soy.

'experiment with more complicated outlines, which were essentially a combination of the basic silhouettes'

Pouring is a game of angles. Once the milk is silky, it's time to fill the cup. Start in the middle and move the jug to a 45-degree angle. If you increase the angle too far, or move the spout too close to the edge, the milk will turn flat. A 90 degree pour will result in a lot of froth, similar to the effect of a babycino.

She believes, with practice, anyone can do latte art. As a self-taught champion, she said learning is now easier than when she started, as there are extra resources online. Instagram is a fantastic resource, where fans and amateurs can follow leaders in the industry, keep on top of trends and gain new ideas for experimentation. Jibbi thinks sharing and copying is one of the best ways to develop your craft: "When you start to learn somebody's work, you can learn more."

ADDING SOME FLAVOUR

with DaVinci Gourmet

When we say gourmet coffee, we mean those delightful coffees you have when you are looking for a dessert hit, a cool down on a hot day, or a cocktail overload. They are those devilishly wicked flavours that purists might tell you shouldn't be added to a shot of espresso, but thank god we are not all pure!

As with adding sweeteners, soy milk or other concoctions to our coffee, flavours allow us to indulge our inner self by creating the drink we want to drink. And the menu can be limitless. Imagine an Iced Caramel Latte on a hot day? Or an Almond Nut Mocha in the snow? Or try a Choc Gingerbread Dream for dessert!

DaVinci Gourmet has been developing flavours since the 70s, starting operations in Seattle alongside coffee stalwarts like Stumptown and Stewart Brothers Coffee. They have created a palette of flavours that allow baristas to produce a suite of drinks to cater for every possibility.

A similar development is happening with flavour-infused spirits, allowing inspired cocktails to voyage to the next level. It started with vodka and now varieties of flavoured spirits are everywhere – flavoured rum, flavoured whisky, and even flavoured tequila.

Where once the purists poo-pooed the addition of anything to the raw product, today we are seeing creative menus that allow us to enjoy different tastes for different occasions. And although the specialty coffee industry is educating people to enjoy that single origin or single estate, at the same time we are celebrating the unique flavours of coffee as a blend of various origins, of various estates and of various flavours to create imaginative and delicious cups, full of flavour.

DaVinci produces favourite flavours such as Irish Cream, Black Cherry, Caramel, Chocolate and Peppermint, as well as creative digressions such as Passionfruit, Peach, Peanut Butter, and Cookie Dough.

Having grown quite a bit since its start-up in Seattle, DaVinci is now available in more than 50 countries. Their products for the Asia Pacific region are now manufactured in Australia. Dedicated to serving the needs of the specialty coffee industry, DaVinci has made it their mission to create products that bring a unique set of flavours to your usual drinks.

Their flavours hold up under heat and mix evenly within the drink, making sure your last sip tastes as great as your first. And all their Classic and Sugar Free flavours are designed not to curdle milk, making it so that signature lattes are only limited by a barista's imagination.

National Sales Manager, Jurgen Kennedy, said, "With the specialty coffee industry evolving quite rapidly these days, DaVinci is keeping up with the pace. Today we are seen as the pre-eminent producer of flavourful infusions, and we are determined to maintain our commitment to integrity, teamwork and the highest quality ingredients, while creating unparalleled flavoured syrups, gourmet sauces, and chocolate confections.

> "With the specialty coffee industry evolving quite rapidly these days, DaVinci is keeping up with the pace."

ALMOND NUT MOCHA

- 30ml shot fresh hot espresso
- 1 pump Almond 7.5ml
- 1 pump Coconut 7.5ml
- 180ml steamed milk

To make an 8oz beverage you firstly need to extract your espresso into a cup. Add the DaVinci Gourmet Syrups. Stir to combine and top with steamed milk. Garnish lightly and serve.

ICED CARAMEL LATTE

- 3 ice cubes
- 15ml coffee shot – Caramel
- 200ml fresh milk

To make a 210ml beverage you firstly need to add the DaVinci Gourmet Caramel Coffee Shot into a glass filled with 3 cubes of ice. Pour fresh milk over the ice to fill the glass. Stir to combine and serve.

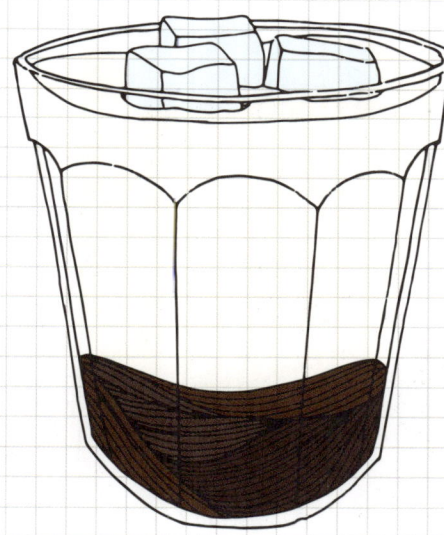

CHOC GINGERBREAD DREAM

- 30ml shot fresh hot espresso
- 1 pump of White Chocolate Sauce 30ml
- 1 pump Gingerbread 7.5ml
- 180ml steamed milk

To make an 8oz beverage you firstly need to extract your espresso into a cup. Add the DaVinci Gourmet Sauce and the DaVinci Gourmet Syrup. Stir to combine and top with steamed milk. Garnish lightly and serve.

Steam Engine | Chatswood

Methods to make coffee

> The choices to brew your perfect cup of coffee are unlimited… from the weird and wonderful to the practical and sophisticated.

SINCE COFFEE WAS FIRST ROASTED, its brewing methods have evolved from the weird and wonderful to the practical and sophisticated. The first espresso machine was first patented in 1901 in Italy and it has been reinvented many times over… And this is all in the search for the Holy Grail – the perfect cup of coffee.

Home machines have become more and more sophisticated over the years, emulating shop style espresso machines, and more recently offering a pod experience that, dare I say it, can be nearly as good. When I was growing up, everyone had a percolator or filter machine for 'after dinner' coffee that was served to guests. Our everyday coffee was instant.

Thank goodness, today, instant is just not acceptable. I can't remember the last time I drank a cup of hot water pretending to be coffee. However, the choices today can make it confusing to understand which method you should choose to make your perfect cup, or what you might like to purchase for a home machine. The following pages are designed to help you understand some of the more common methods, including Espresso, Cold Drip, Stove Top, Pour Over, AeroPress, Chemex, Syphon and French Press.

AEROPRESS

The AeroPress' compact, robust design makes it ideal for travellers or for single-cup brewing at home.

It is a full immersion method, where all the coffee is completely submerged in water for the duration of the brew, before being passed through a filter.

GRIND Medium-fine grind (14g)
BREWING TIME 2-2½ mins
YOU WILL NEED
• AeroPress
• Disc Filter
• Pouring Kettle
• Scales
• Your Favourite Mug
• Water (200ml)
• Fresh Coffee (15g)

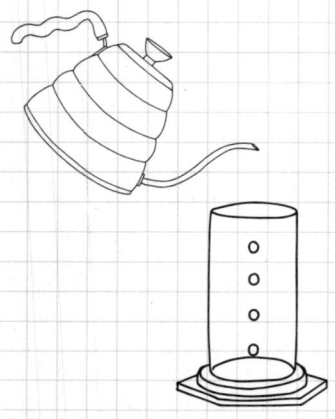

STEP 1: Pre heat your AeroPress by running some hot water through it. For filtration you can use the disc or paper filter. If you are using paper you will need to pre-wet it.

STEP 2: Grind out your coffee and put it into your preheated AeroPress.

STEP 3: Pour in all your water and give it a really good stir to make sure there are no dry pockets of coffee and everything is saturated. Cap it off and wait for 1 minute.

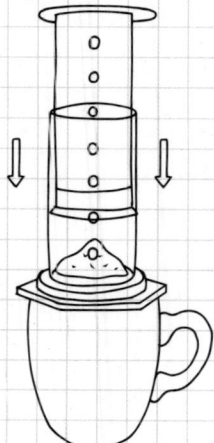

STEP 4: Once the time is up invert it and press it into your favourite mug.

67 Union St Deli | McMahons Point

In The Annex | Glebe

CHEMEX

Mistaken for vases and hourglasses since 1941, the invention of Dr. Peter Schlumbohm will have you brewing a great filter cup of coffee in no time.

The Chemex uses a filter method for brewing, so it will produce clean, tasting results.

GRIND Medium-coarse (25g)
BREWING TIME 3-4 mins
YOU WILL NEED
- Three Cup Chemex
- Folded Chemex Filter Paper
- Pouring Kettle
- Scales
- Water (320ml)
- Fresh Coffee (25g)
- Your Favourite Mug

STEP 1: Weigh out your coffee and grind it. Place the folded filter into the Chemex, then pre-wet with hot water to remove papery taste and to pre-heat your vessel.

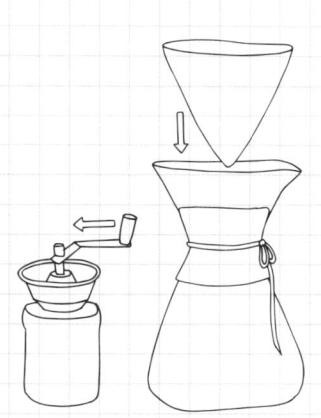

STEP 2: Discard the hot water and add your coffee to the filter. Give it a shake to make sure everything is evenly distributed.

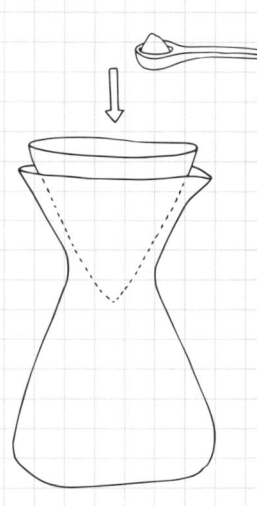

STEP 3: Add around 50ml of water from the pouring kettle, just enough to saturate the coffee but not enough that it is going to bleed through the filter. Let it rest for 30 seconds. Using the pouring kettle, begin to add water by pouring in small, slow circles from the centre spiralling out to almost the edge then spiral back in to the centre. When the water level drops, resume pouring.

STEP 4: It should take around 3 minutes for the brewing time. If it takes longer, you may need to adjust your grind: if it's taking too long – grind it coarser; too quick and lacking flavour – grind if finer. Once it has dripped through, discard the filter, pour into your favourite mug and enjoy!

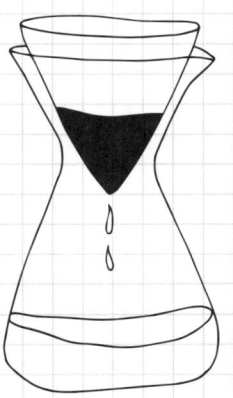

METHODS

COLD DRIP

This brewing method will take slightly longer than your 'Back to the Future' marathon.

When this thing gets up to 88kph... I mean when this coffee hits your taste buds, you're going to taste some serious flavours. A rich, bold flavoured coffee that is often likened to a coffee liqueur.

GRIND Coarse (80g)
BREWING TIME 7 hours
YOU WILL NEED
- Cold Drip
- Paper Filters
- Cold Water (600ml)
- Fresh Coffee (80g)
- Ice (to serve)

STEP 1: Start by rinsing the paper filters with warm water to get rid of any paper taste. Take your coffee chamber, and insert one paper filter followed by the metal filter.
Grind your coffee and add on top of the metal filter. You will want a flat, even surface, so give the coffee a shake and a firm tap to settle it.

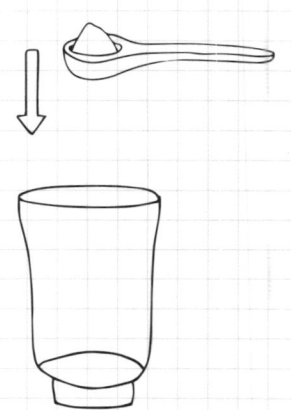

STEP 2: Place the second paper filter on top of the ground coffee - this will help the water to disperse evenly across it. Slide the coffee chamber into place. Make sure the drip tap is secured in the off position (full left) before filling the chamber with water.

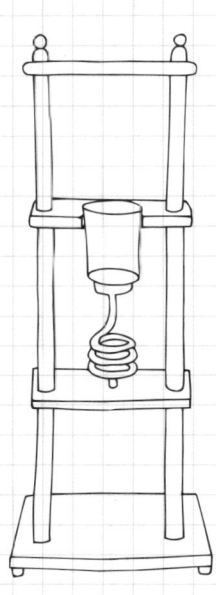

STEP 3: Slide the catching vessel in place and ease on the tap to about 2-3 drips per second. Keep the drips at this speed until you can see that the top 2cm of coffee is saturated (approximately 30 minutes).

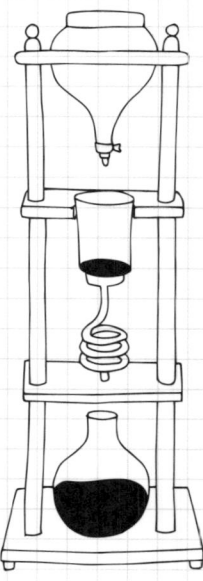

STEP 4: Slow the drip down till it drips at roughly one per second - try to maintain this speed through the rest of the brew. The whole brew should take around 7 hours. You will know it is complete once the top chamber is empty and water drips only occasionally from the coffee chamber.

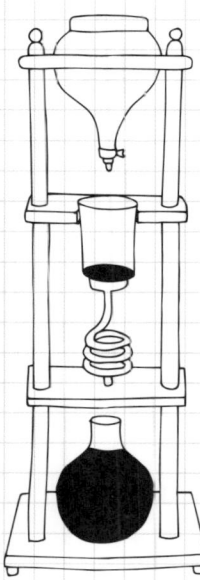

Ritual Coffee Traders | Northbridge

67 Union St Deli | McMahons Point

ESPRESSO

A good espresso has the power to make or break one's day. It is such a volatile process, as you are sending so much pressure through a small biscuit of coffee.

If you follow these easy steps using fresh, good quality coffee you are sure to hit the nail on the head, or at least get the perfect espresso into the cup.

GRIND Finely ground (19-21g)
BREWING TIME 20-30 seconds
YOU WILL NEED
- Espresso machine
- Tamper
- Your favourite espresso cups

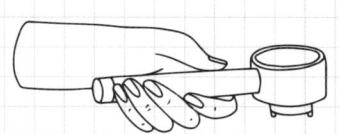

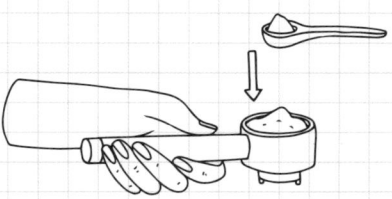

STEP 1: Preheat your cup with hot water and set it aside.

STEP 2: Remove your portafilter and using a cloth wipe it out to make sure it is clean and dry.

STEP 3: Grind and dose your coffee into the portafilter basket. It should weigh somewhere between 19-21g.

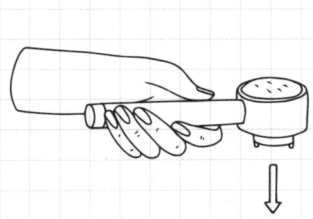

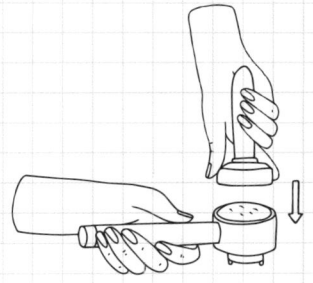

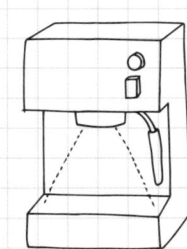

STEP 4: Tap the portafilter once or twice to settle the coffee in the basket and then distribute the grounds evenly with your finger.

STEP 5: Using your tamper, tamp the coffee ensuring it sits flat and level allowing for an even extraction.

STEP 6: Flush (purge) your grouphead with water for a few second to clean it from any old grinds. Remember that cup you preheated? You might want to discard the water now.

STEP 7: Insert portafilter into the grouphead and start the brewing process. Place your favourite cup under the portafilter and watch the espresso pour. It should come out as a steady stream gradually increasing in speed and take 20-30 seconds. If it looks pale, tastes thin and a little weak, adjust your grind finer. If it pulls too short, looks too dark, and tastes bitter, adjust the grind coarser.

FRENCH PRESS

This is one of the easiest ways to start brewing coffee at home. All you will need is fresh coffee, scales, grinder, plunger and water.

The result is a heavy-bodied coffee with a super simple process.

GRIND Coarsely ground (22g)
BREWING TIME 4½ mins
YOU WILL NEED
- Three Cup Glass Plunger (400ml)
- Water (350ml)
- Stirrer
- Your Favourite Mug

STEP 1: Measure out your coffee (22g) and water (350ml). Grind your coffee a little coarser than you would for a drip grind.

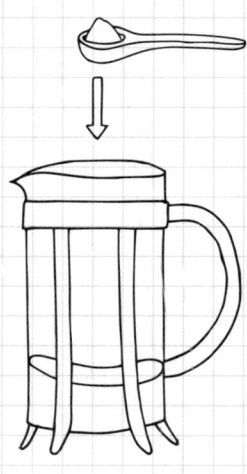

STEP 2: Preheat your vessel with hot water then discard it and add your ground coffee.

STEP 3: Pour the water you measured out on top of your grounds right up to the top, ensuring even coverage and that everything is saturated. Once you've poured in the water wait 30 seconds then knock down the bloom by folding the coffee down with a spoon to make sure everything extracts evenly.

STEP 4: Put the lid on it so the heat doesn't escape and twiddle your thumbs for 4 minutes. Once 4 minutes is up, push your plunger down and pour into your cup. If you're not going to drink it all at once make sure you still pour out all the coffee. If the water is in contact with coffee, it's still brewing and can become pretty bitter.

THE LITTLE GUY

The Little Guy is the perfect tool for making cafe quality espresso at home. Its internal brewing system accurately controls pressure and temperature, allowing you to extract two full-bodied espresso shots and texture milk to perfection.

GRIND Medium-coarse (25g)
BREWING TIME 3-4 mins
YOU WILL NEED
• Three Cup Chemex
• Folded Chemex Filter Paper
• Pouring Kettle
• Scales
• Water (320ml)
• Fresh Coffee (25g)
• Your Favourite Mug

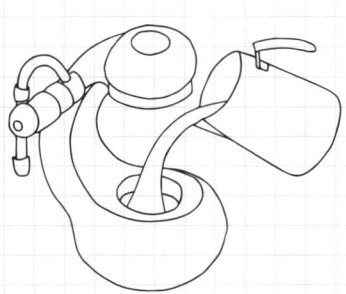

STEP 1: Fill your boiler with cold water and replace cap.

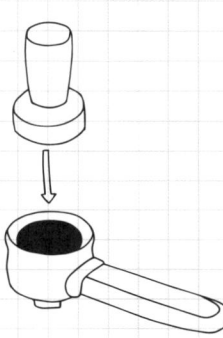

STEP 2: Add your ground coffee to the basket and tamp firmly and evenly.

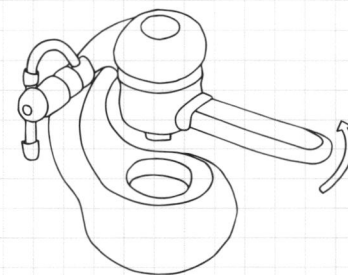

STEP 3: Lock the group handle into place, and place mat and jug underneath before turning on heat source.

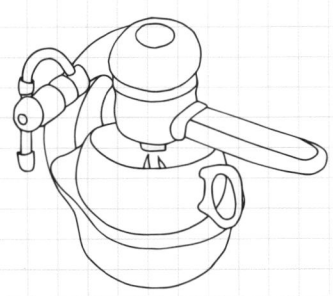

STEP 4: Collect the coffee and pour into your cup.

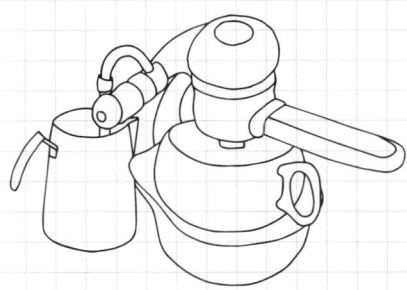

STEP 5: To texture milk insert steam arm into milk jug and turn the steam arm on full. Milk is ready when the side of the jug is just too hot to touch.

STEP 6: Pour milk into your coffee cup and enjoy.

STOVETOP

It may have reached Australian shores as the prized possession in a migrant's suitcase. However from Nonna's windowsills to campsite, for coffee connoisseurs who can't forgo their morning espresso, Stovetop is a very easy method to make a good brew.

GRIND Medium – enough to fill the basket

BREWING TIME Watch for coffee to flow through the top, then take off heat. Time may vary.

YOU WILL NEED
- Stovetop
- Mug
- Water
- Fresh Coffee
- Cold Towel
- Water (320ml)
- Fresh Coffee (25g)

STEP 1: Grind the coffee to a medium grind.

STEP 2: Measure out your water and preheat it before adding it to your mokapot.

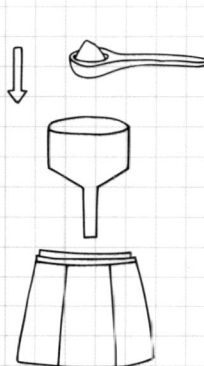

STEP 3: Fill the entire basket with coffee and level it off.

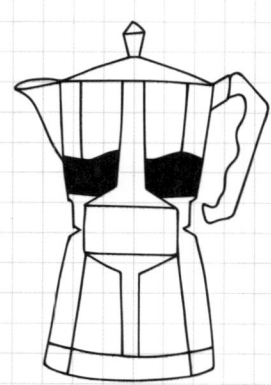

STEP 4: Put together your mokapot and place on your heat source and watch the coffee flow through the top.

STEP 5: Take off the heat and wrap a cold towel around the bottom to stop the brewing process. Pour and enjoy.

Bean Drinking | Crows Nest

Wicks Park Cafe | Marrickville

SYPHON

Although daunting to look at initially, everyone can achieve great results with a Syphon. It has the benefits of a full emersion brewing method, where water is in contact with the ground coffee for the extent of the extraction, as well as the benefit of a clean taste with a filter. The end result is a consistent cup with full body and clarity.

If you are brewing with a new filter, run through the process with no coffee to clean the equipment.

GRIND Medium-fine (16g)
BREWING TIME 4-5 mins
YOU WILL NEED
• Syphon
• Cloth Filter
• Butane burner
• Stirrer
• Water (250ml)
• Your Favourite Mug
• A Lab Coat (for dramatic effect)

STEP 1: Pull the cloth filter over the metal disc, grab the strings and pull them tight. Tie it off and your filter is ready. Secure it to the upper chamber by slipping the chain through the stem and hooking it over the rim. Fill the bottom chamber with water (250ml).

STEP 2: Once it is filled, put on your top chamber. Light your burner and place it under the bottom chamber. The water will vacuum into the upper chamber except for a small amount at the bottom.

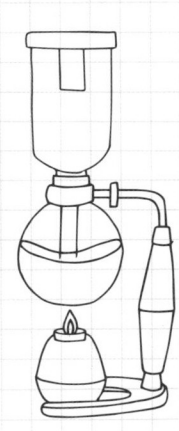

STEP 3: Turn the burner down to a very low boil. Add the ground coffee to the upper chamber and give it a quick stir to saturate the grounds. After 1 minute, knock down the bloom to make sure everything is saturated.

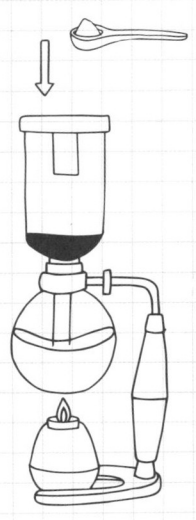

STEP 4: Wait 3 minutes and give it one last stir around the top chamber and kill the flame. This will cause suction from the top chamber and pull the coffee through the filter into the bottom chamber. Pour into your favourite mug and enjoy.

V60 POUR OVER

This Pour Over cone comes in a few shapes and sizes with models made of plastic, ceramic, metal, or glass.

Produced by Hario in Japan, the V60 Pour Over is another easily achieved, filter, brewing method that will produce a clean cup of coffee.

GRIND Medium-fine grind (14g)
BREWING TIME 2-2½ mins
YOU WILL NEED
- 1 cup V60 Pour Over
- 1 cup V60 Paper Filter
- Pouring Kettle
- Scales
- Your Favourite Mug
- Water (200ml)
- Fresh Coffee (14g)

STEP 1: Fold the filter paper and insert into your Pour Over. Place it over your mug and pre-wet the filter as well as warm your brewer.

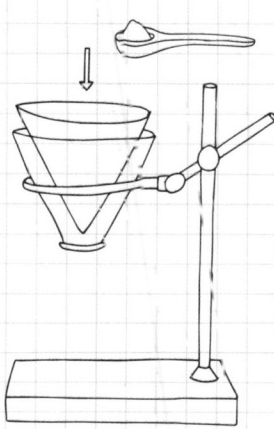

STEP 2: Tip the hot water out of your mug, measure out and grind your coffee and add it to the filter. Give it a shake so it sits flat and even in the filter.

STEP 3: Using the pouring kettle, add around 20ml of water – just enough to saturate the coffee without it dripping through. Let it sit for 30 seconds before adding more water. Pour in small, slow circles, until you have used all your 200ml.

STEP 4: It should take just over 2 minutes for the brew to pour through. If it takes too long and your coffee is bitter, grind it coarser, if it takes less time and your coffee lacks flavour, grind finer.

Steam Engine | Chatswood

AUSTRALIAN SPECIALTY COFFEE ASSOCIATION

by Brent Williams
President of ASCA

In Seattle in April 2015, our own Sasa Sestic, the winner of the Australian Specialty Coffee Association (ASCA) Australia Barista Champion, took home the title as the world's best barista.

This is an incredible achievement for the Australian specialty coffee industry, and ASCA is proud to have played a central role. As a fully volunteer-run organisation, we work hard all year to organise state and national competitions, with the sole purpose of choosing the best barista to represent Australia on the world stage. That this representative was able to take the world title shows how strong we are as an organisation, and indeed as an industry as a whole.

Many may think it's incredible that barista competitions have risen to the level that they have today. Baristas invest thousands of dollars and hundreds of hours to train to compete. At the Melbourne International Coffee Expo, where Sasa was crowed the Australian champion, the grandstands were packed from morning until night with an audience keen to witness who would take on the coveted titles.

These competitions are about a lot more than fun and games. In fact, they are highly competitive arenas that help lift the standards of the specialty coffee industry. It's kind of like F1 racing, although our every day cars don't have the features of speed cars, they are all better as a result of the elite competition.

We encourage anyone who is looking to get involved in the specialty coffee industry to join up with ASCA. Whether as a competitor, volunteer, or spectator, by engaging with ASCA you are playing a part in the future of the industry.

ASCA is the country's pre-eminent coffee industry association. Founded in 2001 by a group of coffee enthusiasts, today ASCA is the country's largest industry body, with its members spread throughout the country.

For the past decade and a half, ASCA has taken a lead role in organising the country's coffee competitions, feeding into the World Barista Championships and associated events. ASCA is the sister association to the Specialty Coffee Association of America (SCAA), Specialty Coffee Association of Europe (SCAE) and other specialty coffee associations around the world, together making up the largest network of coffee associations globally.

More than just competitions, ASCA offers an exciting line-up of networking events, training opportunities, mini competitions and more. Taking place around the country, there is something for everyone, ranging from new entrants in the industry to top leadership.

Join ASCA today to take advantage of:
• Networking and professional development events
• Free entry to ASCA events
• Special promotions
• Training opportunities
• Access to competitions
• Usage of ASCA members' logo

The opportunity to connect with and contribute to Australia's specialty coffee community.

For more information please visit our website
australianspecialtycoffee.com.au

Dose Espresso | Willoughby

VENUE CATEGORIES

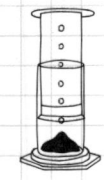
ALTERNATIVE BREWS AVAILABLE

BUSINESS MEETING BREW

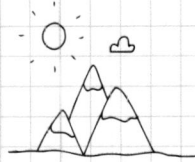
CAFFEINE HIT WITH A VIEW

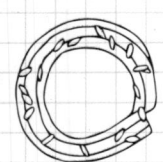
CAKES AND COFFEE, NO KITCHEN

COFFEE DATE

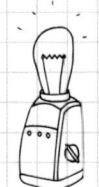
COFFEE GADGETS AVAILABLE

EVERY HIPSTER AND HIS DOG WILL BE HERE

HOLE IN THE WALL

IN HOUSE ROASTING

MADE FOR MORNING RUSH MADNESS

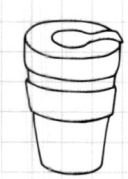
PICK UP YOUR KEEPCUP HERE

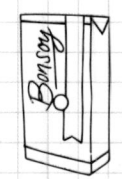
WE USE BONSOY

CAFE VENUES

SYDNEY CBD 110

NORTH OF THE CITY 158

EAST OF THE CITY 244

SOUTH & WEST OF THE CITY 326

REGIONAL NSW 414

Opera Bar Cafe | Sydney

SYDNEY CBD

SYDNEY CBD

1 Brew Collective	119	
2 Cabrito Coffee Traders	120	
3 Cafe Tramezzini	123	
4 Encasa Deli	124	
5 Ground Control Cafe	127	
6 Gumption by Coffee Alchemy	128	
7 Jim (The)	131	
8 Kingswood Coffee	132	
9 Klink Handmade Espresso	135	
10 Livelo Espresso & Kitchen	138	
11 Marcelle	141	
12 Marlowe's Way	142	
13 Mecca Coffee	145	
14 Metropole	146	
15 Nook Urban Fresh Bar	149	
16 Opera Bar Cafe	150	
17 Pablo & Rusty's 161	153	
18 Salvador Cafe	154	

CITY SIDE BARISTAS

BREW COLLECTIVE — Jay Bartho

I HAVE MY COFFEE…
Lightly roasted and black.

IF I WASN'T A BARISTA I WOULD BE…
The world's greatest guitarist

WHEN I'M NOT MAKING COFFEE I AM…
The world's greatest guitarist

CABRITO COFFEE TRADERS — Adrian

MY FAVOURITE BREWING METHOD IS..
I like the look of a Chemex, a Kalita tastes better.

I HAVE MY COFFEE…
Like my underwear – black and delicate

IF I WASN'T A BARISTA, I WOULD BE..
I'd like to be a photographer, probably unemployed

GROUND CONTROL CAFE — Tutti

WHEN I'M NOT MAKING COFFEE I AM…
Fixing things and watching movies.

IF I WASN'T A BARISTA, I'D BE…
An artist/sculptor.

I HAVE MY COFFEE…
Short black at work, mocha when out

KLINK HANDMADE ESPRESSO — Gwenvael Le Joeloux

MY FAVOURITE BREWING METHOD IS..
Espresso

IF I WASN'T A BARISTA I WOULD BE…
Living on the street, probably…
or a specialist of constitutional law

FORGET COFFEE, MY FAVOURITE PLACE TO EAT OUT IN SYDNEY IS..
This is where I'm bound to say in my girlfriend's kitchen

NORTH

CITY SIDE BARISTAS

MARLOWE'S WAY — Hyrum Bishop

IF I WASN'T A BARISTA, I'D BE…
Free! No, would probably have tried to pursue something in sports or music.

WHEN I'M NOT MAKING COFFEE, I AM…
Seeing gigs, music, skateboarding, DJing when I can.

FORGET COFFEE, MY FAVOURITE PLACE TO EAT OUT IN SYDNEY IS…
Chinatown! No specific place, I like to mix it up. Love the authenticity.

NOOK URBAN FRESH BAR — Yogesh Adhikari

MY FAVOURITE BREWING METHOD IS…
AeroPress.

WHEN I'M NOT MAKING COFFEE I AM…
On the beach, at the pub or gym.

GIVE ME A QUOTE…
Drink coffee, smile and get stuff done.

PABLO & RUSTY'S — Philip Pollen

MY FAVOURITE BREWING METHOD IS..
Coffee + water.

IF I WASN'T A BARISTA, I WOULD BE..
A whiskey barman.

WHEN I'M NOT MAKING COFFEE I AM…
Probably practising Ninjitsu.

SALVADOR CAFE — Felipe Afonso Jacob

I HAVE MY COFFEE…
My first one is always a double latte.

MY FAVOURITE BREWING METHOD IS…
Espresso via Synesso.

IF I WASN'T A BARISTA I WOULD BE…
I would be illegal in Australia or a kids' Capoeira instructor.

Livelo Espresso & Kitchen | Sydney City

BREW COLLECTIVE

SHOP 2, LOWER GROUND FLOOR, MARGARET ST, SYDNEY · 0405 546 544 · BREWCOLLECTIVE.COM.AU

MACHINE: La Marzocco GB/5
GRINDER: Mazzer Robur E & Major and a Ditting Bulk Grinder
BEANS: Charlie Coffee
BREWING METHODS: Espresso, Filter, Cold Brew

CHARLIE COFFEE, THE BOUTIQUE ROASTERS BEHIND THE SNEAKY GRIND, OPENED A NEW CAFE IN THE CBD IN AUGUST 2014 – MEET BREW COLLECTIVE. The cafe is a favourite of inner city folk, corporate types on their way to work and coffee enthusiasts who will travel past any number of cafes on their way to Brew Collective.

For Manager, Jay Bartho, and Head Roaster, Saxon Griese, coffee is a passion and their lifeblood. Charlie Coffee does all roasting for the cafe themselves and has even coined a new term for the way they roast their signature house blend – 'New Sydney'. It's lighter than where Sydney has been traditionally, but dark enough to maintain that bit of body that carries it through the milk.

Currently the house blend contains beans from Peru and Ethiopia and as enthusiastic roasters, they're always sourcing new origins for their singles and filters; in fact, they are currently setting up their own project in Uganda.

Brew Collective is committed to providing quality filter coffee, which is certainly growing in popularity. The coffee is a little more subtle than espresso, but gives you "much more to think about," said Saxon. He recommends trying it from the batch brewer, or brewed right before your eyes as a pour over on the V60. For black coffee lovers who have only ever tasted espresso coffees, it's time to meet your new best friend.

At Brew Collective, the staff are almost as passionate about tea as they are about coffee. They source their tea from Teacraft, an artisan tea merchant that sources all of its tea ethically and travels the world to ensure their offerings reach the highest standards. Teacraft bypasses the traditional western route of buying tea from wholesalers in Europe and goes straight to the source, carefully selecting leaves from the teas' places of origin. Teacraft call it the "Tao of tea craft." Try the Egyptian Ice, if you're in on the right day. It's a blend of hibiscus and rose petals with silver jasmine, Ceylon orange pekoe and rock sugar – the perfect pick-me-up on a hot day.

Customers can buy bags of Charlie Coffee beans to take home; either pre-bagged, or as their own personalised order from Brew Collective's wide green bean selection. Just let them know how you want it and they'll make it so! If you're not sure how you like it, be sure to join Brew Collective's monthly coffee tasting session, where you can taste the month's special coffee offerings and listen to the expert baristas tell you all about the coffees' characteristics.

> 'If you're not sure how you like it, be sure to join Brew Collective's monthly coffee tasting session...'

CABRITO COFFEE TRADERS

10-14 BULLETIN PL, SYDNEY · 02 8065 8895 · CABRITOCOFFEE.COM

MACHINE: La Marzocco and Mirage Speedster
GRINDER: Mazzer Robur, Mazzer Kony, Mahlkönig EK43
BEANS: Own Blend
BREWING METHODS: Espresso, Cold Drip, Filter

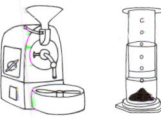   

HOUSED IN ONE OF CIRCULAR QUAY'S ORIGINAL BUILDINGS, IN THE HOME OF SYDNEY'S VERY FIRST NEWSPAPER, TODAY YOU WILL FIND CABRITO COFFEE TRADERS. Owners, Kit Cheong and Michael Cookson, opened the cafe a week before Christmas in 2012 with their own roaster in-house, to give them full control over the quality of coffee from bean through to cup.

Kit and Michael both have backgrounds in the hospitality industry and met while working together on a project. They discovered they shared a common vision to create a retail experience where consumers could see the coffee process of roasting green beans through to brew methods and culminating in a quality cup. The ability to control the quality of the end product is a big part of their proposition. Another big focus of their business philosophy is to make specialty coffee accessible and they are always looking to help their customers broaden their coffee knowledge, as well as their methods of consumption.

To that end, Cabrito Coffee Traders always has a single origin coffee roasted for espresso on offer, which changes fortnightly. It also features a monthly guest roaster for its filter coffees, which provides an opportunity to showcase coffee from other specialty coffee roasters from around Australia. It offers a range of brew methods for those looking to broaden their horizons away from espresso, with pour overs, batch brews and cold drip coffee available.

'...their own roaster in-house, to give them full control over the quality of coffee from bean through to cup.'

The house blend at Cabrito was specifically developed to shine when used in milk-based coffee. It's made from an Ethiopian Harrar, which is naturally processed, and washed beans from Colombia, Papua New Guinea and Costa Rica. They roast to a medium/dark level to ensure it cuts through milk well and the bean proportions and origins change slightly based on the harvest differences each year.

The team at Cabrito has worked hard to create an environment where people can take a break from their busy office day, chill out and relax or meet with friends and colleagues. They recognise that as important as the coffee is, it is one part of a larger experience, so they focus very strongly on providing the best customer service possible and creating an environment with a fun, welcoming vibe.

The Cabrito team loves being able to contribute to their customers' daily ritual and relish the chance to talk coffee with whoever is keen. And they've got a lot to say on the subject. "Coffee is amazingly different, by roast, origin, bean, process style and brew method, so the point of interest might come through in the aroma, taste, mouthfeel or finish. If the coffee's got something interesting to talk about in one, some or preferably all of the above, then great!" said Michael.

For an ever-changing coffee line-up, in house roasting and breakfast and lunch (served Monday to Friday), get yourself down for a slice of Sydney's history at Cabrito Coffee Traders.

CAFE TRAMEZZINI

SHOP 3 CNR OF BATHURST & PITT ST, SYDNEY · 0422 622 876 · FACEBOOK.COM/CAFETRAMEZZINI

MACHINE: Wega Concept
GRINDER: BNZ
BEANS: Di Bella Coffee
BREWING METHODS: Espresso

A crowd gathers in a narrow cafe, tucked away from the chaos of George and Pitt Streets in Sydney's CBD. It's 8am and Cafe Tramezzini is in full swing – men and women in suits stand patiently by the main attraction: the large coffee machine supplying their morning brew.

This narrow space has been servicing the city workers since 2008, but current owner, Stan Mao, has been at the helm since 2011. Having studied business management, he opted for a caffeine-charged life, using his skills to build up a list of regulars that rely on his team for their morning coffee hit. Stan has a strong belief in fast, efficient service and always remembers his customers' names. For him, there isn't anything better than seeing patrons walk out the door with a coffee in hand and a smile on their face.

After many hours of tasting various blends, Stan is confident in his decision to use Di Bella's Felici Blend, a sharp and full-bodied offering with balanced notes of dark chocolate and a subtle acidity. Earthy flavours are tinged with spices and nuts, with its sweetness cutting through the milk beautifully.

Di Bella sources beans through the Crop to Cup program, ensuring high sustainable standards and the delivery of premium green beans all year around. Long-term reciprocal relationships have been established with farmers in Brazil, Peru, Panama, Costa Rica and Guatemala, just to name a few, giving Di Bella the ability to match green bean origins to their blend profiles.

The space sits on the corner of Pitt and Bathurst, occupying a tiny space that many would walk by everyday without noticing. Recycled floorboards make up most of the décor, with a small chandelier over the counter and comfortable benches lining the walls. A cozy, cushioned seating area is tucked away at the back of the cafe, dotted with a diverse customer base, ranging from construction workers to CEO's. The coffee counter dominates the entrance, with a simple menu written on the blackboard above.

True to its name (tramezzini means sandwich), come lunchtime a selection of traditional Italian sandwiches is on offer and thick slices of Vienna sourdough are filled with fresh produce. From Italian sausages and rare roast beef with caramelized onion, to burgers, BLT's and club sandwiches there is something for everyone. Keep your eye on the constantly changing specials board too.

Watch the city pass you by from the front glass windows, escape the hustle and bustle by retreating to the tables out the back, or grab a takeaway on your way to work – any which way, Cafe Tramezzini has you covered.

> '...there isn't anything better than seeing patrons walk out the door with a coffee in hand and a smile on their face.'

ENCASA DELI

135 BATHURST ST, SYDNEY · 02 9283 4277 · ENCASA.COM.AU

MACHINE: Phonica
GRINDER: BNZ
BEANS: Calima Coffee
BREWING METHODS: Espresso

CBD

IN THE BOTTOM OF A LITTLE PINK BUILDING, SQUEEZED IN AMONGST SKYSCRAPERS ON BATHURST STREET IN THE CBD, YOU WILL DISCOVER ENCASA DELI, A CAFE OFFERING GREAT COFFEE AND SPANISH PRODUCE BY THE SAME PEOPLE WHO OWN AND RUN ENCASA RESTAURANT IN PITT STREET.

Pachi and Maria wanted to bring great coffee, at a reasonable price, to the CBD masses. In 2011 the pair, coupled with a healthy dose of Latin style customer service, opened Encasa Deli.

Encasa Deli uses coffee from Australian coffee roasting and wholesale company, Calima Coffee. Calima Coffee uses 100% Colombian coffee, from the Cauca region of Colombia, which is now referred to as the Calima region. It's one of the major coffee growing areas of Colombia, given the rich nutritious soil and the altitude of the area. It's been called 'the richest coffee in the world' and is repeatedly tested to ensure quality standards are met.

The promise of a deli is readily upheld and you won't be able to stop yourself from browsing the shelves of small goods – beans, condiments, sauces, cured meats, pickles – on offer. The deli case at the front of the shop offers olives in large terracotta bowls, sliced meats, cheeses, all irresistible, while giant salamis hang aloft from the ceiling. If you're eating in, pull up a stool and eat at one of the large barrels, or find a spot along the long skinny table against the wall. Naturally, around lunchtime, Encasa Deli is thriving with local businesspeople, but there's always the odd smattering of Spanish grandmas here too, a decidedly good sign.

The house specialty is the Spanish Bocadillos – Spanish style sandwiches made on freshly baked baguettes. There are all sorts to choose from: Portuguese, with spiced grilled chicken, tomato, rocket and herb aioli; Pepito with eye-fillet medallions, fried egg, cheese, lettuce tomato and aioli; Argentino, with South American sausage and chimichurri, or Boquerones, with white anchovies, confit piquillo peppers and roasted garlic aioli. The list goes on, but suffice it to say, they're all popular! The chimichurri sauce, made from parsley, oregano, olive oil, adobo, and salt and pepper, is particularly popular with the locals.

Encasa Deli is currently open for breakfast and lunch, Monday to Saturday, and will soon be opening for dinner as well. They'll be serving pintxos, a small Basque Country snack served on a toothpick. In Spain, these are eaten in taverns and bars while hanging out with friends; and it's an excuse to socialize. These will be the perfect addition to Encasa Deli's offerings. It is, after all, a little slice of Madrid in the CBD of Sydney.

> '...discover Encasa Deli, a cafe offering great coffee and Spanish produce...'

GROUND CONTROL CAFE

SHOP W4, RAILWAY CONCOURSE, ALFRED ST, CIRCULAR QUAY · 02 9247 4330

MACHINE: La Marzocco
GRINDER: Mazzer Luigi
BEANS: Single Origin Roasters and Killerbee
BREWING METHODS: Espresso, Cold Drip

Beautiful exposed brick together with milk crate tables and top-notch coffee makes Ground Control Cafe a great pit stop for the busy commuters in Circular Quay. After all, how often do you find a gorgeously designed cafe serving up specialty coffee in a train station?

Owner of Ground Control Cafe, Sue Zarea, used to own a photography shop but always had a passion for coffee. It was a passion that wouldn't fade and it led her to embark on a new adventure into the world of coffee and cafes. Sue has made sure Ground Control Cafe, which opened in December of 2013, is a friendly, welcoming space where customers are greeted with a smile and none of the pretension you might find elsewhere.

The coffee is sourced from Single Origin Roasters and the house blend is their Killerbee Blend. It's sourced from Brazil, Rwanda and India, but is seasonally adjusted in order to deliver the desired taste profile. The coffee's natural sugars are developed until the 'sweet spot' is found. Single origin offerings are rotated from different areas – recent destinations include Kenya, Colombia, Honduras and El Salvador. In summer be sure to sample an iced coffee, or a cold drip, or both! The imposing cold drip contraptions line the subway-tiled wall and create quite the impact.

The boutique style of care and attention that Single Origin Roasters gives its customers and products fits well with Ground Control Cafe's ethos. Single Origin responds well to feedback and works with its customers to ensure the beans are delivering the desired taste 100% of the time.

'How often do you find a gorgeously designed cafe serving up specialty coffee in a train station?'

Ordering here you really feel welcomed, appreciated and valued. And without doubt, they're efficient. With a constantly moving stream of commuters, workers and tourists, they need to be. The premises is small, the vast majority of customers order takeaways, but there is room to sit if you prefer. Sandwiches, toasties and pastries are available alongside your coffee seven days a week. The fresh white tile, raw brick wall and benches with soft cushions afford a view out of the plate glass windows and on to the passing parade.

Don't be put off by a queue – order via the iPads at the counter and your coffee will be served up with a smile in no time. Commuters, tourists and local workers all rely on Ground Control Cafe for a quick caffeine fix that doesn't compromise on the quality that Sydney-siders (and Australians in general) have become accustomed to.

GUMPTION BY COFFEE ALCHEMY

SHOP 11, 412-414 GEORGE ST, SYDNEY · 02 9232 4199

MACHINE: Synesso Hydra and La Marzocco Linea PB
GRINDER: Mazzer Robur E, Mazzer Kold, Ditting, Mahlkonig
BEANS: Coffee Alchemy, Goodness Galileo, Paracelsus Punch, Sibila's Brew, Holy Hildegard. Hairy Chest and Knockturn
BREWING METHODS: Espresso, Pour Over, Cold Drip

IN THE HISTORIC STRAND ARCADE ON GEORGE STREET, AMONGST THE STAINED GLASS AND ORNATE TILES, LIES GUMPTION, A CAFE BY COFFEE ALCHEMY. Owner, Hazel de los Reyes, opened Gumption December 2013 and, like its 'mother cafe' (Coffee Alchemy in Marrickville), it serves only coffee – no tea, no food, no other drinks.

There is no question that the focus on coffee ensures that Manager, Lisa Tranter, and her team can focus all of their passion and attention onto their one true love: providing a delicious cup of coffee to their customers. Find a standing spot inside or grab a table out in the glorious Strand Arcade to savour your cup.

Hazel has a lifelong passion for coffee and grew up on her grandmother's farm picking cherries from the trees, and then drying and roasting them herself; she was a seasoned coffee drinker at an extremely young age. But passion for coffee is only half the story, according to Hazel.

"Passion doesn't necessarily make you an artisan," she said. "I think it's more about mastery and skill, it's about developing your craft to produce something wonderful, and when you are curious about something, you can eventually achieve that outcome."

Pretty much every item at Gumption is handcrafted by artisans who make their living from doing just one thing, and doing it well. Just like the baristas and their coffee at Gumption! From the hand-spun brass wall lighting, to the floor-to-ceiling leadlight window at the back of the shop, every item has a story and it all fits in perfectly with the surrounding Strand Arcade.

Hazel said, "The Strand Arcade was built during the height of the Arts and Crafts Movement. Its philosophy was all about bringing together like-minded artisans, focused on honouring the essence of their objects, and the Arcade still respects that sentiment today. That's what we do with coffee, too, it is a craft to us."

Just like Coffee Alchemy in Marrickville, Gumption offers all of its six blends as take-home packs. Named after famous alchemists, the blends include Goodness Galileo, Paracelsus Punch, Sibila's Brew, Holy Hildegard, Hairy Chest and Knockturn – the decaf offering. There are always two single estate coffees ready to take home as beans (or ground), one roasted for espresso and the other for filter.

If pour over is your thing, you'll be able to choose from three to four different single estate farms, or if it's cold drip you're after, you'll have a choice of two to three different single estates on any given day.

Gumption is open seven days a week and until 8pm on Thursdays, so there's no missing out on a fantastic specialty coffee. With so many options on offer here we have no doubt you will need more than one visit to appreciate just how good the coffee is.

> 'From the hand-spun brass wall lighting, to the floor-to-ceiling leadlight window at the back of the shop, every item has a story...'

THE JIM

225 GLENMORE RD, PADDINGTON · 02 8964 8629 · FACEBOOK/THEJIM

MACHINE: Wega
GRINDER: Mazzer Luigi
BEANS: Gabriel Coffee
BREWING METHODS: Espresso

JAMES TRAILL WAS A DEDICATED EMPLOYEE OF CORRETTO'S AND WHEN THE PREVIOUS OWNERS WERE READY TO MOVE ON, THEY OFFERED TO SELL THE BUSINESS TO HIM. James jumped at the opportunity. He was in his mid 30s, had been working at Five Ways, Paddington for more than 12 years and felt he was ready to step up and take it over.

Located in the bottom floor of a traditional terraced house, James' The Jim reopened its doors in December 2014 with a fresh coat of paint and some specifically chosen pieces of art. When you step inside you'll instantly feel like you've entered someone's home or their living room. The clean white décor give it an air of sophistication but the colour coordinated vases and knick-knacks put you right at home. It's tucked away a bit behind the main streets in the lovely Glenmore Road amongst the jacaranda trees – if you want to find it, you will.

James is dedicated to offering good coffee, good products, good service and a great atmosphere. Jack of all trades, he owns, manages and plays Head Barista for the business. For him, coffee is where it's at. "Coffee is a way of life, it's about the interaction and the routine of one's day," he said.

Jim has used Gabriel Coffee in various cafes he has worked at over the years, and it was the obvious choice of supplier for The Jim as well. James went to visit Gabriel Coffee's warehouse and was impressed by the way they worked together and how they interacted. This is exactly what coffee's all about for James - the interaction between people. After meeting Sam De Gabriellan and his staff, there was no question in his mind that this was the coffee company to supply his cafe. James serves exclusively espresso-based coffees, which allows him to focus on making his coffee the best in the area.

The Jim may be a new cafe, but it already has a strong following of Paddington locals. "It's very community based", said James, "we see the same people, at the same time, every day." The Jim serves breakfast and lunch, seven days a week but it's really all about the breakfast. The menu is all about the stacks – bacon, salmon or mushroom stacks, that come with avocado, eggs how you like them, haloumi, house-made relish, and other tasty sides. James plans to open for nights soon, too. No doubt this will mean a rush on the already popular espresso martinis, currently available from 3pm, Wednesday to Sunday.

During summer, there are outdoor tables to take advantage of Sydney's glorious weather, with shade from the awnings that line the terraced buildings. For the colder months there's a fireplace and comfy lounges. It's small and cosy, and well worth seeking out. Take a trip down Glenmore Road soon, you'll see.

> 'The clean white decor give it an air of sophistication but the colour-coordinated vases and knickknacks put you right at home.'

KINGSWOOD COFFEE

SHOP 10, WORLD SQUARE (ENTER VIA GEORGE ST STEPS) · 0447 777 567 · KINGSWOODCOFFEE.COM.AU

MACHINE: La Marzocco GB5
GRINDER: EK 43 & Mazzer Robur E
BEANS: Sensory Lab, Steadfast Blend – Columbia Supremo & Brasil Yellow Bourbon
BREWING METHODS: Espresso, V60 Pour Over, Cold Drip

STROLLING THROUGH WORLD SQUARE, WITH ITS BIG-NAME STORES AND MODERN FIT OUT, IT'S A GREAT DISCOVERY TO FIND THIS HOLE-IN-THE-WALL CAFE, KINGSWOOD COFFEE, WITH ITS CLEAN-CUT WOODEN FRONT AND LARGE OPEN WINDOWS. Mikey Jordan and Dane Ross stand ready to provide Sydney shoppers with specialty coffee at this oasis of elegant design amongst the modern shopper's paradise that surrounds it.

Mikey has spent 20 years working in Sydney's top restaurants and coffee shops and his passion for providing the best possible cup of coffee to his customers has driven him to open Kingswood Coffee. The location couldn't be better. It is here that Chinatown meets the CBD and a never-ending parade of shoppers, corporate types and tower-dwellers pass by all day.

There are no large or decaf coffees here, just the very best Sensory Lab coffee and monthly guest roasters. For their house blend, Mikey and Dane have chosen Sensory Lab's Steadfast for its full bodied, smooth and balanced flavour and for how nicely it pairs with milk. The espresso has milk chocolate notes and hints of red fruit, so is the perfect choice for a milk coffee.

The Steadfast blend is comprised of three coffees, including a regional blend from San Agustin (Colombia), Red Bourbon from Fazenda Rainha (Brazil) and Yellow Bourbon, also from Fazenda Rainha. Fazenda Rainha is a special farm, which has won Cup of Excellence seven times, most recently in 2011. It truly cares about the staff who live on site and provide health insurance, a rare benefit for what are mostly seasonal workers.

The monthly guest roasts come from just about everywhere – Central America, South America, Africa, you name it. The Kingswood Coffee boys carefully choose which roasters to showcase, ensuring their customers can access the very best flavours, hand selected by the experts, for their filter and espresso. V60 and batch brew are also available here.

> '...carefully choose which roasters to showcase, ensuring their customers can access the very best flavours...'

Can we take a moment to step away from the coffee (just a moment, I promise), and talk about the eatables on offer at Kingswood Coffee. Kingswood doesn't have a kitchen; instead, they bring in treats from some of Sydney's finest providers.

There are a variety of croissants and pastries from Penny Fours in Leichardt that sell out daily, so be quick. Kingswood provides three to four different flavoured cheese toasties daily. Toasties are on Brickfields Sourdough and filled with produce from Alexandria's Salt Meats Cheese. Glazed doughnuts have also been a hit with the ever-changing flavours on offer. There's also the 'brewnuts' – what some would call a 'cronut' – from Brewtown Newtown. A towering monument of croissant-meets-donut, the fellas at Kingswood Coffee will smother it with melted Belgian chocolate for you, if you like. And you would like, believe me.

KLINK HANDMADE ESPRESSO

281 CLARENCE ST, SYDNEY · KLINK.COFFEE

MACHINE: La Marzocco, Custom Built – The Workhorse
GRINDER: Mazzer Robur E, Mazzer Super Jolly, Ditting Deli Grinder
BEANS: Golden Cobra (House) Single Origins from all over the globe
BREWING METHODS: Espresso, Cold Drip, Siphon, Pour Over

It used to be the clink, and now it's Klink Handmade Espresso. Since 2010, James Humphreys has headed up this popular central city cafe in what was formerly a Police Station.

The space that now serves morning commuters through a window leading onto the footpath, once held inmates and station officers – the holding cells are still apparent, although more comfortably appointed these days. Lovely high ceilings, old wooden floorboards and gigantic arched sash windows make for a stunning spot to enjoy a cup of coffee.

After years of hard labour in bars, restaurants and wineries in Wellington, Central Otago and across Sydney, James was yearning to find the perfect hole-in-the-wall location and focus on coffee. Before long, his zeal for making coffee found him at the helm of a thriving business. Coffee making seems to have a hold over James; even after hand-making hundreds of espresso coffees daily for years, he never tires in his ceaseless pursuit of the perfect cup.

Head barista duties are shared between James and Gwenvael LeJeloux. They're true hospitality professionals who are ready and waiting for the influx of CBD workers and creative types who crowd the take away window and quickly fill the small 10-seat interior. They never claim to know it all and are always ready to learn, adapt and go right back to square one and figure it out from scratch if needed.

The Golden Cobra supplies the house blend here, chosen for its quality and attention to detail, coupled with its panache and creative flair. Truly great coffee can't be boring and after working with all the major coffee brands, James and Gwenvael couldn't go past The Golden Cobra. The house blend incorporates Brazilian, Colombian, Kenyan and Ethiopian coffees, giving it real soul.

While the morning rush favours espresso coffees, the Klink Handmade Espresso team also provides cold drip coffee, for which they use lighter roasted beans from one farm at a time. On occasion you'll also find syphon and pour over coffee, depending on how much time the baristas have to focus on it. They're not willing to serve you anything less than perfect and insist on giving every cup their full attention.

Klink also serves simple, healthy, quality food for breakfast and lunch. Artisan sourdough bread is at the heart of the menu selection. An interesting range of special dishes is also offered from time to time.

Klink Handmade Espresso is housed in a gorgeous three-storey period building right next to Town Hall Station in central Sydney. There's even an art gallery upstairs, so pull up a stool by the wall of hessian coffee sacks from around the world and enjoy a cup or three of pure love.

> 'Lovely high ceilings, old wooden floorboards... make for a stunning spot to enjoy a cup of coffee.'

Brew Collective | Sydney City

LIVELO ESPRESSO & KITCHEN

263 CLARENCE ST, SYDNEY · 02 9090 2120 · LIVELO263.WIX.COM/LIVELO

MACHINE: La Marzocco
GRINDER: Mazzer
BEANS: Livelo House Blend and Single Origin
BREWING METHODS: Espresso, Cold Drip

LIVELO ESPRESSO & KITCHEN IS A RARE FIND IN THE HEART OF SYDNEY'S CBD. Situated near Town Hall and the QVB, Livelo is a small family run cafe with a truly unique décor. Brother and sister team and business owners, Carmelo and Livia Cisca, (hence the name Livelo;) opened the doors to their dream cafe in mid December, 2014. Livelo has an authentic Italian influence brought to life by Carmelo, a passionate barista and Livia, a sensational chef, who have combined their knowledge to bring amazing coffee and delicious homemade food to their customers.

The décor at Livelo Espresso & Kitchen is second to none. Carmelo and his father Joe, sole-handedly crafted this unique, rustic masterpiece. The interior of the cafe is made from recycled materials. You will see wooden pallets suspended from the ceiling, reclaimed doors and industrial lighting. Old timber pallets have been resurrected to form the unique dining tables in the cafe.

Aside from the eye-catching décor, you will be awoken by the strong aroma of freshly ground coffee emanating from behind the La Marzocco coffee machine. Coming from a big Italian family, head barista, Carmelo said that coffee is more than just a beverage, it's a way of life. Therefore, Livelo has its own unique blend of coffee, specifically designed by Carmelo and his father Joe. Coffee beans from around the world were strategically combined to bring a strong, nutty chocolate flavour to the palette. Livelo's signature blend showcases the delectable flavours of coffee beans from Colombia, Brazil, Ethiopia, Papua New Guinea and Indonesia. Livelo serves a unique and modern form of Cold Drip coffee, each month sourcing various single origin beans and perfectly matching them with exotic fruits to enhance the full-bodied taste of the coffee. For a delightful afternoon treat, Livelo offers a refreshing affogato to keep you going during those days that never end.

Not only is the coffee amazing, but head chef, Livia is always cooking tantalising meals in the kitchen. If you really want to take advantage of the Italian influence, be sure to order the Linguine Bolognese, which uses Nonna's timeless recipe. Or try the signature pasta dish, Linguine Livelo, Livia's rich tomato and cream sauce with grilled chicken, topped with enoki mushrooms. Livelo offers many culinary options. They serve a range of delicious made-to-order pastas, burgers, sandwiches, salads as well as seasonal dishes and soups.

'The three most important things to any Italian are, family, food and coffee.'

Also available at Livelo are a number of affordable and enjoyable catering services, bringing that homemade feeling to business meetings and the office lunchroom. Everything at Livelo is passionately made in-house and delivered on the day by the friendly staff.

The three most important things to any Italian are, family, food and coffee. At Livelo that is exactly what they are about. So on your next trip to Sydney's CBD or if you are lucky enough to work or live nearby, this small family run cafe is a must see!

At Livelo, quality coffee and food is always served from the heart.

MARCELLE

127 MACLEAY ST, POTTS POINT · 02 9331 6483 · MARCELLEXO.COM

MACHINE: La Marzocco Linea Classic
GRINDER: Mazzer
BEANS: Allpress Carmelo and Full City
BREWING METHODS: Espresso

FRIENDS WHO THREW PAPER PLANES AT EACH OTHER IN SCHOOL HAVE ENDED UP BUSINESS PARTNERS IN THE SOPHISTICATED CAFE, MARCELLE. Co-owner, Nigel Rae, and best friend, Andrew Stals, cemented their friendship along with Andrew's wife, Gillian, by making their dream of opening a business together a reality.

Nigel has been in the hospitality industry for more than 30 years, both in Australia and overseas. After a stint at Perisher Valley Hotel, he returned to Sydney with a growing passion to open his own cafe, placing an emphasis on consistently great coffee and high quality French food. Couple this with Gillian's experience in law and business and Marcelle was born.

It has just been given a fresh makeover, courtesy of local designer, Gary Skinner, who has injected white-tiled walls, exposed bulbs and natural timber finishes into the airy space, resulting in dimly lit and cozy interiors. A front-and-centre counter displays pastries and other baked goods from Brasserie Bread, tempting passers-by.

If the pastries don't catch you, the wafting smell of Allpress coffee will. Marcelle uses the full-bodied and distinctly caramel-flavoured Carmelo Blend for white coffees. It consists of beans from Brazil, Colombia, Guatemala and Sumatra, with the Brazilian and Sumatran beans providing the base of the blend. The Colombian and Guatemalan beans deliver chocolate and caramel flavours and are the main sources of acidity. If dairy is your enemy but coffee your friend, Bonsoy and almond milk are also on offer.

Short and long black aficionados will appreciate the long, fruit flavours and spicy finish of the Full City Blend, used for black coffees. It combines the rich body and sweetness of Brazil beans with the fruity acidity of beans from Ethiopia and Kenya.

Non-coffee drinkers, don't despair: the non-caffeinated options are nothing to sneeze at. The salted caramel milkshake is almost a meal on its own, while the house-made chai tea with ginger and spices will transport you to the sub-Asian continent in just one sip. Tea devotees will love the organic teas by Ovvio and the house-made hot lemon and ginger tea with raspberries.

> 'You'll find another ten reasons to stay in the form of the wholesome French menu, designed by a one-hatted chef.'

You'll find another ten reasons to stay in the form of the wholesome French menu, designed by a one-hatted chef. The menu is seasonal, but highlights include sweet polenta porridge with vanilla and raspberries; baked eggs with bacon, tomato and marinated mushrooms; the Reuben toastie with corned beef, swiss cheese, sauerkraut and mustard; and the maple-roasted pumpkin salad with Persian feta, rocket, puffed quinoa, orange and pomegranate. Those on the run can also order most menu items to go.

Sitting opposite the iconic El Alamein Fountain on the bustling Macleay Street, Marcelle is the ideal spot to watch the colourful passing parade of Potts Point, coffee in hand.

MARLOWE'S WAY

CORNER OF BRIDGE LN & TANK STREAM WAY, SYDNEY · 0432 487 598 · MARLOWESWAY.COM

MACHINE: Synesseo
GRINDER: Mazzer Robur E
BEANS: The Little Marionette, Jungle Boogie
BREWING METHODS: Espresso, Cold Drip

   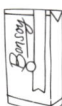

CBD

MARTIN AND CLARISSA JOHANNESSEN HAVE CREATED EXACTLY THE SORT OF PLACE THEY'D LIKE TO HANG OUT IN; SOMEWHERE THAT SERVES GREAT COFFEE, PLAYS RECORDS, SELLS RECORDS, HAS LOCAL ART ON THE WALLS, AND SERVES FOOD AS WELL AS BOOZE. They've found the perfect location, too – in a heritage building right in the middle of the city. The Tank Stream was the first supply of water to the colony of Sydney, and Martin and Clarissa hope they can continue to supply a city with its sustenance: great coffee.

Martin has worked in a number of cafes, and in his spare time would buy and play records as well as occasionally making music himself. As a florist, Clarissa made and played with flowers. The pair always spoke about opening a licensed, city-laneway cafe and eventually found the perfect spot.

It may be situated in the middle of the city, but Marlowe's Way truly feels like a locals' hangout; there's a real community vibe here, where the customers are known by name and if they're short on cash, they just fix it up later. There's such a relaxed atmosphere that you'll think you've stumbled into someone's living room.

Marlowe's Way serves The Little Marionette coffee. When they found this site they spoke to lots of suppliers, but Ed from The Little Marionette was the only one they felt really believed in them and the site. Marlowe's Way started with a specialised blend, Bankistan, that referenced their location in the financial district. The blend has since been refined, modified and improved on and the new house blend, Jungle Boogie is even better. It's close to the original in profile, but has even more body. The blend is made up of coffees from Ethiopia, Rwanda, Colombia and India – as Martin puts it, "nearly all the rhythms of the world are covered!"

> '…there's a real community vibe here, where the customers are known by name and if they're short on cash, they just fix it up later.'

If it's rhythm you're keen on, you're in luck, as the records are always on rotation here. It is open Monday to Friday for breakfast and lunch, and the cafe well and truly slips into bar mode on Wednesday, Thursday and Friday evenings. There is beer on tap and featured artwork on the walls, which changes every three months. Clarissa's Dad, Carmine, makes pasta sauces, soups and other authentic regional Italian dishes, and Martin's Mum makes the slices and syrup cakes, which sell out as soon as they hit the counter.

Managers, Bronwyn Coker and Hyrum Bishop, stand proud behind the Synesso machine, serving espresso and cold drip to the suits, brokers, lawyers, bankers, start-up entrepreneurs, computer wizards, conservatorium kids, administrators, dancers and anyone else who comes their way. This isn't a city cafe, it just happens to be in the city.

MECCA COFFEE

67 KING ST, SYDNEY · 02 9299 8288 · MECCACOFFEE.COM

MACHINE: Spirit
GRINDER: Mazzer Robur and Mahlkönig EK43
BEANS: Own Blend, and showcase from different regions
BREWING METHODS: Espresso, Batch Brew (Fetco)

THE MECCA COFFEE EMPIRE GOES FROM STRENGTH TO STRENGTH, AND IT KEEPS ON GROWING. The coffee company sources, roasts and serves its own coffee, bringing some of the best coffees in the world to its customers in store, through its retail outlets and by supplying cafes right up and down the east coast of Australia.

Paul Geshos is the owner and director of Mecca, and he is quite the force in the local and international coffee industry. The first venue in the Mecca family to open was the cafe on King Street, which in its time has witnessed many cafes open and close nearby, while it keeps growing and adapting. The manager of ten years, Alex Kum, has inspired many a coffee professional and impressed countless customers, with his discipline, determination, dedication and relentless work ethic.

With equal determination and dedication, Sam Sgambellone joined the team alongside Paul to open up a kiosk style espresso bar in Circular Quay. The Kiosk was initially intended as a short-term project but more than seven years on, Mecca CQ still remains. The longevity of the cafe and the brand is supported by Mecca's pride in helping its staff follow their coffee dreams. Whether assisting them to enter coffee competitions, enabling them to work through the ranks or simply teaching them more about the world of coffee, Mecca is dedicated to staff development.

In 2011, Paul and Sam continued the Mecca vision to develop a third cafe, at the much loved location in Ultimo. A space much bigger than its two counterparts, it has become a primary location for many coffee drinkers and fanatics to come together to listen, learn, play and even compete.

Mecca sources as much of its coffee as possible directly from farmers. It works hard to build strong relationships with the farmers and workers, which helps Mecca understand its communities, farming systems, ethics and the coffees it produces. This connection to origin affords Mecca the opportunity to ensure the quality of the product, and in turn a chance to support the local communities and the individual workers.

'The longevity of the cafe and the brand is supported by Mecca's pride in helping its staff follow their coffee dreams.'

When assessing a coffee, the representation in the cup is not the only thing the Mecca sourcing team looks for. They look for coffees that are in season, organic where possible and that are grown and processed in socially and environmentally responsible ways.

Mecca's signature blend is a seasonal and ever-evolving blend that is packed with character all year round. It's delicious taken black as well as with milk. As the seasons change, the personality changes with them, but the quality remains constant.

With a growing list of cafes and retail outlets, Mecca is here to stay. Keep an eye out for many exciting new additions to the family coming soon!

METROPOLE

SHOP 56, GROUND FLOOR, QVB, SYDNEY · 02 9267 1122 · FACEBOOK.COM/METROPOLEQVB

MACHINE: La Marzocco Lina PB, Custom Built
GRINDER: Mazzer Robur and Mini for decaf
BEANS: Grinders, Crema Blend and Organic
BREWING METHODS: Espresso

METROPOLE COMES FROM THE GREEK WORDS MEANING MOTHER AND CITY/TOWN. It was used to refer to cities with whom Greek antiquities retained cultural and political connections. Nik Spartan's cafe, Metropole, retains these family connections; it's an owner-operated, family-run business, with that good old-fashioned service of yesteryear.

Nik started working in the family deli and milk bar when he was five years old. He grew up loving coffee and people so much that he just had to own a cafe when he grew up. The result is Metropole, a cafe on the ground floor of Sydney's iconic Queen Victoria Building.

Open for breakfast and lunch daily, Metropole sees everyone from high school kids to 90-year-old regulars on a daily basis. Located in the middle of the stunning central walkway, Metropole is hard to miss, but just in case, it's the one surrounded by people enjoying their Grinders coffee and Jersey Milk.

Head Barista, Chris Argirousis, can be seen enjoying a macchiato, or three, as he brews up coffees for the shopping-weary of Sydney. It is a very welcome rest spot after you tire from lifting all those shopping bags. The Grinders 100% Arabica Crema house blend has a medium body and is rich, with sweet acidity and a sweet fruity flavour, so it was an obvious choice for the house blend. Metropole also serves Grinders Organic Blend, which has a long, smooth aftertaste of fruit and chocolate.

'...owner-operated, family-run business, with that good old-fashioned service of yesteryear.'

For the hungry, there's an all-day breakfast menu that uses only free-range eggs. Try the Spanish Omelette, with chorizo, mushroom, feta and spinach; or Victoria's French Toast, with banana and maple syrup. The curved service area features glass cabinets that are filled with light bites and bakery items; the pear and raspberry bread or the freshly made waffles are likely to tempt you.

For something larger, the Pulled Pork Roll with crunchy coleslaw and Asian dressing is very popular; as is the Atlantis Sandwich, smoked salmon, Spanish onion, cream cheese, watercress and avocado. If you're being virtuous, there's a great collection of Health Kick Salads to choose from – kale and quinoa, beetroot and chickpea, roasted pumpkin and wild rice. You can then choose a protein to add to your salad – smoked salmon, grilled chicken breast, tuna or prosciutto. With pasta and soup also available and acres of sweet treats in the counter displays, including the 'cronut deluxe', there's something to keep you at Metropole all afternoon.

Fresh bottled juices and iced coffees stand ready to drink and specialty accompaniments for your Grinders coffee, such as Parisian eclairs, Italian tiramisu and black forest cake, will have you dropping into the QVB more than you ever planned.

NOOK URBAN FRESH BAR

83 CLARENCE ST, SYDNEY · 02 9299 5050 · FACEBOOK.COM/NOOKURBANFRESHBAR

MACHINE: Synesso Hydra
GRINDER: Mazzer Robur E and Mahlkönig EK43
BEANS: House Blend, Sensory Lab, 'Seamless', Showcase Blends: Different specialty coffees from Melbourne, Sydney and overseas
BREWING METHODS: V60 Pour Over, Cold Drip, Batch brew

JAMIE SHIN AND MARK DUNNE DRANK ONE CUP OF COFFEE AT ST ALI IN MELBOURNE, AND THAT WAS ALL IT TOOK. They were so impressed by the flavours and the outstanding roasts they found in Melbourne, they decided to bring a taste of Melbourne to Sydney. At the time, there weren't many places in Sydney where you could find a coffee from the cousins down south; noOk urban fresh bar set out to change that.

The result is a house blend from St Ali's Sensory Lab, and a showcase of blends from what is truly a laundry list of the best Australian roasters: Mecca, Seven Seeds, Proud Mary, Coffee Alchemy, Reuben Hills, Sample, 5 Senses, Clement, Stump Town, Square Mile, Market Lane, Coffee Supreme, Double Roasters and Ona Coffee.

The coffee is mostly served to busy business folk, out and about in the CBD with little time on their hands. The folks at noOk urban fresh bar have created a little oasis of calm right in the centre of our busy city – a sort of urban farm gate. It's a relaxed feeling of a country market, with rustic tables, flowers, fresh fruit, and homemade sodas. Head Chef, Robert William Oey, prepares healthy, seasonal dishes using the best quality organic ingredients available. Enjoying breakfast and lunch is like stepping off the treadmill of life and into a (albeit extremely trendy) country cafe.

'Enjoying breakfast and lunch is like stepping off the treadmill of life and into a (albeit extremely trendy) country cafe.'

But back to the house blend: 'Seamless' from St Ali. It is a seasonal blend, currently made up of produce from local Colombian growers (50%), Colombia ADPASO (25%) and Panama Finca Santa Teresa (25%). It makes for a clean and balanced cup, with a light taste and crisp acidity. Rich sweet cherry leads to soft cocoa and a lingering citrus finish. With milk, the coffee presents cherry and creamy malt flavours.

Head Barista, Yogesh Adhikari, prepares blends and single origins for espresso, V60 and cold drip. He likes to offer a selection of coffee not just from Melbourne or Sydney, but also from all over the world.

The single origin choice changes from time to time; it's currently Nicaragua Los Polvorines, from the San Fernando region. The first coffee plantations in the area were introduced in the 19th century. Production expanded, but the civil war of the 1970s and 80s forced many producers to abandon their properties. Peace was declared in 1991 and many growers returned to build today's community, which is thriving. The name Los Polvorines is an acknowledgement of the region's war torn history: during the conflict, many areas built polvorines, or magazines, to store food, personal items and ammunition. Today these structures yield to the lushness of the jungle.

Open Monday to Friday for breakfast and lunch, noOk urban fresh bar is putting the 'fresh' into CBD life.

OPERA BAR CAFE

LOWER CONCOURSE LEVEL, SYDNEY OPERA HOUSE · 02 9247 1666 · OPERABAR.COM.AU/S/CAFE

MACHINE: La Marzocco GB5
GRINDER: Mazzer Robur E and Mahlkönig EK43
BEANS: Single Origin Roasters, Paradox Blend
BREWING METHODS: Espresso

WHEN THE REVAMPED OPERA BAR OPENED IN DECEMBER 2014, IT TURNED THE RULE OF AVERAGE FOOD OPTIONS NEAR MAJOR TOURIST DESTINATIONS ON ITS HEAD. One part of this change is the Opera Bar Cafe, the breakfast-only, standalone space offering tourists and locals alike a beautiful spot to fill up for the day ahead.

The Solotel Group and renowned chef, Matt Moran's restaurant group MorSul, are behind the relaunch. Awarded the ten-year lease in August 2014, the group recognised the need for a cafe in the Opera House precinct, allowing everyone to start their day nestled between two of Sydney's most famous landmarks, the Harbour Bridge and the Opera House.

The design also received a makeover that was a collaboration between Solotel's Creative Director, Anna Solomon, Interior Designer, Nina Maya, and Architect, Chris Grinham, of Humphrey + Edwards. The result: honey-tone wood interiors and bronze and brassy finishes, as well as a brand new colour palette of blue, green and grey, inspired by the colours of the harbour. They've retained what Opera Bar was known for: its seamless blend of outdoor and indoor dining and tables under the iconic white shades.

Coffee comes courtesy of Sydney-based, Single Origin Roasters. It uses Paradox for its house blend, which consists of light to mid roasted beans from Indonesia, Ethiopia, Brazil and Kenya. This combination results in flavours of forest berry, hints of spice and bittersweet chocolate, and a lingering finish. The blend is seasonally adjusted with fresh harvest single origin coffees to deliver the desired taste profile. Single origins are also on a monthly rotation for discerning palates looking for something new. Espresso isn't the only brewing method either; cold brew is also on the cards. The team are creating some homemade flavours by putting a twist on the traditional and sprucing it up with a lime on the side.

Non-coffee drinkers haven't been forgotten, with a range of handcrafted teas from Truly Tea in Byron Bay, and old-fashioned pink lemonade and cold-pressed juice from Sydney-based, Cali Juices.

The menu is short but sweet, offering simple breakfast classics that range from a fresh fruit salad with mint and sheep's yoghurt to a bacon, egg and chilli jam roll. There's a range of house-made bagels, featuring traditional fillings of smoked salmon and cream cheese or leg ham, tomato and cheddar. Vegetarians aren't left out; a vegetarian bagel and a number of different toast options, including a topping of fig, goat's curd, mint and walnut, also make an appearance. Quinoa bircher with coconut and berries will appeal to those on a health-kick, as will the cacao protein balls and muesli bars sitting in the front counter. House-made muffins, chocolate croissants and the Aussie classic, lamingtons are also available to satisfy any sweet cravings.

'...the breakfast-only, standalone space offering tourists and locals alike a beautiful spot to fill up...'

PABLO & RUSTY'S 161

161 CASTLEREAGH ST, SYDNEY · 02 9283 9543 · PABLOANDRUSTYS.COM.AU

MACHINE: Synesso Hydra
GRINDER: Nuova Simonelli Mythos and Mahlkönig EK43
BEANS: Pablo & Rusty's House Blend
BREWING METHODS: Espresso, Cold Drip, Filter

KNOWN TO SYDNEY LOCALS AS '161', PABLO & RUSTY'S HOME IN THE CBD HAS BECOME 'THE' DESTINATION FOR SPECIALTY COFFEE IN THE CITY CENTRE. Opened in August 2013, it is a recent addition to this specialty roaster's story. The team wanted to create a space in the heart of the city where you could always find an exceptional coffee, a place to sit and enjoy it along with food of equal calibre.

The space at 161 is warm and inviting, an oasis amidst the hustle and bustle of the CBD. Warm blackbutt timber lines the ceiling and glass walls keep the noise out but let the light of the skyline in. High ceilings give a sense of space; 161 is many a CBD worker's favourite place to relax and recharge before heading back out into the city life.

Head Barista, Phil Pollen, works alongside a dedicated team to brew Pablo & Rusty's House Blend and wide range of filter offerings, straight from their roastery. The current house blend is made from specialty coffees from Ethiopia, Panama and Brazil; all sourced directly from the farmers at origin. It is a sweet and complex, fruit forward coffee with tasting notes of brown sugar, milk chocolate and red berries. Pablo & Rusty's 161 also offer cold brew coffee, perfect on steamy CBD afternoons.

All of the staff are trained to meet the highly held standards at Pablo & Rusty's. They each participate in monthly workshops at the dedicated roastery training bar (these are also available to wholesale customers), which ensure that coffee knowledge and skills are kept up to date.

A range of single origin and filter coffees are always available here and the staff are more than happy to help you choose exactly the right coffee for you; just ask! Delectable breakfasts and lunches are available six days a week (Monday to Saturday); offerings include Potted Duck Rillettes with spiced quince, or the Slow Braised Lamb Shank with chestnut and Jerusalem artichoke puree. The menu is always seasonal, sustainable and tasty – just like the coffee.

'...the staff are more than happy to help you choose exactly the right coffee for you; just ask!'

As well as a gorgeous cafe space, 161 serves as a wholesale supply hub, allowing potential cafe customers to taste and explore a full range of coffees. There's also a round table, where public cupping sessions are held for customers – a great way to brush up on your coffee knowledge or take your appreciation for coffee to the next level.

Whichever day of the week you visit, you'll be greeted with the warmest welcome, the best coffee and a great bite to eat.

SALVADOR ESPRESSO BAR

32 KINGS LN, DARLINGHURST · 02 9331 0071 · SALVADORCOFFEE.COM.AU

MACHINE: Synesso
GRINDER: Mazzer Luigi
BEANS: Salvador Coffee, Kings Lane Reserve
BREWING METHODS: Espresso, Filter, Pour Over

  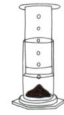 

THE SALVADOR COFFEE ETHOS IS SIMPLE – TRAVEL, TASTE, INNOVATE. Owner, Marcio Brito buys his coffee wherever he finds good beans, from the Americas to Africa and Indonesia. Salvador Coffee aims to discover the berry, chocolate, stone fruit and caramel sensations in the coffee bean and then deliver that joyful complexity to you in a cup.

Travelling from a young age, there's a depth to Marcio's passion. He respects coffee culture and from where his beans are sourced. Before launching Salvador, Marcio went to Brazil, explored coffee farms and growing regions, consumed a lot of good coffee and totally immersed himself in the local coffee scene.

On his return, Marcio found a location he loved, in a small laneway in Darlinghurst, and Salvador Coffee was born. Named after his grandfather, Salvador Quintana, it's a small split level space, with a mezzanine over the brewing area, which highlights the cafe's main focus: the micro-roastery.

Natural recycled timbers dominate the palette, acting as foundations for the counter and the custom-built tables designed for coffee cupping. These organic tones also form the aesthetic platform for the bags of take-away beans and hessian sacks full of the good stuff nestled under the stairs.

The purpose designed cafe layout allows customers to peer up at the roasting magic happening above them or spill out onto the footpath, taking a seat on reclaimed school chairs.

'…it's a small split level space, with a mezzanine over the brewing area…'

King's Lane has a rich history, previously playing host to the razor gangs and 1920s red light districts. These days, it's a melting pot of creative people and is just as exciting, if a lot less dangerous.

Marcio recently returned to a coffee cooperative in Brazil to taste and select a variety of beans for the cafe's Brazil Blend and single origins. He's now the only roaster in Australia to import these beans, which have a great depth of flavour as a result of the region's geographical fingerprint and terroir. Given the ode to his grandfather, it's no wonder Marcio has a specialty Brazilian coffee as his favourite blend.

If you want to try something else, the King's Lane Blend is fruity, bright with chocolate notes and sweet finish, a seasonal coffee designed to reflect the ever-evolving area the cafe lives in.

As an aside to the roastery and the espresso bar, there's a small selection of pastries, organic spelt scones, sandwiches and a seasonally edited selection of weekly specials. Choices range from a healthy light breakfast, such as the muesli with yoghurt to the highly acclaimed avocado toast with Persian feta and fanned tomato slices on top. The delicious simplicity is a perfect lazy morning breakfast for local residents and those who work at home and there are also sandwiches on the run for Salvador's busy business clientele. But the focus here is clear – an exciting, thorough and ever changing variety of in house specialty coffee.

DRINK...

COFFEE
- NO MILK — 3
- WITH MILK — 3.5
- SOY — 0.5   ALMOND 1.0
- EXTRA SHOT — 0.5

TAKE 'IT' AWAY
- SMALLEST — 3
- SMALL — 3.5
- BIG (DOUBLE SHOT) — 4.5

TEA — 4
HOT CHOCOLATE — 4

FIZZY & JUICE — 4

GUEST RØASTER ... MARVELL ST
　　SINGLE O ... KENYA · MUGAGA
　　COLD DRIP ... RWANDA · RULI
　SLO... FILTERS ... RWANDA · MBLIMA
　　　　　　　　COLUMBIA · EL ESPEJO
　FAST FILTER ... ETHIOPIA · KOLOWA

BEANS 250 GRAMS ... HOUSE 12.5 / SINGLES FROM 17

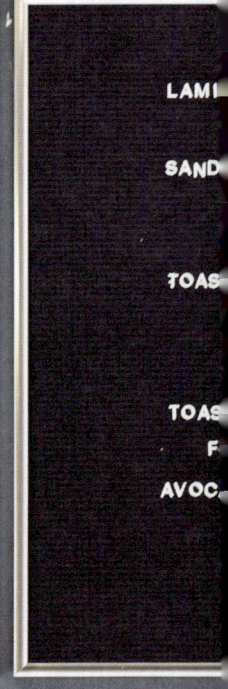

Cabrito Coffee Traders | Sydney

Steam Engine | Chatswood

NORTH OF THE CITY

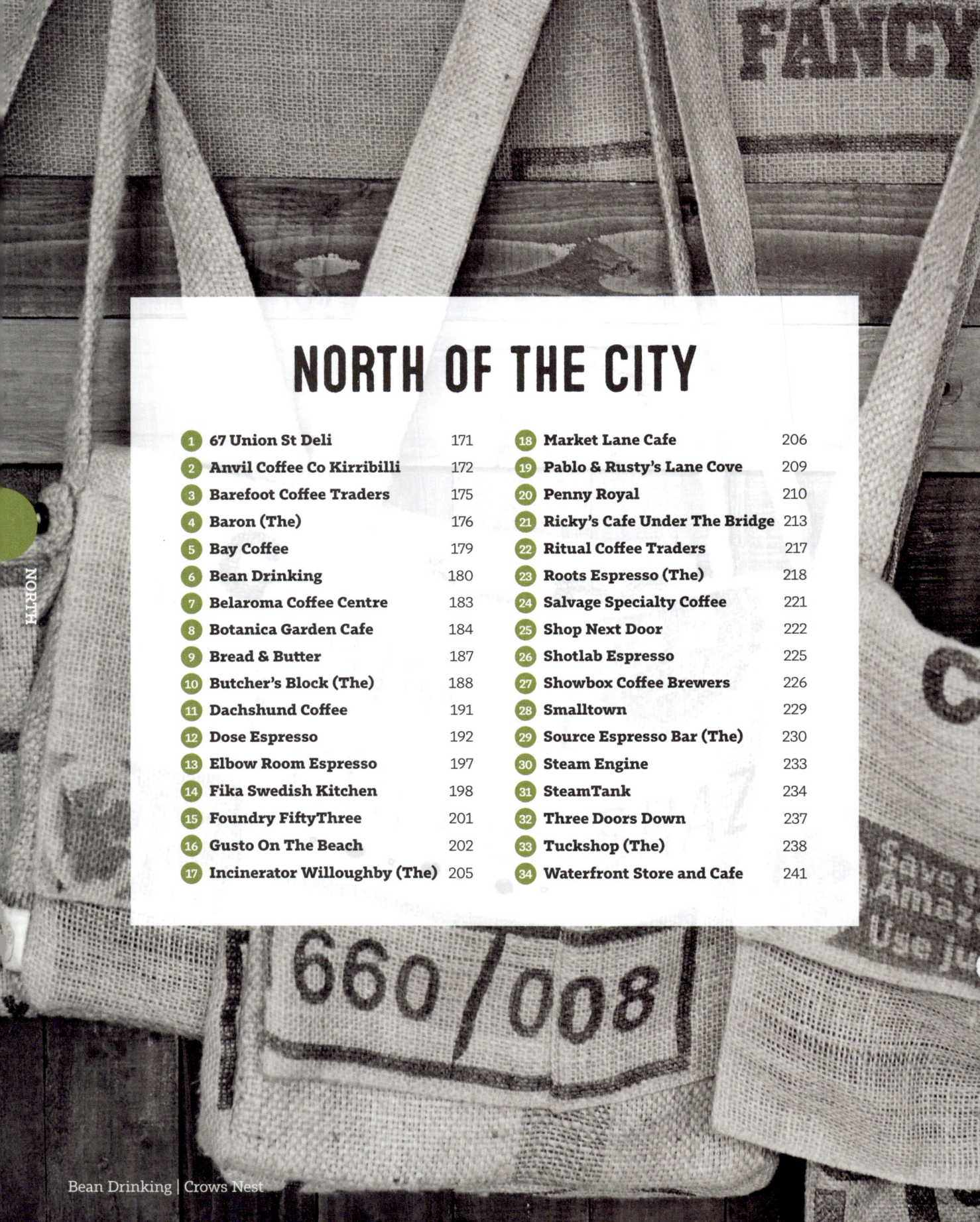

NORTH OF THE CITY

1	67 Union St Deli	171
2	Anvil Coffee Co Kirribilli	172
3	Barefoot Coffee Traders	175
4	Baron (The)	176
5	Bay Coffee	179
6	Bean Drinking	180
7	Belaroma Coffee Centre	183
8	Botanica Garden Cafe	184
9	Bread & Butter	187
10	Butcher's Block (The)	188
11	Dachshund Coffee	191
12	Dose Espresso	192
13	Elbow Room Espresso	197
14	Fika Swedish Kitchen	198
15	Foundry FiftyThree	201
16	Gusto On The Beach	202
17	Incinerator Willoughby (The)	205
18	Market Lane Cafe	206
19	Pablo & Rusty's Lane Cove	209
20	Penny Royal	210
21	Ricky's Cafe Under The Bridge	213
22	Ritual Coffee Traders	217
23	Roots Espresso (The)	218
24	Salvage Specialty Coffee	221
25	Shop Next Door	222
26	Shotlab Espresso	225
27	Showbox Coffee Brewers	226
28	Smalltown	229
29	Source Espresso Bar (The)	230
30	Steam Engine	233
31	SteamTank	234
32	Three Doors Down	237
33	Tuckshop (The)	238
34	Waterfront Store and Cafe	241

Bean Drinking | Crows Nest

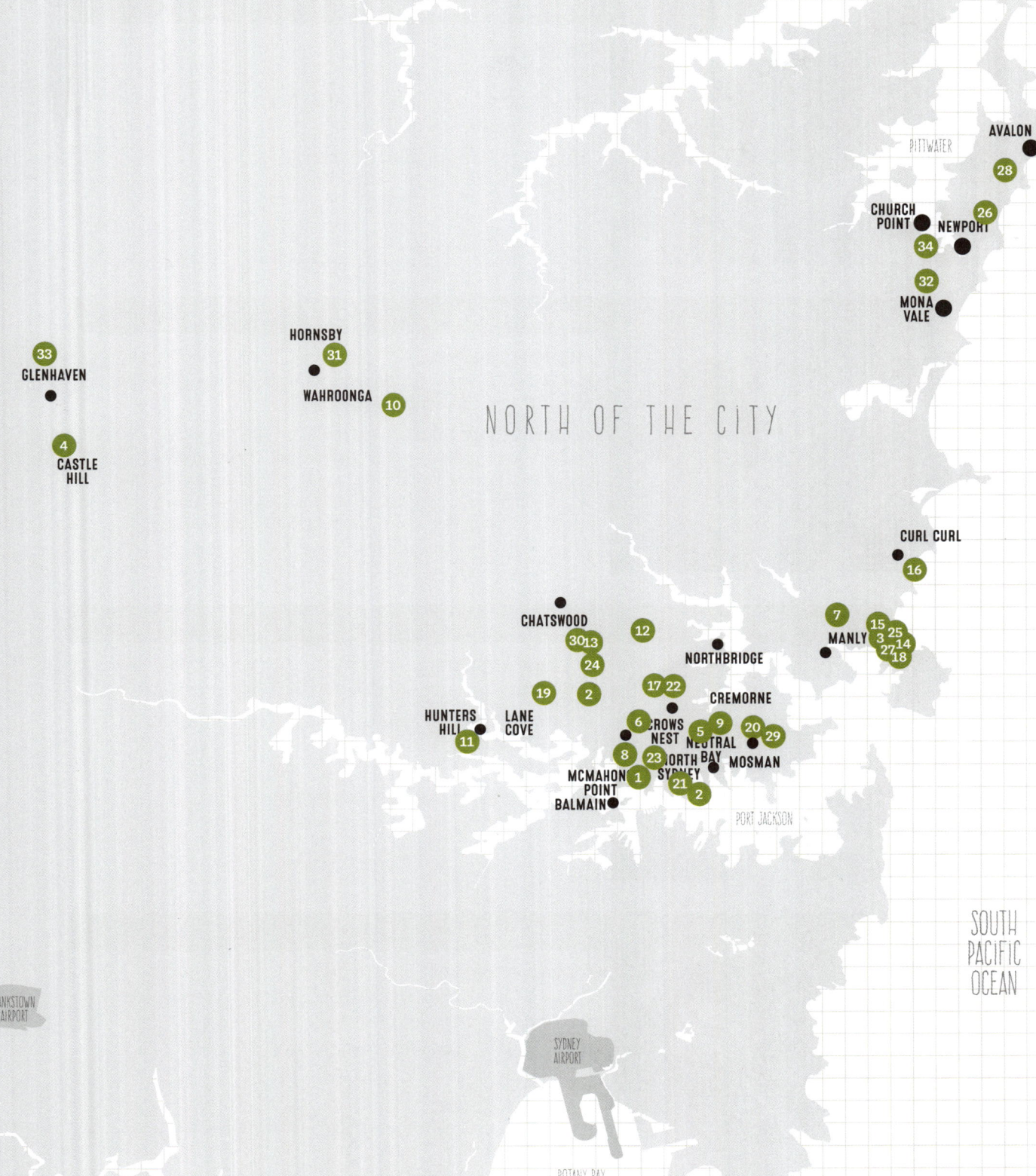

NORTH SIDE BARISTAS

67 UNION ST DELI — Kieran Mackenzie

I HAVE MY COFFEE…
Long, sweet and black.

IF I WASN'T A BARISTA I WOULD BE…
Nowhere near as cool as I am now.

WHEN I'M NOT MAKING COFFEE I AM…
Surfing.

BAREFOOT COFFEE TRADERS — Alex Richards

I HAVE MY COFFEE…
Black! Half full please. Washed down with a cheeky double rizzy flat white in a tulip cup.

WHEN I'M NOT MAKING COFFEE, I AM…
Spreading the word to people that we are all tiny specks on this planet, no one's existence is more or less important than another's; there is an unfathomably large and unknown universe out there… so as Bob Marley sang "don't worry, be happy."

THE BARON — Sam Taylor

GIVE ME A QUOTE…
Coffee like food, is an expression of the person making it.

FORGET COFFEE, MY FAVOURITE PLACE TO EAT OUT IN SYDNEY IS…
Bodega.

WHEN I'M NOT MAKING COFFEE I AM…
Hanging with my wife and three kids.

BAY COFFEE — Bruno Seabra

I HAVE MY COFFEE…
Everyday, at any moment that feels right: before work, during work, enjoying time with friends.

IF I WASN'T A BARISTA, I WOULD BE…
A pilot.

GIVE ME A QUOTE…
If you think you are too small to make a difference, try sleeping with a mosquito.

NORTH SIDE BARISTAS

BEAN DRINKING
Gareth Williams

IF I WASN'T A BARISTA, I'D BE…
A greenkeeper.

WHEN I'M NOT MAKING COFFEE I AM…
Trying to keep my girlfriend happy!

GIVE ME A QUOTE…
I would have said "death before decaf" but ours is really good!

BELAROMA COFFEE CENTRE
Sam McLoughin

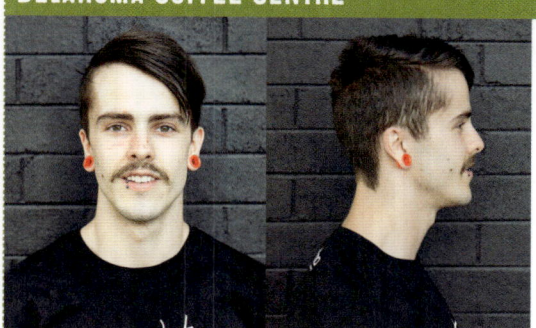

I HAVE MY COFFEE…
Black on single origin.

FORGET COFFEE, MY FAVOURITE PLACE TO EAT OUT IS…
Meat and Wine Co.

WHEN I'M NOT MAKING COFFEE, I AM…
Seeing live music or drinking craft beer with friends.

BOTANICA GARDEN CAFE
Ann Ngo

I HAVE MY COFFEE…
Everyday.

WHEN I'M NOT MAKING COFFEE, I AM…
Being a boss, waiter, dishwasher, mum and friend.

FORGET COFFEE, MY FAVOURITE PLACE TO EAT OUT IN SYDNEY IS…
Mum's house.

DOSE ESPRESSO
Nic Blair & Sam Gibson

MY FAVOURITE BREWING METHOD…
Nic: Pour Over.
Sam: AeroPress.

IF I WASN'T A BARISTA I WOULD BE…
Nick: Broke.
Sam: A customer.

WHEN I'M NOT MAKING COFFEE I'M…
Nick: Drinking it.
Sam: Getting my sweat on.

NORTH SIDE BARISTAS

ELBOW ROOM ESPRESSO — Clare Kwon

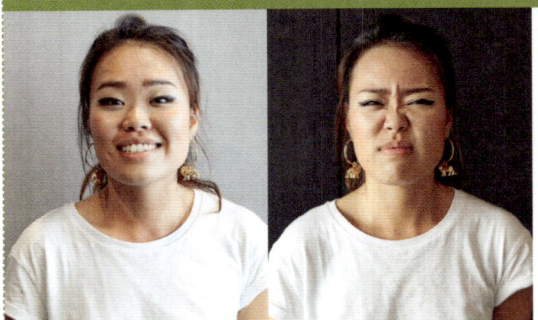

I HAVE MY COFFEE…
Black as black can be.

IF I WASN'T A BARISTA, I'D BE…
An environmental engineer.

WHEN I'M NOT MAKING COFFEE I AM…
At the gym.

FIKA SWEDISH KITCHEN — Kieran James

I HAVE MY COFFEE…
In the morning to get the creative juices flowing.

IF I WASN'T A BARISTA, I'D BE…
A motor sport photographer.

WHEN I'M NOT MAKING COFFEE, I AM…
Spending my time with family, the missus, friends and my two kitties.

FOUNDRY FIFTYTHREE — Alisdair Walter

MY FAVOURITE BREWING METHOD IS…
Pour Over.

IF I WASN'T A BARISTA, I'D BE…
A customer.

MY FAVOURITE PLACE TO EAT OUT IN SYDNEY IS…
Chica Bonita, Manly.

GUSTO ON THE BEACH — Michael

I HAVE MY COFFEE…
Short long black (aka piccolo long black, aka 'the Princess').

MY FAVOURITE BREWING METHOD IS…
The Clever.

IF I WASN'T A BARISTA, I'D BE…
Catching a chairlift up a mountain and riding my bike back down. Then repeat. Oh and get paid for it.

NORTH SIDE BARISTAS

PABLO & RUSTY'S — Ben Richardson

MY FAVOURITE BREWING METHOD...
Any that showcase cleanliness and complexity e.g. Kalita Wave.

WHEN I'M NOT MAKING COFFEE I AM...
Trying to take over the world/impress the wifey.

DID YOU KNOW?
Ben will be representing NSW and Australia at the 2015 World AeroPress Championships in Seattle.

PENNY ROYAL — Chloe Donnelly

I HAVE MY COFFEE...
Double riz ¾ latte.

IF I WASN'T A BARISTA, I'D BE...
A Z-Grade celebrity.

WHEN I'M NOT MAKING COFFEE, I AM...
Paying bills.

RICKY'S CAFE UNDER THE BRIDGE — Ricky

I HAVE MY COFFEE...
Short and black.

IF I WASN'T A BARISTA, I'D BE..
A gourmet traveller.

WHEN I'M NOT MAKING COFFEE, I AM...
In search for the best laksa in Sydney.

RITUAL COFFEE TRADERS — Alex Savidis

I HAVE MY COFFEE...
Any way necessary – I'm an addict.

IF I WASN'T A BARISTA, I'D BE...
Famous.

WHEN I'M NOT MAKING COFFEE, I AM...
Buying sneakers.

NORTH SIDE BARISTAS

THE ROOTS ESPRESSO — Brett Conway

I HAVE MY COFFEE…
Half full and black.

MY FAVOURITE BREWING METHOD IS…
Siphon.

IF I WASN'T A BARISTA, I WOULD BE…
A Barrister.

SALVAGE SPECIALTY COFFEE — Toby Culter

MY FAVOURITE BREWING METHOD IS…
Kalita Pour Over.

FORGET COFFEE, MY FAVOURITE PLACE TO EAT OUT IN SYDNEY IS…
Mary's in Newtown. Might not be the glam but ticks all the boxes in my books.

WHEN I'M NOT MAKING COFFEE, I AM..
Chilling with my wife Ammanah and three kids, Asha, Axle and Phoenix. When I'm not doing that, it's all about bikes.

SHOTLAB ESPRESSO — Heather Booth

I HAVE MY COFFEE…
In the morning usually, and I like to start with a piccolo and then a single origin long black.

IF I WASN'T A BARISTA, I'D BE…
A yoga teacher.

WHEN I'M NOT MAKING COFFEE, I AM…
Enjoying yoga or the outdoor lifestyle of the northern beaches.

SHOWBOX COFFEE BREWERS — Bo Hinzack

I HAVE MY COFFEE…
At 6am.

WHEN I'M NOT MAKING COFFEE, I AM…
Ordering more, listening to 90s music and loving my family.

GIVE ME A QUOTE
Always try the mistakes!

NORTH SIDE BARISTAS

SMALLTOWN — Reece Beuzeville

MY FAVOURITE BREWING METHOD IS…
Cold Drip.

WHEN I'M NOT MAKING COFFEE, I AM…
DJ'ing, playing guitar and taking photos.

IF I WASN'T A BARISTA, I'D BE…
A volunteer for Australia Post.

STEAM ENGINE — Roland Davies

MY FAVOURITE BREWING METHOD IS…
V60 Pour Over.

I HAVE MY COFFEE…
Filter(ed).

FORGET COFFEE, MY FAVOURITE PLACE TO EAT OUT IN SYDNEY IS…
In my mum's kitchen!

THREE DOORS DOWN — Daniel Murray

I HAVE MY COFFEE…
Black.

IF I WASN'T MAKING COFFEE, I'D BE…
A professional NFL player.

FORGET COFFEE, MY FAVOURITE PLACE TO EAT OUT IN SYDNEY…
Anything Mexican, Thai or Indian.

THE TUCKSHOP — Dan Dematos

MY FAVOURITE BREWING METHOD IS…
V60 Pour Over.

IF I WASN'T A BARISTA, I WOULD BE…
Mechanic.

WHEN I'M NOT MAKING COFFEE, I AM…
Making love.

Life without coffee is a life not lived

Three Doors Down | Mona Vale

67 UNION ST DELI

67 UNION ST, MCMAHON'S POINT · 02 7901 9217

MACHINE: La Marzocco Linea PB
GRINDER: Grinder
BEANS: Single Origin Roasters, Reservoir
BREWING METHODS: Espresso, AeroPress, Cold Brew

With a resume that includes the illustrious Boathouse at Palm Beach, Gareth Elliot and partner, Emily Witte, were in search of something they could call home. Their next venture was never going to be just another cafe, and 67 Union St Deli has turned the traditional recipe on its head.

The pair has combined a deli, cafe and homewares boutique and housed it all in a two-storey heritage listed building on picturesque Union Street. They have retained its deli origins, focussing on coffees as well as take away sandwiches and salads during the week, before expanding to an all-day menu on the weekends.

Large communal tables dot the space which is decorated with throws and brightly coloured pillows that are also for sale. Indoor plants bring the outside in, as does the glass counter full of fresh produce. Everything you see you can take home – for a price. This includes the patterned tea towels hanging on the wall, the house-made granola near the cash register and the chilli plants sitting under the menu blackboard.

The coffee isn't forgotten amongst all of the produce. Head Barista, Kieran Mackenzie, works his espresso magic with the Reservoir Blend from Sydney-based Single Origin Roasters. The origin of the beans changes with the seasons, but previous batches have included produce from India, Rwanda and Ethiopia. With flavours of ripe stone fruits, it has enough caramel flavours to keep sugar addicts enjoying the body without having to add to the taste. The structured and vibrant acidity, delicate body and clean finish make it perfect for milk-based coffees.

Filter fans will appreciate the roast from Reuben Hills; adventurous types will value the AeroPress and cold brew options made with a single origin bean on rotation. Both Gareth and Kieran are particular fans of the AeroPress, noting it's "just a preferred flavour loved by all coffee lovers".

The final element of 67 Union St Deli's recipe is the home-style menu, designed by Spanish chef Brenton Gomez, also a Boathouse alum. It changes regularly, but includes favourites such as poached eggs and ham on sourdough, bircher with honey, figs and yoghurt, and avocado and heirloom tomatoes on toast. Everything that can be grown in the garden out back is, upping their environmental credentials and ensuring everything on your plate is fresh as ever.

Weekday warriors will love the variety of lunch options that are perfect for a picnic in nearby Blues Point or Waverton Park. Weekend wooers are guaranteed a morning of entertainment, whether it be picking up some fresh tomatoes or sitting on the crates for a leisurely chat and a beautifully brewed coffee.

> 'Everything you see you can take home – for a price.'

ANVIL COFFEE CO KIRRIBILLI

KIRRIBILLI COMMUTER WHARF, HOLBROOK AVE · 0451 151 737 · ANVILCC.COM.AU

MACHINE: La Marzocco Linea PB
GRINDER: Mazzer Robur, Mahlkönig EK
BEANS: House Blend
BREWING METHODS: Espresso, Chemex, AeroPress, Cold Brew

EVEN WITH ALL THE OTHER QUIRKS ANVIL COFFEE CO HAS GOING FOR IT, YOU REALLY CAN'T GO PAST ITS LOCATION AS THE MOST SERIOUS DRAW CARD. Located at the Kirribilli Commuter Wharf, Anvil Coffee Co has the perfect view out across the harbour. Watch the ferries pull in and out against the backdrop of Fort Denison, Shark Island and the shoreline of Neutral Bay. It's the sort of place that reminds you that we're living in the world's most beautiful city!

The décor here is very fitting – industrial, maritime… some have dubbed it wharf chic. With huge windows, lots of small tables and million dollar views, Anvil Coffee Co is literally perched right over the water.

Owners, Paul Makomaski and Rani Reddy, both decided to leave their office jobs and operate a cafe, and they've hit the jackpot here. The clientele is local; the location means there's not a lot of passing foot traffic, which makes for a really friendly, familiar vibe. Paul and Rani roast their own coffee these days, making their own house blend from three beans from Ethiopia, Colombia and Kenya. The roast is defined by the flavour profile they're after and that's best summed up in one word – chocolate.

The breakfast and lunch menu offerings are simple, made with the best quality ingredients and a fantastic attention to detail. For those with a sweet tooth, try Something Sweet – house ricotta, roasted rhubarb, ginger maple syrup and old-fashioned crumble on sourdough. For Something Savoury, it's chorizo, smashed peas, broad beans, leek and pecorino roman with a watercress and herb salad on sourdough. For those after some hearty comfort, try the Smithie Roll – olive oil Panini, Bangalow double smoked ham off the bone, winter slaw, house onion jam and a poached egg.

But the dish that has the blogosphere talking is the Buttered Arabian Eggs – poached eggs, Greek yoghurt, garlic, chilli and lemon juice burnt butter, with mint on sourdough. This dish has converted many a commuter, who now make the journey across the harbour for one reason only.

There's no question that you've got to try an in-house roasted coffee, but while you're there, why not also try one of Anvil Coffee Co's milkshakes… choose from rhubarb and vanilla, or blueberry and lavender. Divine. There's also a tremendous range of teas for our non-coffee drinking friends, as well as cold brew, cold drip and filter for a break from the old flat white.

Anvil Coffee Co on Kirribilli Commuter Wharf is open seven days a week, which is fantastic news. Delay your crossing and pop in for a quick bite and a coffee, and we guarantee you'll be seduced by the view, the coffee and those Buttered Arabian Eggs!

> 'The roast is defined by the flavour profile they're after and that's best summed up in one word – chocolate.'

BAREFOOT COFFEE TRADERS

18 WHISTLER ST/1 WENTWORTH ST, MANLY · 0416 343 999 · BAREFOOTCOFFEE.COM.AU

MACHINE: Synesso Hydra
GRINDER: Mazzer Robur and Mahlkönig Ek43
BEANS: Toby's Estate, Fairtrade Organic Blend and monthly guest roasters
BREWING METHODS: AeroPress, Moccamaster, Cascara, Cold Drip

THE ETHOS AT BAREFOOT COFFEE TRADERS IS SIMPLE – DO ONE THING AND DO IT WELL. 'Know what you are and know what you're not. Don't be afraid of either.' This is the owner "Squids" motto. This resolution holds true on both the drinks and food front, with great coffee and delicious homemade waffles. That's it. Well, sure, you can order a tea, or a sparkling water but why would you, when you've got experts like owner, Steve Eden and Manager, Alex Richards at the helm?

Head Barista, Josh Howorth, is truly passionate about pouring the perfect cup and at Barefoot Coffee Traders that means no decaf and no large coffees – just the very best taste from the very best beans.

Steve "Squid" has chosen a Toby's Estate fair trade organic blend as his house blend as he wanted a coffee with a strong, rich body to cut through the milk, but one that would also provide a sweet flavour. Each month a guest roaster is chosen by asking various destinations to send them samples. The Barefoot team cups and scores them and then selects its favourite to be the guest roast. Barefoot Coffee Traders sources from a variety of origins including South America, Africa and Indonesia.

The vibe at Barefoot Coffee Traders is that of a community; the regulars are there daily, sometimes up to four times a day! Alex is committed to facilitating a closely bonded, passionate team and it shows in the service. The full time staff stick around year after year, which makes for fantastic customer relations. Customers tend to stick to their favourite Barefoot, either the 'old shop' on Whistler Street, or the 'new shop' on Wentworth Street, but visitors are guaranteed a top class coffee no matter which location they wander into.

Barefoot Coffee Traders came about when owner Steve recognised a definite philosophical shift in coffee consumers' moods, desires and expectations during the mid 2000s. Australian coffee drinkers were growing up, becoming more educated and hence, more demanding. Coffee was now the star, and specialty roasters, such as Toby Smith, were appearing on the scene. Steve put together a team of dedicated baristas and opened Barefoot Coffee Traders with one size coffee, no decaf and one food product.

'Head Barista, Josh Howorth, is truly passionate about pouring the perfect cup... that means no decaf and no large coffees...'

Simplifying and specialising has done Barefoot Coffee Traders a great turn – the waffles are a local favourite, and can be ordered plain, with, salted caramel and/or with ice cream. Simple but fantastic! As well as a top class espresso, customers at Barefoot also enjoy AeroPress, Moccamaster and Cascara coffees.

With a large open window looking out onto Whistler St, and raw brick and green tiles lining the walls, Barefoot Coffee Traders has an airy, relaxed feel that you'd expect in Manly. Customers perch on boxes, elbows on the windowsill, looking out at the passing parade. Life is simple here, simple but special.

THE BARON

SHOP 461 CASTLE TOWERS, 6-14 CASTLE ST, CASTLE HILL · 0433 950 434 · WHOISTHEBARON.COM

MACHINE: La Marzocco Linea PB
GRINDER: Mahlkönig EK43 and Mazzer Robur A
BEANS: Single Origin Roasters, Reservoir Blend
BREWING METHODS: Espresso, Cold Brew

MATT STONE, RICKI ROW AND MIKE ICO ARE THREE MATES who decided that no-one in Castle Hill was serving proper, specialty coffee and fresh, local food – at least not with any kind of style. After a few too many drinks one night, the boys decided that if no-one else was going to do it, they should.

The three boys all work at The Baron now, alongside Manager (and Head Barista), Sam Taylor, who has been in the coffee industry for over 10 years and lives and breathes the stuff. They are all staunch coffee lovers – they drink it, they work with it, and when they aren't working, they're in other Sydney cafes enjoying it.

The Baron serves coffee sourced from Single Origin Roasters, and uses Single O's Reservoir blend as their house blend. Matt, Ricki, Mike and Sam think Reservoir is the tastiest blend to have with milk and suits Castle Hill perfectly.

There's flavours of forest berry, hints of spice and a bittersweet chocolate reveal throughout the cup, with a long lingering finish. Sourced from Aceh, Sumatra Indonesia, Mutovu, Rwanda, Kong cooperative and Yirgacheffe, Ethiopia, Reservoir is a blend of layered complexity and has quickly become Castle Hill's favourite coffee.

When choosing their coffee supplier, the three mates did the rounds, visiting, cupping and tasting. They were three guys who loved coffee, but had never actually run a cafe before. They met with many suppliers who threw all sorts of offers at them – free machines, wind breakers etc, but when they met with Single Origin Roasters, it was a different story. The folks at Single Origin were, shall we say, mildly concerned that these three blokes were wanting to serve their coffeeno experience, and no track record to back them up.

Mike said they were basically interrogated. Single Origin was concerned about their brand being represented at a cafe that was run by people who didn't know what they were doing. To Mike, Ricki and Matt, this was a good sign. It showed them that Single Origin truly cared about their coffee, were passionate about their reputation and selective in their wholesale customers. Rather than just take the money, they wanted to make sure their precious coffee would shine to its full potential. And shine it does.

The end of the story is, of course, a happy one. The Baron serves up Single Origin coffee, and as honourable as their concerns were, Single O needn't have worried – these guys know what they're doing. Visit The Baron in the Castle Tower and you'll see what we mean.

> 'They are all staunch coffee lovers – they drink it, they work with it...'

ORIGIN OF THE WEEK:
GUATEMALA CEYLAN
ORGANIC.

TRY OUR COLD DRIP
PERFECT FOR THOSE HOT DAYS.

Bay Coffee™

WE'RE PASSIONATE
ABOUT BLENDING &
ROASTING UNIQUE
& RARE COFFEES

WE ONLY ROAST IN SMALL BATCH LOTS
TO ENSURE THE COFFEE IN THIS BAG IS
AT ITS ABSOLUTE PEAK.

ROASTED & PACKED BY BAY COFFEE. 2/214 MILITARY RD,
NEUTRAL BAY NSW 2089 PH: 1300 767 754

BAYCOFFEE.COM.AU

BAY COFFEE

GROSVENOR LN, NEUTRAL BAY · 1300 767 754 · BAYCOFFEE.COM.AU

MACHINE: La Marzocco & Slayer
GRINDER: Mazzer Robur
BEANS: House Blend, Bay Roast
BREWING METHODS: Cold Drip, Pour Over, Espresso

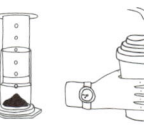

THE FOLKS AT BAY COFFEE SIMPLY AREN'T SATISFIED WITH PROVIDING THEIR CUSTOMERS WITH JUST A FANTASTIC CUP OF COFFEE. They always have, and always will, roast their own beans in-house at their Neutral Bay micro-roastery.

Owner, David Rosa, opened Bay Coffee in 1997, having grown tired of working in corporate multi-nationals by the age of 27. His passion for coffee led him into the coffee game and he learned his craft with the assistance of several coffee roasting industry peers in Melbourne. After working in Melbourne, he headed north to Sydney where he set up the Neutral Bay micro-roastery, and hasn't looked back since.

Head Barista, Bruno Macagi de Seabra, is as well travelled as the single origin, fair trade, directly farm-sourced beans he so lovingly roasts. Hailing from a coffee producing region in Brazil means Bruno truly appreciates every stage of the coffee process. Ultimately though, he's motivated by the customers; their smiles and compliments make him feel grateful to work in an industry that inspires such passion.

Bay Coffee's ongoing journey to source beans from right across the globe makes it possible for customers to sample featured coffees from not only South America, Africa and Indonesia; but also from nearby Tweed Heads Hinterland and even Yemen. David and Bruno search out coffees that best represent their origins. They're not afraid to challenge their customers' palates and always assist in the tasting process by offering tasting notes and cupping sessions.

Bay Coffee's house blend, Bay Roast, is a customer favourite, with its smooth and full body, fruity aroma and chocolaty undertones. Also on offer are eight rotating coffee blends and single origins to sample as a pour-over in store, or as beans to take home. The origins change seasonally and there's always a rare or unique coffee for customers to try. Try the Slayer for a real kick, as pour-over or using the cold drip brew method.

'...a popular haunt for locals who appreciate watching their coffee being roasted right in front of their eyes.'

Tucked away in Grosvenor Lane the Bay Coffee cafe and micro-roastery has always been a popular haunt for locals who appreciate watching their coffee being roasted right in front of their eyes. The focus here is squarely on the coffee, but this is complemented with a beautiful selection of handmade bakery treats and light breakfast and lunch options.

Being roasters, Bay Coffee naturally provides coffee beans online, which means anyone can access the freshest coffee, lovingly roasted and shipped direct to their door. Bay Coffee also supplies wholesale roasted coffee to an ever-growing client base of cafes all across NSW providing equipment, training, support and maintenance, alongside its high quality coffee beans.

BEAN DRINKING

SHOP 1, 13 ERNEST PL, CROWS NEST · 02 9436 1678 · BEANDRINKING.COM.AU

MACHINE: Slayer
GRINDER: Mahlkönig EK43, Mazzer Robur E
BEANS: Roastworks Coffee Co.
BREWING METHODS: Nitro Cold Brew On Tap, Pour Over, Cold Drip, Batch Brew

KEITH REAY'S ORIGINAL RELATIONSHIP WITH COFFEE WAS ELEMENTARY AT BEST: the caffeinated wonder simply got him through long days while working in the IT industry. It wasn't until he opened a sample bag of beans from Yirgacheffe in Ethiopia that his journey with the brew really began. As a result, Bean Drinking was born.

The espresso bar and micro-roaster sits in the middle of Ernest Place, sprouting the artisan coffee message to the workers and locals in Crows Nest. While he may not have started in coffee, Keith's passion to explore the multitude of elements including origins, roasts, brews and extractions, is incredibly obvious at Bean Drinking, where coffee is first and foremost.

The space takes on the look of a coffee emporium, with clocks showing the time in major coffee regions, coffee-sack artwork, chalk-art drawings of the stages of growth of a coffee plant and the tap of Nitro coffee on the main counter. There's a dedicated 'brew bar' laden with alternative brewing methods for you to experience, but the piece de resistance is a customised SLAYER, a hand built coffee machine that allows the barista behind it to produce the most delicious espresso beverages, each of which is weighed and timed to ensure consistency and quality in the cup. Leading the charge here is Manager, Patrice Dayde, an enigmatic Frenchman and ex-Sommelier who is blessed with a wealth of hospitality experience.

'…the roaster quickly outgrew its space and moved into a nearby warehouse as it expanded towards wholesale.'

The choice of beans come courtesy of its in-house roaster Roastworks Coffee Co. Originally located in the cafe, the roaster quickly outgrew its space and moved into a nearby warehouse as it expanded towards wholesale. The cafe uses two house blends. The first is Boots, a lighter roast named in honour of a pair of Keith's much-loved cherry red Doc Martens. It features naturally processed beans from the Yirgacheffe region in Ethiopia and Sertaozinho in Brazil, resulting in a floral aroma with an upfront taste of sweet berries and a lingering cacao flavour. The second is Latin American, a traditional blend of fully washed South Central coffees.

At any one time, you can also find two rotating espresso single origins and two or three filter options, leaving customers spoilt for choice. Cold drip, sparkling cold drip, cascara, pour over, batch brew, nitro coffee on tap, and hand-bottled iced coffee are also on offer for those interested in alternative brewing methods, or just looking for a cold caffeinated solution to a hot day.

Coffee may come first, but the food doesn't sit far behind. Head Chef, Ben Davis and his team have designed a menu full of fresh and seasonal produce, dishing up plates with a creative twist on traditional cafe fare. One last suggestion – try the Coffee Flight and start your own journey of coffee discovery.

BELAROMA COFFEE CENTRE

75 KENNETH RD, MANLY VALE · 02 8966 4345 · BELAROMACOFFEE.COM.AU/

MACHINE: UNIC Stella di Caffè
GRINDER: Anfim and Mythos
BEANS: Belaroma House Blends
BREWING METHODS: Cold Drip, Pour Over, Moccamaster

  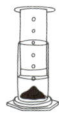 

TUCKED AWAY IN THE BEACHSIDE SUBURB OF MANLY VALE IS A COFFEE ROASTER PERFECTING ITS COFFEE OFFERINGS. Belaroma believes there is no excuse for drinking a bad cup of coffee and what started as roaster and factory has expanded to a much loved brand with an adjacent cafe.

Belaroma's Manly Vale cafe is inundated with staff that know there's no excuse for a bad cup of brew. Sam McLoughlin is in charge of the business, having turned his reliance on caffeine to be a 'morning person' into a full-time career.

The light-filled space places an emphasis on stained wood furnishings, with a long bench playing host to the customised Stella di Cafe coffee machine. Large windows let loads of light in, but when the skies are grey, huge retro green lights ensure you can see your plate. The large communal table in the middle of the space is perfect for perching with the paper and coffee or you can get close to the action by sitting on the 'brew bar' and watching the baristas work their magic. The balcony, with its huge retractable awning is ideal for lunch in the sun.

Having a roaster at your doorstep means the baristas at Belaroma Coffee are spoilt for choice. They use Octavia for their house blend, which features beans sourced from Colombia, Sumatra, Costa Rica and just 10% from Nicaragua. It's roasted lightly in small batches, resulting in an outstanding complexity and smoothness as well as sugary and floral aromas. Hints of nutmeg and other spices blend with delicate roasted notes to provide a clean acidity and no hint of bitterness.

AeroPress, cold-drip, pour over and moccamaster all appear on the menu, and all coffees start with a double ristretto base. 87 point plus single origins are also on a rotation for locals looking to try something new.

While the focus may be on coffee, the kitchen is by no means neglected. Led by Head Chef, Chris Blatchford, the team of chefs produce street-style breakfast and lunch meals, drawing on ingredients from some of the key coffee growing regions where they also source their green coffee beans. As a result, there are flavours of Mexico, Costa Rica, Brazil and Indonesia on the menu, including wraps and rolls spiced up with jamon, chorizo and salsa. They also look locally for produce, favouring the northern beaches and Hunter Valley – a region close to Chris' heart.

For coffee that's withstood the test of time and a menu that more than holds its own against some seriously good brew, Belaroma delivers.

> '...what started as roaster and factory has expanded to a much loved brand with an adjacent cafe.'

BOTANICA GARDEN CAFE

61A BAY RD, WAVERTON · 0432 689 555 · FACEBOOK.COM/BOTANICAGC

MACHINE: La Marzocco
GRINDER: Mazzer Robur E
BEANS: Pablo & Rusty's House Blend
BREWING METHODS: Espresso, Filter

BRING A TOUCH OF SERENITY TO YOUR DAY WITH A STOP AT BOTANICA GARDEN CAFE IN WAVERTON. This idyllic setting will have you relaxing with a steaming cup of coffee in no time.

The wood framed structure has a cabin-in-the-woods feel. Eclectic decorations of photographs, vintage signs and birdcages are scattered on the walls, while a perfect mismatch of tables, couches and pillows fill the space. Look up and you will see teapots and flowers adorning the roof. Outside you will find a small waterfall and a fish-filled pond.

Nathan, a fine dining chef, and Ann, a former CS officer for banks, met, fell in love and created this haven. Nathan is a skilful chef who can make pretty much anything and when you combine this with Ann's creative eye and passion for delivering a good cup of coffee, it's no wonder such an amazing sanctuary was born.

In 2012 they were at a crossroads in their lives, choosing between making lots of money or being with their two babies. They chose living life to the fullest and their family. Nathan said their focus had always been to "deliver the best, to show our passion and love for what we do, and not go after the money".

Nathan and Ann are both religious coffee drinkers and Ann said, "Coffee not only gives you a kick to start the day but is also a means time for a catch up and conversation." Ann and Nathan are big believers in giving back to the world and donate all tips to various charities as well as donating vouchers for school raffles. They also support arts, sustainability and all things good for Mother Earth. It is this ethos that influenced their decision to stock Pablo & Rusty's House Blend.

Pablo & Rusty's Roasters are dedicated to sustainable practices and enforce it into all processes, from bean to bag. The first time Ann and Nathan tried their blend, they had to have another cup. They knew that it was the coffee they wanted to share with their customers.

The house blend offers a sweet and complex, fruit forward flavour with tasting notes of brown sugar, milk chocolate and red berries. This irresistible Pablo & Rusty's House Blend is offered alongside Vietnamese Coffee Drips – a dark and sweet flavour with a velvety, chocolate taste.

Botanica is open for breakfast and lunch seven days a week, offering a fusion of good ol' homemade food and modern Australian/Asian twists. Try their Signature Sandwich – chargrilled Scotch fillet, melted Swiss cheese, house-made beetroot relish and pickles, Dijon aioli in toasted Schiacciata bread served with their homemade slaw or triple cooked hand cut chips. Botanica Garden Cafe is a place that welcomes customers of all ages, from young and old, to artists and families – and it is even dog friendly!

'Ann and Nathan are big believers in giving back to the world and donate all tips to various charities...'

BREAD & BUTTER

89 PARRAWEEN ST, CREMORNE (ENTER VIA 392-394 MILITARY RD) · 02 9909 2496

MACHINE: La Marzocco GB/5
GRINDER: Mazzer Luigi
BEANS: Barrtel One Coffee Roasters and Guest Roasters
BREWING METHODS: Espresso, Chemex, Pour Over, Cold Drip, Cold Brew, AeroPress, French Press

FROM THE SAME PASSIONATE AFICIONADOS AT MANLY'S FOUNDRY 53 COMES ANOTHER FAVOURITE LOCAL CAFE IN CREMORNE – BREAD & BUTTER. Part of a unique retail offering, this hipsters' paradise is a collection of retail, gallery and hospitality spaces, hidden behind a conventional street frontage.

All aspects of the venue are interconnected through doorways and laneways, but all lie in separate buildings or floors around a large courtyard. What you find when you penetrate the façade is something truly special: a furniture, art and clothing store stocking local designers' and artists' work, fair trade and recycled products; Sweeney's Barber, a vintage barber with a traditional chair where you can experience a cut throat shave, a vintage haircut and an aged scotch; a bar, Sidecar, serving up beautifully crafted cocktails and matched charcuterie plates; and of course, Bread & Butter, providing Barrel One Coffee Roasters' beans in a rustic but comfortable garage space.

The intimate cafe, managed by Michael Tyson and Alisdair Walter, pairs Barrel One beans, sourced from Tanna Island in Vanuatu, with freshly baked goods, breakfast and lunch favourites, and live music every second Sunday. Huge murals grace the walls, and herb gardens and green walls abound, providing fodder for the kitchen. Relaxing in the sunny courtyard with a perfect pour over, cold drip or AeroPress, you'll forget you're in the middle of a city, smack bang between two busy roads.

'Part of a unique retail offering, this hipsters' paradise is a collection of retail, gallery and hospitality spaces, hidden behind a conventional street frontage.'

Sourcing their coffee directly from the producers on Tanna Island means the folk behind Bread & Butter know their farmers, care about their lives and working conditions, and allows Bread & Butter to donate machinery and funding for projects at the cooperatives and estates.

The locals live and work at the base of the Mt Yasur volcano, whose ash clouds contribute to what is considered some of the most organic and natural farming land in the world. Each farmer owns one or two acres of garden, where they grow coffee for Bread & Butter, but also taro, cassava, peanuts, cabbage and other vegetables to either sell, or use for their families. This intercropping system means the farmers' land can give them fresh produce as well as providing them a cash crop.

Bread & Butter's coffee is a great point of difference for them – they know it intimately because they have been there right from planting to brewing; they know the producers and their staff take great pride in educating customers about their blends, and what the coffee means for the farmers who produce it. They take their coffee seriously, but offer service that is friendly and helpful.

As well as their delicious coffee creations, Bread & Butter also offers organic, fresh, healthy food that aims to land beyond your regular cafe fare. Their chefs have backgrounds in gastronomy and food matching which would allow them to work in some of the finest Sydney restaurants, but the challenge and opportunity to create their own works of art means it's in Cremorne they stay!

THE BUTCHER'S BLOCK

15 REDLEAF AVE, WAHROONGA · 02 9487 8136 · THE-BUTCHERSBLOCK.COM

MACHINE: La Marzocco GB/5
GRINDER: Mazzer Robur
BEANS: Allpress Carmelo
BREWING METHODS: Espresso

FATHER AND SON TEAM, GEORGE AND ANTHONY KARNASIOTIS, OPENED THE BUTCHER'S BLOCK IN WAHROONGA IN 2013. The name, and the one of a kind fit-out, pays homage to the long line of butcher shops that have at some stage in history inhabited the space.

Set in the leafy green suburb of Wahroonga, The Butcher's Block offers something unique to the area – a smart cafe offering specialty coffee and a colourful menu of breakfast and lunch temptations. It's a place where the father and son team can work side-by-side for the first time. Having said that, Anthony has grown up working for George in all his other ventures, including delis, chicken shops, takeaway shops and cafes.

The Butcher's Block sees business meetings, university students and long, leisurely lunches. The one thing they all have in common is their enthusiasm for the Allpress Espresso. George and Anthony couldn't be happier with Allpress, and neither could their customers. The father and son find Allpress has a respect for the product and the industry which really impressed them, and the commitment to their customers and the support they offer has guaranteed that Allpress will be supplying all The Butcher's Block coffee for the foreseeable future. The house blend is the Carmelo Blend; medium roasted, using the hot air roasting method, with beans from Colombia, Sumatra, Brazil and Guatemala. It's lively and full-bodied, with distinct caramel flavours.

> 'It's a place where the father and son team can work side-by-side for the first time.'

Alongside the house blend, The Butcher's Block also offers a rotating selection of single origins, sourced from places such as Costa Rica, Ethiopia, Guatemala, Brazil, Papua New Guinea, Indonesia, Colombia and Yemen.

Floor Manager, Rocco Mammone, has his own love affair with coffee. Being of Italian background, coffee played a large role in Rocco's upbringing. From a young age, Rocco would sit with his Nonno, sharing stories and an espresso – definitely an acquired palate at a young age. Together with Head Barista, Vikrant Joshi, Rocco takes care of his customers with true dedication.

The food (and the crockery) is vibrant in colour, balanced in flavour and extremely popular. The early morning tradies making their way down from the Central Coast pop in for the 'one pan' breakfast of fried eggs and bacon, sourdough and house tomato sauce. Teachers and parents on their way to the start of the school day rush in for a specialty coffee; the mums and dads come back once free of the kids for the polenta porridge with rhubarb compote, walnut crumble and almonds.

The Butcher's Block is open for breakfast and lunch, but keep an eye out next door. George and Anthony are currently fitting it out to open as a night time bar and bistro, called The Butcher's Apprentice. I wonder who will be working in there?

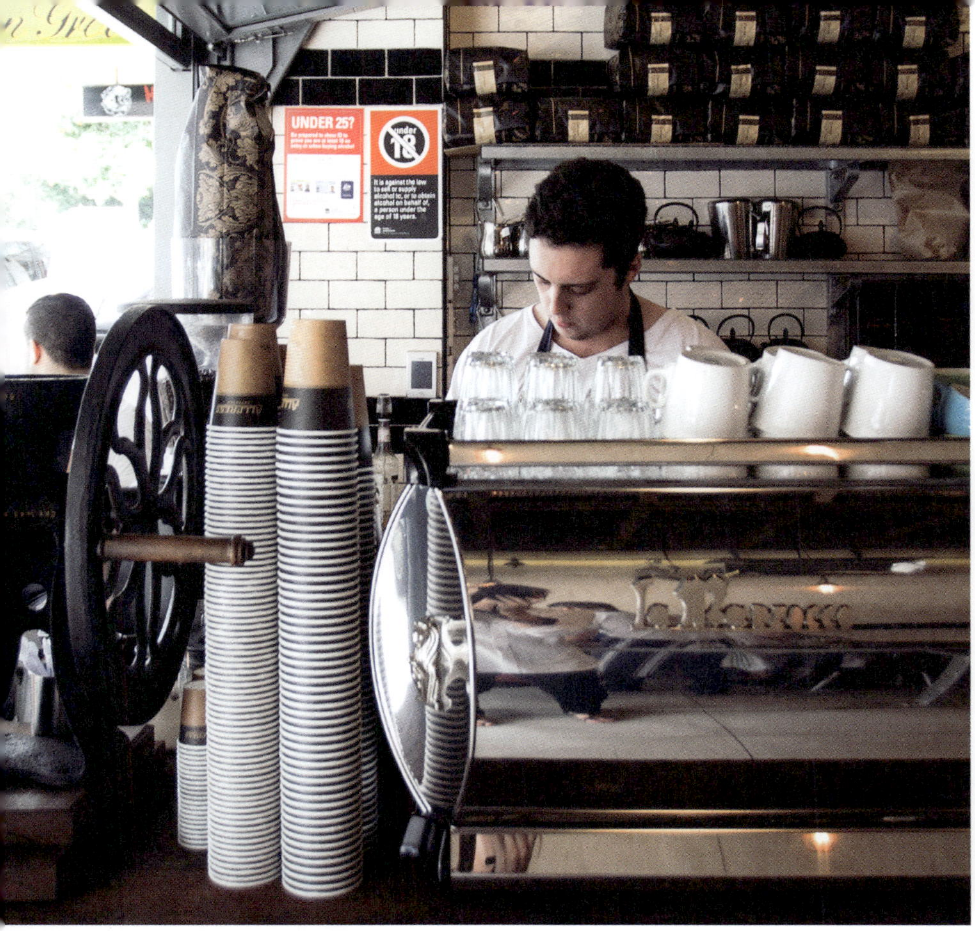
UNDER 25?
under 18
THE BUTCHERS BLOCK
Specials
Crusty Baguette
Hotdog of lamb
Merguez snow pea
Salad and a poached
egg $15.-
Sweet potato and
speck risotto
$23
46
45
THE
BUTCHER'S
BLOCK

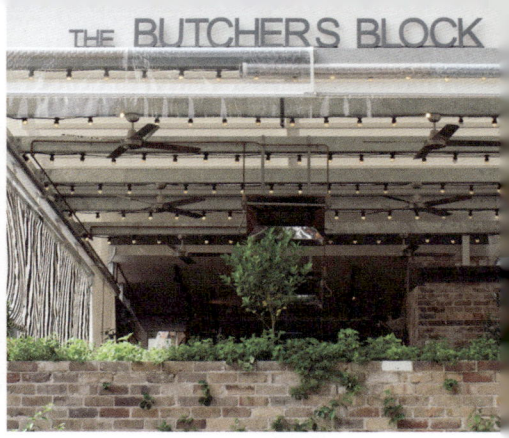

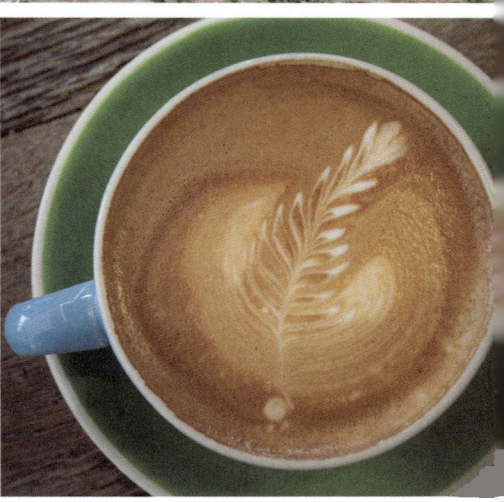

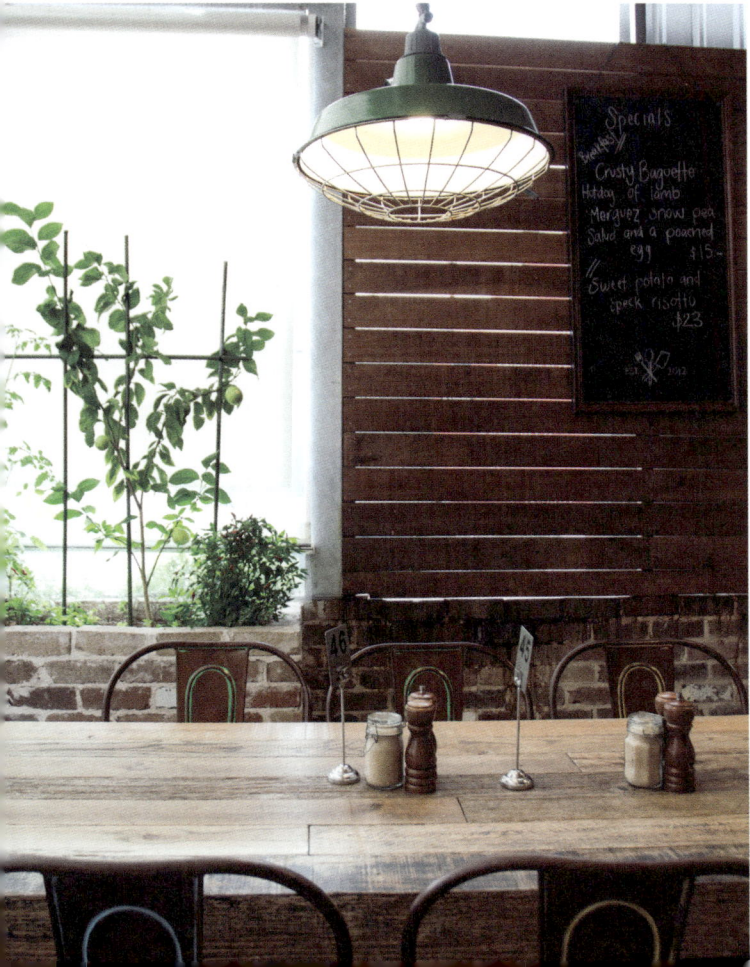

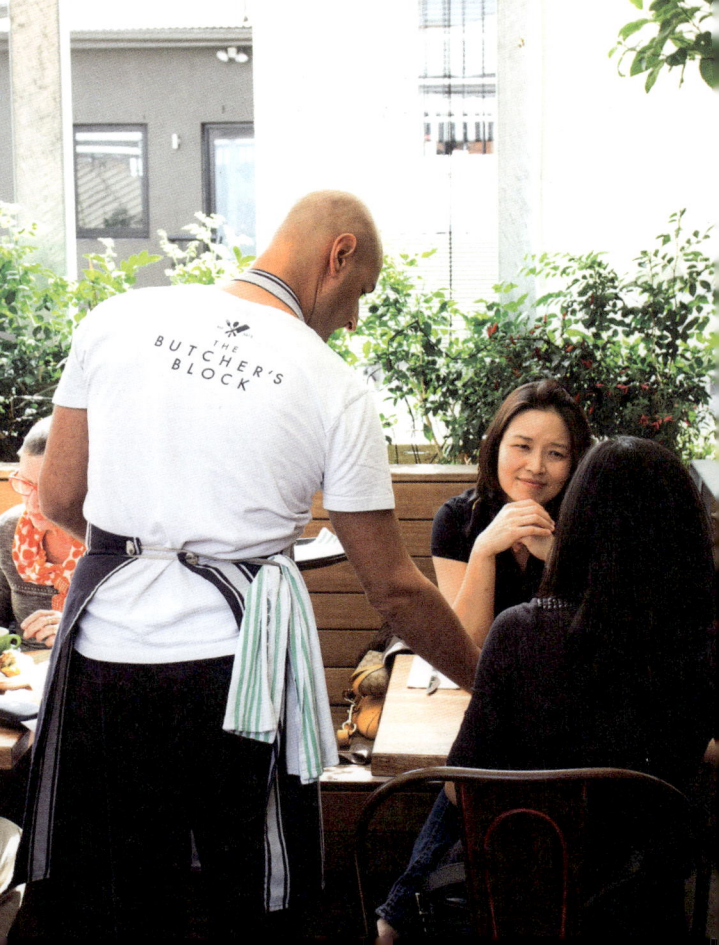

DACHSHUND COFFEE

4/64-68 GLADESVILLE RD, HUNTERS HILL · 02 9879 4619 · COMESITSTAY.COM.AU

MACHINE: Highly modified Synesso Cyncra and Fetco
GRINDER: Mazzer Robur E and Mahlkönig EK43
BEANS: Fat Poppy Blend
BREWING METHODS: Espresso, Cold Brew, Batch Brew

As you peer through the enormous glass walls and catch a glimpse of the polished concrete floors and large green enamel lights, you'll instantly be tempted to enter this cafe and join the friendly, bubbling atmosphere. Go right ahead, at Dashshund Coffee in Hunter's Hill, it's an open invitation to do what the doggy would do – come, sit, and stay.

In 2014, together with business partner and longtime friend, Rob Stein, twin brothers Matt and Alex Williams opened this charming cafe. It's a long-yearned-for chance for the trio to share their passion for good coffee and utilise the hospitality skills they've honed over the years. Rob and Matt have experience working in Canada with 49th Parallel Coffee Roasters and this is the third cafe Alex has helped set up. Their collective experience working with notable names is also worth mentioning, Alex with Pablo & Rusty's and Rob with Sensory Lab. The boys are intrigued and excited by coffee – this dark liquid that is a mainstay in forging relationships, starting conversations and playing such a steady part in their everyday lives.

There's the constant shifting and changing of the product, which keeps it exciting too: new seasons, new coffees and the constant search for the perfect shot. Dachshund Coffee exclusively uses Fat Poppy Coffee, chosen for its consistency and quality. The house blend is a seasonal espresso blend designed with milk-coffee drinkers in mind, but is delicious black too. The flavour profile is a sweet toffee from honeycomb, combined with chocolate covered blueberries. It has a full body, refined acidity and fruit driven sweetness. Sounds divine, yes? Currently, the blend consists of a pulped natural coffee from Brazil for that low down punch, while a natural Ethiopian Yirgacheffe yields the sweet berry flavours.

Brewing on a highly modified Synesso Cyncra and a Fetco batch brewer, Matt, Alex and Rob also offer bottled cold brew in the warmer months. They want to help people understand that using a batch brewer, while perhaps losing some of the romanticism of manual brewing, provides a reliable and consistent taste.

'Together with Sasha Jade, owner of Fat Poppy Coffee, the Dachshund team has tasted and sampled coffees from just about every notable roaster in Australia...'

Together with Sasha Jade, owner of Fat Poppy Coffee, the Dachshund team has tasted and sampled coffees from just about every notable roaster in Australia, as well as many from around the globe, in order to be sure of their selections. Sasha's exceptional palate and quirk for the unusual ensures she supplies cafes with some of the finest coffees available, including natural process coffees, which are often overlooked by roasters.

Besides the tremendous coffee, Dachshund Coffee serves breakfast and lunch seven days a week. It's food you'd be happy eating day in, day out – and feel good about. There's also the occasional chance for sweet indulgence, of course.

The venue in this quiet, harbourside suburb is small and intimate. It's a welcoming and vibrant setting, frequented by young families, retirees, 20-somethings and school kids. On a good day, you might even see a Dachshund!

DOSE ESPRESSO

SHOP 6 183-191 HIGH ST, WILLOUGHBY · 02 9967 2552 · DOSEESPRESSO.COM.AU

MACHINE: La Marzocco Linea PB
GRINDER: Mazzer Robur E and Kony E
BEANS: Gabriel Coffee, Dose Blend
BREWING METHODS: Espresso, Cold Drip, Pour Over

   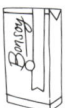

SAM GABRIELIAN IS THE OWNER OF GABRIEL COFFEE, WHICH SUPPLIES FRESHLY ROASTED, SPECIALTY COFFEE TO CAFES ACROSS SYDNEY. He and his partner, Vincent Capozzi, decided that they needed to get closer to the front line, and decided to open a cafe where they could serve their customers face to face. This became a reality in 2011 when the pair opened Dose Espresso in Willoughby, after travelling around Australia and overseas searching for the best coffee experience.

They decided on Willoughby because there wasn't anyone offering coffee the way they wanted to in the area. And what a great decision it was, as they are now Willoughby's go-to cafe for unique single origins and a popular house blend. The exclusive house blend, Dose, is roasted by Gabriel Coffee, of course, and consists of five origins. It has plenty of body and sweetness and gives a dark chocolate Toblerone finish. Delish! In white coffees, the house blend has body and in black it exhibits sweetness. In addition to rotating single origins and the popular house blend, Dose also offers cold drip, iced coffee and pour over V60.

With the support of Gabriel Coffee the team of professionals at Dose are able to indulge their passion for coffee and its philosophy to continue chasing the perfect cup. There are so many factors to consider, from the quality of the beans, the age of the bean and the equipment, down to the precision, passion and dedication that is shown – and it's the barista's responsibility to ensure this all comes together day in day out. Thankfully the staff here thrive on the fun, fast working environment and add to the positive vibe of the place.

The La Marzocco Linea PB takes care of the coffees, while the kitchen pumps out breakfast and lunch for the hungry clientele. Who knows what specials will be on offer when you visit, but if you're lucky you'll see the Mexican six hour pulled pork bean salad with roasted corn, capsicum, jalapeños and coriander, topped with sour cream and lime. For something sweet, try the Pannetone French toast with caramalised nectarine, cherry mint salad and maple syrup. There's as much love poured into the food here as there is into the coffee and that's saying something. The dedicated team is committed to handcrafting both the coffee and the food to the highest possible standard.

'...the staff here thrive on the fun, fast working environment and add to the positive vibe...'

Dose sees a constant flow of locals – young families, young adults, retirees, health nuts, you name it. And it's not surprising. Willoughby was recently named the third biggest coffee consuming area in Sydney, after the CBD and Mascot, and Dose has been at the forefront of that movement. The Willoughby locals are connoisseurs – come check out their local and see why.

Market Lane Cafe | Manly

DEATH
-before-
DECAF

ELBOW ROOM ESPRESSO

6A SPRING ST, CHATSWOOD · 02 7900 9833 · INSTAGRAM @ELBOWROOMESPRESSO

MACHINE: La Marzocco GB/5
GRINDER: Mazzer Robur E
BEANS: 5 Senses and alternating coffee from the world
BREWING METHODS: Cold Drip, Hario V60 Pour Over, AeroPress

It's difficult to walk by this little gem in Chatswood without peeking inside to take a look. The funky tunes spilling onto the street are an invitation to look through the long, glass windows and take a step inside. Once you're through the doors I can guarantee you'll want to take a seat and soak up the atmosphere.

Owners Christine Cho and John Kwon opened Elbow Room Espresso in late 2013 with one goal in mind: to deliver great quality coffee. Chatswood had always been a bustling area but there was one essential thing missing. "Chatswood used to be one of the big shopping districts with nowhere to go for great coffee and we had always been dreaming of some kind of revolution," said John.

A caffeine-induced revolution is exactly what they brought to the area, with customers travelling from near and far to enjoy their smooth blends. Christine and John had already struck up a love affair with 5 Senses Coffee years before on their travels to Melbourne, falling in love with its quality, consistency and flavour. John said, "Along with an irresistible flavour, 5 Senses Coffee builds relationships with the people farming their coffee in source countries and supports them with education, equipment and commitment."

Dark Horse is the 5 Senses blend of choice at the cafe, a combined blend of three distinct coffees – YIRGZero from the Yirgacheffe region of Ethiopia, Tiga Raja from Simalungun in Northern Sumatra, and Los Santos from Guatemala. The resulting blend is a distinctly flavoured coffee that showcases a citrus vibrancy balanced out by sweet, creamy notes of caramel.

Determined to keep their offering fresh and constantly evolving, Christine and John ensure their coffee is regularly rotated. "We also put a big effort into the brew bar trying seasonal, filter-roasted, single origin beans," explained John. Alongside espresso, they also offer batch brew, a brew coffee made with the finest filter roasted single origin coffee. Since demand for filter coffee has increased in Elbow Room this clever alternative allows them to increase the speed and volume of delivery and reward their customers with a lower price point.

'A caffeine-induced revolution is exactly what they brought to the area…'

John encourages the staff to follow their mantra to "always strive to elevate your craft". Not only do the head baristas John and Clare offer 5 Senses Coffee alongside a variety of other international roasteries, but they are also trained to deliver coffee via Cold drip, Hario V60 and AeroPress. And it doesn't stop there. Tory, the Head Chef, rules the kitchen for breakfast and lunch offering up his own "funky, fun and tasty seasonal menu to get along with smooth medium roasted coffee."

The friendly staff at Elbow Room Espresso are a tightknit family brought together by this all consuming love for coffee. Christine believes that coffee "brings otherwise strangers together, binds them to a shared passion and a bizarre love."

FIKA SWEDISH KITCHEN

5B MARKET LN, MANLY · 02 9976 5099 · FIKASWEDISHKITCHEN.COM.AU

MACHINE: La Marzocco
GRINDER: Mazzer Luigi SRL
BEANS: Campos Superior
BREWING METHODS: Swedish Brew Coffee

   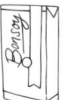

THE SWEDES HAVE A SPECIAL WORD FOR THE TIME IN THE DAY WHEN YOU TAKE A BREAK FOR COFFEE AND A BITE TO EAT, TO CATCH UP WITH FRIENDS, OR JUST STEP AWAY FROM THE RAT RACE FOR A MOMENT. This 'special time' is called 'fika' and was the inspiration behind the cafe set up by three Swedish ladies who now call Manly home.

Linda Stanes, Sophie Zetterberg and Diana Chirilas all grew up in Sweden and then moved to Sydney. Whenever they could catch up, the conversation often turned to all the things they missed about Sweden and they wondered why no one had brought together all the best things about Swedish culture to blend with modern Australian cafe culture.

The idea grew strength and the concept was born. Fika Swedish Kitchen opened on Swedish National Day in 2013.

Linda has a strong background in hospitality, while Diana and Sophie work in the design industry and have an eye for all things Scandinavian. These talents combine to create this airy, clean-lined cafe with Swedish yellow and blue highlights throughout. The only Swedish cafe in Sydney, Fika Swedish Kitchen is open for breakfast and lunch every day and dinner Wednesday to Saturday.

Head Barista, Kieran James, sources Fika's coffee from Campos – the only cafe serving up Campos coffee in the heart of Manly. Kieran and the team value Campos for its high quality, great taste and the fact that they visit every producer to make sure the coffee is being produced ethically and sustainably. The house blend, Campos Superior Blend, won Gold in the 2013 Royal Tasmanian Agricultural Show for Plunger Category and Silver for Espresso. It has a butterscotch base with slight fruity highlights, a rich body, a sweet finish, and a fantastic dimension. The three primary producers of the Superior Blend include Baroida Estate in Papua New Guinea, El Manzano in El Salvador, and Santa Anna in Rwanda.

Fika Swedish Kitchen also offers Swedish brew coffee, a lighter coffee traditional in Sweden, with a less intense taste than espresso coffee. Perhaps many Australians don't realise that the Swedish are as passionate about coffee as we are. Restaurants even provide free brew coffee with their meals as it's a given that you'll want one. Sophie and her siblings once gave a portable espresso machine to their mother for Christmas, to ensure they always had good coffee, no matter where they were.

> '...all the best things about Swedish culture to blend with modern Australian cafe culture...'

If you're after lunch, try the ever-popular Skagen – toasted sourdough piled high with a traditional prawn mix, or for dinner it's got to be the Swedish meatballs with mashed potatoes, gravy and lingonberry jam. Even if you find yourself in between meals, it's time to fika at Fika! The spirit of Scandinavia is alive and well in Manly!

FOUNDRY FIFTYTHREE

SHOP 1/53 PITTWATER RD, MANLY · 02 9977 7740 · FOUNDRYFIFTYTHREE.COM.AU

MACHINE: La Marzocco GB/5
GRINDER: Mazzer Robur Luigi
BEANS: Barrel One Coffee Roasters and guest roasters
BREWING METHODS: Espresso, Chemex, Pour Over, Cold Drip, AeroPress, French Press

FOUNDRY FIFTYTHREE IS TUCKED AWAY FROM THE GLITZ AND GLAMOUR OF MANLY BEACH, HARBOUR AND WHARF, AND AS A RESULT IS THE PLACE LOCALS PREFER TO CATCH UP WITH THEIR FRIENDS AND A DAILY COFFEE. Set on Pittwater Road just blocks from the beach and wharf, the cafe is always busy and full of the sounds of local laughter and gossip as well as people doing business on their laptops or holding informal meetings.

With wide bi-fold windows creating lots of light and bringing in breezes from the ocean, the seating varies from low stools, high stools, or comfy lounges. The baristas know their customers well, and, "Just the usual today?" is a question often asked at this local favourite.

Foundry FiftyThree prides itself on its intimate knowledge of its coffee and always has on offer an array of seasonal single origins and blends. Owner, Robbie Fazey, and Managers, Michael Tyson and Alisdair Walter, have established a direct trade relationship with the coffee farmers of the INIK cooperative on Tanna Island in Vanuatu. Buying directly from Farmer Co-operatives and Estate farms allows Foundry Fiftythree's owners to work intimately with their suppliers; it also gives them the chance to fund projects and donate equipment directly to the farmers.

Living in the shadow of Mt Yasur volcano, Tanna Island is considered one of the most organic places on earth. The active volcano is referred to by the local Ni-Vanuatuaians as 'the mother of the land'. The volcano produces ash clouds daily, which are blown northwards, where they fertilise the farmers' land. Mt Yasur Volcano provides vital organic nutrients to the soil, which in turn produces some of the finest 100% organic coffee beans available.

As well as the coffee from Vanuatu, Foundry Fiftythree offers weekly single origin espressos and filters, guest roasts, French press, cold drip, cold brew, V60, AeroPress, pour over and chemex. There is something here for every coffee connoisseur. While you're enjoying a single origin brew, or the house special blend, 'Solera' (featuring sweet cocoa aromas, intense dried apricot notes and a chocolaty, nutty body), be sure to purchase a suspended coffee so that someone in need can enjoy a break too.

Alongside your specialty coffee, be sure to experience a healthy and hearty breakfast or lunch prepared by Chef Kshitji Yogi. All produce is freshly sourced from local boutique suppliers, and is mostly organic. The cafe is positioned amongst gyms, surf and bike shops, and only blocks from Manly beach.

Kshitji creates food that matches the locals' active and healthy lifestyles. Everything but the bread is freshly made in-house. For breakfast, try the signature chorizo 'dog' with sofrito, green eggs and houllumi, or choose from a variety of mueslis or a BLT with herbed aioli.

The unique interior of Foundry FiftyThree speaks to owner Robbie Fazey's enthusiasm, and university training, in design. "I knew from a young age I wanted to create interesting and unique venues", Robbie said. Graffiti sprayed brick tables, communal dining, free flowing interior – Foundry FiftyThree is the ultimate in urban cool.

GUSTO ON THE BEACH

SOUTH CURL CURL SLSC, CARRINGTON PDE, SOUTH CURL CURL · 02 9939 5689 · GUSTOCOFFEE.COM.AU

MACHINE: UNIC Stella di Caffè
GRINDER: Nuova Simonelli – Mythos Clima
BEANS: Gusto Manna Blend and Gusto Single Origin
BREWING METHODS: Technivorm Moccamaster

The team at Belaroma Coffee Roasters have travelled north, opening a new flagship cafe for its Gusto brand called Gusto on the Beach, located at South Curl Curl Beach in the Surf Life Saving Club. It is a relaxed haven for locals and surfers alike.

The roasters, as long-term supporters of the club, supplied the coffee to the previous management. When they decided to move on, Gusto moved in, eager to elevate the quality of coffee to match the great location.

With just a small strip of pavement between the cafe and the sand, the cafe is perfectly placed to serve the needs of early morning swimmers, families doing nippers and surfers taking a break from the waves.

The renovated space reflects its ties to the Surf Life Saving Club, with the yellow, blue and white colours of the volunteers' cap prominently featuring. Clean white walls offset bright yellow stools surrounding timber tables with colourful crockery. Wide French doors open up to reveal unbeatable views of the beach, and a host of outdoor seating sits at the front and side of the building.

Gusto on the Beach is a key cafe for the Gusto coffee brand, showcasing the best of Gusto coffee. Arabica beans are sourced from all four corners of the world and roasted in a state of the art Brambati roaster that provides a gentle and consistent roasting process. Each blend is small batch roasted, ensuring the high quality is maintained. There are three blends under the Gusto heading: Salida del Sol, Arleccino and the house blend Manana.

The Manana blend cuts through milk beautifully, featuring a full body with notes of caramel, spice and cocoa after taste. It has a medium acidity and high floral aromas, with flavours of dark chocolate and spice. The Arleccino blend is a big coffee, with a substantial body and slight hint of sweetness. Liquorice and dark chocolate flavours shine through when served black; with milk it resembles caramel fudge in liquid form. Salida Del Sol is reminiscent of fresh cedar combined with dark honey and delicate citrus. The espresso is medium bodied, rich with spice and notes of cardamom. Combined with milk, it produces a sweet toffee flavour.

Batch brews made on lightly roasted, 87 point plus single origins are available on rotation as an espresso or long black. Alternative brewing methods such as technivorm and mochamaster are also available

The menu isn't forgotten either, with simple but effective breakfast and lunch options. One of their biggest sellers is the toasted Wee Bit Seedy muesli with blended acai berry and summer fruits, but there's also brunch with bacon and egg rolls, and Longboards, with eggs, smoked salmon, brie and avocado. Lunch options include Israeli cous cous salad and brioche buns filled with slow-cooked pulled pork, as well as a range of wraps and sandwiches.

> '...early morning swimmers, families doing nippers and surfers taking a break from the waves.'

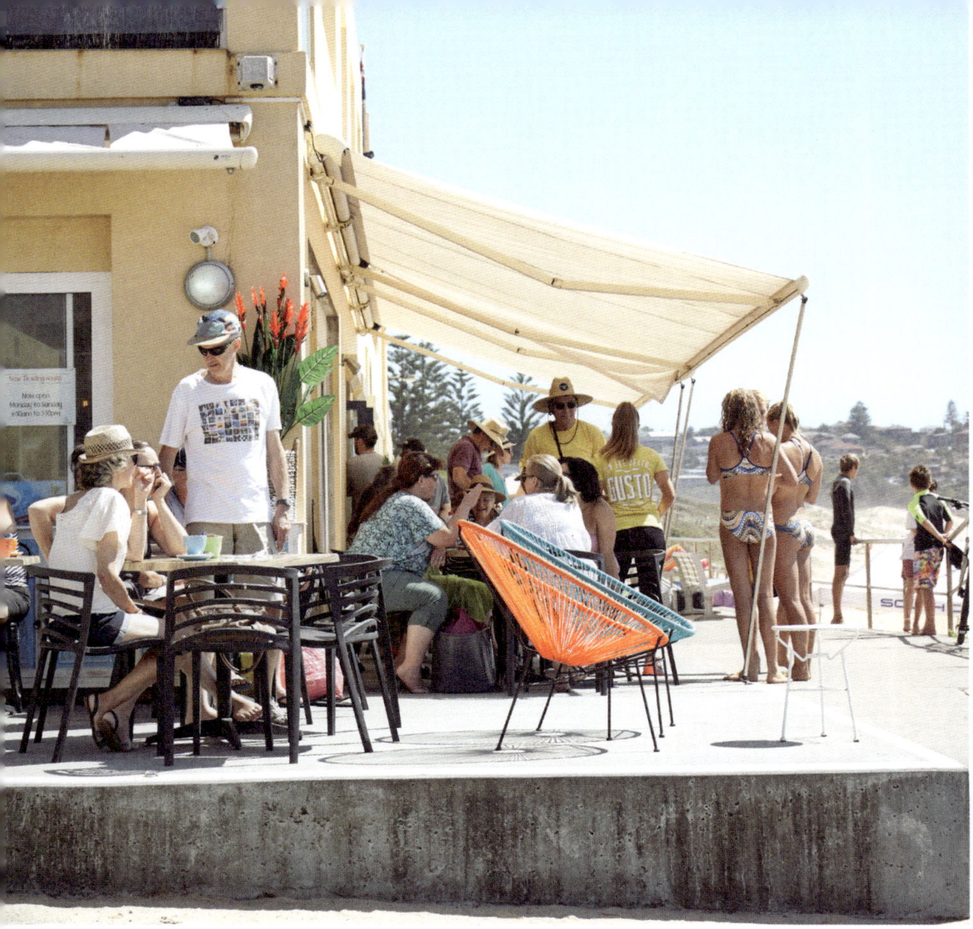
GUSTO

GUSTO
ESPRESSO COFFEE

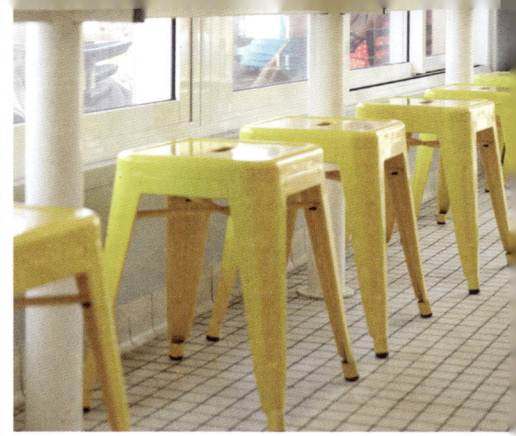

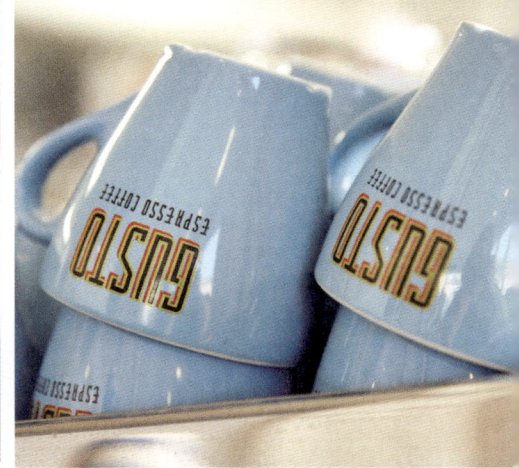

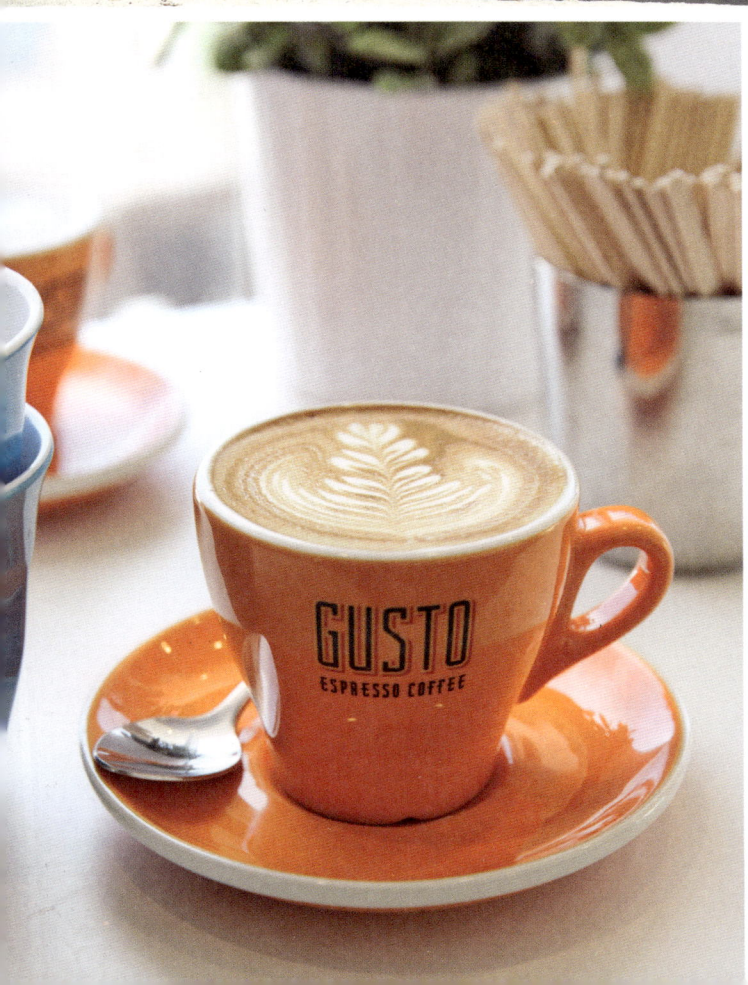

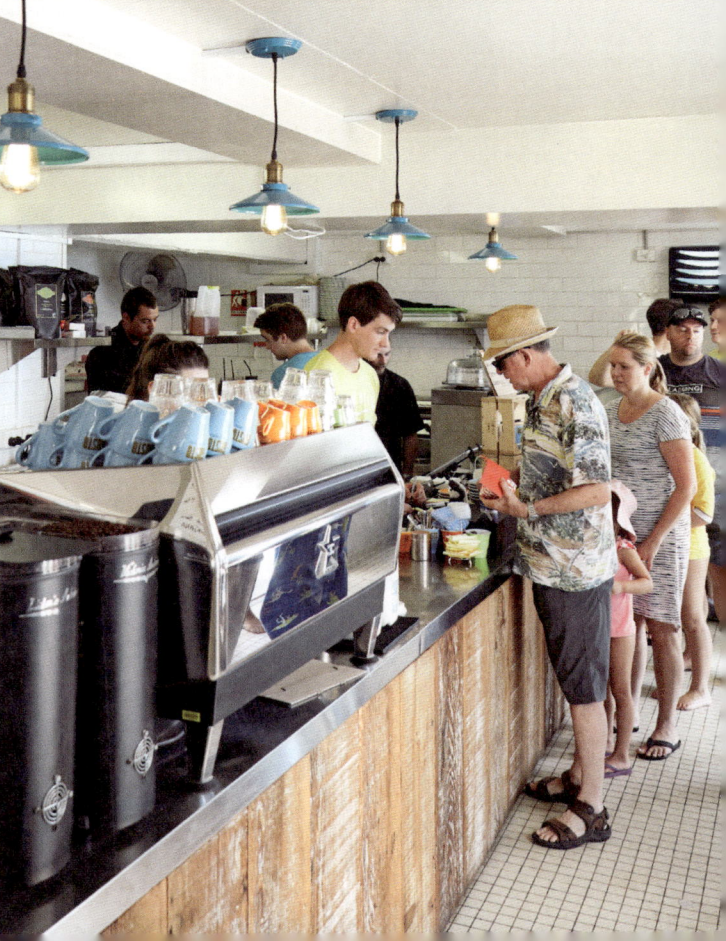

TREATS

LAMINGTONS $4.8
CINNAMON SCROLLS $4.8
CRONUTS - CHOC HONEYCOMB $5.5
         - CINNAMON $5
MUFFINS $5
BANANA BREAD $4
ORANGE FLOURLESS $5.5
CARROT CAKE $5.5
LEMON MERINGUE $5.5
CHOCOLATE SALT CARAMEL $6

SEASONAL BLEND COFFEE $15

THE INCINERATOR WILLOUGHBY

2 SMALL ST, WILLOUGHBY · 02 8188 2220 · THEINCINERATOR.COM.AU

MACHINE: Synesso Hydra 3 Group
GRINDER: Mazzer Robur E
BEANS: Grounds Roasters House Blend
BREWING METHODS: Espresso

THE GROUND FLOOR OF THE 1930S WALTER BURLEY GRIFFIN-DESIGNED, WILLOUGHBY INCINERATOR IS NOW HOME TO A SUITABLY STYLISH CAFE AND COFFEE DESTINATION, KNOWN SIMPLY AS THE INCINERATOR.

The striking design starts right from the front door, with its asymmetrical metal design work and distinctive peaked roof. Situated on the edge of the Willoughby Centennial Parklands, The Incinerator is the perfect spot for a relaxed breakfast inside an historic building by one of Australia's most popular architects.

Opened in February 2014, The Incinerator serves restaurant quality food and top coffee. In fact, Jonathan Slingo believes that coffee is "the centerpiece of the business." Jonathan sources coffee from The Grounds Roasters because, in his words, it has "the best beans in Sydney." Jonathan works with The Grounds, not only because of the flavour and consistency of its blend, but also because of the service and passion that is shown by its staff. This passion for flavour, consistency and service is certainly a shared ethos between roaster and brewer. Just to prove the point, there is no head barista here, it's simply about the entire team working together.

The centrepiece of the open kitchen is the wood-fired oven, which supplies diners with Wood Roasted Barramundi, served with white asparagus, burnt butter and lemon, and the Wood Roasted Chicken and Quinoa Salad, with smoked yoghurt, peas and green chilli. Also worth trying is the Pressed Lamb Shoulder, served with spiced pear chutney and mint and fennel salad. The menu is seasonal and changes regularly, so you're sure to find something fresh and in season when you visit.

The striking interior design and warm ambience make The Incinerator a great place for events. It seats 50 people inside, or up to 100 standing. The intimate dining space sits under the pitched ceiling and exposed beams.

There is outdoor seating as well, taking in views of the parklands. Just outside the large double doors, which let in a fresh breeze, you can't help but admire the public artwork by renowned artist Richard Goodwin. Titled 'Exoskeleton Lift', the large-scale fabricated polished stainless steel structure encloses the outdoor lift and makes a fascinating addition to the already iconic property.

Jonathan and his team spent their first year in business keeping the coffee offerings simple and getting it consistently right. They honed their espresso skills to perfection and are now starting to diversify their coffee offerings. Keep an eye out for single origin offerings in the near future. They've got their breakfasts and lunches down to a fine art now and works of art they truly are. Dinners will be starting soon too. The only way for The Incinerator is up!

> 'This passion for flavour, consistency and service is certainly a shared ethos between roaster and brewer.'

MARKET LANE CAFE

SHOP 9 37-39 THE CORSO, MANLY

MACHINE: La Marzocco
GRINDER: Mazzer Robur R and Mazzer Major
BEANS: Allpress Carmelo
BREWING METHODS: Espresso

   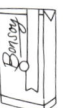

MARKET LANE CAFE IS SMACK BANG IN THE MIDDLE OF THE BUSTLING SUBURB OF MANLY, YET IT MANAGES TO BE AN OASIS OF CALM AWAY FROM THE FRENZY OF THE MAIN DRAGS. Owners, Jim and daughter Isobella Buda, know very well that there are more than 30 cafes in Manly alone, and that there's no grand slam as far as standing out from the crowd. Instead, the difference is in the detail and the passion, and they have both of them in spades.

Market Lane Cafe is compact - a little hole in the wall, with seating inside and out in the lane. It has managed to tread that fine line of being just where you want it while also feeling out of the way and secret.

Jim, with a lifetime of caffeine addiction, has imbued his children with the love of the bean. Today they're serving Allpress coffee to the dedicated clientele of Manly locals, surfers, yoga mums, businessmen and women and a healthy dose of Lycra-clad cyclists.

"We want life to be simple," Jim said, and as a result, they serve only espresso-based coffee. Jim and Isobella, together with Manager and Barista, Liv Ferreira, found that their constantly preferred coffee was from Allpress.

As far as selecting their house blend, Jim and Isobella were after a strong, smooth blend. The only way to go was Allpress' Carmelo Blend – such a popular choice across Sydney, and for good reason. It's lively and full bodied, just as Market Lane Cafe wants, and has distinct caramel flavours. It may be popular across Sydney, but if you want an Allpress coffee in Manly, Market Lane Cafe is the only place you'll find it!

Situated in a lovely courtyard in one of Manly's best laneways, Market Lane Cafe gets the best of the winter sun during the colder months and is shaded and cool during summer. The cafe prides itself on almost total in-house self sufficiency with all cakes, bars, muffins etc baked daily in house.

Jim and Isobella believe that cafes are complex ecosystems of small details, and if you can get this right then everything else will flourish. Life dwells in the details.

It is open seven days a week, from early morning until late afternoon, so there's no reason you can't make more than one stopover during the course of the day. Pull up a cane chair out the front, settle in beside the blonde wood façade near the large wooden bar, and watch Manly life ebb and flow before your eyes.

We'll leave you with wise words from Jim – "For all of us, the prism of life has more depth with coffee".

> 'The difference is in the detail and the passion, and they have both of them in spades.'

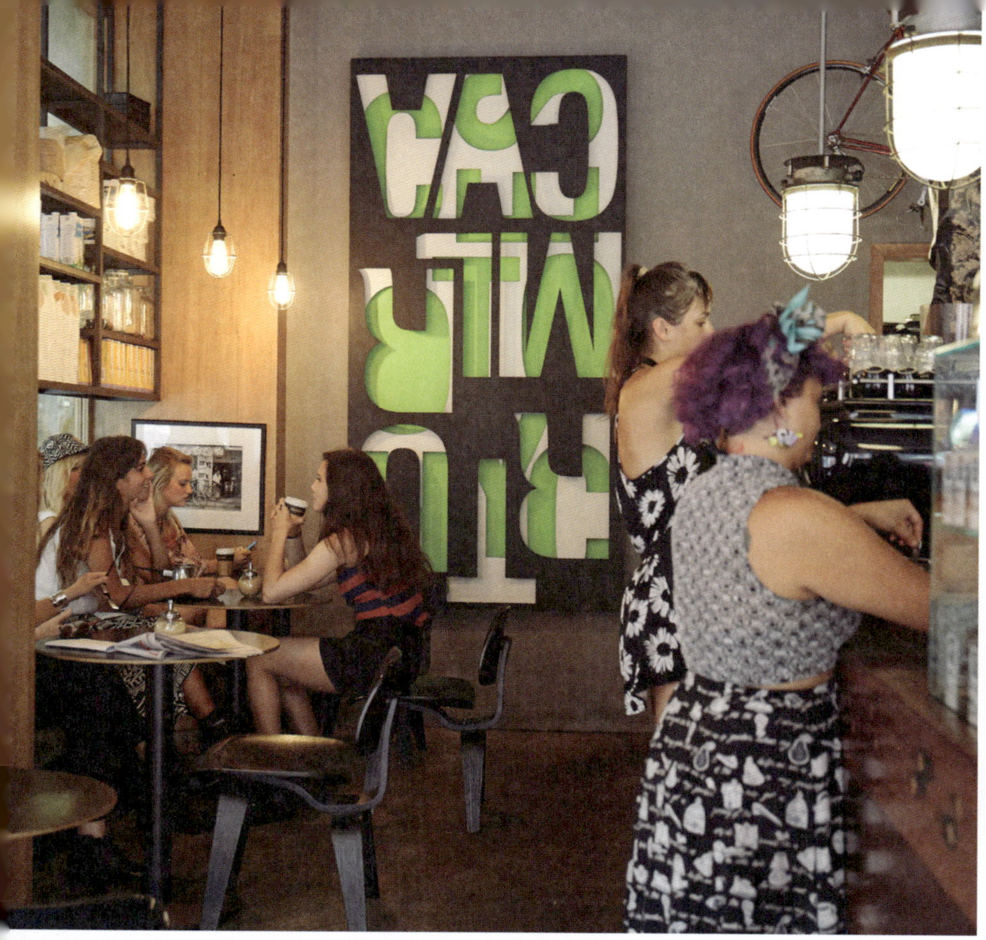

ALLPRESS
ALLPRESS
ALLPRESS

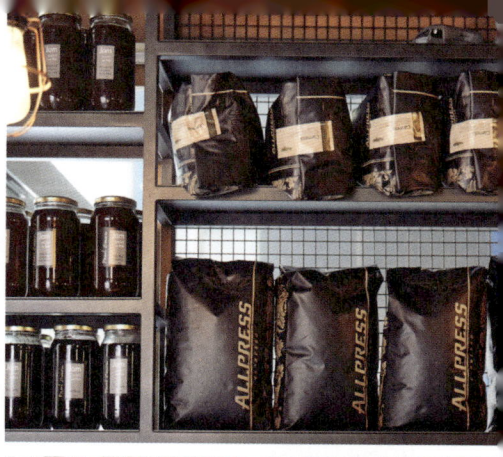

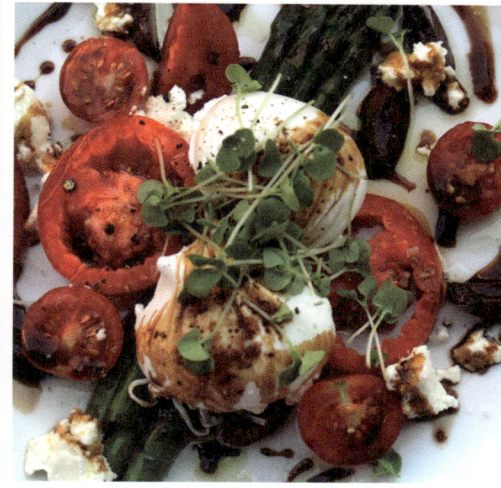

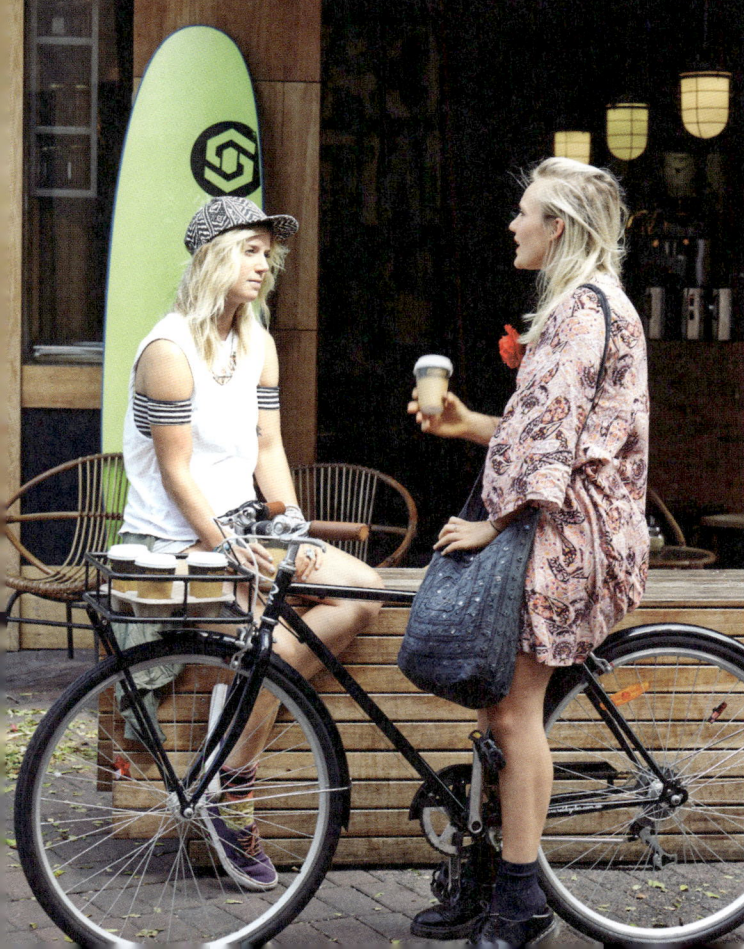

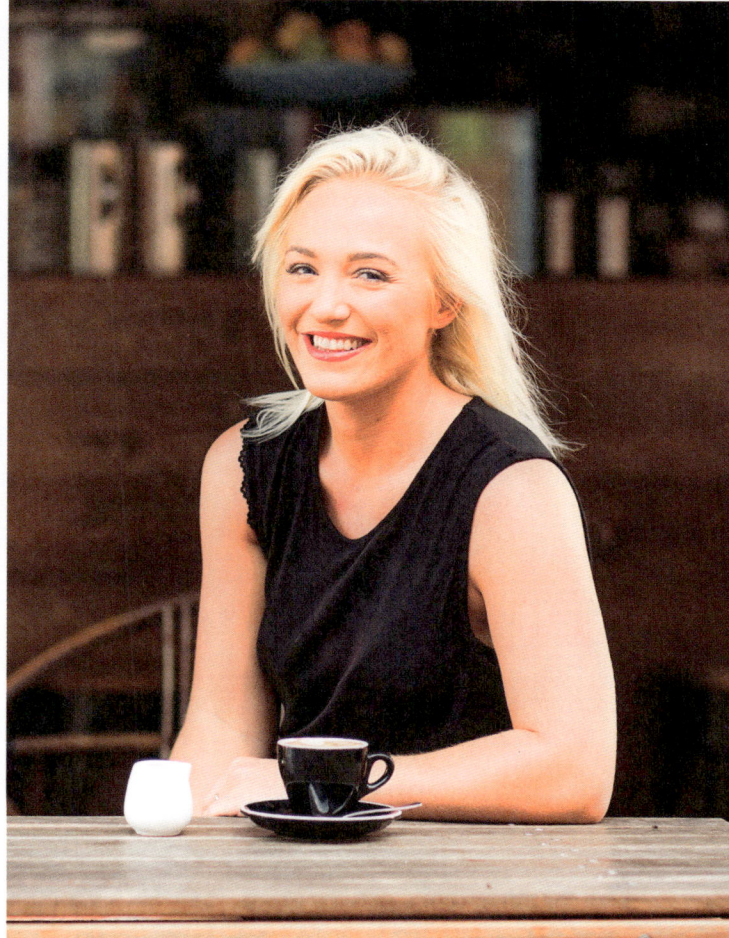

PABLO & RUSTY'S LANE COVE

SHOP 13 LANE COVE PLAZA, 123 LONGUEVILLE RD, LANE COVE • 02 9418 8005 • PABLOANDRUSTYS.COM.AU

MACHINE: Synesso Hyrda Gen 2
GRINDER: Mythos and Mahlkönig EK43
BEANS: Pablo & Rusty's House Blend
BREWING METHODS: Espresso, Cold Drip, Filter

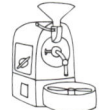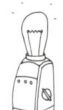

PABLO & RUSTY'S LANE COVE, A LOCAL COFFEE HUB SITS BETWEEN THE CITY AND THE SUBURBS AND RIGHT IN THE HEART OF THE COMMUNITY, WHERE LOCALS GATHER TO MEET, SHARE STORIES AND CATCH UP ON NEWS, ALL OVER A DELICIOUS SPECIALTY COFFEE.

Sustainability is vital to Pablo & Rusty's operation and here you'll find only freshly harvested coffee that is sustainably and ethically produced. They work directly with the farmers who produce the beans whenever possible. This allows them to continue researching new and innovative agricultural and processing methods to achieve the best specialty coffee at harvest.

Head Barista, Ben Richardson, is part of the QA team at Pablo & Rusty's and heads up the team of baristas at Lane Cove. Dedicated to quality, Ben can be found between the P&R stores – at wholesale cafes brewing Pablo & Rusty's or at the training bar and roastery cupping the latest coffee offerings and creating new brew recipes for the P&R clients.

Amongst the ever-changing coffee offerings at Pablo & Rusty's Lane Cove is the San Agustin from Guatemala. Harvested between January and April, just before the new rains come for the next season, the cherries are carefully picked by hand and delivered to the mill at Santa Clara each day between 4pm and 7pm. They're then fermented for up to 20 hours, dried on raised beds for 15 to 20 days and then milled right there on site. Excellent as a filter brew, maximising floral aromatics and sparkling acidity with a sweet and syrupy lemon cordial flavour.

The food is carefully selected and sourced from suppliers who operate with similar ideals to P&R. Generally partnering with local, small, artisan producers, Pablo & Rusty's make sure that the produce they buy in for their seasonal menu is traceable and sustainably sourced.

> 'Pablo & Rusty's entire ethos centres around making a positive contribution...'

Pablo & Rusty's entire ethos centres around making a positive contribution – to the farmers and producers at origin, to the environment and to their customers. One taste of their coffee proves they're right on point.

It's not hard to see why the locals flock to this corner cafe in the heart of Lane Cove. P&R sits within the bustling plaza and is a core part of this community hub. The industrial warmth of its zinc and copper finishes are complimented with glass-jar lights and milk crate pendants. The staff are friendly and coffee focused professionals, ready to brew the latest filter coffees or single origins. Coffee is their core product, and this influences everyone and everything in store.

PENNY ROYAL

2/563 MILITARY RD, MOSMAN • 0416 452 644 • FACEBOOK.COM/THEPENNYROYAL

MACHINE: La Marzocco Linear 3 Group
GRINDER: Mazzer Robur
BEANS: Campos
BREWING METHODS: Espresso, Cold Filter

LOCATED ON MILITARY ROAD, THE PENNY ROYAL HAS AN EDGY VIBE THAT OWNER, CHLOE DONNELLY, HAS MADE HER OWN. The Penny Royal turns up the quirkiness with walls adorned with black sketch graffiti, name stamps on the cups and recycled crates that substitute as tables spill out into the laneway. Alternative classics pumping from the sound system complete the street grunge vibe.

You can lend thanks to Chloe for the eclectic feel of this cafe. After three years of working at the Penny Royal, Chloe took over ownership to re-brand the business. "After applying for a bar job eight years ago and becoming the barista with no experience, I found passion in making that perfect cup of coffee and wanted to make it my career," she said.

A tiny 17 square metres, The Penny Royal caters to the masses on a daily bases with pride and passion. This hole in the wall cafe takes up a small lane of Mosman with limited seating but big demand. Most days have a waiting list, but don't be deterred, the coffee is well worth the wait. Staying devoted to the Campos Coffee roast at various places over the last three years, Chloe said, "I preferred the flavour profile and found it was best suited to both black and milk coffee. The Penny Royal pumps out the best quality coffee at high intensity to supply Mosman's coffee cravers."

You can find Owner and Head Barista, Chloe, behind the bar everyday alongside her highly trained sidekicks, dishing out the Campos blend to Penny Royal regulars and newbies alike, doing what they love. Serving up Campos Superior Blend and a rotation of single origins of the week, Chloe has sought to expand and push the limits of what can be done in such a small area. Superior Blend is toffee based with a tinge of fruity underlines. It has a rich, bold intensity capped off by a sweet butterscotch finish so it's no wonder people are lining up out the door to grab a steaming cup.

Complementing the coffee is an ever-changing breakfast and lunch menu. Chloe puts as much use as possible to the small space insisting on serving up a seasonal menu that caters to the weather. In winter you can find a slow-cooker special to warm your tum and in summer you can feel fresh with an abundance of healthy dishes packed full with flavour. With a gym so close, the cafe offers up a post-gym protein bowl and special dietary dishes are all on offer, from gluten-free to paleo.

The Penny Royal is truly worth the mad rush through the door but you should also check out its small brew bar next door, showcasing different brewing methods and single origin specialty coffee alongside retail pickles, hot sauces and maple syrup from America.

> 'Chloe has sought to expand and push the limits of what can be done in such a small area.'

RICKY'S CAFE UNDER THE BRIDGE

SHOP 6, ENNIS RD, MILSONS POINT · 02 9955 8875 · RICKYSCAFEUNDERTHEBRIDGE.COM.AU

MACHINE: La Marzocco GB/5
GRINDER: Anfim
BEANS: Allpress Carmelo
BREWING METHODS: Espresso

RICKY OCAMPO TOOK WHAT WAS ONCE THE VILLAGE BUTCHER SHOP IN KIRRIBILLI AND CONVERTED IT INTO A CAFE, RETAINING ITS ORIGINAL INTERIOR. It's not his first venture, not by a long shot. Ricky has been in the Sydney food industry since 1992. He first opened a cafe in Kirribilli in 1995 out of desperation – he was sick of having to go to the next suburb for a latte! He also ran Carabella, the first Spanish restaurant on the lower north shore. Now after a three year break to travel and try new flavours, Ricky is back, with his cafe under the bridge. Which bridge? Yeah… that famous one.

A coffee drinker since 10 years old, Ricky is now serving up espresso to commuters using the nearby Milsons Point Station, to tourists exploring the Kirribilli area (perhaps after doing the long hike over the bridge) and Kirribilli locals like Ricky, who just want a good quality, local coffee near home. No 10-year-old customers these days, though.

Ricky's Cafe Under the Bridge, managed by Ricky's sister Lulu, is open for early breakfast to late lunch, Monday to Sunday. You can be sure of an excellent menu because Ricky is totally dedicated to food. He grew up in a family of food lovers, and has travelled extensively to taste and learn about other cuisines. His curious tastebuds have led him to some of the off the beaten gourmet paths of Europe and Asia, from the locals' favourite sausage kiosk in Salzburg to the trattoria with the tastiest and darkest squid-ink pasta in Venice.

A typical selection at Ricky's Under the Bridge might include, for breakfast, Ricky's Homemade Granola with fresh fruits, Kangaroo Island yoghurt and chia seeds, or walnut loaf with pears, Piemonte white truffle honey and fresh ricotta. If you're in the area for lunch, head under the bridge for some olive sourdough, served with organic chicken fillets, sun-dried tomato pesto, avocado and mesclun. Ricky spent a long time sourcing the perfect sourdough – one with the perfect balance of crusty and sour that can be so elusive. In addition to the fantastic bread, there's croissants and pastries from artisan bakers. You can even buy the bread from the cafe to take home with you.

> 'Ricky is back, with his cafe under the bridge. Which bridge? Yeah… that famous one.'

The menu changes regularly, with the seasons, and includes some super foods to charge you up. Try a juice with acai berries or a smoothie with chia seeds. The honey, as mentioned, comes all the way from Italy – the very best white honey from Piemonte. The Italian flavour continues in the flatbreads with potato, oregano, tomato and prosciutto.

The coffee decision is easy here – Ricky's Cafe Under the Bridge serves up espresso-based coffees, and only espresso-based coffees. Sourced from Allpress Sydney, Ricky is clear about the coffee – you just have to try it!

Market Lane Cafe | Manly

RITUAL COFFEE TRADERS

1/160 SAILORS BAY RD, NORTHBRIDGE · 02 9967 2007 · RITUALCOFFEETRADERS.COM.AU

MACHINE: La Marzocco Linea PB
GRINDER: Robur E and Mahlkönig EK43
BEANS: Gabriel Coffee Monte Carlo
BREWING METHODS: Cold Drip, V60 Pour Over, Espresso

RITUAL COFFEE TRADERS IS THE NEW HEALTH NUT ON THE BLOCK, BRINGING THE MOST VIRTUOUS OF DISHES TO NORTHBRIDGE LOCALS SINCE NOVEMBER 2014. It's all about the raw, the vegan, the dairy free, the gluten free, the healthy and the holistic, and serves delicious and guilt-free sweet treats. And what's more, the staff here also happen to be coffee experts.

Co-owner, Sam Gabrielian, is the man behind Gabriel Coffee, which supplies cafes across NSW with its popular blends, so you know the coffee is going to be amazing. And Alex Savidis comes to the business with 13 years' experience as a barista. Naturally, Alex also acts as Head Barista here. He loves the fact that with coffee, there's always something new to try and the ways we select and prepare coffee are constantly evolving. Alex loves experimenting with the countless methods of preparing and extracting the coffee to get the very best out of it for his customers.

Ritual Coffee Traders naturally uses Gabriel Coffee with the Monte Carlo blend as its house staple. It has a full-bodied chocolate taste that gives coffee lovers a satisfying kick. Monte Carlo is made up of a four-bean blend with coffees from Papua New Guinea, Sumatra, Kenya and Ethiopia: some washed and some naturally processed. Sam and Alex prefer roasts with chocolate notes for milk-based coffees, so Monte Carlo works well in the ever-popular lattes and flat whites. For the black coffees, they look for sweet, floral and fruity beans.

We've already mentioned the health-focused menu but it's well worth trying something new. Ritual Coffee Traders is the first to retail Hippie Lane organic, raw and vegan treats, all of which are refined-sugar free, dairy free and mostly gluten free. There's a Mean Green Smoothie for those feeling virtuous or an Acai Bowl with berries, cacao, maca powder and Hippie Lane's Rawnola. But never fear, there are also egg and bacon rolls as well as sandwiches and wraps on offer too. The most popular lunch items by far are the falafel bowls and the nourish bowls (try the Rainbow Nourish Bowl if you can).

'You'll see coffee lovers perched on milk crates under the shade of the towering gum tree...'

This geometrically inspired, hole-in-the-wall cafe isn't big, but it's airy and opens right out onto the street. You'll see coffee lovers perched on milk crates under the shade of the towering gum tree and locals lining the walls on the banquette seating. A floating 3D ceiling, truly one of a kind with its geometrical design, is a stand out feature of the space. It is modern, clean and slick with light woods and black countertops. You might find that the glowing blue neon sign, handmade for the cafe is what lures you inside.

THE ROOTS ESPRESSO

SHOP 7 / 2 ELIZABETH PLZ, NORTH SYDNEY · THEROOTSESPRESSO.COM.AU

MACHINE: La Marzocco Linea PB
GRINDER: Mazzer Robur and Ditting
BEANS: Single Origin Roasters, Reuben Hills, Seven Seeds, Dukes
BREWING METHODS: Espresso, Pour Over, Syphon

NORTH OF THE BIG BRIDGE AND UNDER A LITTLE FOOTBRIDGE, SITS THE ROOTS ESPRESSO – A COFFEE LOVER'S OASIS IN THIS CORPORATE ENCLAVE OF NORTH SYDNEY. Here, the baristas may be cool and relaxed but they are as passionate about coffee as baristas come. Corporate types mingle with original hipsters, united in their quest for a smooth, delicate pour over; a rich and well-balanced espresso; or a worth-writing-home-about syphon coffee.

Owner, Brett Conway, and Head Barista, Adam Hooker, pump out the seasonal brews while their stereo pumps out the best of 1990s hip hop. The industrial-chic interior, with 'the roots' spelled out in glowing Neon on the wall, resembles a scientist's laboratory where beakers of brewing coffee sit proudly on the counter for all to marvel over.

Brett Conway has worked in hospitality since the tender age of 14. Previously part owner of The Brewery Espresso in Erskine Street, Brett then moved on to spend two years at Three Blue Ducks. Now he provides the good stuff to North Sydney hipsters and suits – and hipsters in suits. Brett's interest in coffee? "What's not to like?" he asked.

The fully washed, rich and well balanced house blend sits alongside El Salvador's 'La Fany' with its sweet, juicy and effervescent Washed Bourbon, and its syrupy, hazelnut and plum Natural Bourbon. Other varieties hail from Colombia, Honduras, Rwanda, Ethiopia and Panama, to name but a few.

> '...pump out the seasonal brews while their stereo pumps out the best of 1990s hip hop.'

Head down on the first Thursday of every month for a free cupping session, but make sure you RSVP. It's open to the public and the perfect way to get a greater appreciation for the black stuff you wake up thinking about every morning.

Alongside the seasonal bean offerings from Single Origin Roasters, Reuben Hills and Dukes, The Roots Espresso also serves innovative comfort food that wouldn't be out of place in a cafe in New York City. Not to be missed is the 12-hour Brisket Roll with beetroot slaw and pickle or the Yeezus Burger, which is also developing a cult following. There is also a selection of healthy salads to choose from.

The Roots Espresso is open for breakfast and lunch, Monday to Friday. It's become a work day must for the local business types, who love the healthy Blackberry Bircher Muesli with apple, almonds, seeds, currants and mulberry compote. There's always a selection of sweet bites, too – house baked dulche de leche muffins make the morning that bit easier.

The Roots have even taken over Next Door, aptly named "The Roots Next Door" providing cured meats and cheese by the gram with a serious selection of local wines and killer cocktails from 12 till late Wednesday to Friday.

For a smashing coffee and some hip-hop to start your day, there's only one place to go – under the bridge downtown!

SALVAGE SPECIALTY COFFEE

5 WILKES AVE, ARTARMON · SALVAGECOFFEE.COM

MACHINE: Synesso Hydra
GRINDER: Mazzer Robur E and Mahlkönig EK43
BEANS: Artificer Specialty Coffee
BREWING METHODS: Espresso, Batch brew, Kalita Pour Over, AeroPress, Cold Brew

THREE MATES, NOT HAPPY WITH THE COMPROMISING STANDARDS IN THEIR WORKPLACE, WERE SITTING IN A COURTYARD IN ARTARMON ONE NIGHT EATING RAMEN, WHEN THEY SAW AN EMPTY SHOP SITTING JUST ACROSS THE WAY. The cogs in the brains turned, and on Australia Day 2013, the three mates opened Salvage Specialty Coffee. Their one resolution? To only serve to their customers what they would want to be served, from the coffee, to the food, even to the Jersey milk. They treat each product with respect, and never compromise on quality. They source locally where they can, and certainly only serve what they personally endorse. The people of Artarmon lived happily ever after – The End.

Well, there's not really any end in sight here, actually. Toby Cutler, Dan Yee and Matt Goto aren't going anywhere. They are part of the long coffee chain and they respect their part in bringing top quality black gold to their regulars! Toby said, "The beauty is that every link in the chain of the journey of coffee is integral to the final product in the cup. From the farmer growing and processing, the buyer selecting and finding the best, through to the roast, to the barista understanding the best way to represent the coffee in the cup. The process has become a lot more personal of late when it comes to representing the care and attention that each person in the chain has put in."

The three mates/owners rotate days running the bar, and log their parameters daily in order to constantly improve and maintain a consistent product between the individual operators.

The house blend at Salvage is a seasonal blend focused on best showcasing the coffee in milk as well as producing an interesting and complex espresso. Coffee used in the blend changes regularly, depending on what is in season. The coffee is by Artificer Specialty Coffee and is roasted by Dan Yee and Shoji Sasa.

Salvage Specialty Coffee also offers batch brewed coffee and hand brewed coffee – generally aeropress, or barista Toby's personal favourite, Kalita pour over. There's also the extremely popular cold brewed coffee, made using a full immersion brew. The boys pump out the Artificer Specialty Coffee espresso on a Synesso Hydra machine.

The food here (breakfast and lunch) looks like something out of a fine dining restaurant – beautifully presented, with delicate flavours.

It's a small menu (generally 6-7 food items), with a couple of longstanding menu staples. The food changes regularly dependent on the season. If you're lucky, you might be there on a day they're serving their Beetroot Cured Salmon, with horseradish crème fraiche and radish, apple and sorrel salad. A hot weather favourite is the Kingfish Ceviche with watermelon granita, cucumber and olive. Swap your boring eggs on toast for Salvage's lightly smoked trout and asparagus with free range eggs, blood orange hollandaise and sorrel on toast. You won't regret it.

> '...seasonal blend focused on best showcasing the coffee in milk as well as producing an interesting and complex espresso.'

SHOP NEXT DOOR

46-50 PITTWATER RD, MANLY · 02 9977 5569 · THESHOPNEXTDOOR.COM.AU

MACHINE: Faema
GRINDER: Mazzer Luigi
BEANS: Eight-O-Eight
BREWING METHODS: Espresso

ONLY IN MANLY WOULD YOU FIND A COMBINED SURFBOARD-CUM-COFFEE SHOP JUST A SHORT STROLL FROM THE BEACH. Having already established The Shop Next Door as a spot to grab an eclectic surfboard or new pair of boardies, the owners saw an opportunity for expansion when the homewares store next door closed down. Knocking a hole in the wall, The Shop Next Door was born.

Having already built up a large fan base of surfers and beach babes looking for that something special surf-wise, it wasn't hard for the crew to expand. The transformation was gradual; one day there was a fridge, and soon a counter, coffee machine and furniture followed. The owners planned to focus on coffee and juice, but customers kept looking for food, and so they opened a kitchen too.

The space maintains the easygoing vibe of the retail store next door, with a blue and white colour scheme and simple furniture. Local flowers line the window sills, housed in old Orchard Street juice bottles and hanging plants dot the entrance, emphasising the cafe's dedication to organic produce. Natural products are littered all over the place, with Orchard Street juices and smoothies, Vegan Teahouse treats and other organic brands making an appearance.

Amongst all this healthiness lies the blue-and-white-accented coffee machine, producing espresso-based varieties with Will & Co beans. The Shop Next Door chose the Bondi-based brand after striking up a friendship with Co-founder of Will & Co, Sam Coombes. He had chosen Sam's brand Critical Slide Society to feature in the surf shop, at the time he happened to be looking for beans for the new cafe. They use Eight-o-Eight as their house blend, which features 100% Arabica beans sourced from Guatemala and Brazil. It is medium-bodied, finely balanced blend with a sweet floral aroma, crisp acidity and caramel finish.

> '...take a breather with a coffee and breaky or grab a take away and amble your way down to the beach for a swim or surf.'

Those who can't have dairy will delight in the lactose-free options: coconut, almond and soy milk are all on offer, as well as gluten free, dairy free and sugar free treats. You can also nurse a cup of tea courtesy of Melbourne-based Prana Chai, who mix tea leaves with spices and honey by hand, or for the caffeine-free you can try Mayde Organic hand-blended tea.

The food follows the same healthy line, with everything on the menu satisfying the organic criteria. Breakfast, lunch and snacks are available every day, including avocado with sunflower sprouts on Spring Wellness sprouted loaf, home-made chia seed muffins and vegan nachos.

Just two blocks from the beach, the Coffee Shop Next Door is the ideal spot to take a breather with a coffee or grab a take away and amble your way down to the beach for a swim or surf. We know just the place to grab your gear…

SHOTLAB ESPRESSO

SHOP 1, 326-330 BARRENJOEY RD, NEWPORT · 0406 537 784 · SHOTLAB.COM.AU

MACHINE: Synesso Cyncra
GRINDER: Mazzer Robur E, Mazzer Kony E
BEANS: Background Coffee
BREWING METHODS: Espresso, Cold Drip, Pour Over, AeroPress

   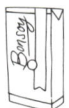

SHOTLAB ESPRESSO IS PART SPECIALTY COFFEE LABORATORY, PART COFFEE RETAIL OUTLET AND PART CAFE, STOCKING AND BREWING EXCLUSIVELY BACKGROUND COFFEE.

Background Specialty Coffee Roasters trades directly with the coffee growers, ensuring a fair go for the farmers – operating socially responsibly is at the top of the list of priorities here. The micro-roastery ensures full traceability of its beans and its house blend is made using the best crop of high quality seasonal specialty coffee beans. For the farmers, it means security and a direct relationship with their buyers, and for Newport locals, it means access to an extremely good cup of coffee.

Being a retail outlet for Background Specialty Coffee Roasters ensures that the staff not only understand the entire process of coffee harvesting and roasting, but also are able to control many of the variables necessary in delivering the perfect cup. ShotLab Espresso has a passion for sharing its knowledge about coffee and educating its customers on the experience and excitement of it all.

Owner, Lecio Resmini knows that coffee is more than just a drink – it's an experience and a lifestyle. Together with Head Barista, Heather Booth, and Manager, Carol Alcazar, they are ready and waiting to provide fantastic service and information about the beans, the blends, and the process. Just ask!

Background House Blend incorporates Kelagur Heights Geisha Grade AA (India), which has fruity, sweet and smooth notes, Ipanema Microlot (Brazil), which is bright, citrusy and well balanced, Nairobi Grade AA (Kenya), an award winning Golden Bean that tastes chocolaty and rich, and Yirgacheffe Grade 1 (Ethiopia), which is delicate and floral. The result is a perennially popular blend that is super smooth and sweet at the same time, while still retaining its natural floral and fruity notes when served black.

In the hotter months, be sure to try the iced latte, the cold drip or the iced mocha – Lindt chocolate is used in the mocha, which elevates it to a completely new level. If plunger coffee is more your thing, that's cool too. Or branch out and try the AeroPress or Chemex for something completely different.

'The micro-roastery ensures full traceability of its beans and its house blend is made using the best crop...'

Alongside the Background Specialty Coffee Roasters, ShotLab Espresso serves homemade food for breakfast and lunch. If you're there for brunch, make sure to try the ShotLab Espresso Legendary Brekky Wrap – homemade hashbrown, spinach, salsa, boiled egg, cheese and avocado. For a healthy lunch, try a Brazilian Superfood Acai Bowl made with homemade granola, or for a sweet treat with your coffee, you can't go past the signature treat Anzac Cup with Spanish caramel and top of Swiss chocolate.

Right near Newport Beach, with a bright and open feel, ShotLab Espresso is populated by tradies, locals, mothers with babies and surfers; lots of positive, appreciative customers with high expectations. Coffee sacks are upcycled into chair covers and cushions, which perfectly complement this light, beachy cafe.

SHOWBOX COFFEE BREWERS

19 WHISTLER ST, MANLY · 02 9976 5000 · SHOWBOXCOFFE.COM.AU

MACHINE: La Marzocco Linea
GRINDER: Mahlkönig EK43 and Mazzer Robur E
BEANS: Mecca Dark Horse, a rotating brew bar and espresso options
BREWING METHODS: Espresso, Cold Brew, V60 Pour Over

BO HINZACK OPENED SHOWBOX COFFEE BREWERS ON VALENTINE'S DAY, 2014. An auspicious date, as the cafe has certainly received a lot of love since it opened its doors. Serving up coffee from a variety of specialty roasters like Mecca, Reuben Hills and Single O, Showbox fills a gap in Manly with their innovative health-oriented menu that offers more than just salads and smoothies.

Bo, previous owner of The Penny Royal, has been in the industry for about 12 years. He is inspired by the changing nature of the natural coffee product, and chooses his beans and blends from varying suppliers. He knows that when it tastes good, it doesn't matter where it's from. Bo and his team offer what they are interested in trying and order based on their findings, regardless of the popularity or location of the supplier. Most important is the taste, but staying close to companies who have direct relationships with their producers is also essential. The relationships that suppliers have with their farmers and the positive impact companies can have on the farmers' lives are at the forefront of coffee selection at Showbox Coffee Brewers.

The cafe takes its name from a theatre in Seattle that opened in the late 1930s and showcased a diverse range of music, from punk to swing to grunge. The ethos of offering a variety of experiences and creating a community with a variety of products is what spoke to Bo, and made Showbox the natural choice of name. Alongside a vast choice of blends and origins, customers also have the choice of V60, cold brew and during winter, batch brew.

Open for breakfast and lunch, the menu is as innovative as the coffee selection. Considering Showbox's focus on healthy food, it's a surprise to see a doner kebab (silver bullet) on offer for breakfast. This kebab, however, is poles apart from what you might find being devoured outside a nightclub. Instead it is offered as a roti-style bread encasing 24-hour slow-cooked beef, with charred eggplant, hummus, and refreshing tabouli and yogurt. For the uber healthy there's Hawaiian chopped raw fish (poke poke) on black wild rice, or the ancient grain and seed loaf served with smashed avocado, feta and habernero oil. The menu also takes its inspiration from locations across the globe, from Hawaii and South East Asia to the Middle East and the menu is always being adjusted depending on the season.

The industrial inspired décor is a nice change from the (understandably) beachy vibe found in many seaside cafes. Set back from the main drag, away from the beach, it's in a location designed for locals and any tourists willing to step off the Corso. Pipes line the walls and ceiling, and customers Bo fondly describes as "barefoot and interested" inhabit the red-and-white vintage tables.

> '...customers Bo fondly describes as "barefoot and interested" inhabit the red-and-white vintage tables.'

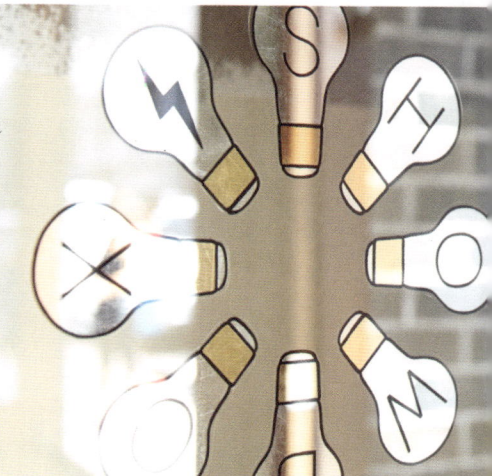

SMALLTOWN

SHOP 1/21-23 OLD BARRENJOEY RD, AVALON · 02 9443 2286 · FACEBOOK.COM/SMALLTOWN

MACHINE: La Marzocco Linea PB
GRINDER: Mazzer Robur E and Mahlkönig EK43
BEANS: Single Origin Roasters – Killer Bee and Single Origin of the week
BREWING METHODS: Espresso, Cold Drip, V60 Pour Over

  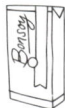 

FOR SO MANY, COFFEE IS A DAILY RITUAL – A MUST-HAVE BEFORE FACING THE DAY. For those in the coffee industry especially, it's so much more than that. It's a lifestyle, a passion, a way of life. Raul Hammerschmitt and Harry Dodson, owners of Smalltown, are no different. In fact, they're up there amongst the biggest coffee devotees you'll find in New South Wales.

To them, coffee is not just about "waking up'" or "becoming more productive", but it is about that unique process that can only apply to completely natural products. Coffee is a gift from nature that we are all still experimenting with and learning about.

Raul comes to Smalltown with seven years' experience working as a barista in cafes around the northern beaches. Harry is a qualified chef, having worked in restaurants in both Australia and Canada for the past ten years. They both manage the business, alongside Katrina Smith. To all of them, coffee is a joy. It is an ongoing journey of the palette but is also an intriguing field to continue to examine. They each take pride in learning more about its roots, processes and geographical influences.

At the cafe, a block back from the beach, Raul and Harry serve coffee from Single Origin Roasters, featuring the Killer Bee blend as their house blend. The house blend is seasonally adjusted and varies in origin to create the desired profile and find that "sweet spot" that accommodates the customers' desire for milk-based coffees. In fact, knowing the big milk drinking culture in Sydney as well as everyone's preference for a sweeter tasting coffee, helped them make their choice of coffee from the beginning.

The Killer Bee Blend has tasting notes of dark honey and tropical fruit, with a creamy finish and mild acidity. Smalltown also showcases lighter roasts and single origins to meet the growing interest in black and filter coffee.

Smalltown goes above and beyond the other coffee styles available in the neighbourhood, offering V60 pour over, cold drip, Inside Out almond milk, Bonsoy and various single origin coffees.

At Smalltown, food offerings are as serious as the coffee. The breakfast and lunch menus are reflective of the seasons and as such, are relaunched every three months. Smalltown offers quirky twists on classic dishes, such as rose water pears, edible flowers and lavender peach compote. They use a sous vide machine for all soft eggs and the menu often features handcrafted burgers, quality seafood, indulgent weekend delights, gluten-free baked goods, cold pressed juices and vegetarian options. The staff are committed to maintaining strong relationships with their suppliers, in order to provide their customers with something special that they can trust and enjoy

At Smalltown, you'll find a consistent stream of locals returning time after time for quality food and excellent coffee.

> 'Coffee is a gift from nature that we are all still experimenting with and learning about.'

THE SOURCE ESPRESSO BAR

6/914 MILITARY RD (ENTER VIA RAGLAN ST) MOSMAN · 02 9969 1368 · THESOURCEESPRESSO.COM.AU

MACHINE: La Marzocco Strada
GRINDER: Mazzer Robur and Mahlkönig
BEANS: Own Blend, Roasted on premises
BREWING METHODS: Pour Over, AeroPress, Batch Brew

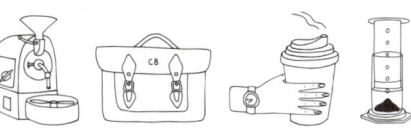

Allan Simpson and Peter Friedmann are owners of various restaurants and want to offer Mosman locals and visitors the very best in coffee and food. Their mission is to ensure an experience so good that it will ensure return visits over and over again. Together with Head Barista BJ, they have achieved exactly this with The Source Espresso Bar. Roasting their specialty single origin coffee on-site three times a week and creating their own signature house blend goes a long way to ensuring The Source remains a firm local favourite.

The Source Espresso Bar's Lucky 7 Blend is created using the freshest crop of green beans from Africa and Central America, and changes with the season. At time of printing, the seasonal blend was made up of Ethiopian coffee from Sidamo and Kenyan Othaya coffee from the Nyeri region. The house blend is roasted to retain the natural sweetness of the coffee bean and gives a lasting taste, which follows you well into the day. It features sweet notes of blueberry, caramel chocolate and balanced acidity, with lemon curd flavours.

The Nyeri region of Kenya is home to numerous coffee farms, most of them on the foothills of the Aberdare Mountains. There are 23 active cooperatives operating in the region, which are comprised of a membership base of over 78,000 individual farmers. The 'Kenyan Kamagogo' beans also come from this region and are available for purchase, as well as to enjoy in the cafe.

The Mosman and North Shore locals have been frequenting The Source since it opened in 2006. They keep returning because of the way The Source baristas meet their specialised requirements and can engage them in deep conversation about the ins and outs of the coffee trade. With specialised knowledge and high expectations from their customer base, it's no wonder The Source Espresso Bar was voted Best Bean to Cup Café in Sydney by The Sydney Coffee Guide.

Alongside espressos, The Source also offers filter coffee, AeroPress, batch brew and the ever-popular milk coffees.

It's not all about the coffee here, though. The diverse and innovative breakfast and lunch menu was created alongside Jane Grover, of Naked Food fame, and is available Monday to Sunday. The all day breakfast and light meals are the perfect accompaniment to the excellent coffee. Try the Sweet Corn and Zucchini Fritters with Avocado Salsa, Poached Egg and Bacon for breakfast, or the Smoked Ocean Trout Salad with Horseradish Dressing for lunch. Breakfast is available all day, too, so lazy weekend mornings are sorted.

The recently refurbished, industrial-chic fit out adds a touch of cool, and as it is conveniently located right next to a large, free public parking area, you can take your time and relax!

'Their mission is to ensure an experience so good that it will ensure return visits over and over again.'

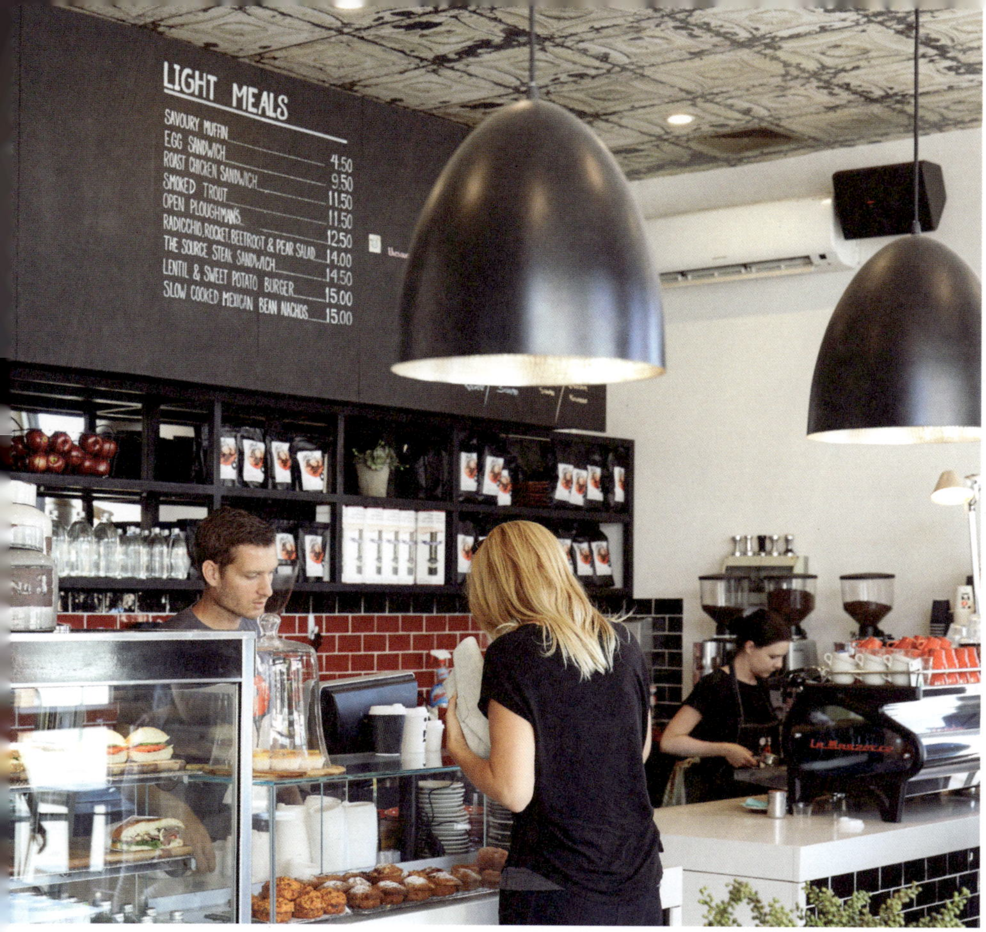
LIGHT MEALS
SAVOURY MUFFIN 4.50
EGG SANDWICH 9.50
ROAST CHICKEN SANDWICH 11.50
SMOKED TROUT 11.50
OPEN PLOUGHMANS 12.50
RADICCHIO, ROCKET, BEETROOT & PEAR SALAD 14.00
THE SOURCE STEAK SANDWICH 14.50
LENTIL & SWEET POTATO BURGER 15.00
SLOW COOKED MEXICAN BEAN NACHOS 15.00

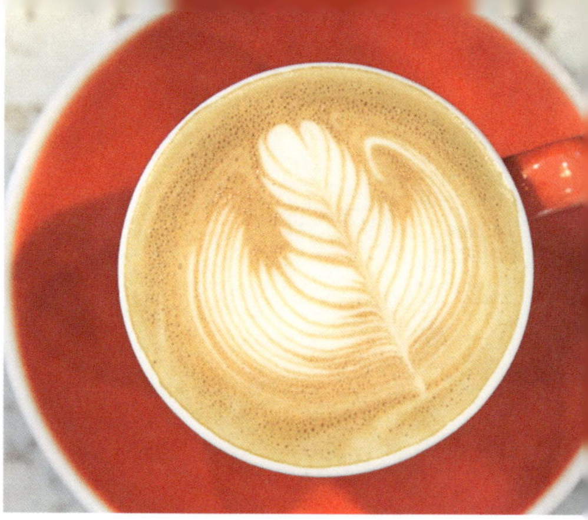

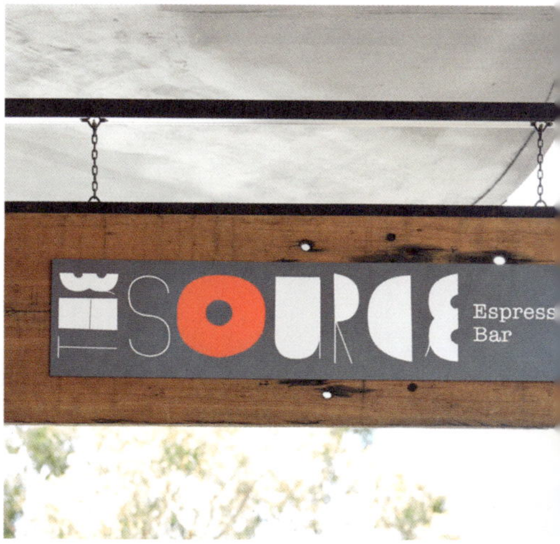
THE SOURCE
Espress
Bar

TRADING HOURS
MON-FRI
6AM-2:30PM
SAT-SUN
6AM-3PM
ESPRESSO
FILTER

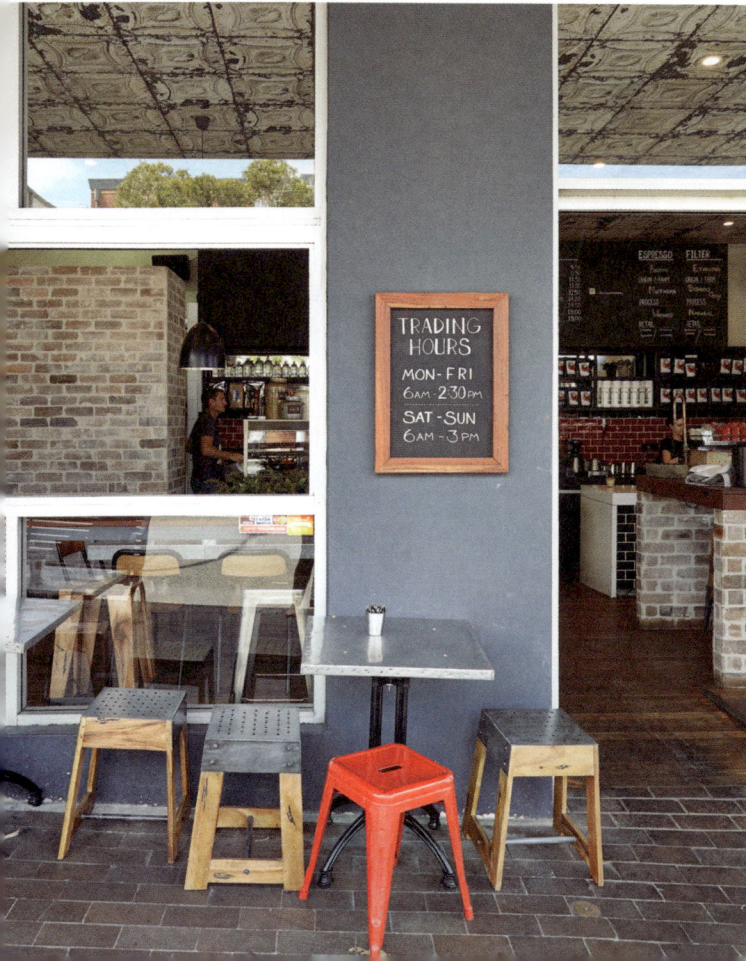

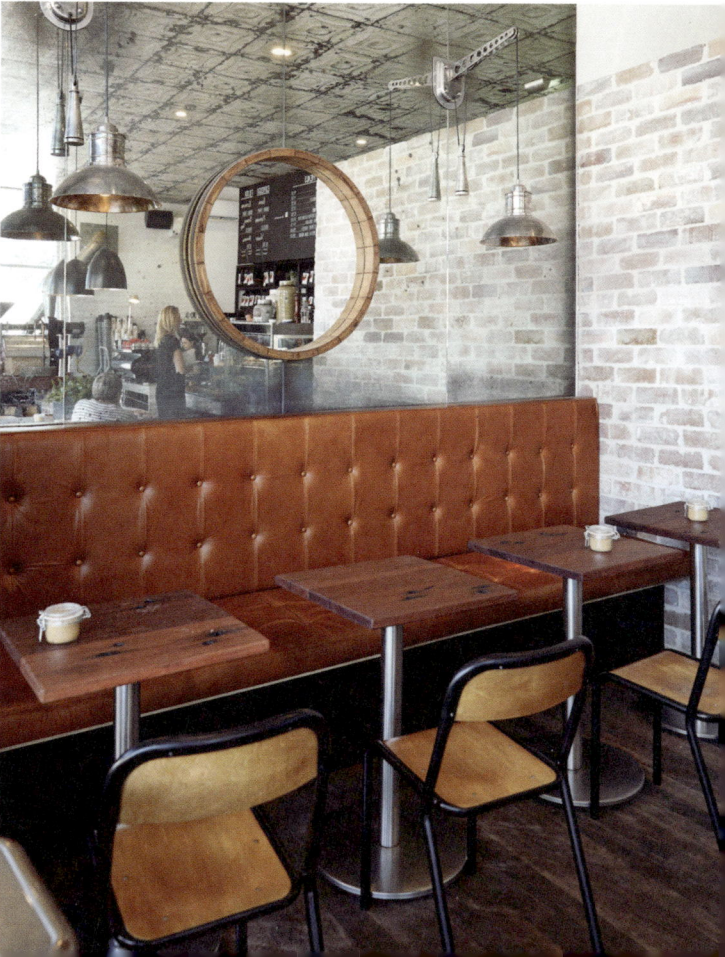

STEAM ENGINE

SHOP 25A, LOT 3 - 436 VICTORIA AVE, CHATSWOOD · FACEBOOK.COM/STEAMENGINECOFFEE

MACHINE: La Marzocco FB/80
GRINDER: Mazzer Robur E and Ditting KR1203 Deli
BEANS: Toby's Estate TSE Vapor Blend
BREWING METHODS: Espresso, Syphon, V60 Pour Over, AeroPress, Cold Drip, Cold Brew

What do you get when you add two best mates from high school, an uninspiring empty shell of a shop, and an obsession with coffee? The ultra-cool Chatswood coffee mecca, The Steam Engine.

Roland Davies and Samuel Werrett don't just have an interest in coffee; they have an obsession. When they dreamed about opening a cafe together they were only half serious, but when this site popped up, they took one look at it, and it was go time! The pair set out to bring specialty grade coffee to their customers in Chatswood.

The Steam Engine may be in what Roland describes as a bland urban area, but the boys have made sure their 23 square metres of coffee paradise spices things up for the locals. The curved ceiling, with gorgeous red detailing, makes you feel like you're in the carriage of a Victorian era steam train carriage – hence the name, right? Despite its size, there's a truly social atmosphere here, with plenty of regulars and a healthy dose of banter.

Roland and Sam are as passionate about their supplier, Toby's Estate Coffee Roasters, as they are about their cafe. After touring their facilities and sampling their coffee, there was no doubt that Toby's would be the one and only supplier to The Steam Engine. Their attention to detail, the fact that they cup every single batch and test every bag of every blend for consistency – what more could coffee lovers ask for?

The house blend is Vapor, which consists of beans from 8 different origins from Africa, South America and Central America. It is designed to pair beautifully with milk, however at about the 10 day aging mark it also pulls a full-bodied, clean long black. Mid palate, it is all black forest, full of chocolate with hints of cherry, pecan and blackberry.

The Steam Engine constantly rotates their single origins, offering two different origins each week. The staples tend to be single components of the house blend, the highlights of which are from Ethiopia, Panama and Costa Rica. There's a steady stream of amazing single origins from Panama, thanks to Toby's Estate owning a farm there and having control beyond just buying and roasting. Roland and Sam's favourite is the Panama Finca Santa Teresa Batista Honey Gesha – quite the mouthful, in both senses of the word. Also available are V60 pour over, AeroPress, syphon, cold drip and cold brew.

The Steam Engine opens for breakfast and lunch from Monday to Saturday. Keep an eye out in 2015 for monthly After-Dark Brewing Sessions, for those with a passion to learn and talk coffee. And even if you're lacking a little passion, these young men have plenty to spare.

> '...there's a truly social atmosphere here, with plenty of regulars and a healthy dose of banter.'

STEAMTANK

SHOP 3, PEDESTRIAN OVERBRIDGE, HORNSBY RAILWAY STATION, HORNSBY · STEAMTANKCOFFEE.COM.AU

MACHINE: La Marzocco, Strada
GRINDER: Mazzer Robur E and Mahlkönig EK43
BEANS: Mecca, Reuben Hills, Small Batch, Seven Seeds, Marvell St
BREWING METHODS: Espresso, AeroPress, Pour Over, Ratio Brewer, Cold Brew

 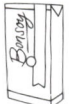  

FOR TOO LONG, THE COMMUTERS OF HORNSBY EXISTED IN A DIRE COFFEE DROUGHT. Not an ethically sourced, seasonal coffee bean to be seen. It's a wonder they ever made it to work awake. In March 2014, Mitchell Hayes and Natasha Kumar put an end to that drought by opening SteamTank, an espresso bar that injects a warm and inviting vibe into what can be a cold and bleak railway concourse.

Mitchell and Natasha met at university while studying biochemistry and microbiology, but quickly decided they'd rather swap the test tubes for the grinder and opened a cafe together. They're absolutely obsessed with coffee and have been for quite a while: Mitchell was working in his parents' coffee shop well before the age most of us started working and Natasha spent a year travelling through Brazil, where she spent some time on a coffee plantation and fell in love with the entire process.

This joint passion has translated into a welcoming place where customers are empowered to start their day on the right track. For those grabbing a coffee during the morning rush, the team at SteamTank serve up consistently excellent coffees in a timely fashion, ensuring no one is ever late. Or, if you want to step out of the rat race and take a moment to relax, there are lean bars and friendly faces in the small but welcoming space.

The house blend here is Dark Horse from Mecca Coffee Roasters. It's a seasonal blend and changes frequently. It usually contains three coffees: one from Central America and two from Africa, typically including at least one naturally processed coffee. The crew at SteamTank are big fans of Ethiopian coffees. Ethiopia is the one place in the world where Arabica is harvested from wild grown forest trees and some small plantations. Mitchell explained, "in the cup this translates to a beautiful complexity and variety of flavour coming from Ethiopian coffees."

'...everything on the menu is obtained from ethically sound sources so you can feel good about what you're drinking and eating.'

SteamTank will only use coffees that have been sourced transparently, that is, they can be traced back to either the cooperative who produced it (for African coffees) and often the farmer themselves (in the case of Central and South American coffees). This promotes better quality, prevents corruption and ensures a fair price for the farmers.

Open until 3pm during the week and 1pm on Saturday, SteamTank also offers a variety of healthy food options to eat in or take away. Naturally, everything on the menu is obtained from ethically sound sources so you can feel good about what you're drinking and what you're eating.

With such a strong focus on uncompromising quality, don't you wish your commute took you through Hornsby station?

THREE DOORS DOWN

12/24 WARATAH ST, MONA VALE · 0404 562 337

MACHINE: La Marzocco Linea PB
GRINDER: Mazzer Robur E, Mazzer E, Mahlkönig EK43
BEANS: Three Doors down HB by Pablo & Rusty
BREWING METHODS: Batch Brew, Espresso, Cold Drip

 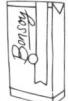  

HIDDEN DOWN A LANEWAY IN MONA VALE, THREE DOORS DOWN IS THE BRAINCHILD OF TOMER ELNEKAVE, WHO HAS BEEN A BARISTA FOR MANY YEARS AND OPENED A CAFE IN THE TYPE OF LOCATION HE LIKES TO DRINK HIS COFFEE – TUCKED AWAY FROM THE MAIN DRAG AND OFF THE BEATEN PATH. Three Doors Down opened late in 2013 after a renovation, which turned the space into an industrial-style cafe with a warm and inviting feel.

Offering espresso, batch brew and cold brew, Mona Vale locals drop by for coffee dates and catch ups, with everyone from young mums and bubs to retirees soaking up the atmosphere and the custom house-blend.

Tomer sources his coffee from Pablo and Rusty's, who created a custom house-blend for Three Doors Down. It is a seasonal blend that is altered to keep its delicious taste profile year round, and generally consists of beans from Latin America and Africa. Some of the beans are washed and some are natural, creating a distinct cacao flavour with a berry fruit finish. Tomer and the suppliers successfully achieve a unique flavour with a roast profile that exhibits the characteristics of each origin.

Tomer and Barista, Daniel Murray, strive to provide the best possible cup of coffee, every time. They're obsessive about brewing accuracy and really understand the importance of consistency. All of the baristas, including Hila Zabari, have several years' experience and are focused on providing their customers with exceptional service and a consistently excellent cup of coffee. The cafe is set up with a La Marzocco PB espresso machine and different machines for grinding – a Robur E and a Mahlkönig.

People come for the coffee, but they stay for the food! Try the Shakshuka – baked eggs in a spicy tomato sauce, served in the pan with sourdough and homemade labna cheese. Or go for the delicious Smashed Avocado with house made pesto, halloumi cheese and roasted tomato. For something a little more substantial, try the smoked trout and avocado salad served on potato hash with lime and black pepper aioli.

> '...opened a cafe in the type of location he likes to drink his coffee – tucked away from the main drag'

The interesting and exotic flavours continue with heirloom tomato bruschetta with feta, pine nuts and pomegranate molasses. For a sweet treat, is there anything more appealing than Israeli chocolate brioche? Not in our book.

The up-cycled brick walls and recycled timber fixtures create a warm atmosphere here. It's just a coffee-lover owner and his coffee-loving team, turning up to work everyday with one aim – making their customers the best cup of coffee they've ever had. Simple!

THE TUCKSHOP

78 GLENHAVEN RD, GLENHAVEN · 0433 950 434 · TUCKSHOPCOFFEE.COM.AU

MACHINE: La Marzocco Linea
GRINDER: Mazzer Robur A
BEANS: Single Origin Roasters, Reservoir
BREWING METHODS: Espresso, Cold Brew

THE THREE FELLAS BEHIND 'THE BARON' FELT THAT, AFTER TWO YEARS OF SMOOTH SAILING IT WAS TIME FOR A NEW VENTURE. The Baron's still going strong of course; they've just now added 'The Tuckshop' to their portfolio. Matt Stone, Ricki Row and Mike Ico, together with Nathan Hindmarsh, took over what was a local takeaway joint in Glenhaven, and turned it into The Tuckshop. They wanted to retain the takeaway shop concept, but twist it up with what they knew, which is great food and excellent coffee.

The result is a takeaway cafe that serves its food in Biopak packaging, rather than on plates and in bowls, where the customers grab a blanket and head over to the park across the road to enjoy their burgers, all day breakfasts and Single Origin coffee. Open seven days a week, The Tuckshop is a local treasure to Glenhaven residents, who share it with tradies working in the area and uni students during the week.

Choosing the coffee supplier for The Tuckshop was a no brainer – the guys were so happy with their supplier at The Baron, Single Origin Roasters, who gave them the third degree when they wanted to serve Single O coffee in their first cafe, which they opened with zero cafe experience whatsoever. They did want a house blend that was a bit different to what they offer at The Baron, however – a point of difference between the two businesses, and something that would suit Glenhaven folk in particular. That led The Tuckshop crew to 'Reservoir', Single Origin Roaster's signature blend. Its structured and vibrant acidity and flavours of ripe stone fruits suits The Tuckshop down to the ground. Currently made from coffees from India, Rwanda and Ethiopia, the blend is adjusted seasonally with fresh harvest single origin coffees, to ensure it continues to deliver the desired taste profile.

Dan Dematos manages the business alongside the owners, and also acts as head barista. Dan was previously a customer of The Tuckshop. He then quit his desk job to make coffee at a local cafe, and it wasn't long before he was making his way over to work behind the La Marzocco Linea at The Tuckshop. As well as the standard espresso coffees, he serves cold brew – black or with milk – and a rotating single origin offering, if the customer asks for it.

For a hole-in-the-wall takeaway cafe, you'd be surprised at the quality of food that comes out of the kitchen. The Tuckshop prides itself on being exactly that, after all, – a tuck shop – from the original use of the word, meaning to 'tuck into a meal'. And tuck you will; the Glenhaven location means access to fresh, organic produce on a daily basis from some of Sydney's best farmers. The menu's simple but comprehensive: an All Day Menu featuring breakfast standards, 'The Tradie Roll' and 'The Breakfast Box' (boiled egg, avocado, confit mushroom, cherry tomato, kale and herbs), a Burger menu, and 'Salad and Things'. There's a kids' menu for 'Little Tuckers', too. All in all, as they say at The Tuckshop, "it is what it is!"

> '…customers grab a blanket and head over to the park across the road to enjoy their burgers, all day breakfasts and Single Origin coffee.'

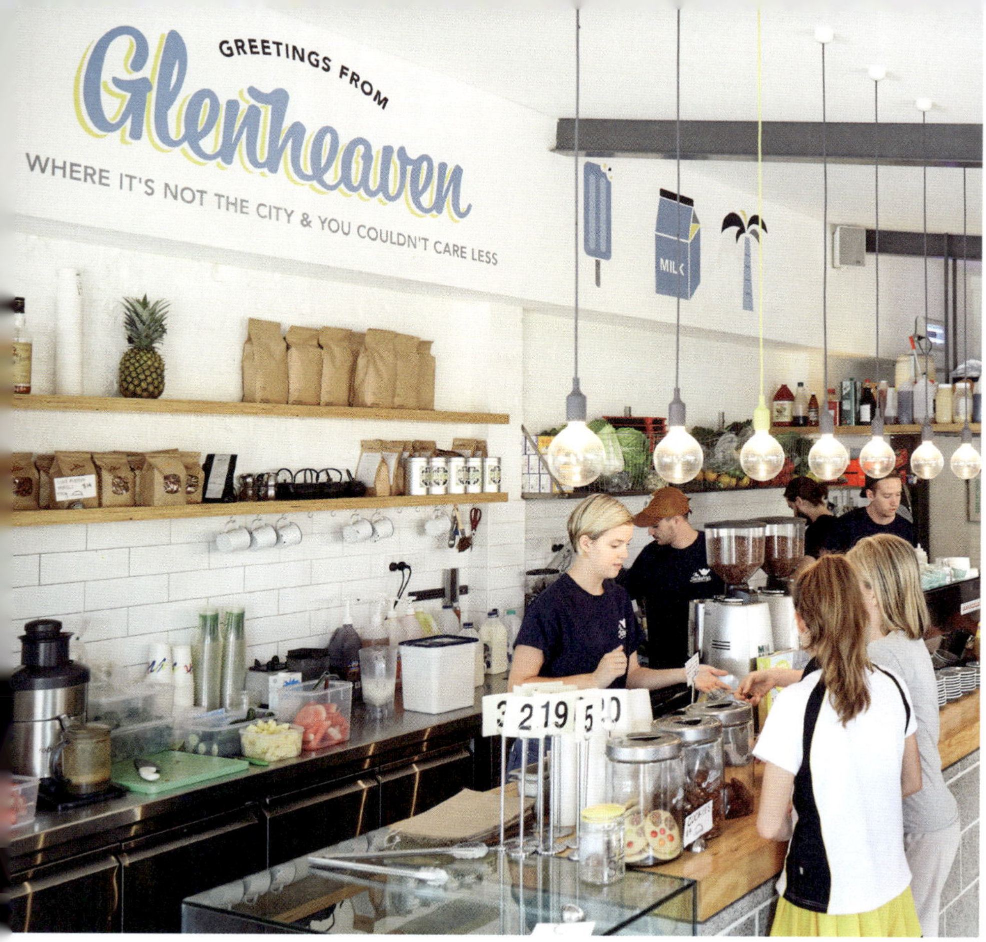
GREETINGS FROM
Glenheaven
WHERE IT'S NOT THE CITY & YOU COULDN'T CARE LESS
MILK
The Tuckshop
Bonsoy

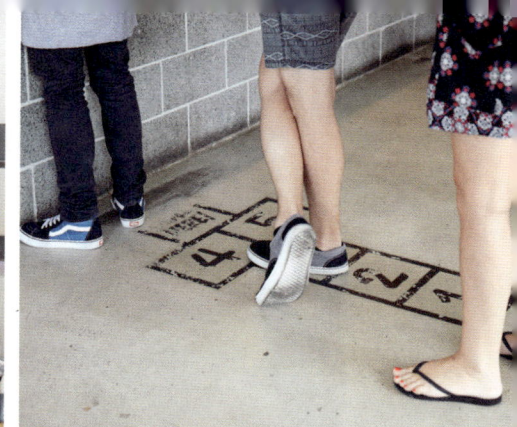

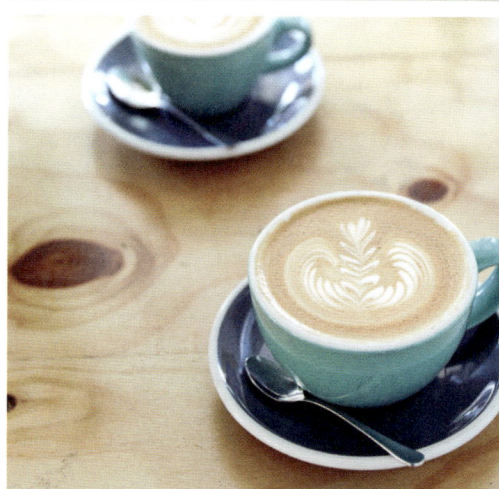

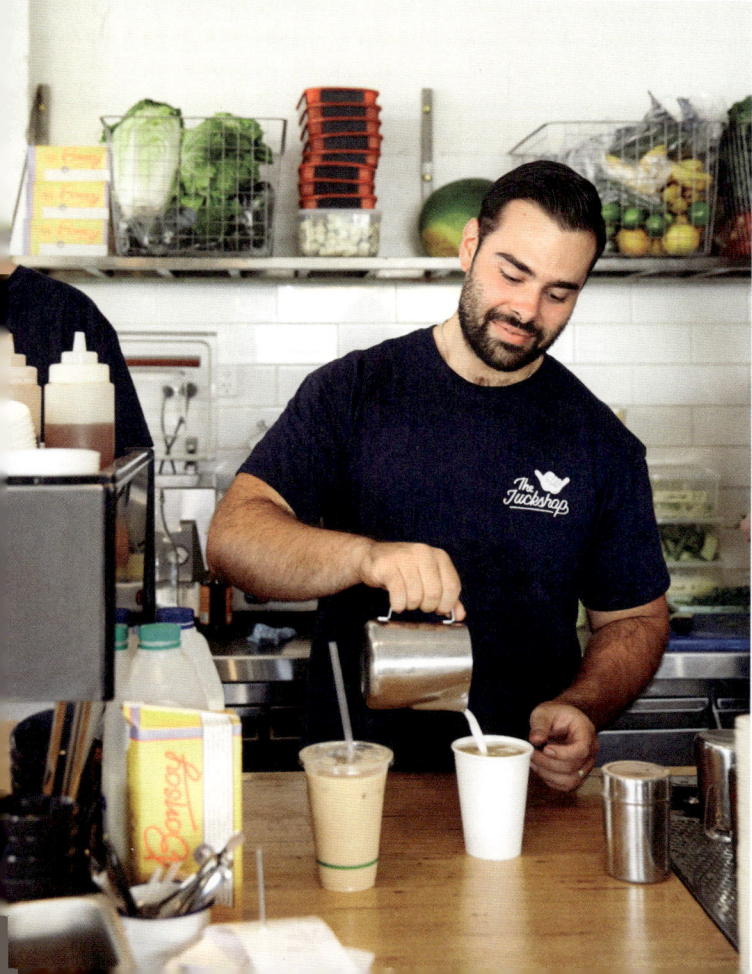

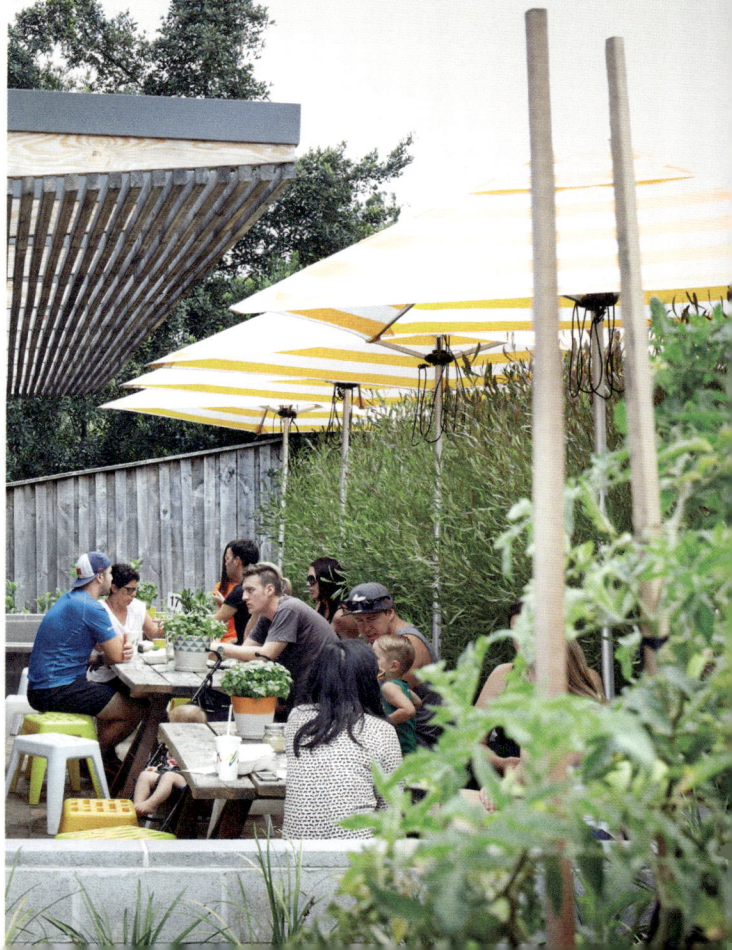

WATERFRONT STORE AND CAFE

1860 PITTWATER RD, CHURCH POINT · 02 9979 6633 · WATERFRONTSTORE.COM.AU

MACHINE: Wega Vela
GRINDER: Mazzer Robur E
BEANS: Own Blend, Romeo Coffee
BREWING METHODS: Espresso

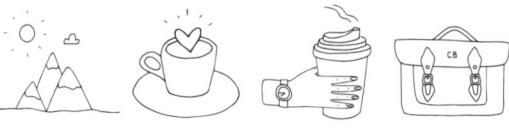

Set on a wooden deck perched above sparkling Pittwater, Waterfront Cafe serves up fantastic coffee, food and views. With a scattering of boats and yachts and Scotland Island just a stone's throw away, it's the perfect place to escape to before a busy day.

Not only does Waterfront Cafe serve up great coffee and breakfast, it is also a general store, heritage Post Office, restaurant, take-away and bottle shop – basically Church Point's one-stop shop for locals or those passing by on boat.

With so many areas to look after, it can be easy to think that the quality of coffee may be left behind, but that is certainly not the case. The Waterfront Cafe has its own blend which is roasted by their very (own SCAA licensed) Coffee Q grader Tony Macri of Romeo Coffee Roasters.

The seasonal blend served at Waterfront is 100% Arabica, comprising 60% Tanna Island, Vanuatu, 20% Pocos Caldas, Brazil, and 20% Tolima Tres Santos, Colombia. This blend is based on Romeo Coffee's direct trade relationships and the cupping qualities of each coffee.

Tanna Island, part of the Vanuatu island nation, provides a body coffee that blends really well, giving a great cut through the milk. The Colombian, cultivated in Tolima Tres Santos, is wonderfully fragrant and balanced. Flavours include sweet raisin and cocoa throughout and a clean finish of cranberry and apple. The Brazilian beans are grown on a legendary mountain on the Boa Vista Farm in Pocos De Caldas in Brazil. Andre Sanches grows some of the finest coffee in the region on his self-titled estate, and Tony said that this lot in particular blew him away with its complexity and brightness.

Romeo Coffee has a bean to cup policy and Tanna Island has been the hero of the cup in many of its blends. When the tiny island was almost obliterated by Cyclone Pam recently, CEO of Romeo, Tony Macri, turned around to offer support to the farmers by organising fundraisers, with the money being handed over to rebuild their community and coffee plantations. He has also committed to pay premium prices for future coffee.

> 'Church Point's one-stop shop for locals or those passing by on boat.'

Tea-lovers are well looked after too. Alongside classic Chai and English Breakfast Tea there are unique flavours like Honeydew Green tea and Fruits of Eden. Enjoy a big breakfast with your coffee or tea, or opt for something different like scrambled truffle eggs or avocado cups. The breakfast menu is as extensive as the dinner and lunch menu together, so your food experience can be as unique as the ever-changing view.

Whether you're a tourist, traveller, sailor or local, breakfast, coffee and morning haze over Pittwater Harbour is a bucket-list item not to be missed; and the Waterfront Store and Cafe is the only place to get all three with such incredible quality.

*Coffee first
Schemes
later*

Showbox Coffee Brewers | Manly

Articifer Coffee | Surry Hills

EAST OF THE CITY

EAST OF THE CITY

1. 22 Grams — 257
2. Ampersand Cafe & Bookstore — 258
3. Artificer Specialty Coffee Bar and Roastery — 261
4. Bellagio Cafe — 262
5. Book Kitchen (The) — 265
6. Brooklyn Hide — 266
7. Bunker (The) — 269
8. Cafe Con Leche — 270
9. Café Hernandez — 273
10. Coffee Tea & Me — 274
11. Cook & Archies — 277
12. Corduroy Cafe — 281
13. Devon Cafe — 282
14. Di Bella Coffee Roasting Warehouse — 285
15. Edition Coffee Roasters — 286
16. Filosofy — 289
17. Flat White Cafe — 290
18. Joe Black — 293
19. Latteria — 294
20. Nelson Road Tuckshop — 299
21. Orto Trading Co — 300
22. Reformatory Caffeine Lab, The — 303
23. Room 10 Espresso — 304
24. Rose Bay Diner — 307
25. Royal Darlinghurst (The) — 308
26. Sample Coffee Pro Shop — 311
27. Sensory Lab — 312
28. Shop and Wine Bar (The) — 315
29. Stop Valve Espresso — 316
30. Single Origin Roasters Surry Hills — 319
31. Sly Espresso — 320
32. Uliveto — 323

Di Bella Roasting House

EAST SIDE BARISTAS

AMPERSAND CAFE & BOOKSTORE — Renald Vettese

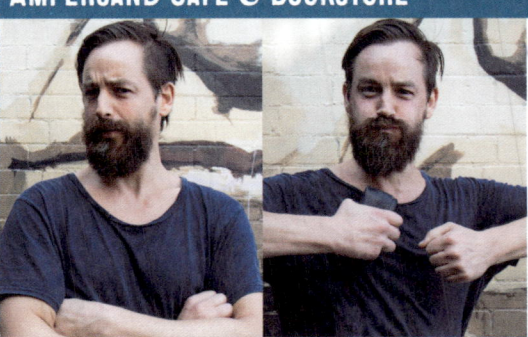

I HAVE MY COFFEE…
Strong, short espresso or macchiato.

IF I WASN'T A BARISTA, I WOULD BE…
A plastic surgeon.

FORGET COFFEE, MY FAVOURITE PLACE TO EAT OUT IN SYDNEY IS…
Fleetwood Macchiato, Newtown. It has a nice vibe and is near home.

ARTIFICER SPECIALTY COFFEE BAR AND ROASTERY — Dan Yee

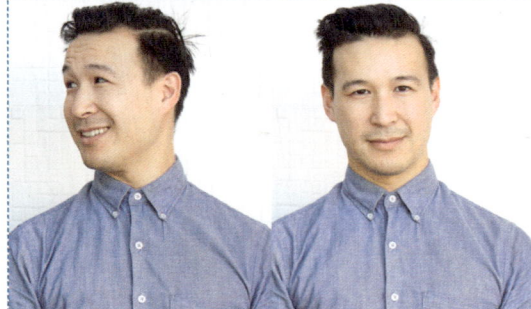

WHEN I'M NOT MAKING COFFEE, I AM…
Eating and sleeping.

FORGET COFFEE, MY FAVOURITE PLACE TO EAT OUT IN SYDNEY IS…
Bulletin Place.

GIVE ME A QUOTE
I like to keep coffee real without the "latte art."

THE BOOK KITCHEN — Emma Rule & Lucas Blackman

I HAVE MY COFFEE…
Emma: And I want another immediately.
Lucas: Rarely, but soy with honey.

IF I WASN'T A BARISTA, I'D BE…
Emma: A chef or food editor travelling the globe.
Lucas: Shaking your cocktails.

MY FAVOURITE BREWING METHOD IS…
Emma: Espresso.
Lucas: Espresso.

BROOKLYN HIDE — Matthew

IF I WASN'T A BARISTA, I WOULD BE…
Rich.

FORGET COFFEE, MY FAVOURITE PLACE TO EAT OUT IN SYDNEY IS…
I prefer to pack a lunch and head to a park.

WHEN I'M NOT MAKING COFFEE I AM…
I own my business… I don't have a life.

EAST SIDE BARISTAS

THE BUNKER — Cesar Augusto Echeverri

I HAVE MY COFFEE…
Short and black or on a double ristretto piccolo.

MY FAVOURITE BREWING METHOD IS…
Pour Over.

IF I WASN'T A BARISTA, I'D BE…
An animation director.

CAFE CON LECHE — Robert Saunder

I HAVE MY COFFEE…
Short black and then a double latte.

WHEN I'M NOT MAKING COFFEE I AM…
Reading, playing music.

GIVE ME A QUOTE
"Art is never finished, only abandoned." – Leonardo Da Vinci

COOK & ARCHIES — Jakkraphat Sawangsangeattana (Pure, for short)

I HAVE MY COFFEE…
Latte with cold milk.

IF I WASN'T A BARISTA, I'D BE…
An IT wizard. I'm great with computers.

FORGET COFFEE, MY FAVOURITE PLACE TO EAT OUT IN SYDNEY IS…
My girlfriend is a great cook. So I like to eat at home.

CORDUROY CAFE — Con

I HAVE MY COFFEE…
First thing in the morning.

IF I WASN'T A BARISTA, I WOULD BE…
Travelling the world.

FORGET COFFEE, MY FAVOURITE PLACE TO EAT OUT IN SYDNEY IS…
Alongside my wife.

EAST SIDE BARISTAS

DI BELLA ROASTING HOUSE — Jeffrey

WHEN I'M NOT MAKING COFFEE I AM…
Riding my motorcycle.

I HAVE MY COFFEE…
Piccolo.

FORGET COFFEE, MY FAVOURITE PLACE TO EAT OUT IN SYDNEY IS…
Movida.

EDITION COFFEE ROASTERS — Corie Joel Sutherland

MY FAVOURITE BREWING METHOD IS…
Pour Over.

IF I WASN'T A BARISTA, I'D BE…
John Mayer… but seriously, I wanted to be a famous guitarist and composer.

WHEN I'M NOT MAKING COFFEE, I AM…
Studying language, spending time with my family.

JOE BLACK — Pippo Chaiyasirinroj

IF I WASN'T A BARISTA, I'D BE…
A graphic designer (print) for a magazine, or in advertising.

WHEN I'M NOT MAKING COFFEE, I AM…
Playing games and keeping up to date on the music I like.

MY FAVOURITE BREWING METHOD IS…
Cold Drip.

LATTERIA — Nikel Patel

I HAVE MY COFFEE…
Before life begins.

IF I WASN'T A BARISTA, I'D BE…
A great husband.

WHEN I'M NOT MAKING COFFEE, I AM…
Looking for a wife.

EAST SIDE BARISTAS

NELSON ROAD TUCK SHOP
Trent Bramley

IF I WASN'T A BARISTA, I WOULD BE…
A Chopper Pilot.

MY FAVOURITE PLACE TO EAT OUT IN SYDNEY IS…
Kitchen By Mike in Rosebery for brunch.
Cho Cho San for dinner.

WHEN I'M NOT MAKING COFFEE I AM…
Trying to find someone to make one for me..

ORTO TRADING CO
Louise Hunt

I HAVE MY COFFEE…
First thing in the morning.

IF I WASN'T A BARISTA, I'D BE…
A winemaker.

WHEN I'M NOT MAKING COFFEE, I AM…
Renovating my house.

ROOM 10
Bettina Kurth & Andrew Hardjasudarma

IF I WASN'T A BARISTA, I WOULD BE…
Bettina: A designer of some sort.
Andrew: A car racer.

WHEN I'M NOT MAKING COFFEE I AM…
Bettina: On my road bike or cooking dinner.
Andrew: Serving customers.

MY FAVOURITE BREWING METHOD IS…
Bettina: Espresso and AeroPress.
Andrew: AeroPress at home, espresso at work.

ROSE BAY DINER
Benny Sweeten

I HAVE MY COFFEE…
Black.

WHEN I'M NOT MAKING COFFEE, I AM…
Building cafes.

MY FAVOURITE PLACE TO EAT OUT IN SYDNEY IS…
Longrain or Nomad.

EAST SIDE BARISTAS

THE ROYAL DARLINGHURST — Morgan Knight

I HAVE MY COFFEE…
Double ristretto piccolo.

IF I WASN'T A BARISTA, I WOULD BE…
A paramedic.

MY FAVOURITE BREWING METHOD IS…
AeroPress.

SAMPLE COFFEE PRO SHOP — Toby Wilson

MY FAVOURITE BREWING METHOD IS…
Pour Over.

FORGET COFFEE, MY FAVOURITE PLACE TO EAT OUT IN SYDNEY IS…
This Must Be The Place (cocktail bar).

WHEN I'M NOT MAKING COFFEE, I AM…
Playing piano.

THE SHOP AND WINE BAR — Mike Haskas

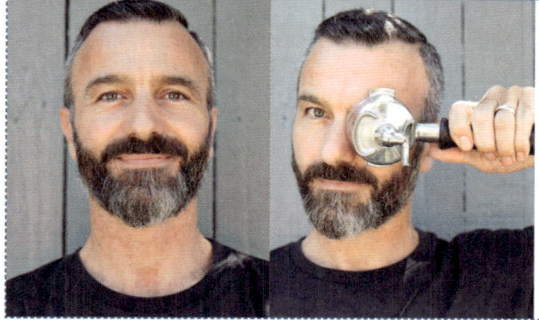

I HAVE MY COFFEE…
White for brekkie, black for lunch.

FORGET COFFEE, MY FAVOURITE PLACE TO EAT OUT IN SYDNEY IS…
My wife's kitchen.

WHEN I'M NOT MAKING COFFEE, I AM…
Loving life as a husband, father and surfer.

STOP VALVE ESPRESSO & BAR — Bom Tarin Sathukarn

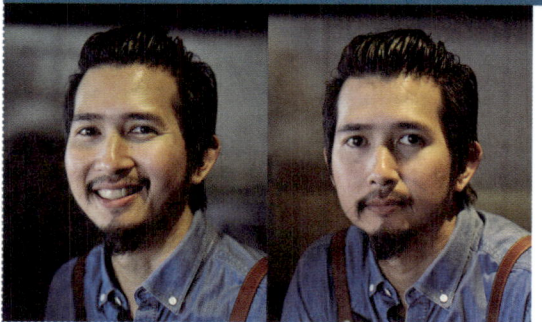

MY FAVOURITE BREWING METHOD IS…
At the moment, a V60 Pour Over.

FORGET COFFEE, MY FAVOURITE PLACE TO EAT OUT IN SYDNEY IS…
I'm Thai and love spicy food! Gaysorn Thai serves great southern Thai food.

WHEN I'M NOT MAKING COFFEE, I AM…
Chasing up my 3 year old daughter.

EAST SIDE BARISTAS

SLY AT SURRY HILLS — Alexander 'King Brown' Zamfir

I HAVE MY COFFEE…
Black. A short long black. We call it a 'schlong'.

IF I WASN'T A BARISTA, I'D BE…
A shoe shiner on the streets.

WHEN I'M NOT MAKING COFFEE, I AM…
Writing a book of poems.

ULIVETO — Chai Pranomrum

I HAVE MY COFFEE…
Double shot long black.

IF I WASN'T A BARISTA, I'D BE…
A cocktail pro.

WHEN I'M NOT MAKING COFFEE, I AM…
Following the stock market.

EAST

Ampersand Cafe & Bookstore | Paddington

"You can do it"
- Coffee

blasted with a shot gun
left out overnight in the rain
betrayed by a friend
stranded in a foreign country
overwhelmed by the kindness of a stranger
floored by the stars in the desert sky
licked by a dog
stood on, shouted at and gave back as good as you got
danced till breaking point
and sang your song with everyone watching
travelled, with depth, soul and life
you, me
us

22 grams the weight of experience

22 GRAMS

166-168 BELMORE RD (ENTER VIA HIGH ST), RANDWICK · 02 9398 2277 · FACEBOOK.COM/22GRAMSCAFE

MACHINE: La Marzocco
GRINDER: Mazzer Robur E, EK, Nuova Simonelli Mythos
BEANS: Dark and Handsome
BREWING METHODS: Espresso, Pour Over

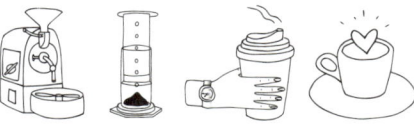

The owners of 22 grams, Doug and Hazel, believe that near enough is not good enough when it comes to specialty coffee. Their team of talented baristas live up to expectations by creating great freshly roasted espresso for the appreciative locals.

Doug and Hazel, who both have extensive experience in hospitality, joined forces to create 22 grams and it has quickly become somewhat of a Randwick institution. 22 grams' coffee fixation saw the purchase of a 5kg Probat roaster, with seasonal beans sourced from far and wide and roasted in-house.

The 22 grams team use washed, honey, pulp natural, and dry processed beans, and strive to produce a consistent, full-bodied house blend, with pronounced caramel sweetness and a clean finish. Current bean selection includes Ndaroini Kenya, Sonora Costa Rica, Mormora Guji Ethiopia, and Pocos de Caldas Brazil, to name a few.

The 22 grams coffee philosophy is summed up by Doug and roaster Jeff, "making a good coffee is, with sufficient practice, easy. But great coffee requires a zealous attention to detail and a willingness to fixate on an abundance of minuscule factors, which, only if you get them right, come together to create an awesome experience."

The coffee bug has well and truly made its way into the veins at 22 grams, and the result is a coffee experience like few others. Since the team started roasting in-house the focus has been on developing the perfect warm-hug wake-up experience of their milk blend, a sophisticated blend for their black espressos, and dropping some accentuated fruit bombs as well as a more nuanced attack with their selection of filter brews. At 22 grams roasting and brewing coffee has become a daily meditation, a chance to get in flow, chase perfection and create a distinct coffee experience.

22 grams has a faithful following of regulars, many of whom work at the nearby Prince of Wales and Sydney Children's hospitals and there is also a lively crowd who wander over from the University of New South Wales. Hazel and Doug take delight in providing an oasis for customers to let their hair down, take a deep breath and smell... the coffee. Hazel reflects, "The thing I've always loved about coffee is that it's five minutes of me-time, having something I love, just the way I want it, and then I can re-enter the world energized."

"...it's five minutes of me-time, having something I love, just the way I want it..."

The look of the cafe is warm and rustic with exposed walls contrasted by warm lighting. The irresistible muffins, cakes and pastries are baked daily and the meals are bursting with freshness and flavour. Open seven days a week for breakfast and lunch, and catering to gluten free customers too, there's something for everyone at 22 grams.

AMPERSAND CAFE & BOOK STORE

78 OXFORD ST, PADDINGTON · 02 9380 6617 · AMPERSANDCAFE.COM.AU

MACHINE: La Marzocco
GRINDER: Mazzer
BEANS: Allpress Carmelo
BREWING METHODS: Espresso, Cold Drip

DOES ANYTHING PAIR BETTER WITH A GREAT CUP OF COFFEE THAN A BOOK? They are two things so many of us are passionate about, and at Ampersand Cafe and Book Store, there's the perfect balance. A unique combination of ambience, authentic food, Allpress coffee and diverse books lining the walls, Ampersand Cafe and Book Store has been the go-to spot for Paddington book lovers and coffee aficionados for more than 10 years.

The heritage-protected building is filled with antique décor, but there's nothing stuffy and dusty about this bookshop cafe. There's a modern vibe, great energy and a bustling atmosphere.

Irene Goldsworthy took over the business in 2014 and together with her 'trusted lieutenants,' manages the day-to-day operations of this literary destination. With a long family history in the hospitality industry, Irene is passionate about delivering a unique dining and coffee experience. "Coffee is the glue that binds every cafe," Irene said, and of course she's right. That glue binds tightly at Ampersand Cafe; it's been using Allpress' Carmelo Blend for years. It has a strong following among the Ampersand regulars – ask them, and they'll tell you it's the best bean in town.

The Allpress Carmelo Blend is a medium roast blend featuring coffees from Colombia, Sumatra, Brazil and Guatemala. It is lively and full bodied and offers distinct caramel flavours. You'll most likely find it difficult to decide where you want to sit and settle in with your Carmelo Blend; will it be outside in the sun, watching the world go by, or on one of the three levels amongst the books?

Head upstairs for Fiction, where you can find a cozy table nestled amongst the shelves, or outside under the striped awning, admiring the book-themed street art on the alleyway walls. If you prefer to be front and centre, grab a tall wooden stool at the front counter. The library in the basement doubles as a quirky and unique place to hold events.

In recent years Ampersand has won multiple coffee and food-related awards, and Head Barista, Renald Vettese hails from Paris and has been at Ampersand for nearly eight years – he is something of a local institution. Be sure to pop in and say 'bonjour.'

Warm days call for a cold drip or a cold brew, and cooler days are made for snuggling up in a vintage armchair under the eclectic chandeliers and floor-to-ceiling bookshelves, groaning with tomes. There are over 30,000 second-hand books here to be perused, so settle in!

> 'A unique combination of ambience, authentic food, Allpress coffee and diverse books lining the walls...'

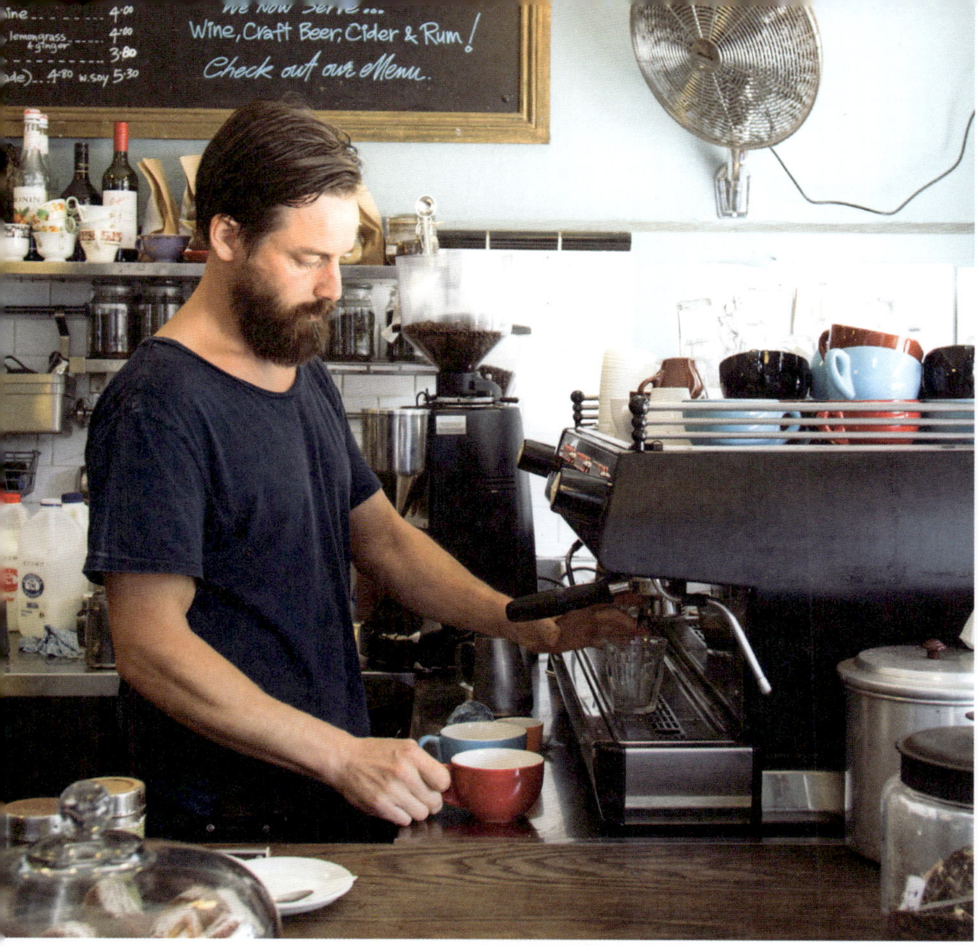
Wine, Craft Beer, Cider & Rum!
Check out our Menu

THE CLOISTER AND THE HEARTH
CHARLES READE
FICTION
No. 29
EVERYMAN'S LIBRARY
DENT
DUTTON
THE SMALL HOUSE AT ALLINGTON
Anthony Trollope
THE WORLD'S CLASSICS
OXFORD
FRAMLEY PARSONAGE
Anthony Trollope
THE WARDEN
Anthony Trollope
217
THE WORLD'S CLASSICS
OXFORD
DOCTOR THORNE
ANTHONY TROLLOPE
298
THE WORLD'S CLASSICS
OXFORD
Sylvia's Lovers

AMPERSAND
BOOKS
BOUGHT & SOLD

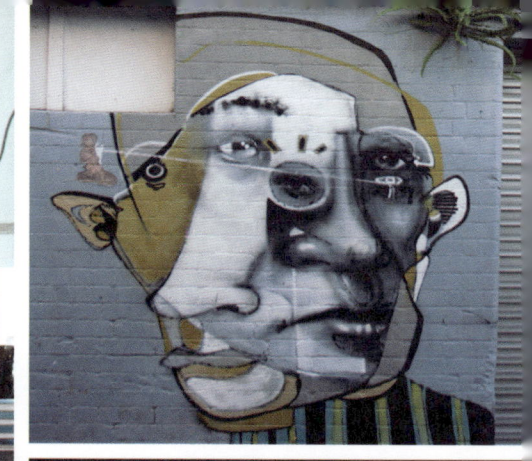

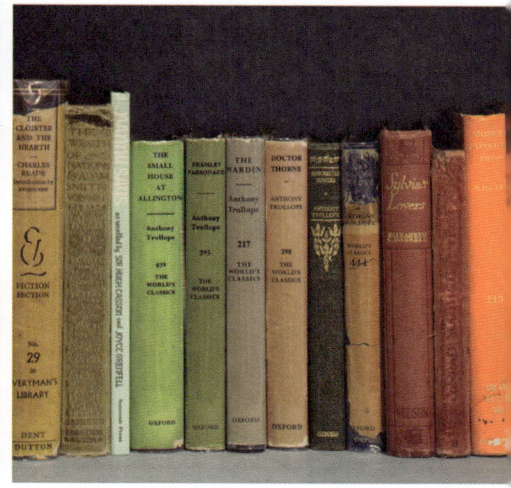

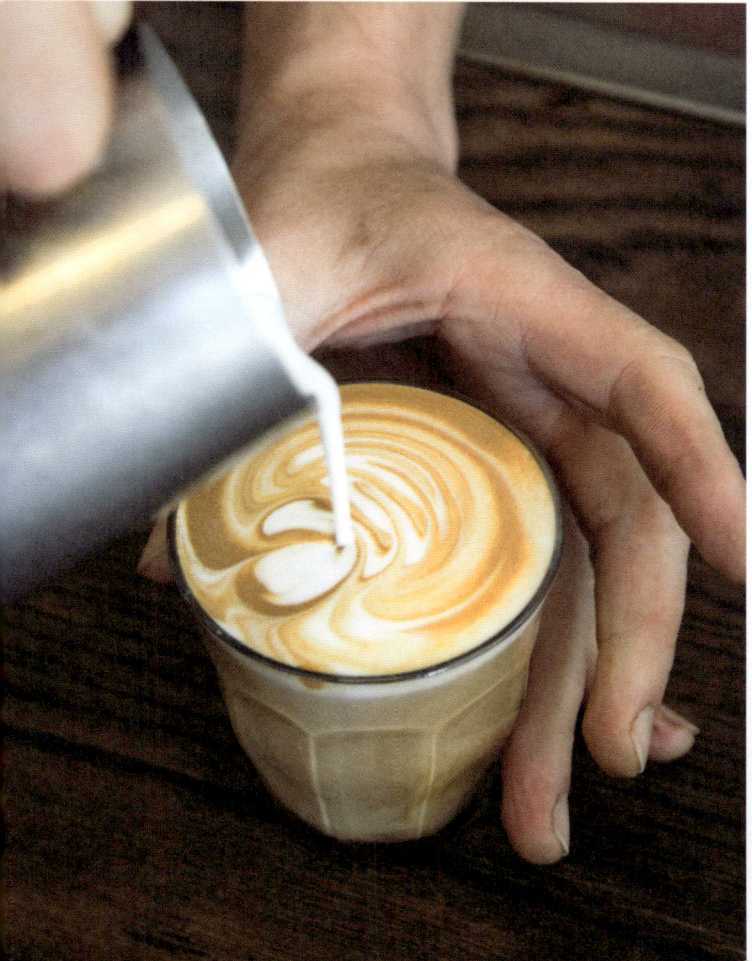

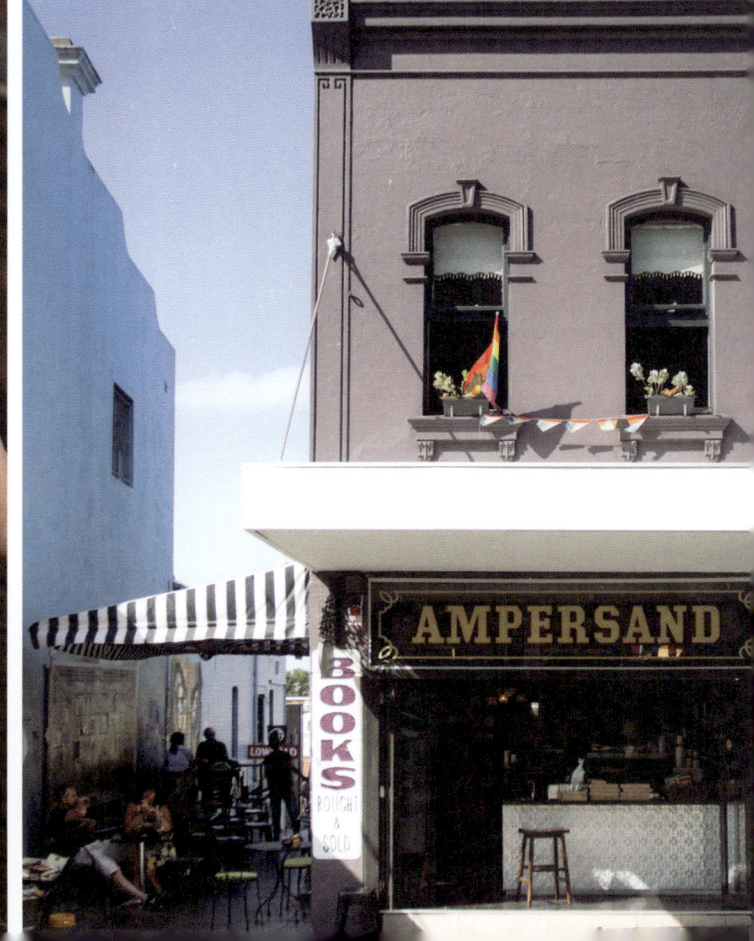

ARTIFICER SPECIALTY COFFEE BAR AND ROASTERY

547 BOURKE ST, SURRY HILLS · 0401 265 220 · ARTIFICERCOFFEE.COM

MACHINE: Synesso Hydra
GRINDER: Mazzer Robur E, Mahlkönig EK43
BEANS: Artificer Seasonal
BREWING METHODS: Espresso, Pour Over, Cold Brew

At Artificer Specialty Coffee Bar and Roastery, they take that word 'specialty' seriously, very seriously indeed. Owners, Managers and Head Baristas, Dan Yee and Shoji Sasa provide specialty coffee, and only specialty coffee to their customers. No tea, no milkshakes, no breakfast, just the very best in quality coffee, served up by these award-winning baristas.

Dan hails from Air Coffee and Salvage, while Shoji comes to Artificer from Single Origin and Mecca. Coffee is in their blood and setting up Artificer allowed them to take full control of the selection of coffee, the roasting, the brewing, the customer service and the atmosphere, from start to finish. They focus on the correlation between roasting and brewing and best representing coffee's unique qualities.

The space here is small – and that's on purpose, too. It's tailored and designed for the service and preparation of coffee and the space also limits the number of customers so that the quality of the product is maintained. Customers order at the bar so that Dan and Shoji can guarantee they, as the baristas, can communicate directly with their customers and tailor the coffee precisely to the customer's needs. This is specialty coffee made approachable – without the smoke and mirrors Dan and Shoji detest. It is two guys, making excellent coffee, simply but brilliantly.

Dan and Shoji source their beans from Kenya, Ethiopia, Guatemala and Bolivia, and do all the greens' selection, roasting and brewing in house. Espresso, filter, cold brew and cascara are all offered. The blends are seasonal and tend to feature lighter roasts. Being seasonal, there's always a change in flavour profile as the months go by, but no change in quality.

If you ask Dan Yee what his favourite coffee is, he'll tell you it's black – and would you expect anything else? No sullying of the flavour with milk for Dan! He likes to keep coffee real, "without the latte art", he said.

It's no surprise that Dan thinks he would have ended up in design if it wasn't for his love affair with coffee. The venue here is slick, with light ameri-oak walls, sleek bare wall lighting and understated bench seats. It's ultra cool without feeling pretentious.

So whether it's the Kolowa (Ethiopia), Las Illusiones (Guatemala), Muwa (Kenya), or another specialty bean Dan and Shoji have selected, roasted and brewed up for you, you're sure to appreciate the love, care and attention that has gone into every cup at Artificer Specialty Coffee Bar and Roastery – it's their one true love, after all.

> 'This is specialty coffee made approachable – without the smoke and mirrors...'

BELLAGIO CAFE

285 BRONTE RD, WAVERLY · 02 9387 1562 · BELLAGIOCAFE.COM.AU

MACHINE: La Marzocco Linea
GRINDER: Mazzer Robur E, Mazzer Robur
BEANS: Campos
BREWING METHODS: Espresso, Cold Drip

The graffiti-mural on the corner of Bronte Rd and Albion Street in Waverly might be what first catches your eye, but it's the friendly service and homely atmosphere that will have you returning to Bellagio Cafe over and over. This 10 year old cafe is renowned for its family-friendly atmosphere, its smooth blend of coffee and irresistible selection of outstanding homemade pastries.

Felix Clark opened Bellagio Cafe in 2004 wanting to create a coffee hub in the eastern suburbs. Felix's ten years' experience in tending and managing bars, restaurants and pubs equipped him with all he needed to purchase Bellagio and make it his own. Four years ago he met his wife, Corinna, who contributed her own wealth of knowledge to the table. Her experience as a chef, as well involvement in the nutrition and personal training industries, allowed the pair to create a truly memorable cafe experience at Bellagio.

Over the past decade, Felix and Corinna have watched the local area grow and develop. They now know most customers by first name and have watched as children have grown into young adults. The manager, Mary-Ann Urquhart, has experience in the coffee industry as well as managing bars and restaurants. Mary-Ann believes "service is king and shouldn't be stuffy or contrived."

> '...family-friendly atmosphere, its smooth blend of coffee and irresistible selection of outstanding homemade pastries.'

With its proximity to local schools and Queens Park, it's no wonder there is a playground out the back, stocked with toys to amuse children of all ages. This setup allows parents to relax inside or lounge on the sun-drenched deck and quietly enjoy a cup of Campos Coffee.

The Campos Superior Project is truly a special coffee and Head Barista, Emma Cowan, expertly works through the many coffee orders. The blend is based on the best coffee from the best producers around the world. Felix said, "Campos keeps a very close relationship with all its suppliers to create an amazing house blend. We originally went to Campos 10 years ago for their exacting procedures and processes in selecting and roasting. We were one of their early customers and have enjoyed an amazing partnership together as both companies have grown."

Bellagio Cafe is open for breakfast and lunch seven days a week, with breakfast offering up all the classics as well as a couple of stand-out dishes. Whether you're coming for a long coffee date, or you're popping in for a takeaway cup, we suggest you don't leave without grabbing something for morning tea. The extensive selection of bread and pastries are made at their bakery, The Nelson Road Tuckshop, and the sauces, fermented pickles and smoked meats are made on site. 'Felix the Jam Man' condiments are also for sale.

THE BOOK KITCHEN

255 DEVONSHIRE ST, SURRY HILLS · 0420 239 469 · THEBOOKKITCHEN.COM.AU

MACHINE: La Marzocco
GRINDER: Mazzer Robur E
BEANS: Single Origin Roasters, Yeehah
BREWING METHODS: Espresso

SET IN AN OLD GARAGE IN SURRY HILLS, WITH AN ABUNDANCE OF CHARACTER, IS THE BOOK KITCHEN, A CAFE AND RESTAURANT OWNED BY AMELIA AND DAVID BIRCH SINCE FEBRUARY 2010. The Book Kitchen has been a favourite of Surry Hills locals for longer than that, though – the venue celebrated its 10th birthday at the end of 2014.

Amelia and David have 30 years' experience in hospitality between them. When Amelia was working at Glass Brasserie, and David as Sous Chef at Selah, they wanted some time off to get married. They couldn't get the time off, so both resigned (ahh, true love knows no bounds!). Their new-found freedom was the catalyst for their purchase of The Book Kitchen and they've never looked back.

The Book Kitchen has been serving Single Origin Roasters' Yeehah blend for years. Once Amelia and David took over, they went in for a cupping and tried three or four other blends, with the idea of updating their house blend. At once they decided they could never change. Yeehah was here to stay.

The blend is sourced from various origins, adjusted seasonally. Currently the blend features beans from Tata Estates, India, Aceh, Sumatra Indonesia, and Merthi Mountain, India. The seasonal adjustments ensure the taste profile remains as desired: voluptuous and sweet, with flavours of caramel, raisin and macadamia. It's weighty, and textured, and served with love by head baristas, Emma Rule and Lucas Blackman. Restaurant Manager, Bridget Raffal, is also a coffee lover. She respects and loves the element of alchemy involved in coaxing complex flavours and aromas out of something so small.

Breakfast and lunch are available seven days a week, with dinner also available from Wednesday to Saturday. If you're in for lunch during summer (the menu changes with the seasons, and always uses fresh produce), try the Poached Salmon Salad; soba buckwheat noodles, wakame, herbs, chilli, soy mirin dressing and candied ginger, or the Pulled Chicken Sandwich with avocado salsa, char-grilled corn, snowpea leaf and jalapeño mayo. For dinner, be sure to order the Seared Scallops with fennel puree, radish and crispy gnocchi, or the Heirloom Tomatoes with grilled haloumi, white anchovies, croutons and basil.

A recent renovation has been a major turning point for The Book Kitchen, which now boasts a contemporary space with white walls and high ceilings, lots of wood, a charcoal pressed tin bar and copper finishes. The walls are lined with cooking books, for purchase and for perusing while you're enjoying your Single Origin Roasters brew.

To finish off your visit try an affogato – that's two more shots of Yeehah coffee, vanilla ice cream, hazelnut biscotti and Frangelico or Amaretto. You'll come for the food and stay for the coffee.

> 'The seasonal adjustments ensure the taste profile remains as desired: voluptuous and sweet...'

BROOKLYN HIDE

226 COMMONWEALTH ST, SURRY HILLS · 02 9211 6448 · BROOKLYNHIDE.COM.AU

MACHINE: La Marzocco
GRINDER: Mazzer Luigi SRL
BEANS: The Little Marionette and House Blend
BREWING METHODS: Espresso

THERE'S A LITTLE SLICE OF BROOKLYN IN SURRY HILLS THESE DAYS, BOTH IN NAME AND IN SPIRIT. When you're feeling like a proper bagel and a great coffee, there's really only one place to go. Brooklyn Hide on Commonwealth Street opened in mid 2013, and serves a fantastic array of real bagels, as well as some other out of the ordinary cafe fare. Oh, and don't forget the wonderful Little Marionette coffee, too.

Owners, Matthew Forsdike and Michael 'Ginger' Munro, met while doing their chefs apprenticeships and forged a bond that led them to opening their own cafe. It's undeniably a hipster hangout, with a no nonsense approach – just really good food, everything made in-house, and good coffee to go with it. And if you're in a hurry they're ready, willing and able to make your order via Beat the Q.

Drop in to Brooklyn Hide and you're quite likely to see Matthew with his nose in the top of a new bag of Little Marionette beans, breathing in the goodness of that wonderful smell before he starts brewing them up for his regulars. Matthew and Michael pride themselves on making great coffee and Little Marionette was an easy choice for them as far as beans go. The Little Marionette house blend has a chocolate flavour that punches through milk, while as an espresso it shows a bright acidity and sweetness with notes of citrus finish with bittersweet chocolaty goodness.

> 'When you're feeling like a proper bagel and a great coffee, there's really only one place to go.'

You obviously can't head to Brooklyn Hide without trying a bagel. You can either select your type of bagel and then your spread (like poppy seed bagel with jalapeño cream cheese, or cinnamon and raisin bagel with apple and cinnamon cream cheese), or you can select from the Signature Bagel menu. Each Signature Bagel is given a New York–inspired name and will transport you straight from Sydney to the Big Apple. The Hells Kitchen features prosciutto, avocado, feta, rocket and lime, while the Manhattan promises in-house cured lox, cream cheese, rocket and honey vinegar. The Brooklyn Hide bagel is worth naming a cafe after – braised pork shoulder, dill pickles, apple jam, mayo and rocket. Amazing.

There's also a cafe menu featuring granola, avocado toast and baked eggs, as well as some more NYC inspired fare: pastrami sandwich with Swiss cheese, Russian dressing, sauerkraut and bagel chips, and potato hash with tomato chutney, spinach, eschallots, mushroom and spiced egg.

If you're an almond milk fan, you're in luck – the boys at Brooklyn Hide make their own, fresh every morning. It's blended with fresh dates, and it's delicious. It's open for breakfast and lunch, Monday to Saturday, proudly bringing a little slice of the New York City to Sydney, in the form of a round, boiled bread treat, perfectly chewy and guaranteed to please.

THE BUNKER

339 LIVERPOOL STREET, DARLINGHURST · 02 8094 9308 · FACEBOOK.COM/THEBUNKERCAFE

MACHINE: La Marzocco Linea
GRINDER: Mazzer Robur, Mazzer Robur Electronic, Mazzer Super Jolly
BEANS: Campos Coffee, Superior Blend
BREWING METHODS: Espresso, Cold Drip

Tight, cosy and tucked away, The Bunker could not be more appropriately named. This self-proclaimed hole-in-the-wall cafe has been transformed into a place for people to get close and enjoy each other's company. With bare, stone walls, mismatched chairs and wooden tables, it really is the perfect place to hunker down with a good coffee.

Cesar Augusto Echeverri, the Manager and Head Barista, grew up running through the coffee fields of Colombia. Even though he's far away from the fields, Cesar still feeds his love of coffee at The Bunker, trying to provide a taste experience with every cup and providing service with a smile.

"Is important to know how to brew coffee but I think it is more important to know how much work is put in on the farm process," he said. "A lot of baristas don't realise how much work is involved in making a kilogram of coffee or how many hands and steps help those little coffee beans to be ready to be ground."

With such love for his coffee origins, you can guarantee Cesar trusts the beans he buys. Campos Coffee has proven their loyalty to The Bunker with the effort they put into providing high quality coffee. The blend of choice, Superior Blend, is from Papua New Guinea, and has been grown by the Colbran family for three generations. Cesar describes it as having "a silky, brown syrupy magic body, finishing with an amazing after taste in your palate." There is also a cold drip on offer, which is one of the great prides of The Bunker.

To complement the mismatched and casual bunker-feel, breakfast and lunch is served on the kind of second-hand crockery that reminds you of home. Don't be fooled by the size of the venue because the menu is anything but small. Unsurprisingly, the bacon and maple syrup topped Bunker crumpets are a breakfast favourite on this ever-changing menu. Lunch brings sandwiches and salads brimming with smoked salmon and slow-cooked lamb. And don't forget those ever-addictive cronuts!

'Everyone is brought together by the good food and good coffee in a home-style simplicity...'

Most people try to shun the hipster label but The Bunker embraces their crowd, loving anything as mismatched and unique as the building itself. Expect to get cosy with actors, directors, models and every other creative and their laptop, as well as the devoted Darlinghurst residents, coined 'Bunkerees.' Everyone is brought together by the good food and good coffee in a home-style simplicity and closeness where no one can take himself or herself too seriously.

Even though The Bunker is built on rough wood, metal and concrete, you can expect to be greeted by plastic animals, friendly hairy faces and, as always, coffee made with love.

CAFE CON LECHE

104 FITZROY ST, SURRY HILLS · 02 9331 8157 · FACEBOOK.COM/CAFECONLECHE

MACHINE: Etnica
GRINDER: BNZ
BEANS: Colombian Connection
BREWING METHODS: Espresso

CAFE CON LECHE IS A CELEBRATION OF ALL THINGS COLOMBIAN. It permeates through every area of the business, from the coffee and the cuisine, to the owner and the manager. The name, Cafe Con Leche, is a Spanish term for coffee with milk… not your ordinary latte, but a 1:1 mix of strong espresso coffee and scalded milk.

Joaquin Herrera moved to Australia 15 years ago from, you guessed it, Colombia. Raised in a family that has been running a restaurant for 40 years, it's no surprise that once in Australia, Joaquin opened his own cafe that would showcase the food and coffee of his native land.

Coffee is a large part of Colombian culture and has been a passion of Joaquin's for many years. He has chosen to offer coffee at Cafe Con Leche that comes exclusively from Colombia. The house blend is made from 100% Colombian beans and is roasted locally. The beans come from the Huila region and are sourced through the supplier, Colombian Connection. It's a medium light roast that is smooth and creamy.

The welcome is warm and genuine, the decor rustic and inviting and the out of the way location makes Cafe Con Leche something of a hidden gem. And yet it's always buzzing with customers. Head baristas, Rob Saunder and Cesar Vela, serve up the Colombian espresso on their Etnica machine. Cesar is from Colombia too; ask him for a Tinto – a Colombian coffee that equates to an extra long black. The strong, but never bitter, Colombian Connection coffee really sings when served like this.

We may be focused on the coffee here, but let us just cover one particular non-coffee related quirk of Cafe Con Leche. It's the hot chocolate with cheese. Nope, that's not a typo. It's a favourite of the Cafe Con Leche regulars and is worth trying, if only to say you've had it. The cheese doesn't melt, it goes soft and mixes in a strange but satisfying way with the sweet hot chocolate.

> '…the out of the way location makes Cafe Con Leche something of a hidden gem.'

One of the menu highlights is the Arepas (little pancakes), one filled with cheese, one with corn, and served with little pots of trimmings: avocado, salsa, pulled pork and sour cream. In the cooler months, go for the soup of the day, which could well be the fantastic Caldo de Costilla – beef rib soup with potato and coriander.

Cafe Con Leche is open for breakfast and lunch, Monday to Sunday. Sit back and enjoy the Latin music drifting in from the kitchen, mingling with the smells of South American cuisine and fantastic Colombian single origin coffee.

CAFÉ HERNANDEZ

60 KINGS CROSS RD, POTTS POINT · 02 9331 2343 · CAFEHERNANDEZ.COM.AU

MACHINE: Conti
GRINDER: Mythos
BEANS: Hernandez Coffee, Spanish Blend
BREWING METHODS: Espresso

THE PATRIARCH OF CAFÉ HERNANDEZ, JOAQUIN HERNANDEZ SENIOR, OPENED THE CAFE IN 1972, HAVING MOVED TO SYDNEY FROM HIS NATIVE SPAIN. In Spain, he worked as a quality controller of raw coffee beans as they entered the country, so you could say he knows a thing or two about the humble bean. Joaquin Snr started roasting coffee at Café Hernandez in Potts Point, and the longevity of the business speaks for itself – it's still going strong, 43 years later.

The cafe is now owned and managed by Joaquin Snr's son, Joaquin Keno Hernandez. He oversees the onsite roasting, and it's a good thing they've got so much coffee moving through every day – because they're open 24 hours a day, 7 days a week. The cafe has an artistic, bohemian ambience, and welcomes in customers at all times of the day and night, for a boutique specialty coffee from their large range of blends. The coffee is also available to take home – Café Hernandez takes order by telephone, internet or in person.

Joaquin Hernandez Senior designed the blends and the way to roast Café Hernandez's single origins in the 1970s, and his son Keno carries that tradition on to this day. He uses only the best quality Arabica beans, and "roasts single origins to various degrees to arrive at the most favourable outcome," Keno said.

In the cafe, they offer eight different single origins, as well as their Spanish, African and French blends. The African blend has a strong, aromatic, rich chocolaty flavour, while the French blend is expertly blended to form a coffee with medium strength body and flavour.

The Spanish Blend is a combination of a large variety of coffees, expertly blended to produce a strong, full bodied aroma with a rich flavour. To take home, the New Guinea blend is a refreshing fruity flavoured coffee with a light to medium body, while the Ethiopian blend has an excellent, full bodied flavour with a medium roast. The Nicaragua Gold coffee is noted by its particularly large bean. It's roasted to a fairly high level, and gives an aromatic, quite sharp flavour with good body. And the list goes on, and on – you will be well and truly spoiled for choice at Café Hernandez.

'...welcomes in customers at all times of the day and night, for a boutique specialty coffee from their large range of blends.'

The menu features some of the Spanish treats Joaquin Snr remembers from home; Sobresado, (Spanish spread), Jamon Serrano, Chorizo, Arroz con Leche, and Churros. Try the Horchata, a cool, sweet, traditional Spanish drink made from the root of the chuffa plant, which takes a bit like almond milk.

You'll find Café Hernandez coffee being served in many local businesses, including at the Ritz Cinema in Randwick, One Earth Café and Paradise Marina on the water's edge at Forster. Hernandez coffee is also available to buy at Kemenys Supermarket; it has been for over 20 years.

The Potts Point 24 hour precinct is lucky Café Hernandez is there, keeping them going right through the night, every night.

COFFEE TEA & ME

87C MACLEAY ST, POTTS POINT · 02 9332 2717 · COFFEETEAANDME.COM.AU

MACHINE: La Marzocco
GRINDER: Mazzer Robur Electronic
BEANS: Campos Superior
BREWING METHODS: Espresso

  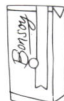 

COFFEE, TEA & ME IS ONE OF FOUR CAFES OWNED BY COFFEE AFICIONADOS, NIC KAT, EREZ SHARABANI AND NOAM KATZIR. The Redfern cafe started them on their journey to create great coffee experiences, and serve Jerusalem style bagels.

The Potts Point Coffee Tea & Me may be small, but it doesn't feel cramped. Customers are intertwined with baristas and wait staff, and everyone cosies up to make it work. There's a Soho feel here, and not just because of the bagels on the menu – it's in the artsy, upcycled furniture and décor and the ultra-cool but at the same time, warm and fuzzy vibe.

The owners have a strong passion for coffee and come from barista backgrounds. This knowledge has helped inform their choice to use Campos Coffee's Superior Blend as the house espresso blend. The talented team of baristas work tirelessly to serve up the delicious blend; it has a toffee base and a rich body with a sweet butterscotch finish. It won Gold at the 2013 Royal Tasmanian Agricultural Show in the plunger category, and silver for espresso.

The Superior Blend is made up of beans from Papua New Guinea from the Baroida Estate, beans from El Salvador from the family-owned El Manzano farm in Santa Anna, and a Rwandan coffee from emerging powerhouse, Nyabumera, in the Western District.

As much focus and pride goes into the cafe's food as it does into the coffee here. Coffee Tea & Me proudly bakes all of its bread and many of the sweet treats too. The bagels come filled with everything from the classic ham, cheese and tomato or roast beef to avocado and cheese or spicy tuna and cheese. They're soft and crunchy, just delicious. For any time of the day (up until 8pm!) you can try the bacon, egg and cheese bagel.

> '…cosy nooks to settle into with an espresso and a magazine.'

The menu may feature bagels and pastries but it also offers nutritious and vibrant salads. You can be sure that there is a strong focus on healthy, whole foods here and the staff are committed to using fresh, local produce. Coffee, Tea & Me is committed to using environmental packaging for its products and is conscious of its impact on the environment.

Local Sydney hipsters, mums and dads, professionals, celebrities and all walks of life spill out of the cafe onto the footpath. Inside there's rustic wood floors, recycled, just about everything, and cosy nooks to settle into with an espresso and a magazine.

COOK & ARCHIES

4/14 BUCKINGHAM ST, SURRY HILLS · 02 9310 3933 · COOKANDARCHIES.COM.AU

MACHINE: La Marzocco
GRINDER: Mazzer
BEANS: Single Origin Roasters, Killerbee
BREWING METHODS: Espresso

  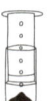 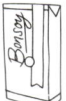

IN 2005 AFTER MANY YEARS OF OWNING A VARIETY OF BUSINESSES VICKI AND STEVE MANAKAS BOUGHT COOK & ARCHIES. Since then it has become an integral part of their family and they've lost all interest in owning anything else. It's no surprise the entire family works here and their kids have grown up behind the counter.

Hidden away in Surry Hills, Cook & Archies is set away from other cafes and stores, which only adds to its charm. Local residents, people working in the area and foodies who seek it out especially, fill the tables. The customers love Head Barista, Jakkraphat Sawangsangeattana, who they call 'Pure' for short. Pure is known to be quite the artist, both when making coffee and sketching on paper. His love for coffee and his drive to produce the best cup every time has made Pure a very popular figure here.

Cook & Archies serves Single Origin Roasters' Killerbee blend as its house blend, and it's a hit. Killerbee is a sweet blend and features a flavour profile of dark honey and toffee, with tropical fruit sweetness. The blend is adjusted seasonally to make sure it conforms to the desired flavour profile. Currently, Killerbee is made up of beans from Colombia, Caldono, Sertao, Brazil and Mahonda. At other times of the year, you might taste other origins. Whatever it takes to achieve that long milk chocolate finish.

A modern Australian cafe with a Greek twist, Cook & Archies sells out of its lunch display on a daily basis. The takeaway lunch trade here is bustling, no doubt due to the high quality ingredients and the constantly updated menu. But if you have the time, be sure to sit in for lunch and set aside some time to choose something from the extensive menu!

> 'It's no surprise the entire family works here and their kids have grown up behind the counter.'

Check out the Instagram account to keep up with the changing menu, but it's always fresh, seasonal and delicious, with a Mediterranean twist. Try the Wagyu Beef Burger with bacon, Gruyere cheese and dill pickles served with beer battered fries, or the Citrus and Dill Cured Ocean Trout with poached eggs, potato galette, baby beetroot and goat's curd. Or try the Braised Beef Brisket with beetroot relish. There's also a great selection of salads, including Halloumi and Watermelon Salad with plum tomatoes, cucumbers, capers, sumac and mind.

Vicki and Steve's passion for food and coffee keeps them both driven to try out new ingredients and keep on top of food trends. After all, it's what keeps the customers coming back.

STEP ASIDE MORNING THIS IS A JOB FOR COFFEE

Articifer | Surry Hills

CORDUROY CAFE

4/14 FOSTER ST, SURRY HILLS · 0418 297 834

MACHINE: La San Marco with custom leather panelling
GRINDER: Mazzer Robur
BEANS: The Little Marionette, Blend 11
BREWING METHODS: Espresso, Cold Drip

HUSBAND AND WIFE TEAM, CON AND KARA TERZIS, HAVE BEEN WORKING IN HOSPITALITY ALL THEIR LIVES. After they got married a few years back, they decided to celebrate by buying a cafe together. They came upon Corduroy Cafe in Foster Street, Surry Hills, which had already been up and running for a couple of years. Perhaps some might warn against newly-weds going into business together, but Con and Kara truly love what they do, they love working together and strive every day to provide the best experience possible for their clientele.

A skinny hole-in-the-wall cafe, Corduroy Cafe's front opens right onto the street, with a distinctive wooden bar front and their La San Marco, with custom leather panelling, standing proud and luring the customers closer. It's not unusual to see customers gathered on the footpath in front of the store while their coffee's being brewed just to their liking.

Con and Kara's coffee philosophy is simple but honest. "Coffee is a part of everyday life, which we want to share with everyone," Con said. "There's so much to learn and so little time!" Con plays the part of Head Barista at the cafe, while Kara manages the food – a light breakfast and lunch menu that perfectly complements their coffee offerings.

When the Corduroy Cafe first opened, it was owned and managed by Nigel Park, from Brighton the Corner, and Ben Stronarch, Head Roaster at The Little Marionette. Naturally, Corduroy Cafe served The Little Marionette coffee. Con and Kara have kept this tradition going, and use TLM's Blend 11 as their house blend.

"After becoming familiar with The Little Marionette, their coffee is hard to resist," said Con. The house blend features coffees from Colombia, Nicaragua and Indonesia. The proportions change over time to retain the taste; the roasters keep a keen eye (and their taste buds!) on the blend to make sure it delivers the exact flavour profile they're after.

Corduroy Cafe also serves up other blends from The Little Marionette; keep an eye out for coffees from Kenya, Colombia, Nicaragua, Mexico, Ethiopia, Indonesia and Costa Rica. If it's a hot day, be sure to try the cold drip at Corduroy – it's a local favourite. The clientele you'll find here are mostly made up of those working in local businesses. They take a moment out of their day (or moments, several times a day!) to gather on the pavement before heading back in to the office.

Con and Kara have a fairly simple aim, really, and it seems to be coming to fruition. "We are just a small operation, trying to offer people some great coffee, and food at reasonable prices," said Con. Sounds like Corduroy Cafe is in good hands.

> '…customers gathered on the footpath in front of the store while their coffee's being brewed…'

DEVON CAFE

76 DEVONSHIRE ST, SURRY HILLS · 02 9211 8777 · DEVONCAFE.COM.AU

MACHINE: Synesso Sabre 2
GRINDER: Mazzer Robur E, Mahlkönig EK
BEANS: Coffee Alchemy, Goodness Galileo
BREWING METHODS: Espresso, Cold Drip, V60 Pour Over, Chemex

OF ALL THE STREETS IN SURRY HILLS, DEVONSHIRE STREET ISN'T EXACTLY THE CENTRE OF THE FOODIE MOVEMENT THAT THE SUBURB IS KNOWN FOR. However, Devon Cafe, situated just a hop, skip and a jump away from Central Station, is leading the way, offering a fine-dining approach to casual cafe food alongside delicious specialty coffee.

Derek and Noni Puah are the husband-and-wife team who own and manage Devon Cafe, focussing on locally sourced, house-made ingredients. They have also partnered with chefs that have extensive experience in fine dining restaurants. Their choice to source coffee beans from Coffee Alchemy was not only because it is a highly rated Sydney coffee roaster, but also because there was an element of pride at being offered an Alchemy account.

Head Barista, Keith Klein, has always had a strong interest in coffee, working at a number of cafes when he finished school and during his travels around the UK. Upon returning home Keith ran his own mobile cafe in the Northern Rivers on New South Wales, before coming to Devon Cafe. "Coffee exceeds the bounds and hours of a 'day job' and is a personal passion," he said. "I see a long and adventurous journey ahead for myself in the world of coffee."

The house blend here is Goodness Galileo, it has a bold flavour and tastes like sweet dark chocolate and caramel, with a very long finish. There are also single origin espressos for specialty brews, including cold-drip and Chemex, as well as milky iced coffee. Single origins come from a number of specialty roasters: Industry Beans, Reuben Hills, Grace & Taylor Coffee Company, Marvell Street Coffee Roasters, Sample Coffee Roasters and Moonshine Coffee Roasters.

When it comes to food, fine dining at cafe prices is the theme of the menu. Growing up on the island of Penang in Malaysia helped Head Chef, Zach Tan, develop a love for the region's famous hawker street food. He trained at Le Cordon Bleu in Sydney and worked at Jimmy Liks and Pier before spending time at Guillaume in Bennelong, where he met his future right-hand woman, Jacqui Ektoros. Every dish on the menu is worth trying, but if you absolutely have to single one out, ask for Breakfast with the Sakumas – miso-grilled king salmon, smoked eel croquette, 63 degree egg, radish petit salad and Kewpie mayo.

> '...offering a fine-dining approach to casual cafe food alongside delicious specialty coffee.'

The cafe's interior boasts similar credentials to its food, having been specially designed by acclaimed interior designer, Matt Woods. Blonde plywood clads the walls, covering the walls, ceiling, counter and furniture. A thin blue line runs over the tabletops and benches, as well as up the walls and onto the ceiling, uniting the aesthetics of the space. The outdoor courtyard features graffiti by street artist Numskull and creates a look and feel that is entirely unique, much like its coffee and food. And the coffee is so good that Derek opened another cafe on Danks Street.

DI BELLA COFFEE ROASTING WAREHOUSE

2/50 HOLT ST, SURRY HILLS · 02 9699 9656 · DIBELLACOFFEE.COM.AU

MACHINE: La Marzocco
GRINDER: Mazzer
BEANS: House Blend
BREWING METHODS: Espresso, Cold Drip

DI BELLA COFFEE IS AUSTRALIA'S LARGEST SPECIALTY COFFEE ROASTER, HAVING STARTED AS A SMALL ROASTING OPERATION IN THE SUBURBS OF BRISBANE IN 2002. Di Bella Coffee supplies their high quality fresh coffee to some of Australia's best cafes and restaurants. In 2010 they opened headquarters in China and since then, retail operations in India and wholesale business in New Zealand have followed.

Mirko Morello keeps the coffee brewing for Sydneysiders at the Di Bella Coffee Roasting Warehouse in Surry Hills. Opened in 2010, single origins are roasted in-house and one single origin and two blends are offered daily. The house blend here is 'Felici', one of Di Bella's most popular blends. While its origins aren't disclosed, we do know that it is made up of seven varieties, including washed, semi-washed and natural processes. The blend was chosen because it can be enjoyed in all types of coffees. It's sharp and full bodied, with a smooth and rounded profile that features cacao and rich dark chocolate aromas, complemented by luscious chocolate flavours and a subtle acidity that is sure to leave you smiling!

Mirko has found that his customers are cultured and very knowledgeable about coffee. The large, spacious cafe has plenty of room for meetings and group catch-ups with friends and the knowledgeable staff, led by Head Barista, Vinnie, are always keen to chat about their favourite bean. What better audience for a roaster than such switched on patrons?

Di Bella sources the beans for its blends from Cuba, Brazil, Peru, Ethiopia, India, Colombia, Mexico, Costa Rica and Panama. Amongst its single origin offerings is the India Monsoon Malabar Single Origin, which has an interesting life before reaching your cup. After being picked and processed, the coffee rests in a specially designed shed without walls and is exposed to the strong monsoon winds for up to 3 months. This alters its flavour characteristics and gives it the dark cocoa and sweet cedar notes. It's even perfect when cold filtered and served on ice.

Di Bella Roasting Warehouse in Surry Hills opens for breakfast and lunch. Try the soft shell crab burger for lunch, or good old Avo, Chilli Eggs for brekky. The decor is fresh and modern, with floor to ceiling windows on the street front letting in loads of lovely light. There's coffee-related gear for sale, as well as large show pieces like the huge copper roaster taking pride of place.

With sweet treats to take away, and a constantly changing lunch special, you're sorted in the food department. And where better to get your morning brew than straight from the roaster's... roaster?

'And where better to get your morning brew than straight from the roaster's...roaster?'

EDITION COFFEE ROASTERS

265 LIVERPOOL ST, DARLINGHURST · EDITIONCOFFEEROASTERS.COM

MACHINE: La Marzocco Linea PB
GRINDER: Mahlkönig K30 Vario, Mahlkönig EK43
BEANS: Edition Coffee Roasters
BREWING METHODS: Espresso, Cold Brew, AeroPress, V60 Pour Over, Batch Brew

WHEN YOU WALK THROUGH THE OPEN DOORS AT EDITION COFFEE ROASTERS YOU WILL INSTANTLY FEEL THE CALM, WARM AND CHARMING VIBE OF THE PLACE. Owners, Daniel Jackson and Corie Sutherland focus their energy on serving flawless single origin coffee here. They believe that the high quality coffee they buy can be best showcased when it is roasted and served on its own, allowing the flavour of the origin to really shine through.

At Edition Coffee Roasters you can expect great attention to detail, an enthusiastic explanation of your coffee's origins, and a calm, poised, dignified cup – just like the owners. Daniel and Corie work with integrity, passion, pride, a bit of class and style, and respect. The two have a strong believe that "there is a real magic in coffee. A collective togetherness, all striving for better."

This isn't Daniel's first venture, as co-founder of Clover in Annandale and Room 10 in Potts Point he brings with him a wealth of invaluable knowledge about the coffee industry. Corie is well versed in the art of coffee too, having worked at Mecca Coffee and Toby's Estate. It was at the World Barista Championships in 2013 that he discovered the enormous potential of single origin coffee. It was here that he met Gwilym Davies who served him an Ethiopian Yirgacheffe as both an espresso and a milk-based coffee. The flavours blew Corie's mind. He said it tasted like strawberries and smelt like flowers. It instilled in him a love for single origin coffee and a passion to bring excellent coffee to the people of Darlinghurst. The cafe on Liverpool Street is quaint and inviting, with a mostly white interior, light wood tables and hints of Japanese design. The menu takes its inspiration from a place even further from Sydney: Scandinavia. The signature dish is the Smorrebrod – smoked king salmon on rye bread with pickled vegetables, radish and roe. There are plenty of fresh, healthy breakfast and lunch options to choose from too, with delicate flavours and gorgeous presentation.

'It is one of the first places in the world you can sample Elixir coffee...'

Currently Daniel and Corie buy green coffee from Lattorre and Dutch Coffee Traders. They attend cupping sessions to taste various origins and pick the best flavours to showcase at Edition. The origins currently featured are very floral and acidic, allowing the flavour to cut through milk and shine as black or milk-based coffee. Edition Coffee Roasters also serves V60 pour over, AeroPress, cold brew, batch brew and Japanese drip.

It is one of the first places in the world you can sample Elixir coffee, a recipe that only four people worldwide actually know. It looks like whisky, feels like tea, is made from coffee, and tastes like nothing you have had before!

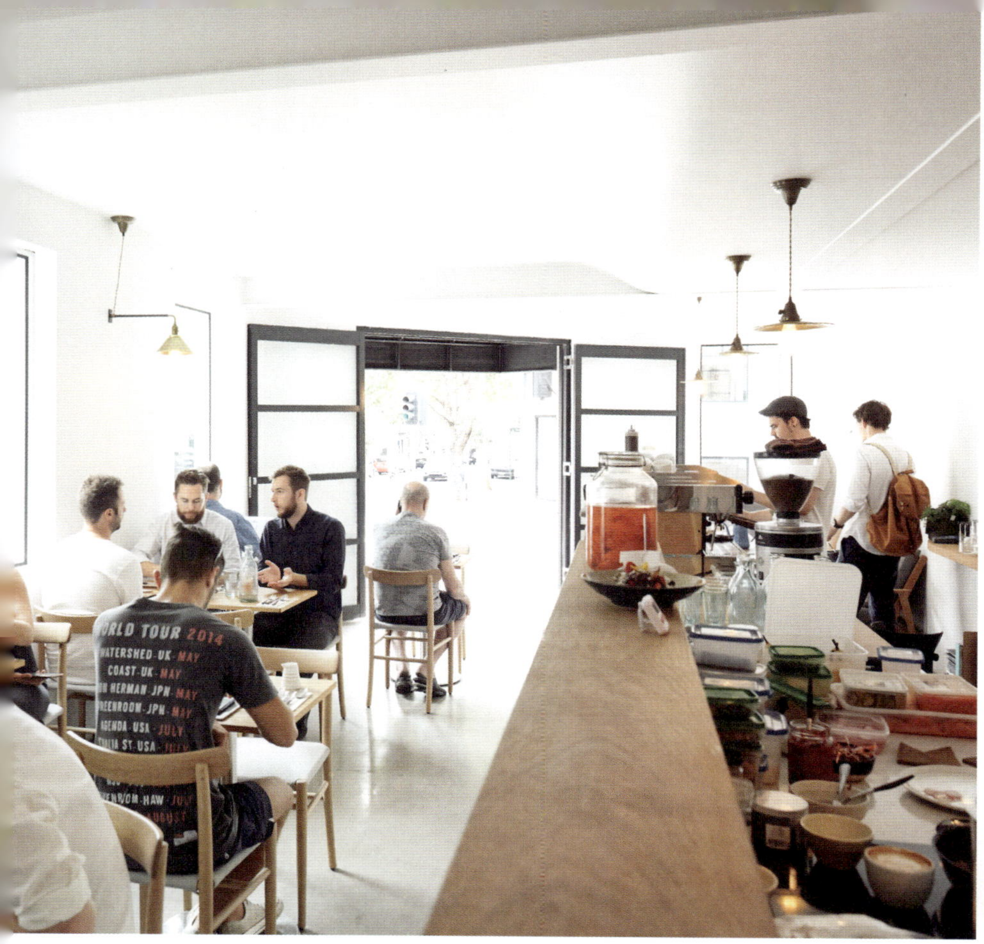
WORLD TOUR 2014
WATERSHED·UK·MAY
COAST·UK·MAY

EDITION

16

LA MARZOCCO

THE ART OF
PORCO ROSSO
BRUT

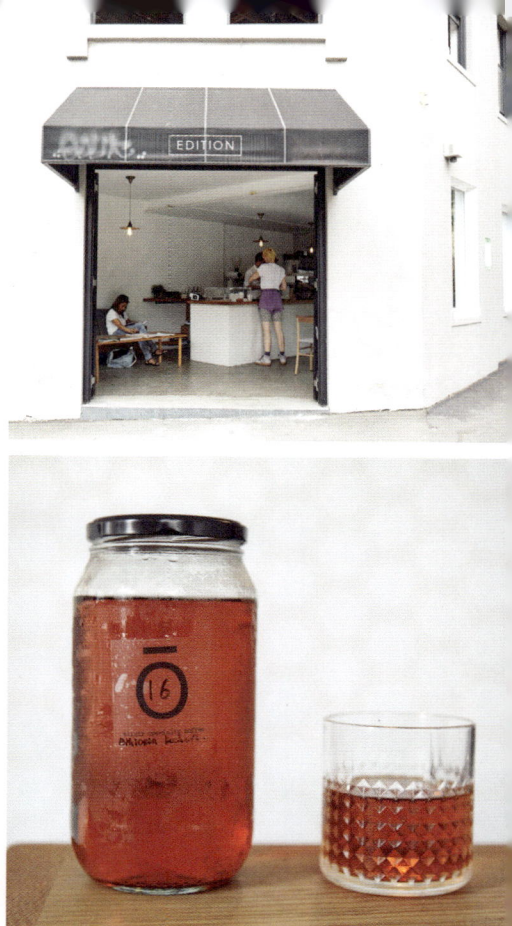

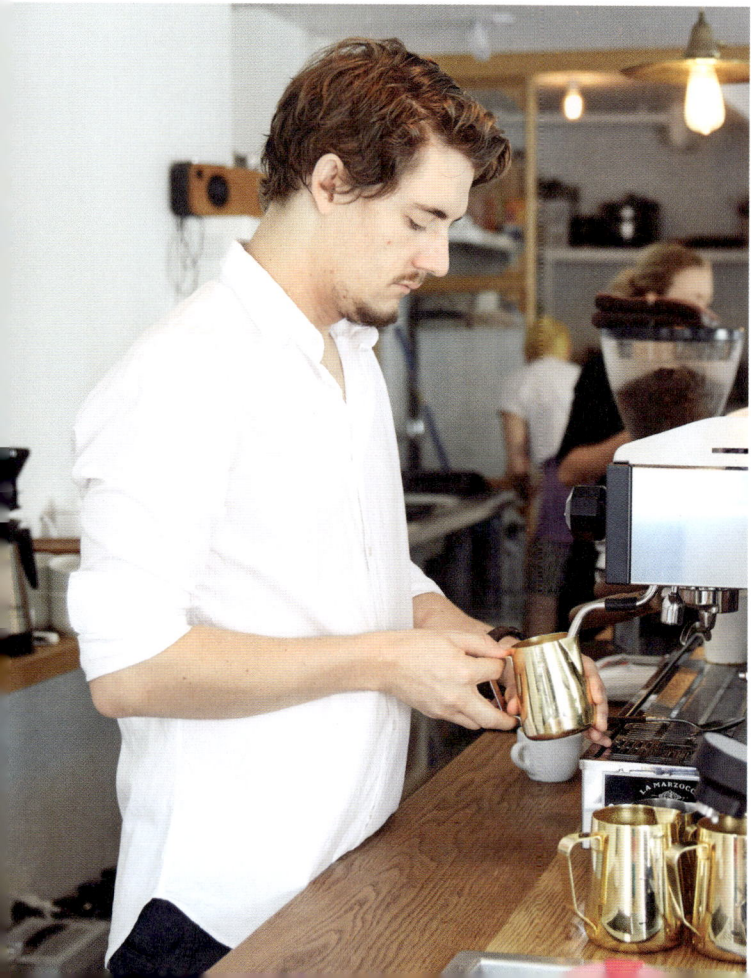

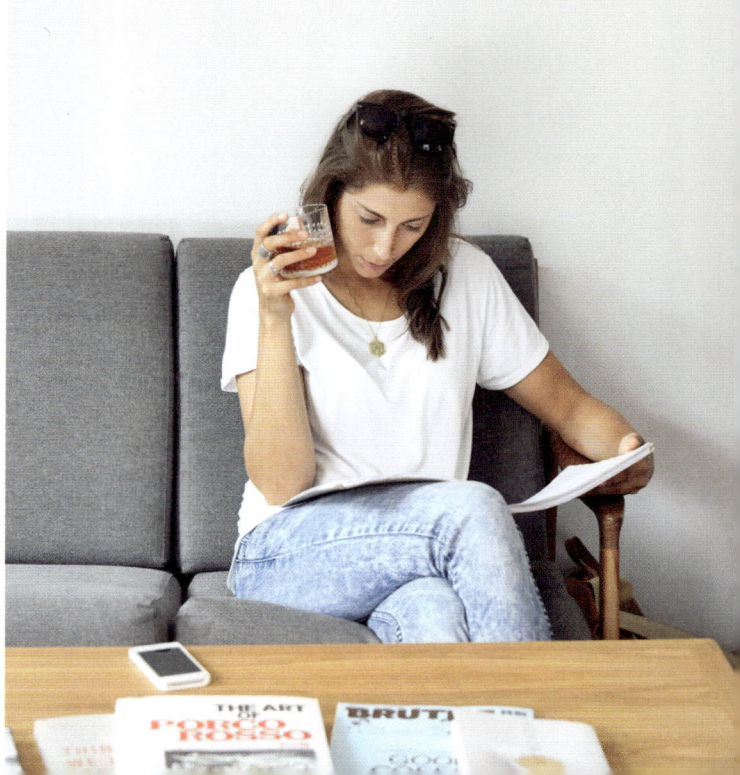

FILOSOFY

CNR OF KNOX LN & BAY ST, DOUBLE BAY · 02 9326 1846

MACHINE: La Marzocco
GRINDER: Mazzer E Robur
BEANS: Own Blend, Quintana Blend
BREWING METHODS: Espresso

How do you turn a small space in an empty laneway into a successful cafe? Marcio Brito, Stephen Balme and their partners took a shell of a coffee shop, added a brand new fit-out, started serving the best coffee in Double Bay, and called themselves Filosofy.

When Stephen had considered opening a coffee shop, he knew it made sense to partner with an experienced operator. Nearly two years after meeting Marcio, who has a business roasting coffee under his own label in Darlinghurst, Salvador Coffee, the space in Double Bay became available.

As Stephen said, "I knew it would work because Marcio's beans and his passion for roasting made it a no-brainer." Marcio created a coffee blend especially for Filosofy clientele, Espresso Quintana, a tribute to his grandfather, Salvador Quintana, and a nod to his Brazilian heritage.

With its huge open window and clever outdoor seating, the cafe has an inviting, casual vibe. Manager and Head Barista, Cris Ferreira, takes his coffee seriously. With more than ten years' experience as a barista, he oversees the brewing of the delicious Espresso Quintana blend. Cris described it as having hints of berry, chocolate, caramel and oranges. It's designed to shine on the espresso machine and cuts perfectly through milk. For coffee aficionados there is always a new single origin on tap that the baristas rotate every week.

Open for breakfast and lunch, seven days a week, Filosofy's menu is simple and healthy. The team manages to turn out a clever variety of food from a tiny kitchen space. Breakfast is big and the cafe is always packed on weekends. You can choose from house-baked fresh muffins, the special Filosofy breakfast, which includes house-made gravlax (cured Atlantic salmon), and the incredibly popular portable bacon and feta omelette. Filosofy sandwiches are great and the cafe also caters to the health conscious, as well as customers seeking gluten free delights, with chia seed puddings, gluten-free bread and gluten-free organic granola.

'Filosofy has become a draw card for all serious coffee drinkers in Double Bay.'

Since opening in late 2014, Filosofy has become a draw card for all serious coffee drinkers in Double Bay and has started to get a reputation around the Eastern Suburbs. Like all good cafes it's all about the coffee, and the atmosphere created by truly service-oriented staff. Filosofy has a great team with energy and a sense of fun that make it an uplifting place to visit.

Although Stephen and Marcio started the cafe with the intention of slowly building the business' reputation, it seems the small space on the corner of Knox Lane and Bay Street has exceeded their expectations in a very short space of time. So pull up a chair at the large, open window and enjoy the freshly brewed coffee and accompanying treats.

FLAT WHITE CAFE

98 HOLDSWORTH ST, WOOLLAHRA · 02 9328 9922 · FLATWHITECAFE.COM.AU

MACHINE: La Marzocco GB/5
GRINDER: Mazzer Robur
BEANS: House Blend
BREWING METHODS: Espresso

IT HAS TO BE AUSTRALIA'S FAVOURITE COFFEE: THE FLAT WHITE. IT'S CERTAINLY THE MOST POPULAR COFFEE IN WOOLLAHRA, AND NO DOUBT THE FLAT WHITE CAFE IS TO THANK. Owner, Bobby Mueller, took over the popular cafe in 2012, which had already been operating for some years, and has specially tailored its house blend to shine brightest in precisely that format.

The clientele know the staff by name and the staff know the clientele not only by name but by order – they're often busy making the coffee before the customer has finished paying. This individual service has guaranteed repeat business and has prompted many a regular to travel two suburbs over for their coffee, or risk parking tickets in the quick dash to get their fix on the way to work.

Manager and Head Barista, Chris Cowan, has been with the Flat White Cafe since it opened its doors and he's a popular face in the local area. He now brews up the three-origin house blend for those in their early twenties, who first started frequenting the cafe with their parents when they were school kids. The community spirit permeates out of the cafe and into the local area, too, with Flat White Cafe supporting local groups like the Woollahra Public School, Queen Street West Woollahra Association and Glenmore Road Public School.

> '…know the clientele not only by name but by order – they're often busy making the coffee before the customer has finished paying.'

The blend here often prompts customers to remark on how lovely and strong it is – coming from Paradox Roasters, it's a blend of beans from Costa Rica, Nicaragua and Ethiopia. The selection of the Costa Rican bean was paramount for a blend that would work well with milk, as its pleasant lemon acidity cuts through and complements the natural sweetness present in Australian milk. The Ethiopian bean, from the Sidamo region, possesses the natural beauty of sweet oranges and transforms into a seductively full, sweet biscuit flavour. The Nicaraguan bean adds a deep, dark base and holds the coffee together. It mellows out the acidity and brings the famous flat white coffee from Flat White Cafe into perfect balance.

The blend makes a beautiful espresso, too, with fruity and chocolaty notes. The beans are roasted in small batches, in a Central Italian style, to optimise the quality and freshness and to ensure the maximum flavour potential is realised. Chris said that this style of roasting brings out a bounteous, fuller, and richer flavour.

Flat White Cafe serves breakfast all day. The portions are generous, the menu is lovely and the produce is fresh. The bread comes from Infinity Sourdough and the cakes, cookies, banana bread and fig and apricot fruit bread is baked in house. Bobby has successfully made Flat White Cafe "a home away from home" for his customers.

IN HOC SIGNO VINCES

JOE BLACK

27 COMMONWEALTH ST, SURRY HILLS · 02 8097 8647 · FACEBOOK.COM/JOEBLACKCAFE

MACHINE: Synesso Cyncra
GRINDER: Mazzer Robur E, Mazzer Luigi SR1 "Mini Man", Marco Pouring Perfection
BEANS: 5 Senses
BREWING METHODS: Cold Drip, V60 Pour Over, Clever Drip, AeroPress

FOR A LITTLE TASTE OF MELBOURNE LANEWAY COFFEE RIGHT HERE IN SYDNEY, HEAD TO JOE BLACK CAFE IN SURRY HILLS. The eclectic decor and an impressive line up of coffee grinders on the counter welcome you into this hipster hangout, famous for its dedication to real coffee.

Owner, Alan Lo, has worked in the food and hospitality industry for nearly 30 years and is passionate about food and culture. He aims to provide a quality cup of coffee with exceptional value for money. His staff are self-confessed coffee nuts too, and they strive to provide the best coffee experience in every cup. They make their best effort to showcase the coffee bean's best taste profile. They see coffee as others see food and carefully consider all of the elements: presentation, taste, texture, flavour, seasonal variation and the ability to elicit different emotions. Each cup holds within it a single experience, something to be remembered.

The Five Senses Dark Horse Blend, a mixture of Ethiopian, Sumatran, Brazilian and Central American beans, was chosen as the house blend due to its ability to provide an exceptionally rounded and complex cup. Joe Black's single origin changes weekly for espressos and filtered coffee. Try the 'Magic' signature coffee: a ¾ cappuccino... deemed magic as, after a few sips, it disappears! Many find it hard to limit themselves to just one; there's a reason this is the most popular coffee.

Joe Black also offers exceptional filter coffees, cold drip, V60, clever drip and AeroPress, as well as syphon coffee. Over time, you might find you have to try them all. The syphon machine stands proudly next to the many coffee grinders, giving the impression that a science experiment is about to take place.

Exposed pipes, bare light bulbs and interesting wallpaper set the vibe for the cafe, which offers a breakfast and lunch menu of classic cafe favourites with a twist. The "Stormin' Norman" is a local favourite – avocado salsa and a poached egg on sourdough toast – and is perfect with a strong, nutty coffee that has a smooth caramel aftertaste.

As offices surround the cafe, many local professionals make a quick stop as part of their daily routine. This quirky and quaint cafe is tucked away down a laneway, keep your eyes peeled for the small sign, or you'll miss it! All in all, the cool but friendly staff, the simple but interesting menu and the hip interiors prepare you for the star: the Five Senses coffee. Enjoy!

> 'Magic' signature coffee: a ¾ cappuccino... deemed magic as, after a few sips, it disappears!'

LATTERIA

320B VICTORIA ST, DARLINGHURST · 02 9331 2914

MACHINE: La Marzocco
GRINDER: Mazzer E
BEANS: Belaroma No. 25 Blend and Single Origin
BREWING METHODS: Espresso, Cold Drip, AeroPress

  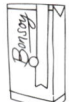 

LATTERIA OPENED IN 1993, AND AFTER ALL THESE YEARS, THE SKINNY LITTLE CAFE IS STILL GOING STRONG. Recently taken over by Alex Rigas, Latteria opens its doors promptly at 5am each morning, serving Belaroma coffee and healthy food options as well.

Alex comes to Latteria from the Lion Corner cafe in Surry Hills and Cappuccino Afloat, which was a regular at a number of organic markets around Sydney. This experience with coffee shines through in her dedication to the brew at Latteria. Alex and the rest of her team aim to consistently create the perfect cup, every single time. Latteria sources beans that are high quality and ethically sourced and bold, as well as searching for unique and interesting single origins and cold drip blends.

The house blend is Belaroma's No. 25 Blend, chosen because of its consistency and its trend towards a darker coffee without being overly acidic. It has a dominant chocolate flavour, the aroma of sweet honey with toffee and a smoky almond base. No. 25 is made from 100% premium Arabica beans from plantations in New Guinea, Costa Rica, Colombia, Sumatra and Brazil. The roasting is a two-phase process, combining caramel roast with a medium roast base. It is perfectly balanced, with full palate coverage and excellent length and has a natural sweetness that balances with the refreshing acidity to leave the mouth clean and fresh.

The 12-hour cold drip is a popular choice too, as is the iced coffee and the affogato made with Maggie Beer's ice cream. Head Barista, Niket Patel, lives and breathes coffee; in fact, he said if he didn't work in coffee, he'd probably have found his ideal wife by now. But the call of the La Marzocco is too strong, and for now his life revolves around the magic bean.

The wooden chairs scattered outside Latteria are the perfect place to perch (if you manage to snare one) and watch the Darlinghurst locals go by. The quality of coffee is only one of the high standards expected in Darlinghurst, and as such Latteria emphasises the best coffee, great service and excellent food.

> '...has a natural sweetness that balances with the refreshing acidity to leave the mouth clean and fresh.'

It may only be 27 square metres, but Latteria delivers delicious breakfasts, including the signature spinach Panini (spinach, buffalo mozzarella and heirloom tomato) to the dedicated regulars. You'll find cyclists, lawyers, politicians, hipsters, businessmen, tourists and even celebrities at Latteria, enjoying the passing parade of characters. The floor staff, chefs and baristas welcome each and every customer with warmth and swift service.

Alex has created a personable and intimate environment smack bang in the middle of a bustling, frenetic part of the city; and that's no mean feat.

Brooklyn Hide | Surry Hills

NELSON ROAD TUCKSHOP

60 BRONTE RD, BONDI JUNCTION · 02 9387 6505 · NELSONROAD.COM.AU

MACHINE: La Marzocco Linea
GRINDER: Mazzer Robur E
BEANS: Campos Superior Blend
BREWING METHODS: Espresso, Cold Drip

POSITIONED IN THE HEART OF BONDI JUNCTION, THE NELSON ROAD TUCKSHOP CATERS TO THE HEALTH CONSCIOUS RESIDENTS OF THE EASTERN SUBURBS. Behind the sleek counter you'll find protein-packed salads and balanced meals as well as a tempting selection of homemade pastries.

Owners, Felix Clark and his wife Corinna Kovner, run the sister cafe, Bellagio, in Waverly which has been operating for over ten years. Their extensive experience in the hospitality industry, including Corinna's experience in nutrition and personal training, has allowed them to create a stand-out healthy dining experience in Bondi.

Determined to uphold their reputation for serving up a stellar cup of coffee, Felix was committed to using Campos Coffee in both venues. He said, "It was unquestionable that we were looking to continue our relationship with Campos when opening Nelson Road Tuckshop. Their support for our business has been paramount over the years."

Fresh juice blends and smoothies are served alongside sought after cups of Campos Superior Blend coffee. Head Barista and Manager, Trent Bramley, has had a close working relationship with Campos in the past, having previously owned his own cafe. Not only is he committed to continuing the strong partnership Felix and Corinna have established, but he also believes "coffee is what wakes us up in the morning and keeps us going in the afternoon." As a general rule, the Tuckshop uses seasonal, single origins for their cold drip set up, although for espresso extractions they don't venture from the Superior Blend for consistency purposes. The Superior Blend has a toffee base with slight fruity highlights, and a rich body with a sweet butterscotch finish.

The bright and light decor of Tuckshop is complemented by a selection of quirky Australian knick-knacks. These additions bring personality to the space and reflect the menu's desire to bring a modern twist to Australian classics. It is open for breakfast and lunch seven days a week and you can pre-order delicious lunch boxes in advance, or build your own lunch from 11.30am onwards.

The Nelson Road Tuckshop prides itself on a strong local following, with no specific demographic. Its close proximity to Bondi's major gyms and its focus on wholesome eating has certainly attracted Sydney's healthy eaters, but you'll also find corporate meetings and coffee dates along this busy sidewalk.

If you can't make it into Tuckshop, you might be lucky enough to stumble across their homemade sourdough and French-inspired pastries featured in some of Sydney's best cafes and restaurants. So keep an eye out!

'...a stand-out healthy dining experience in Bondi.'

ORTO TRADING CO

SHOP 7/38 WATERLOO ST, SURRY HILLS · 0431 212 453 · ORTOTRADING.COM.AU

MACHINE: La Marzocco
GRINDER: BNZ
BEANS: Orto's House Blend
BREWING METHODS: Espresso

ORTO TRADING CO IN SURRY HILLS IS A BIG, GORGEOUS, LIGHT-FILLED SPACE HOUSING WHAT IS REALLY A SMALL, LOCALLY OPERATED BUSINESS. A favourite of foodies and bloggers on the weekends and creative and business types during the week, Orto Trading Co has a constant stream of regulars and first timers.

Owners, Lou Hunt and Chris Low, worked together at Baffi & Mo, a cafe Lou opened in 2008. They are both extremely passionate about coffee; in fact, Lou was the state training manager for Lavazza coffee early in her career. Their joint passion for food, coffee and wine meant that the natural thing to do was to open a cafe or restaurant together. And so in April 2011 they did.

At Orto Trading Co, the pair doesn't complicate their idea of great coffee. They focus on serving fresh espresso-based coffee that is roasted locally. They source their coffee from Arte Cafe, and stick with the house blend. All of the beans used in the blend are premium grade, which means they offer a cleaner flavour. The beans are all washed green beans and sourced from Colombia, Brazil, Uganda, Guatemala, Nicaragua and Papua New Guinea. Orto uses plain packaged coffee, without brands emblazoned across the windows, "this means that the barista, the machine and the coffee really have to stand up", said Lou. Thankfully, it does.

The community feel is alive and well. A stunning bottle display hangs above the bar, with fresh flowers from Lou's private collection. The bricks of the two-story feature wall reveal the paint from the original building; this softens the otherwise industrial space. There's a great indoor-outdoor feeling, with large bi-fold doors opening up to the al fresco courtyard dining space, which holds up to 30 people. The locals often pop in to grab a few chillies or some herbs for their dinner from the Orto pallets on wheels and garden boxes.

'...locals often pop in to grab a few chillies or some herbs for their dinner from the Orto pallets...'

When you visit you'll no doubt be served by one or both of the owners – it's a very hands on, owner-operated establishment. Orto Trading Co is open for breakfast and lunch, seven days a week. It also opens in the evening as a private dining space for 20 or more, bookings essential.

The breakfast menu features dishes such as Carrot Cake Hotcakes, served with toffee pecans, gingerbread, carrot curd and mascarpone; and Southern Fried Chicken Benni on an Orto's English muffin with hollandaise. For lunch, try the Gaffa's Lunch of terrine, Scotch egg, cured meat, cheese and pickles; or the Wagyu Burger on brioche with pickles, mozzarella, beetroot and tomato with polenta chips.

Lou and Chris are trendsetters in the food department and at the top of their coffee game, the result: Orto Trading Co is a genuine, down to earth establishment with a truly welcoming vibe.

"FILTERS"

... THE MAKER SERIES * 90+ PANAMA JU...
...EKISSE N2   * 90+ PANAMA P...
...EKISSE RED   * 90+ PANAMA N...
...MGIN W2   * ETC...
...CHEMBE N2

THE REFORMATORY CAFFEINE LAB

SHOP 7B 17-51 FOVEAUX ST, SURRY HILLS · 0422 011 565 · FACEBOOK.COM/THEREFORMATORY

MACHINE: La Marzocco
GRINDER: Mazzer, Mythos 1, Mahlkönig EK43
BEANS: Own Blend, SQAB and Joker
BREWING METHODS: Espresso, Chemex, Steampunk, AeroPress

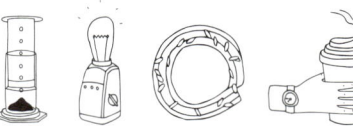

The Reformatory Caffeine Lab really is just that – an interesting mix of cafe, coffee lovers' paradise, and science lab. Mad scientist lab, really, with the eye-catching graffiti artwork on the black walls and metal cages housing bare light bulbs. The cold drip coffee is served in test tubes, for goodness' sake. It's ultra-cool, filled with funky Surry Hills locals and coffee geeks.

Owner, Simon Jaramillo, was born on a coffee farm in Colombia and has been involved with coffee all his life. Being born on a coffee farm, it's well and truly in his veins; he's the fourth generation of his family to be involved in the industry. Owning a cafe is the last link in the chain for Simon on his journey through the wonderful world of coffee. He's been a coffee farmer, a coffee importer, a roaster and now a retailer. Alongside Jet Zhu, he manages the day to day operations of the business, as well as sourcing all the beans and working with the suppliers. Being a coffee farmer himself, he's incredibly fussy about sourcing the best beans, and then he roasts it himself. A true coffee expert.

The Reformatory Caffeine Lab offers just about every style of coffee imaginable: cold drip, V60, chemex, steampunk, espresso, syphon, AeroPress, iced coffee and plunger. They work with seasonal blends that change every three months, and offer two house blends of their own creation.

SQAB is a blend made up of beans from El Salvador, Java and Ethiopia. The Ethiopian beans are natural coffees, the El Salvadorian are fully washed and the Java is a semi-wash. For their Joker Blend, the beans come from Ethiopia, Colombia, Brazil, Kenya and Costa Rica. It's a very complex blend, and more of the coffees are honey processed or washed. The blackboards proudly list the many filter offerings. The Reformatory Caffeine Lab works with top beans, offers a huge range of brew styles and changes its coffee menu every week. There's always something amazing to try.

It is open Monday to Saturday, and while there's no scrambled eggs on toast or bacon sandwiches, (and no tables to eat them at, just a standing bar), there is often an incredible choice of donuts, pastries, croissants etc.

'The Reformatory Caffeine Lab offers just about every style of coffee imaginable...'

If your coffee habits need to be reformed, Simon's your man – he'll take you on a journey around the world, from the farm to the cup. He'll explain to you what you're drinking, what its life cycle has been, how to drink it – everything you need to know to truly appreciate the long journey that ends with the black stuff in your cup.

EAST

ROOM 10 ESPRESSO

10 LLANKELLY PL, POTTS POINT · 0432 445 342 · INSTAGRAM.COM/ROOM10ESPRESSO

MACHINE: La Marzocco Linea PB
GRINDER: Mazzer Robur E
BEANS: Mecca, Darkhorse Blend
BREWING METHODS: Espresso, Batch Brew

DOWN A LITTLE LANEWAY LIES A TINY HOLE-IN-THE-WALL CAFE THAT HUSTLES AND BUSTLES WITH LOCALS AND TOURISTS THAT HAVE ENJOYED A FANTASTIC CUP OF COFFEE. The buzz here is palpable and no-one seems to mind that it's very… intimate.

So cozy is the premises, the staff scamper up and down ladders to grab ingredients that are stacked high, right up to the ceiling. The staff are well versed in crowd control and if the little hole-in-the-wall is full when you arrive, they'll be sure to seat you as soon as they can. In the meantime, have a peek at the menu – you'll need some time to decide.

Owners and Managers, Daniel Blackman and Andrew Hardjasudarma, opened the cafe in August of 2010. They serve what they consider to be the best coffee in the area and offer a food menu showcasing carefully picked, best of the best ingredients from local suppliers. Open for breakfast and lunch, Room 10 Espresso is buzzing all day long.

It serves up Mecca beans to the crowds of coffee lovers – there seems to be a constant queue of takeaway customers but they never have to wait too long as the Room 10 Espresso baristas are experts at creating gorgeous coffees in a hurry. Mecca coffee has a big following and Room 10 Espresso's exceptional baristas really showcase it beautifully. No frills or tricks, just really good coffee. Smooth and bold with cacao notes, rich and smooth with warm caramel notes, intricate latte art – their coffee is impressive.

Aside from the high-demand coffee, people from near and far rave about the Breakfast Rice: a combination of soaked brown and red rice, white and red quinoa, banana, fig, blackberries, rhubarb, yoghurt and cinnamon. With the accompanying breakfast dukkah of almonds, pistachios and spices, this is a firm favourite. Owner and Manager, Daniel, makes a batch every morning and serves it cold through summer and warm in winter.

> '…staff scamper up and down ladders to grab ingredients that are stacked high, right up to the ceiling.'

With kids, bikes, outdoor seating and staff never more than a metre away, the easy going, welcoming vibe here sets Room 10 Espresso apart from the more 'hipster' venues. Don't get us wrong, Room 10 is definitely hip, but it's not pretentious, and the staff clearly love what they do.

Room 10 Espresso has won numerous awards and it's no wonder, this cafe is decidedly on point and is most deserving of its accolades. It's definitely worth taking a trip down Llankelly Place and squeezing in amongst the regulars for the full Room 10 Espresso experience.

ROSE BAY DINER

LYNE PARK, NEW SOUTH HEAD RD, ROSE BAY · ROSEBAYDINER.COM.AU

MACHINE: La Marzocco
GRINDER: Mazzer Robur E
BEANS: Single Origin Roasters, Reservoir
BREWING METHODS: Espresso, Cold Drip, AeroPress

BEN SWEETEN'S REPUTATION PRECEDES HIM. Having learnt his trade at one of Melbourne's crown jewels, Proud Mary, he ventured up north to open Joe Black in Sydney's Surry Hills. Eventually, he couldn't resist the call of the harbour, and opened Rose Bay Diner in 2014.

He recruited some of the best in the business, signing Icebergs and Fratelli Fresh alum, Daniele Trimarchi, as Head Chef. Together, they have turned a former toilet block into a bustling cafe, with diverse breakfast and lunch options, coffee from Single Origin Roasters and ready-to-go picnic hampers, ideal for lunch in the surrounding grounds of Lyne Park.

It's impossible to miss the coffee machine as you walk in here, and that's exactly how Ben wants it. "Coffee is my life," he said. "It's been my life as long as I can remember. It's only natural working with coffee every day, selling it, learning more and more about it."

The machine sits front and centre, both literally and metaphorically. As Head Barista, Ben has invested in finding the perfect blend for his customers, settling on Single Origin Roasters. Having established a good working and personal relationship with founder, Dion Cohen, he found the fantastic culture at the Sydney-based company hard to resist.

Rose Bay Diner uses the Reservoir Blend which features beans from Tata Estates in India, Huye Mountain in Rwanda and Konga Co-op from the Yirgacheffe region in Ethiopia. The result is a bright and sophisticated blend, with flavours of ripe stone fruits and a structured vibrant acidity, full body and clean finish. Noting the number of Sydney-siders that drink coffee with milk, Reservoir was also chosen for its ability to cut through milk well

Black drinkers can try the Colombian Rosalia Conda single origin. The beans are manually processed and dried by Rosalia herself, resulting in creamy milk chocolate and toffee flavours with a honeydew melon sweetness and smooth finish. If that's not enough to satisfy your caffeine appetite, filter and AeroPress are also on offer.

'The coffee may be a main player, but the food more than holds its own.'

The coffee may be a main player, but the food more than holds its own. The menu was written by the founding Head Chef at Proud Mary, and is brought to life by Daniele. Fresh is the focus, with local, organic produce across the menu. Try the Pain Perdu, with brioche, fresh ricotta, strawberries, blueberries, pure Canadian maple syrup and toasted almonds or the Johnny Tightlips, featuring avocado and heirloom tomatoes on toast with shanklish and herbs.

The team at Rose Bay Diner has brought the surrounding parkland in with floor-to-ceiling windows, a timber-roofed courtyard and outdoor tables perfect for pooches. Plants dot the space and large wooden tables evoke a country-life atmosphere. So next time you're looking for somewhere with amazing food and coffee, somewhere outside of the city, head down to Rose Bay and seek this one out!

THE ROYAL DARLINGHURST

128 DARLINGHURST RD, DARLINGHURST · 02 9380 9390 · THEROYALDARLINGHURST.COM

MACHINE: La Marzocco Linea
GRINDER: Mazzer Major and Mazzer Mini
BEANS: The Little Marionette, Her Majesty's Arms
BREWING METHODS: Espresso, French Press

THE LOVE OF COFFEE TRANSCENDS GENERATIONS; IT'S REALLY AND TRULY IN THE BLOOD. Joseph Faggion's grandfather immigrated to Australia from Italy in the early 1930s, lugging with him an espresso machine. He set up one of Sydney's first Italian restaurants, in Martin Place, and passed down the coffee-loving gene to his grandson. Joseph has now taken over The Royal Darlinghurst and like all Australians, a hot cup of coffee is the most essential part of his day.

Located in a leafy residential area, the Royal faces west, so wherever you sit you will catch the beautiful afternoon sun, a welcoming treat in the winter. There is charm in spades here, with dark wood panelling, bookshelves crammed full, brown leather seats and tall windows looking out onto the street. The Royal is all about "good coffee, good friends, and no pretension," said Joseph.

Joseph has always worked in hospitality. He spent the last ten years travelling around the world and worked in many cafes and restaurants along the way. For him, there's nothing better than catching up with great company, in a chilled setting, with plates of good food and cups of great coffee.

Joseph and his team are committed to great coffee, and use Little Marionette's Her Majesty's Arms (HMA) Blend, which was developed specifically for The Royal. It also rotates through a large variety of single origin beans from Colombia, Brazil, Guatemala, and pretty much every South American country, as well as Ethiopia, Hawaii and Kenya. Head Barista, Morgan Knight, uses these single origins for black coffees and if you want something different, French Press is also on offer.

The food is hearty and wholesome, with specialties such as the Signature Royal with cheese, which is made with slow-roasted beef, red cabbage slaw and provolone; or the glorious cider-roasted field mushrooms, with beet relish and avocado on sourdough. The Royal Darlinghurst is open for breakfast and lunch until 4pm, seven days a week, with plans for the near future to open over the weekend until 10pm.

All walks of life pass through The Royal Darlinghurst, from locals to the stars of Australian film. They're all there for a decidedly excellent cup of coffee. "The quality of our bean and the commitment of our team and barista means that you are always guaranteed a top quality drop – it's something that we quite seriously pride ourselves on," Joseph explained. "We know that if they can count on that, our clientele will maintain an unsaid loyalty, which in itself adds to the charm of the cafe".

If you don't have time to try the famous buttermilk pikelets with mascarpone, stewed peaches, pomegranate and honey, at least swing past the coffee window for a quick Her Majesty's Arms takeaway.

> "Good coffee, good friends, and no pretension."

B & E 14·0
W/ HOMEMADE BBQ SAUCE
BIRCHER MUESLI 8·5
W/ FRUIT & YOGHURT
PIKELETS 10·0
W/ BLETTED QUINCE & MASCAPONE
SERANO OPEN 14·0
W/ ONION JAM, PECORINO, ROCKET
CIDER ROASTED MUSHROOM 14·0
W/ AVO, BEET RELISH, FETA
sMOKED sALMON 15·0
W/ RICOTTA, DILL, CAPER

SAMPLE COFFEE PRO SHOP

SUITE 1.03, 75 MARY ST, ST. PETERS · 02 9517 3963 · SAMPLECOFFEE.COM.AU

MACHINE: La Marzocco Linea PB
GRINDER: Mythos One, Mahlkönig EK43
BEANS: Sample Coffee Roasters, Pacemaker Espreso and Single Origins
BREWING METHODS: Espresso, Cold Brew, Batch Brew, V60 Pour Over

   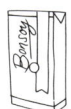

SYDNEY COFFEE ENTHUSIASTS WILL BE VERY FAMILIAR WITH THE SAMPLE COFFEE SURRY HILLS COFFEE BAR, WHICH OPENED IN LATE 2011. The great news is that the owner, Reuben Mardan, has since opened another Sample Coffee location, this time in St Peters. The Sample Coffee Pro Shop opened in February 2015 and is located in a one hundred-year-old factory. It's a modern coffee bar and roastery, which serves breakfast and lunch and offers a wide range of coffee brew gear for sale as well.

Reuben Mardan has well and truly dedicated his career to coffee. With 15 years service to the industry, the diversity of coffee, the opportunity to keep learning and the social aspects of educating customers keeps Reuben as passionate about his chosen profession as he was on day one. "Coffee is a chance to keep learning and connect with the world," he said.

At the Sample Coffee Pro Shop customers can sit at the curved bar and watch as Reuben's team prepare the food and coffee. The bar is tiled in pale grey squares and has a built-in glass case, showcasing the sweet treats on offer. Cold brew is dispensed from bar taps, and the La Marzocco gets a constant workout.

Sample Coffee Pro Shop serves up the Pacemaker Blend as its house espresso, naturally it is roasted in house. Pacemaker is a seasonal blend, meaning it changes throughout the year to uphold its delicious taste profile – at the time the cafe opened it was made from Panama Elida, Ethiopia Hunkute and Colombia Cococentral Lot 1. If you're at the cafe on the right day you can even witness the roasting in action. The 57-year-old Probat UG-15 roaster is still going strong in the adjoining roastery space.

Sample Coffee is always focused on sourcing the highest quality beans, some through direct sourcing and others through small, quality-focused importers. Sample Coffee finds that by focusing on smaller farms in Africa, Central America and South America, it can be sure it's getting cleaner, better quality coffee.

Barista, Toby Wilson, alongside Reuben and the rest of the team, work tirelessly to uphold their point of difference: consistently high quality coffee and exemplary service. They are always willing to educate their customers on coffee, and are continuing to learn themselves. They serve cold brew, batch brew, manual filter and a kombucha-cascara iced tea. They have on staff the current New South Wales Brewers Cup champion, which never hurts.

This big, light, modern space is a tremendous breath of fresh air into a historical building, which now, thanks to Sample Coffee, has a new lease on life.

> '...willing to educate their customers on coffee, and are continuing to learn themselves.'

SENSORY LAB

75-79 HALL ST, BONDI BEACH · 02 9130 7256 · SENSORYLAB.COM.AU

MACHINE: La Marzocco GB/5
GRINDER: Mahlkönig EK43 and Mazzer Robur E
BEANS: Sensory Lab, Steadfast Blend
BREWING METHODS: Espresso, V60 Pour Over, Cold Drip

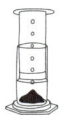

SENSORY LAB IN BONDI BEACH IS THE FIRST SYDNEY LOCATION FOR THIS INFAMOUS COFFEE SUPPLIER. At their cafe-cum-science-laboratory in David Jones, Melbourne, Sensory Lab has wowed the coffee-loving locals with their syphon brewing system, intricate menu listings and white-coat clad servers. While there's less of the beaker and clipboard and more of a cafe feel at Sensory Lab Bondi Beach, locals and the ever-changing transient population of the area are in for a genuine treat at this coffee destination.

With its polishedconcrete floors and walls covered in draped fabric (pinned back by plants in glass containers), there's certainly an industrial-chic vibe to the place. There's no kitchen here – this is a place designed specifically to glorify the beloved bean. Having said that, there is a small selection of pastries and bagels available, which provide the perfect accompaniment to what many locals have dubbed the perfect coffee.

Owned by Salvatore Malatesta and a group of partners who are all in the business, Sensory Lab Bondi Beach is managed by Felipe De Castro Cruz, who moved from Perth to join the expert team. Upholding relationships with producers in various destinations such as Costa Rica and Brazil, the house blend is Steadfast, which currently contains a blend of Colombia San Agustin and Brazil Fazenda Rainha.

Sensory Lab is at the forefront of the specialty coffee movement and places a special emphasis on manual brewing. Offering espresso-based coffees, V60s, AeroPress and the aforementioned syphon, a trip to Sensory Lab is an educational experience as well as a place for a simple caffeine refuel. The knowledgeable staff pride themselves on providing an elevated coffee experience. If you are interested in learning about the roasting and brewing process, just ask!

> 'It is at the forefront of the specialty coffee movement and places a special emphasis on manual brewing.'

Syphon brewing has already proven popular in coffee-mad Melbourne, appearing at a limited number of venues, which include Sensory Lab's two Melbourne destinations and St Ali, Sensory Lab's parent company. Syphon coffee comes served in a glass beaker (think secondary school science class), and is drunk from a cup with a wide bowl, which allows the drinker to experience the coffee's bouquet. It is a science and an art that is up there with wine appreciation!

The beans used in syphon coffee are roasted in a 'filter' style, that is different to those used in traditional espresso. The beans are then ground and steeped in carefully controlled hot water. The coffee is pulled through a fabric or paper filter and poured into the serving beaker. This process allows different flavours to come through; flavours that are lost when beans are brewed at a higher temperature – it is all about subtlety. Taken without milk or sugar, syphon coffee is worth a try, and where better than at Sensory Lab, with the backdrop of Bondi Beach and the sea breeze on your face?

the·shop

THE SHOP AND WINE BAR

78 CURLEWIS ST, BONDI BEACH · 02 9365 2600 · THESHOPBONDI.COM

MACHINE: La Marzocco Linea Classic
GRINDER: Mazzer Robur Continental
BEANS: Gabriel
BREWING METHODS: Espresso

ANTHONY KAPLAN SWORE HE'D NEVER OWN ANOTHER CAFE AFTER OPENING AND CLOSING HIS FIRST ONE IN THE NINETIES. Fast forward to 2004 and he found himself going back on his word, opening The Shop and Wine Bar, the first small bar in Bondi.

The restaurateur and bar owner now has his fingers in a number of different Bondi venues, including The Shop, The Corner House, Panama House and as of November 2014, the revamped Bondi Bowling Club.

The Shop and Wine Bar was his first foray into the bar scene, creating an all-day space offering specialty coffee, breakfast, lunch and dinner, and a great atmosphere. With Anthony in charge of overseeing his many locations, husband-and-wife team, Mike and Lucy Haskas, hold down the fort with Mike caressing the coffee and Lucy manning the kitchen.

If that doesn't have you rushing through the door, the brightly patterned walls and rustic interiors will certainly catch your eye. Wide French doors frame the main entrance, providing access to small tables nestled away near the front counter. A coffee window is covered in potted plants and coffee products; enticing passerbys to grab one on the go. Stools also line the exterior walls, perfect for perching with a coffee or two.

Mike works with Gabriel Specialty Coffee Roasters for his espresso-based offerings, serving a house blend with beans from Kenya, Ethiopia, New Guinea and Sumatra. Called Monte Carlo, it has a full bodied chocolate taste when made with milk. Its medium acidity and syrupy mouth feel gives black coffee lovers a fruity well balanced cup, making it a very satisfying formula. They chose Gabriel Coffee because of owner, Sam Gabrielan's knowledge and talent, as well as his welcoming attitude that made Mike feel part of the family.

Food is available from 7am everyday until late, starting with breakfast bites all the way through to dinner dishes. Choose from the impressive selection of antipasto and cheese platters, homemade burgers and other Italian-inspired plates. Early risers can grab classics with a twist, including the delicious BLT with gherkins and smashed avocado, served with roma tomatoes and basil on wild rice and quinoa bread; or the breakfast salad with hot smoked trout, corn salsa, lentils, peas and avocado. Oversized soft sandwiches are the belles of the ball during the day. Fillings include hot Italian meatballs and poached chicken with chilli jam. There are also generous salads to try, including a seared, chipotle chicken salad with tortilla chips, black beans and corn salsa.

True to its name, when the clock strikes twelve a curated wine list appears alongside the coffee menu for an afternoon pick me up of a different type.

> '…an all-day space offering specialty coffee, breakfast, lunch and dinner, and a great atmosphere.'

STOP VALVE ESPRESSO

70 RILEY ST, DARLINGHURST · 02 9368 7926 · STOPVALVE.COM.AU

MACHINE: La Marzocco Linea PB
GRINDER: Robur & Robur Electric
BEANS: Reformatory Coffee, Stop Valve House Blend
BREWING METHODS: Espresso, Slow Drip

WE CHALLENGE YOU TO WALK PAST STOP VALVE ESPRESSO WITHOUT STOPPING TO TAKE A LOOK AT THE ENORMOUS SHAUN TAN-INSPIRED MURAL, WHICH ACTS AS A SIGNPOST OF WHAT'S TO COME. Painted by artist Heesco, the bright red creature's tentacles extend to the interior of the cafe, joining the visual motif of stop valves – the only remnants of the space's previous history.

Owner, Daniel Corke, found the abandoned storage space while looking for somewhere to fill what he saw as a gap in the market for a meeting spot, where customers could try a specialty coffee offering.

Having already opened Coffee Space in Ballina nearly five years ago, he was well placed to open a city hotspot, but had to literally start from scratch. The chosen location had no water or gas and the only feature left was the sprinkler pipes. Daniel ran with what was left and these stop valves inspired the name and design of the entire venue, including the mural.

In its transformation, the team has retained the original valves, protecting them with a mesh screen. The cafe now has a front-facing coffee bar and timber benches lining the walls of the cafe. The industrial-chic feel of the cafe is maintained with steel highlights and dark grey walls but is truly exemplified with the bright red mural spreading its tentacles from the exterior of the cafe. You will no doubt recognize the iconic 'lost thing,' the main character in Shaun Tan's intricately illustrated book and short film. The outdoor tables unify the space, creating the ideal spot for people-watching along Riley Street.

Daniel found his coffee roast at the Reformatory Caffeine Lab, run by Simon Jaramillo. The roaster's family has been farming coffee in Colombia for over 110 years, meaning he is a bean expert. Stop Valve uses a special house blend that features rich notes with a fruity peach flavour framed by notes of black pepper and star anise. This sweetness is balanced with a bright lime acidity, making it ideal for both milk-based and black beverages.

Stop Valve also rotates single origins from Reformatory every week, with beans coming from places like Sumatra, Kenya, Columbia and Ethiopia. Stop Valve Espresso has only been open since mid-January 2015 and has already engaged a loyal following.

The food lets the coffee shine, with a small selection made in the space-challenged kitchen. Dave Ferreira is behind the grill, producing North American classics such as slow-cooked pulled pork and American fried chicken as well as gluten free options. Keep an eye out for when Stop Valve doubles as a bar Wednesday through Saturday nights.

> 'In its transformation, the team has retained the original valves, protecting them with a mesh screen.'

SINGLE ORIGIN ROASTERS SURRY HILLS

60 RESERVOIR ST, SURRY HILLS · 02 9211 0665 · SINGLEORIGINROASTERS.COM.AU

MACHINE: La Marzocco Linea PB
GRINDER: Mahlkönig EK43 and Mazzer Robur E
BEANS: Reservoir and monthly changing single and reserve origins
BREWING METHODS: Espresso, Hario V60 Pour Over, Cold Drip, Cold Brew, AeroPress

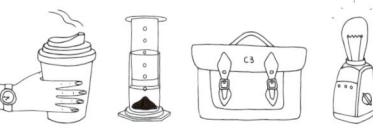

Single Origin Roasters has become synonymous with excellence and innovation in the Sydney coffee world, since first opening in 2003. The company now boasts two cafes, a roastery and a brew bar and its coffee can be found in many of the best cafes across Sydney and Australia. Surry Hills is lucky to play host to its much loved cafe and neighbouring brew bar.

This is where it all started more than 12 years ago. The 15kg roaster, 'Boris' is to thank for many a Sydney-siders' first experience of a single origin, and today the dedicated team continue to serve a changing menu of single origins as well as its signature house blend, Reservoir – named after its beloved home street. The Reservoir Blend is a bright and sophisticated coffee, with flavours of ripe stone fruits, structured and vibrant acidity, a delicate body and a clean finish. It's adjusted seasonally with fresh harvest single origin coffees. Currently it features coffees from Huye Mountain Rwanda, Konga Co-op Yirgacheffe Ethiopia and select co-ops in Kenya.

Innovation is extremely important to Single O, and the dedicated team are certainly leading the way on this one too. The intimate brew bar is tiny in size and doesn't allow for lots of empty milk bottles to be lying around. Dion and Emma Cohen, founders and owners of Single Origin Roasters, approached industrial designer, Ross Nicholls, and engineer, Adam Preston, and asked them to come up with a solution.

The Juggler, a milk-on-tap system for cafes, is the result, and is now being produced for use in cafes all over Australia. Rather than plastic milk bottles, Single O now has milk delivered in 10-litre bags. This forward thinking ensures cafes are left with next to no wastage and baristas don't need to spend time fiddling with the milk bottles.

Open for breakfast and lunch Monday to Friday, with an all-day menu Saturday, Single O Surry Hills is as dedicated to offering top quality food as it is to its coffee service. Try the wrap with coffee spiced chicken, coconut cracked wheat, lettuce and tomato, with an optional super hot sauce challenge. If you're up earlier, try the house-cured bacon and egg roll or the quinoa kedgeree, a favourite that updates seasonally.

They are customer focused, whether in the form of ongoing barista training and maintenance support to its wholesale customers, or through the friendly, welcoming vibe at the cafe. The team are restless creative types, dedicated to their customers and their craft, and they have a great time while they're at it. It's a vibrant, exciting area to enjoy the full trifecta – of great food, great coffee and great service – it's no wonder Single O is a Surry Hills institution.

> 'The 15kg roaster, 'Boris' is to thank for many a Sydney-siders' first experience of a single origin...'

SLY ESPRESSO

212 DEVONSHIRE ST, SURRY HILLS · 02 8399 2041 · FACEBOOK.COM/SLYSURRYHILLS

MACHINE: Spirit Triplette Bastone
GRINDER: Mazzer Robur E and Anfim Barista Dosastore
BEANS: Snow Queen Blend
BREWING METHODS: Espresso, Cold Drip, Pour Over

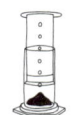

Back when prohibition was in full swing, 212 Devonshire Street played host to gangster-queen, Kate Leigh's 'sly groggeries.' More than 50 years later, on the notorious underworld figure's birthday, the building was reborn as Sly, supplying the people of Sydney with a different type of stimulant – this time legal.

Owner, Dean Wilkinson, is a veteran of the industry, having spent 12 years as a chef and six years in front-of-house roles. Coffee was his drug during his days as a chef, throwing back cup after cup to get through double shifts. It wasn't until he enjoyed a coffee made by an industry professional that he began to appreciate the complexities of the coffee world.

Dean has paid homage to the building's exotic past, stripping the space back to its exposed brick and timber state, using bottles and swinging decanters as light shades. Hats, like those worn by Leigh, line the walls, surrounding a portrait of the woman herself, painted by local artist Madeleine Beckett.

The coffee is another throwback to the cafe's previous incarnation – the custom house blend, provided by Roastworks Coffee Co. is named Snow Queen, a reference to Leigh's cocaine dealing. It features fully washed beans from the San Carlos Community Project in Costa Rica, Guatemala and Santa Rita La Chaparral in Colombia. This results in a robust blend that packs a punch, with an edge of bitterness, and treacle and chocolate notes. Single origin beans are also on rotation, giving regulars and first-timers a chance to try something new. Espresso isn't the only option; cold drip, reverse iced lattes (frozen espresso shots mixed with vanilla and panela, served with cold milk) and pour over are also available.

After scouring Sydney and Melbourne for a supplier, Dean found the Roastworks Coffee Co sitting right under his nose, at his local coffee shop. He chose the Artarmon-based company because it produced exactly what he wanted, it offered great support and the staff were knowledgeable and understanding. Its sustainable practices were also a big draw card.

Toasties and their lesser-known cousins, jaffles, dominate the menu, both served with a very adult twist. The unsealed toasties are filled with porchetta, fennel and apple sauce; or roast mushroom, red sorrel, labna and red onion jam.

Their sealed relatives feature fillings such as duck and chestnut, and d'Affnois and pear. There are also a few non-toasted options, including a mushroom stack and the Notorious P.I.G, a heart-attack-inducing combination of braised pork shoulder, smoked speck and chorizo.

If the authorities are kind, a liquor license is also in the future, allowing Dean and his team to continue Kate's alcohol-serving legacy – legally.

> '...the custom house blend, provided by Roastworks Coffee Co. is named Snow Queen, a reference to Leigh's cocaine dealing.'

ULIVETO

33 BAYSWATER RD, POTTS POINT · 02 9357 7331 · ULIVETOCAFE.COM.AU

MACHINE: La Marzocco
GRINDER: Swift and Mazzer Robur
BEANS: The Little Marionette
BREWING METHODS: Espresso

Already familiar with the cafe industry, Chris Zafeirakopoulos, the blushing owner of Potts Point's gem, Uliveto, was raised in his family-owned city cafe. He pursued a degree in Economics and, naturally, a career in the industry should have followed. Instead, Chris returned to what was familiar.

When he first stumbled upon Uliveto, Chris fell in love. Abandoning the opportunity to work in finance, he couldn't pass up the chance to call this beautiful cafe his own. And in 2013, that's exactly what happened. He now heads up the Uliveto team, including its Le Cordon Bleu Head Chef, Sanghoup Lee ("Mr Lee"), and couldn't be happier.

The north-facing cafe takes advantage of all-day sun and has been likened to an oasis. There's loads of outdoor seating, shaded in summer and heated in winter, and an architect-designed interior featuring a commissioned installation by artist, Gary Carsley. Families with dogs and kids, tourists spending time in gorgeous Potts Point and the committed locals all spend lazy mornings or afternoons relaxing at Uliveto.

Chris is coffee obsessed, filling his days with piccolos and his nights with long blacks. After noticing a decline in quality from his previous roaster, Chris set out to find a roast that no one else in the area used. He settled on Sanchez, by The Little Marionette, and hasn't looked back.

Head Barista, Chai Pranomrum, brews up the espresso on a La Marzocco with a view. Despite his name, Chai's choice is always a double shot, long black.

Chris carries his passion through to the kitchen, sourcing fruit and vegetables from the local market and if it's not Chris down there selecting the produce, it's his Dad who's been in the hospitality industry for over 40 years. Everything is freshly baked and made in-house daily.

> 'The north-facing cafe takes advantage of all-day sun and has been likened to an oasis.'

There's an extensive all day breakfast menu, so your day can start whenever you choose. Select from the usual suspects of Eggs Benedict or a Breakfast Sandwich, or try out the Uliveto Breakfast: two free range eggs with bacon, chicken chipolatas, grilled tomato and toast. Lunchtime brings ever-changing specials including Wild Barramundi with a creamy barley risotto and a pineapple salsa, as well as the popular sandwich menu and other hearty meals. Try the Zatar Chicken – quinoa tabouli with Danish feta and avocado. There are also a great selection of hot meals including burgers, steaks, risotto, pasta, hand-made gnocchi and a bowl of Tasmanian mussels, and salads.

If for no other reason, head in to Potts Point to try the Sanchez coffee blend from The Little Marionette. Chris said it is absolutely amazing at the two and a half to three week mark, and by his calculation, Uliveto is the only place in the area you'll be able to experience it.

Cafe Con Leche | Surry Hills

coffee.
creative
lighter
fluid

Two Chaps | Lilyfield

SOUTH & WEST OF THE CITY

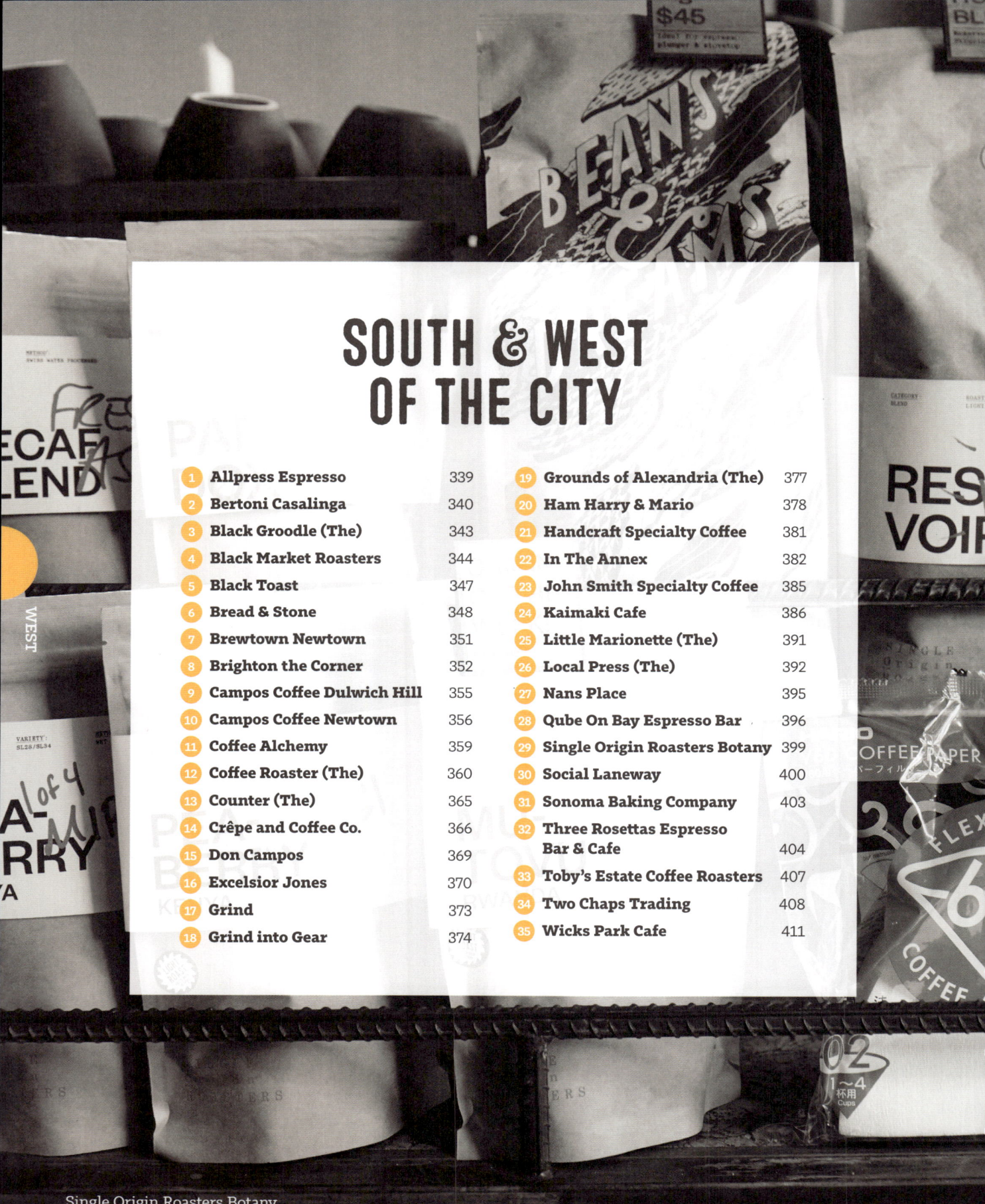

SOUTH & WEST OF THE CITY

1. Allpress Espresso — 339
2. Bertoni Casalinga — 340
3. Black Groodle (The) — 343
4. Black Market Roasters — 344
5. Black Toast — 347
6. Bread & Stone — 348
7. Brewtown Newtown — 351
8. Brighton the Corner — 352
9. Campos Coffee Dulwich Hill — 355
10. Campos Coffee Newtown — 356
11. Coffee Alchemy — 359
12. Coffee Roaster (The) — 360
13. Counter (The) — 365
14. Crêpe and Coffee Co. — 366
15. Don Campos — 369
16. Excelsior Jones — 370
17. Grind — 373
18. Grind into Gear — 374
19. Grounds of Alexandria (The) — 377
20. Ham Harry & Mario — 378
21. Handcraft Specialty Coffee — 381
22. In The Annex — 382
23. John Smith Specialty Coffee — 385
24. Kaimaki Cafe — 386
25. Little Marionette (The) — 391
26. Local Press (The) — 392
27. Nans Place — 395
28. Qube On Bay Espresso Bar — 396
29. Single Origin Roasters Botany — 399
30. Social Laneway — 400
31. Sonoma Baking Company — 403
32. Three Rosettas Espresso Bar & Cafe — 404
33. Toby's Estate Coffee Roasters — 407
34. Two Chaps Trading — 408
35. Wicks Park Cafe — 411

Single Origin Roasters Botany

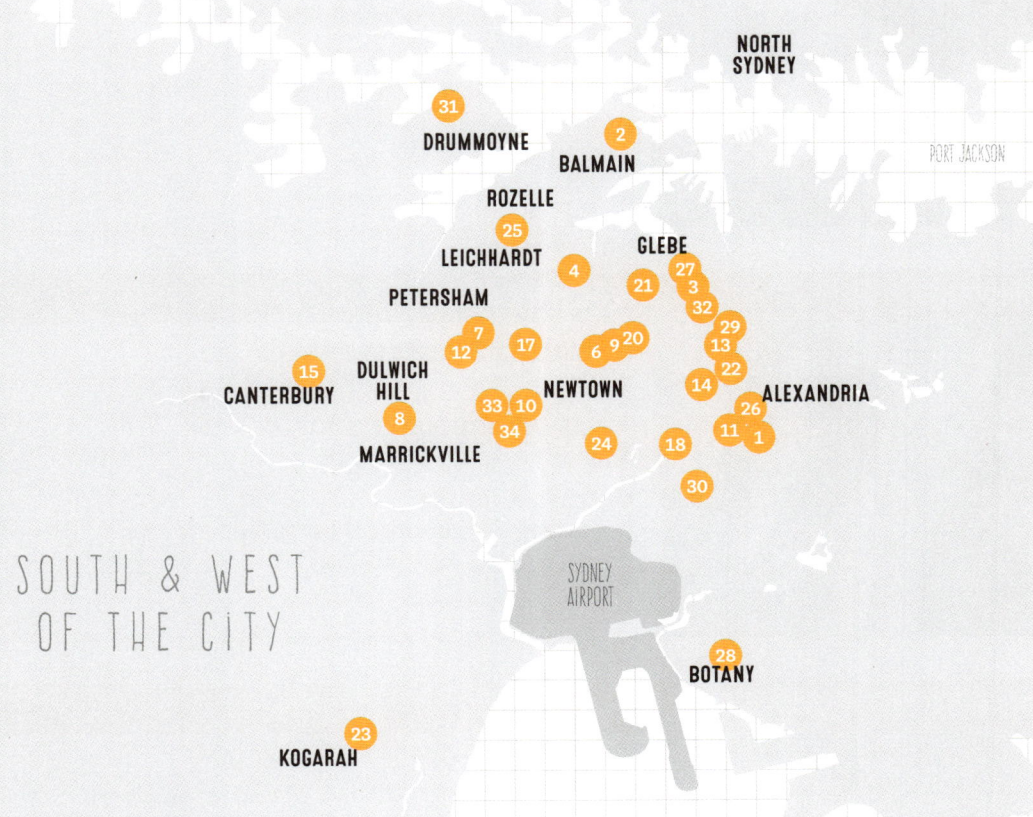

SOUTH & WEST SIDE BARISTAS

BERTONI CASALINGA — Mani

I HAVE MY COFFEE…
Made with love.

MY FAVOURITE BREWING METHOD IS…
French press.

IF I WASN'T A BARISTA, I'D BE…
A tennis pro.

THE BLACK GROODLE — Vivi Thendean

IF I WASN'T A BARISTA I WOULD BE…
A Pilot.

WHEN I'M NOT MAKING COFFEE I AM…
Sipping on wine with friends.

GIVE ME A QUOTE…
The secret of joy in work is contained in one word – excellence.

THE BLACK MARKET ROASTERS — Angus Nicol

I HAVE MY COFFEE…
AeroPress, 4am hand-ground, 88 degrees, single estate, fresh, light roast… heaven.

MY FAVOURITE PLACE TO EAT OUT IN SYDNEY IS…
Sushi Suma – epic sashimi.

MY FAVOURITE BREWING METHOD…
Personal: AeroPress.
Business: Espresso.

BLACK TOAST — Emmy

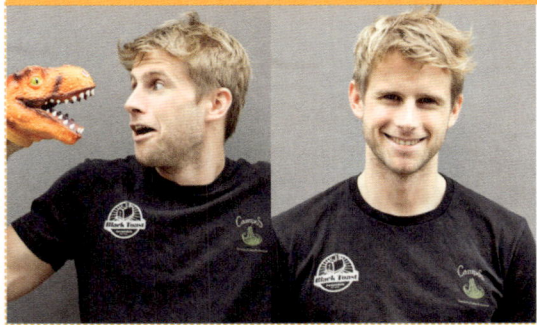

I HAVE MY COFFEE…
Simple creamy latte.

IF I WASN'T A BARISTA, I'D BE…
A bean roaster, coffee is my life.

WHEN I'M NOT MAKING COFFEE, I AM…
Eating, chatting, baking sweets.

SOUTH & WEST SIDE BARISTAS

BREAD & STONE
Shane

I HAVE MY COFFEE…
As a Pour Over, give me a Yirgacheffe please.

IF I WASN'T A BARISTA, I'D BE…
Travelling around Australia playing music for my coffee.

WHEN I'M NOT MAKING COFFEE, I AM…
Coffee hopping with the lads.

BRIGHTON THE CORNER
Nigel J Park

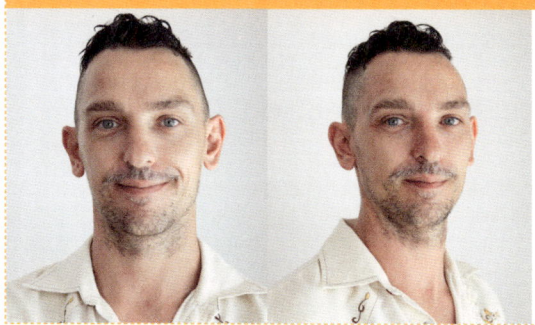

I HAVE MY COFFEE…
Black and long.

IF I WASN'T A BARISTA, I'D BE…
Helping out in the GWS Giants midfield.

WHEN I'M NOT MAKING COFFEE, I AM…
Being the best dad I can.

CAMPOS COFFEE DULWICH HILL
Brendon King

MY FAVOURITE BREWING METHOD IS…
Filter.

IF I WASN'T A BARISTA, I WOULD BE…
An account manager at a Telco.

GIVE ME A QUOTE…
Don't hold knowledge hostage.

CAMPOS COFFEE NEWTOWN
Jadon Irwin

I HAVE MY COFFEE…
As an espresso.

IF I WASN'T A BARISTA, I WOULD BE…
A bartender.

WHEN I'M NOT MAKING COFFEE I AM…
Drinking coffee.

SOUTH & WEST SIDE BARISTAS

THE COFFEE ROASTERS — Dara Chey

I HAVE MY COFFEE…
Short and strong.

MY FAVOURITE PLACE TO EAT OUT IN SYDNEY IS…
Braza Churrascaria, Darling Quarter.

GIVE ME A QUOTE…
Everybody should believe in something; I believe I'll have another coffee.

THE COUNTER — Gabor

I HAVE MY COFFEE…
With milk.

MY FAVOURITE BREWING METHOD IS…
Cold Drip.

WHEN I'M NOT MAKING COFFEE I AM…
Riding my motorbike.

CRÊPE AND COFFEE CO. — Jordan Caibre Zordan

I HAVE MY COFFEE…
In a cup.

MY FAVOURITE BREWING METHOD IS…
Clover or pourover (most clarity of flavour).

IF I WASN'T A BARISTA, I WOULD BE…
President of your country.

DON CAMPOS — David Ruslie

MY FAVOURITE BREWING METHOD IS…
I'll have to go with Clever Coffee Dripper with this one. I get really geeky on it; playing around with grind size, water temperature, steeping time, turbulence, infusion, cold brewing, etc.

IF I WASN'T A BARISTA, I WOULD BE…
Sitting in my tiny little cubicle, in an office, coding away.

MY FAVOURITE PLACE TO EAT OUT IN SYDNEY IS…
Gumshara Ramen! I've been their regular since day one. I'm a big ramen fan, and by far, this is the best one yet in Sydney.

SOUTH & WEST SIDE BARISTAS

HANDCRAFT SPECIALTY COFFEE — John Lee

I HAVE MY COFFEE…
Every hour. Can't live without it. Seriously.

IF I WASN'T A BARISTA, I'D BE…
A car mechanic or racer.

MY FAVOURITE BREWING METHOD IS…
V60 Pour Over.

IN THE ANNEX — Edrick

I HAVE MY COFFEE…
As an espresso.

MY FAVOURITE PLACE TO EAT OUT IN SYDNEY IS…
LP's quality meats in Chippendale. It's owned by Luke Powell who used to be the head chef at Tetsuya's and made up Mary's burgers. Also it's literally around the corner from me!

WHEN I'M NOT MAKING COFFEE, I AM…
I'm trying someone else's.

JOHN SMITH SPECIALTY COFFEE — Hayden Rhys McTaggart

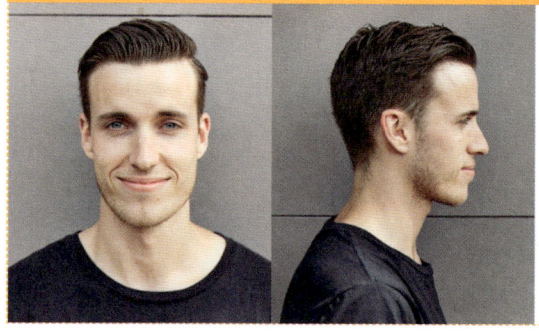

IF I WASN'T A BARISTA, I WOULD BE…
A hand model.

MY FAVOURITE PLACE TO EAT OUT IN SYDNEY IS…
Macciatio.

GIVE ME A QUOTE
There's no excuse for hard poached eggs, especially after I trained eggs.

THE LOCAL PRESS — Arthur

IF I WASN'T A BARISTA, I'D BE…
Homeless.

MY FAVOURITE PLACE TO EAT OUT IN SYDNEY IS…
Pub Life Kitchen, Ultimo (meat heaven!).

WHEN I'M NOT MAKING COFFEE, I AM…
A full time navel gazer.

SOUTH & WEST SIDE BARISTAS

NANS PLACE — Jodie

I HAVE MY COFFEE…
Whenever I want!

MY FAVOURITE BREWING METHOD IS…
Shaken Ice Pour Over.

IF I WASN'T A BARISTA, I'D BE…
A professional tennis player.

QUBE ON BAY ESPRESSO BAR — Jay Park

I HAVE MY COFFEE…
Espresso.

IF I WASN'T A BARISTA, I'D BE…
A trekker.

MY FAVOURITE PLACE TO EAT OUT IN SYDNEY IS…
Longrain.

SINGLE ORIGIN ROASTERS BOTANY — Angus Lindsay & Stephanie Burrows

IF I WASN'T A BARISTA, I'D BE…
Angus: A professional oboe player.
Stephanie: A ballerina.

MY FAVOURITE PLACE TO EAT OUT IN SYDNEY IS…
Angus: Yen's, Redfern.
Stephanie: Wa, Bondi Junction.

WHEN I'M NOT MAKING COFFEE, I AM…
Angus: Indulging in my other love: alcohol.
Stephanie: Cooking.

SOCIAL LANEWAY — Marina Agustina

I HAVE MY COFFEE…
Smooth, creamy warm latter.

WHEN I'M NOT MAKING COFFEE, I AM…
Spending as much time as possible with my little girl.

GIVE ME A QUOTE…
"The trouble with not having a goal is that you can spend your life running up and down the field and never score".
– Bill Copeland.

SOUTH & WEST SIDE BARISTAS

SONOMA BAKING COMPANY — Tomas Slezak

I HAVE MY COFFEE…
Black, always.

MY FAVOURITE BREWING METHOD IS…
Chemex.

IF I WASN'T A BARISTA, I'D BE…
A professional skier.

TOBY'S ESTATE COFFEE ROASTERS — Leanne Foo

MY FAVOURITE BREW METHOD IS…
Espresso – short and punchy like me.

IF I WASN'T A BARISTA I WOULD BE…
An International Tour Guide for Contiki!

MY FAVOURITE PLACE TO EAT OUT IN SYDNEY IS…
My Canh, a Vietnamese restaurant in Bankstown.

UH OH, THIS GUY NEEDS COFFEE + CRONUTS STAT.

Brewtown | Alexandria

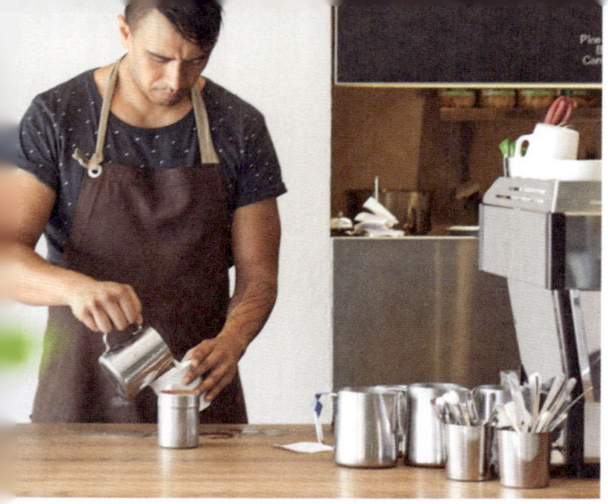

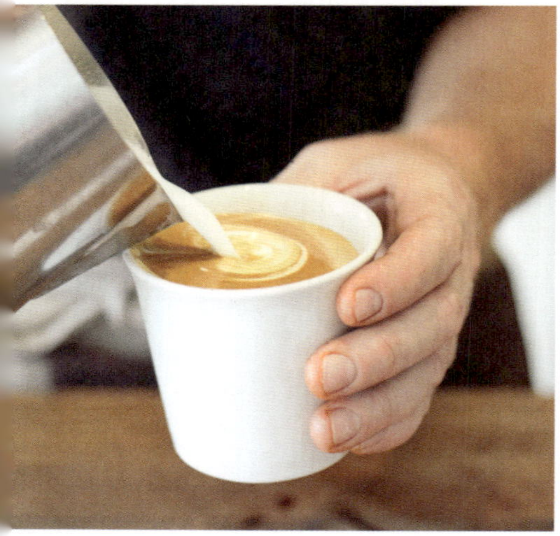

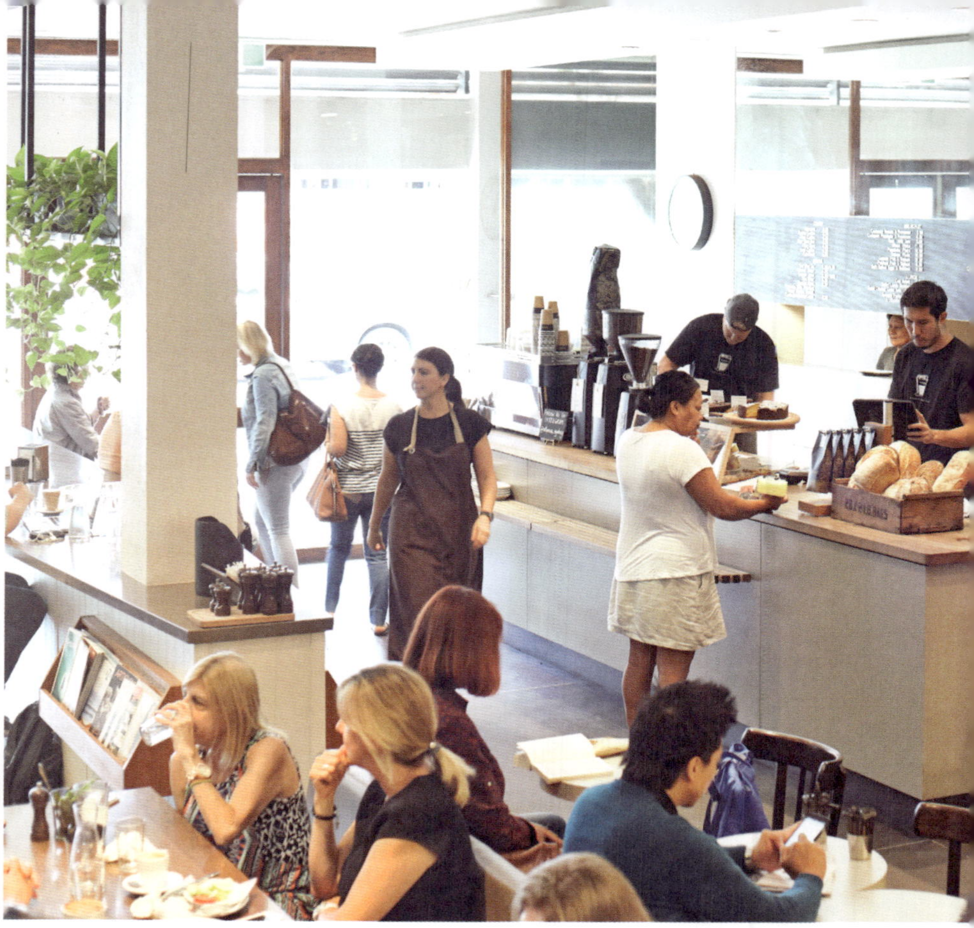

COFFEE
Espresso 3.20
Regular Coffee 3.70
Large Coffee 4.20
Soy / Extra shot 0.50
Filter Brew 4.50
Iced Coffee 4.20
Cold Brew 4.00
DRINKS
Tea/ Mint Tea 4.00 /
Mineral Water 4.50
Orange Juice 3.50 /
San Bitter 3.00
Blended Drink 5.50
Kale Pistachio
Almond
Juice 5.50
LA MARZOCCO

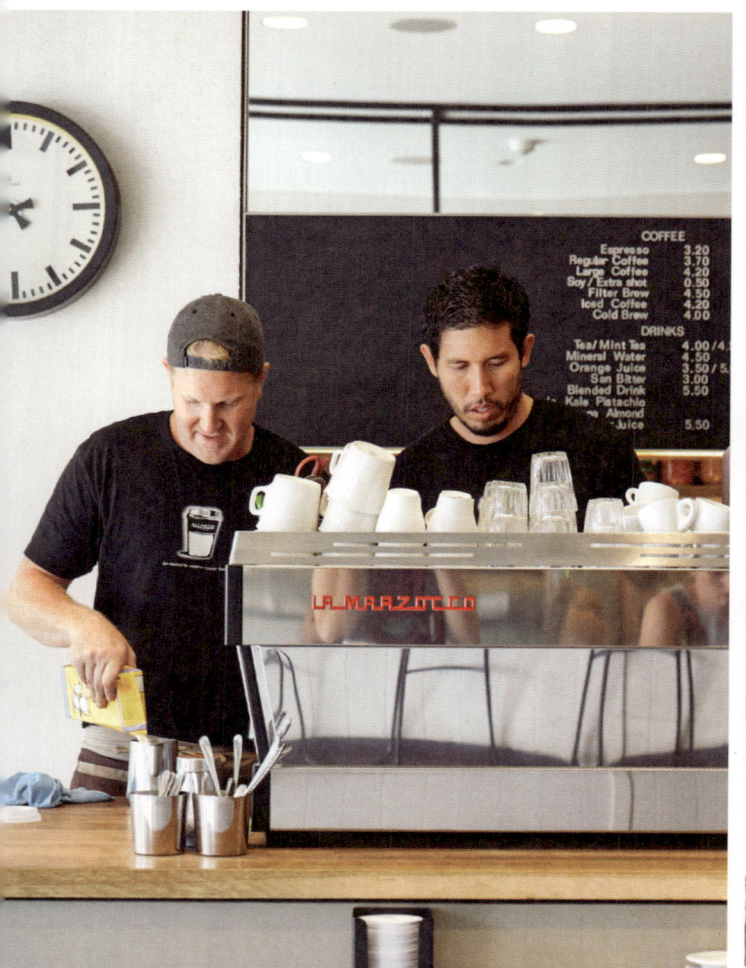

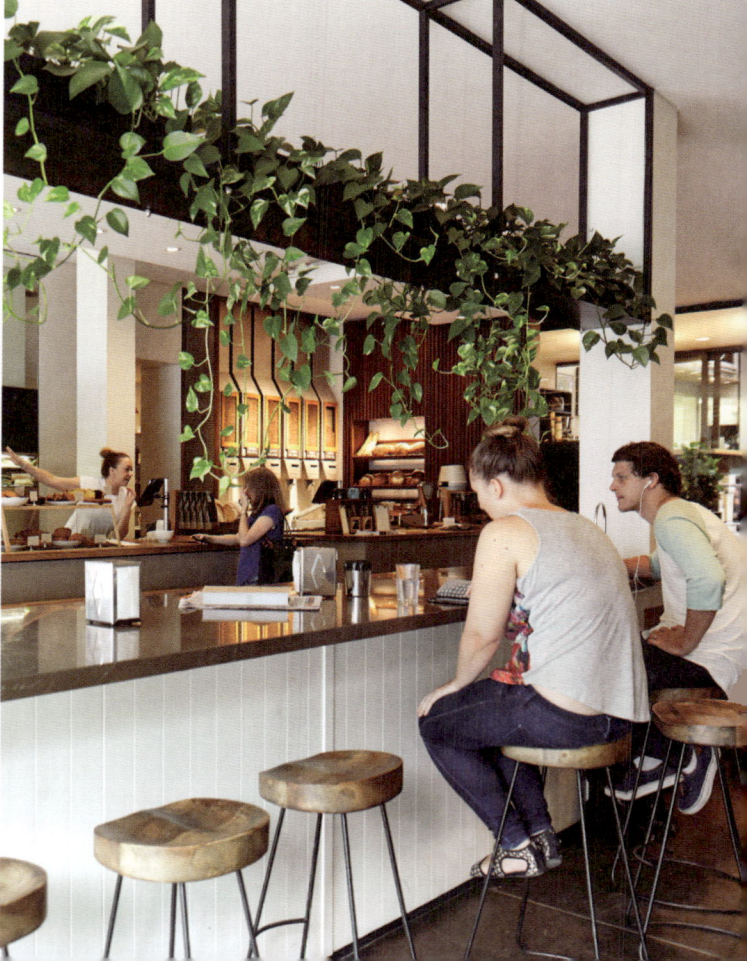

ALLPRESS ESPRESSO

58 EPSOM RD, ZETLAND · 02 9662 8288 · ALLPRESSESPRESSO.COM.AU

MACHINE: La Marzocco Linea PB
GRINDER: Mazzer Robur Auto
BEANS: Own Blend, Allpress Espresso
BREWING METHODS: Espresso, Filter, Cold Brew

MICHAEL ALLPRESS HAS BEEN SUPPLYING FRESH ROASTED COFFEE TO NEW ZEALAND CAFES SINCE 1988 WHEN HE OPENED HIS OWN ROASTERY, ALLPRESS ESPRESSO. In 2001 he decided it was Australia's turn to experience his coffee and together with long time friend, and restaurateur Tony Papas, he established the Allpress Roastery in Sydney. They simultaneously opened the Roastery Cafe, which was one of the first roaster cafes in town.

Where many competitors use drum roasting to roast their coffee beans, Allpress use Hot Air Roasting technology. Hot Air Roasting uses strictly convective heat in a chamber, where beans are suspended in a stream of fluidised hot air. This allows an even heat transfer to penetrate through the beans with no risk of scorching or tainting from residual smoke. Michael believes the flavour advantages are significant and evident in the consistent taste of their coffee – naturally sweet, smooth and a long lasting finish.

The coffee is sourced from various cooperatives and farms from around the world, including a Colombian bean that has been grown exclusively for Allpress. Allpress works directly with the growers and exporters to ensure the bean perfectly fits their cup profile. The relationship the business has with everyone involved in the coffee process is exceptionally important to the team, and their success is no doubt owed to this careful fostering of relationships.

The coffee served up in the Roastery Cafe is Carmelo, but changes between one of four espresso blends Allpress has available. The blends and single origin coffees are poured into countertop hoppers from the roastery and are available to purchase for brewing at home.

The cafe is open for breakfast and lunch Monday to Saturday, and is populated by something of a mixed crew – local families, couples and those who work in local businesses, plus those from the nearby fashion houses. The food offering is simple: good quality products that complement the coffee. Take your pick from one of the popular breakfast plates on offer or choose from the delicious selection of fresh sandwiches including Vietnamese chicken, Mortadella artichoke and mint, or Pork and Watercress.

'Allpress works directly with the growers and exporters to ensure the bean perfectly fits their cup profile.'

As you sit in the cafe you look straight into the roastery where the team are busy roasting, hand packing and preparing the coffee for their wholesale customers. Witnessing the hard work that goes into roasting and preparing these beans will allow you to appreciate your cup even more. You might even catch members of the public attending one of the informative, and extremely interesting, coffee classes.

As well as its cafes and roasteries across New Zealand, Melbourne and Sydney, Allpress has now expanded into London and Tokyo sharing its flavour into like minded communities.

BERTONI CASALINGA

281 DARLING STREET, BALMAIN · 02 9818 5845 · BERTONI.COM.AU

MACHINE: Wega
GRINDER: Mazzer
BEANS: Bertoni Blend
BREWING METHODS: Espresso

BROTHERS, ANTHONY AND ALBERT WERE BOTH WORKING IN CORPORATE SETTINGS IN SOFTWARE AND OPERATIONS, BUT HARBOURING A NOT-SO-SECRET DREAM OF OPENING A CAFE AND SERVING ITALIAN HOME COOKED MEALS, GREAT COFFEE AND PASTRIES. They wanted to create somewhere where they could give a real, traditional Italian experience, with a modern twist. They've since built themselves quite the empire, with cafes right across Sydney.

Anthony and Albert have been drinking coffee since they were teenagers – they were coffee snobs before it was cool. They used to spend their time travelling around Sydney searching for the perfect cup. They've now developed their own blend, the Bertoni Blend, which they say is only for serious coffee drinkers! It has a rich and robust flavour with undertones of chocolate and is roasted exclusively for the Bertoni cafes by Artecaffe. The beans are sourced directly from the growers in Indonesia, Ethiopia, India and Kenya and then roasted and blended in true artisan style. This Bertoni Blend has been developed and refined over the last 11 years. Finally the brothers found their 'perfect cup.'

Anthony and Albert's parents grew up in Italy. Their mother, Mama Maria, in Naples, and their father in Sicily, where he was a farmer. Growing up, their parents taught them that great tasting Italian food needs to be 'semplice' – simple – and only made with the freshest ingredients. They had a constant source of fresh produce from their father's backyard garden and they still hold his traditions close.

All the food in their cafes are cooked on-site daily, just the way it should be.

The very extensive menu has something for everyone. You'd be made of stone if you could resist the bakery offerings, particularly the Bertoni Ciambella, a toasted Italian doughnut with Nutella, or the Sfogliatelle, a classic Neapolitan pastry filled with ricotta and candied orange. The menu recommends you 'don't ask, just order it'; we recommend the same.

> 'The staff know all of the customers, their regular orders and the names of their kids.'

But the most important element that the brothers hope everyone will experience at Bertoni is family. Many of the key staff members have been there for years and several family members work within the stores too. The staff know all of the customers, their regular orders and the names of their kids. And if you're as impressed by the food as we expect, you'll be interested to know that the brothers have produced a cookbook, called 'I Only Eat Bertoni', which ranked number 8 on the NSW Independent Booksellers list. It's the story about the Bertoni journey, the family and their food.

You might be wondering about the name – Bertoni. It sounds like a European name, perhaps from some Italian village. Well, actually, it's quite simple. Albert and Anthony... Bert and Tony... Bertoni!

If you can't make it to Balmain, check out one of their other locations: Balmoral, Kent St Sydney, Farrer Place and Darling Quarter.

THE BLACK GROODLE

55 MOUNTAIN ST, ULTIMO · 02 9281 9161 · FACEBOOK.COM/THEBLACKGROODLE

MACHINE: La Marzocco
GRINDER: Mazzer Robur
BEANS: Di Lorenzo
BREWING METHODS: Espresso

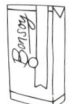   

AFTER TEN YEARS OF OWNING AND MANAGING AN INNER CITY CAFE, KARLOS AZZI DECIDED IT WAS TIME TO OPEN ONE IN ULTIMO. He had spent years watching people come and go from the cafe in Darlinghurst, and witnessed the happiness, and social interaction that coffee brings to a community.

He wanted to provide a venue that was warm and welcoming, and somewhere that locals would enjoy dropping by for a coffee and a chat. Everyone from young designers, architects and marketing executive to teachers and students can be found chilling out here. This industrial, chic cafe has certainly achieved a sense of community by offering a homely place to relax and take a second away from the world.

Walk in to this open, communal environment and the first thing you notice is the wafting aroma of good coffee. The Black Groodle's coffee is well known in Ultimo for the uniqueness of each blend. Karlos said, "We produce damn good coffee, which is deep in flavour with a rich, chocolate, nutty overtone, possesses a hint of sharpness on the tip of the tongue, and has great structure and body. It has a lasting, pleasant aftertaste, without bitterness – just 100% taste!"

A bit hard to resist? The locals certainly think so. Head Barista, ViVi Thendean, pounds away on the La Marzocco espresso machine from breakfast through to afternoon tea, consistently serving coffee with maximum taste.

Open from Monday to Friday for breakfast, lunch and afternoon coffee, it serves up salads and lunches as well as delicious breakfasts. Billed as Street Food Made Local, the cafe is known for its homely food offerings. Glorious salads, brimming with Mediterranean flair and bursts of colour are piled high in bowls ready to be served up alongside a dollop of hummus and some Lebanese flatbread. Pick as many or as few salads as you like, or perhaps go for a wrap. For dessert, you can't go past the Knafeh – a baked cheese with semolina and rose sugar syrup. It's decadent and it'll be a memorable mid-week lunch. There are plenty of smaller sweet treats too, made by in-house chef, Cyrille Launey. Take your pick from brownies, salted caramel bites, muffins, banana bread, hummingbird cake or his famous apple tart … oh and don't forget to try the delicious homemade cashew nut Balawa made by Karlos' mother.

The open kitchen provides customers a chance to watch the kitchen staff producing homemade and old-style, comfort food. White subway tiles line the walls, providing a blank canvas for the daily specials. Steel accents and natural timber furniture, including cute-as-can-be benches, also dot the space, blending the lines between industrial chic and a home-away-from-home.

It may be named after the owner's beloved dog, Jed, a golden retriever cross poodle, but the cafe is an ode to its owner's passion for good coffee, great food and homely ambiance.

> '…achieved a sense of community by offering a homely place to relax and take a second away from the world.'

BLACK MARKET ROASTERS

16 SIR JOSEPH BANKS ST, BOTANY [BY APPOINTMENT ONLY] · 0414 924 685 · BLACKMARKETROASTERS.COM.AU

MACHINE: Synesso Hydra and Ply La San Marco, Custom Built
GRINDER: Mazzer Robur E, Manual, Mazzer Mini and Ditting
BEANS: Own Blend
BREWING METHODS: Batch Brew, Cold Drip, V60 Pour Over, AeroPress, Chemex

BLACK MARKET ROASTERS IS A SMALL-BATCH OPERATION THAT SOURCES, ROASTS AND SUPPLIES SPECIALTY COFFEE TO QUALITY ESPRESSO BARS, RESTAURANTS AND BUDDING HOME BARISTAS. Run by Angus and Jessica Hol, this establishment not only offers up the beans but the brains behind it too, with Barista Courses taught by professional baristas available at their roaster.

Bidding farewell to the corporate industry, Jessica and Angus embraced the hospitality sector and learnt their craft through work at various espresso bars and fine dining restaurants in Sydney. In a bid to learn as much as possible about coffee and cafe culture, Angus boarded a plane to Europe. Travelling the continent, he tasted the coffee and evaluated the atmosphere of cafes, learning about the integral role both play in European lifestyles.

Filled with caffeine and new knowledge, Angus and Jessica embarked on their first venture together in 2010 and opened Swallow Coffee Traders, which continues to be a success. TopHat coffee in Clovelly was next, which has become a go-to spot for many locals looking for quality coffee since its 2012 debut.

Though they source their coffee from all over the globe, Ethiopia and Sumatra remain Black Market favourites when looking for something special. One of Black Market Roasters' favourite Ethiopian regions is Yirgacheffe. It is a small town located in central southern Ethiopia and produces floral and fruity flavours that have much of the specialty coffee industry hooked.

The house blend is currently made up of four origins that each bring a unique characteristic and come together to create a sweet and smooth blend. It contains a Brazilian Sertao for a nice cocoa base, an Ethiopian Sidamo adding a fruity sparkle, a Colombian Tolima giving it a sweet, smooth quality and a spicy Sumatra Wahana, which adds a touch of spice to the blend.

As well as the house blend, single origins are also for sale and alternate on a month-to-month basis. Angus said, "This means our clients can choose from a minimum of three single origins each month or just get a selection of all three to keep things interesting."

Although the roaster is closed to the public, the Barista Courses offered are targeted at beginners, focusing on teaching practical skills that will help students find job placement within the industry. "We have found that while the coffee culture in Sydney has grown rapidly over the years, there are few courses that really give students the skills that they need when working as a barista." With a limit of four students to a class, they are able to tailor each student's requirements to suit his or her skill level.

Watch this space! BMR is looking to expand their retail operations in the CBD.

'...produces floral and fruity flavours that have much of the specialty coffee industry hooked.'

BLACK TOAST

43 BOOTH ST, ANNANDALE · 02 9571 4442 · BLACKTOAST.COM.AU

MACHINE: La Marzocco Line and La Marzocco Linea
GRINDER: Mazzer Robur and Mazzer Super Jolly
BEANS: Campos Superior
BREWING METHODS: Espresso, Cold Drip

SET IN A FORMER 19TH CENTURY FURNITURE FACTORY IN ANNANDALE, BLACK TOAST BENEFITS FROM THE PERIOD FEATURES. High ceilings, expansive floor plan and a sun-filled atrium garden make this vast space, set over two levels, the place to be in the inner west. Decorating the space are eclectic artworks, funky vintage toys and coffee-themed equipment. The exposed joists give hints to the building's age and history.

Black Toast sources its coffee from Campos. The cafe has a long-standing relationship with the company and respect the consistency of the product. Traditional blending methods and cold drip are on offer here, all lovingly prepared by the team of dedicated baristas.

The vibe here is unpretentious, quirky, fun and inviting. Frequented mostly by locals, including plenty of young families and couples, the atmosphere is friendly and the food and coffee offerings are simple but authentic, fresh, local and modern. Open for all day breakfast and lunch from midday, Black Toast boasts a menu that is all about the produce. Hearty and imaginative breakfasts complement the delicious coffee bean aromas on lazy weekend mornings, or for those in a hurry there are freshly baked muffins, mouth-watering sweets, and an array of savoury choices ready to be taken away.

The food is wholesome and nutritious and is sourced from partners who share Black Toast's philosophy on food. Keep it fresh, local and simple. Bread is delivered fresh from the Sonoma Bakery, sweets are from Madhouse Bakehouse, Yael's Cakes, Ms. Cupcake and Madeleine Fine Food. Try the breaky wrap, or the Birdie Brekky – two poached eggs on a homemade potato rostie with Portobello mushrooms, house smoked bacon and avocado. Or for something a little… 'manlier' try the Manwich – double bacon, double egg, smashed avocado, cheese and golden hash browns with homemade relish or BBQ Sauce. You can even purchase a jar of the relish to take home with you along with an array of other Black Toast products that are available.

'It's an art gallery meets a retro homewares store meets an on point cafe…'

The large, diverse space lends itself perfectly to functions of all types, from corporate events to private functions, from art exhibitions to book launches. With plenty of room to mingle, lots of conversation starters hanging from the walls and a team of young and vibrant staff, events are guaranteed to be a hit. Every so often you'll find an interesting event open to the public, like the Black Toast Garage Sale, where customers can take home some of the cafe's unique collection of knickknacks and furniture. Local artists' work is featured on the walls, with the collection changing regularly.

You can relax in an armchair, or sit at one of the aptly vintage, funky op-shop style tables. It's an art gallery meets a retro homewares store meets an on point cafe, and it's no wonder it's so popular.

BREAD & STONE

63 CRONULLA ST, CRONULLA · 02 9444 1188 · BREADANDSTONE.COM.AU

MACHINE: La Marzocco Strada MP
GRINDER: Mazzer Robur E and Mazzer Major
BEANS: Veneziano Bond Street
BREWING METHODS: Espresso, Cold Drip, V60, Cold Brew (flavoured), AeroPress

With a love of fresh whole foods and an undeniable passion for coffee, Bread & Stone is all about getting back to basics. Cronulla's local eatery has something to suit everyone's taste.

Steven and Francine Hackett opened their first cafe in 1998, while also juggling two children and study. Their passion for coffee has only grown since then. They see brews as a lifestyle and a love letter to clients and friends. Two years ago, Veneziano coffee started being distributed in New South Wales, opening a whole new world of coffee to Steven and Francine. They were able to meet other baristas and Latte Art champions and learn from the best, and from this they began their never-ending pursuit for the perfect cup of coffee. Bread & Stone is where the couple can experiment and play with everything they have learnt.

It only makes sense then that Steven and Francine should feature Veneziano coffee in their cafe – they've been hooked on it since they first tasted it in Melbourne. They were blown away by the passion, skill and quality in every seasonal roast. Their house blend, the Bond Street Seasonal Blend, has a syrupy body with berry notes with a brown sugar finish. The decision to use a seasonal blend was important to Bread & Stone because the subtle changes keep the year interesting and matches the seasonality they prize in their food. With 40% from Brazil and two Ethiopian beans, Bond Street was the perfect choice for Steven and Francine because it works well with both black and milk drinkers.

While the couple may be lovers of coffee, they understand that some people just need it to make it through their day. Bread & Stone is filled with everyone from those who enjoy AeroPress and cold drip coffee, to workers who would rather a quick cappuccino with too many sugars. Tea lovers aren't forgotten here either, with a selection of Ovvio organic teas available.

Bread & Stone also caters to the foodies in the area. Produce for breakfast and lunch is locally sourced and made in-house where ever possible. Expect seasonal, healthy fare like quinoa and roast veggie frittatas or paleo brownies and muffins. There are even decadent pastries and donuts loaded with toppings for those looking to treat themselves.

The modern wooden interior of Bread & Stone is filled with hanging plants and bright blue hues, feeling as fresh and clean as their food. It's the perfect place for a quality coffee date and some feel-good food.

> 'They see brews as a lifestyle and a love letter to clients and friends.'

BREWTOWN NEWTOWN

6-8 O'CONNELL ST, NEWTOWN · 02 9519 2920 · BREWTOWNNEWTOWN.COM

MACHINE: Kees van de Westen Spirit
GRINDER: Mazzer Robur E and Mahlkönig EK43
BEANS: Brewtown Coffee Roasters
BREWING METHODS: Espresso, Cold Brew, Pour Over

There's a wealth of experience behind the two men responsible for Brewtown Newtown. Charles Cameron previously managed Single Origin Roasters and Toby's Estate Woolloomooloo, and Simon Triggs was Retail Operations manager for Toby's Estate and owns Gnome Espresso in Surry Hills. These two have had truly extensive careers in the specialty coffee industry, and for them, coffee is an essential part of day to day living.

Together, they now own and operate Brewtown Newtown, a venue that is more than just cafe, more than just a roastery, more than a bakery – it's a one-stop shop. Housed in a beautiful old warehouse that dates back to 1911, Brewtown Newtown serves a seasonal bistro inspired menu, pastries made in house and specialty coffee roasted in house and served as a pour over, cold brew, batch brew and espresso. They've even got a fashion and homewares retail collection upstairs.

The building itself has had its share of diversity, too – at one time or another, it's served as the district ambulance offices, an artificial flower manufacturing centre and most recently, a bookshop. If these walls could talk! The tall ceilings, exposed beams and wooden planks, the hanging pendant lights and raw exposed brick walls – it all combines into a super trendy space with plenty of air and light.

Charles and Simon roast their own coffee, a decision they made so that they could take authorship of their coffee and develop into a coffee wholesaler. They buy from a range of specialty coffee brokers and tend to focus on African coffees. Having said that, the choices of what they buy are all made at the cupping table and based entirely on coffee quality. Charles and Simon like to keep the components of their house blends transparent and generally to two or three different origins; currently their Xanadu blend is Colombia Finca Morella and Brasil Ondas de Mantiqueira. The Metropolis blend (all their blends are named after classic films), by contrast, is all Ethiopian – Wottona Bultuma and Konga Natural.

'...more than just a roastery, more than a bakery – it's a one-stop shop.'

The breakfast menu features everything from grilled black sausage, eggplant puree, fennel and blood orange salad and goat's cheese, to sticky date coconut chai morning pudding with pistachios and dehydrated mandarin. For lunch, there's the Elvis burger – ground beef, savoury brewnut, Canadian bacon, Gruyère and mayo served with chips and relish. Or try the toasted sandwich stuffed with coffee-rubbed beef brisket, smoked eggplant, pickled cabbage, porcini salt and horseradish cream on light rye.

You're most likely familiar with a certain word we just mentioned – the Brewnut. Sydney-siders have been falling over themselves to get to these for some years. Brewtown Newtown's version of a cronut is simply spectacular, and well worth the trip. Pair one with the Xanadu blend, what could be better?

BRIGHTON THE CORNER

49 PALACE ST, PETERSHAM · 02 9572 6097

MACHINE: La Marzocco Strada MP
GRINDER: Mazzer Kony E and BNZ MD 64 Ceramic
BEANS: The Little Marionette and Brighton Black Cat
BREWING METHODS: Espresso, Cold Drip, V60 Pour Over

ON THE CORNER OF TWO PICTURESQUE, LEAFY STREETS IN PETERSHAM, YOU'LL FIND A CHARMING, HISTORIC, CREAM BUILDING WITH A DISTINCTIVE STRIPED BLACK AND WHITE AWNING. It's a good old-fashioned corner shop, Brighton on the Corner, serving great brews and fantastic food.

The awning shades outdoor tables filled with locals and their dogs, enjoying a coffee right on the corner. Inside, there's plenty of seating, with small tables for two lining the long wall, a large communal table in the middle of the space, and window seating, looking out onto the lovely Palace Street. Plants and flowers abound: on the tables in vases, on the windowsills, and hanging in baskets from hooks in the ceiling. It brings a lovely, homely vibe to the smart décor, which features a white subway tiled service area.

Owners, Nigel Park and Michael Coombs, both come to Brighton the Corner with long careers in hospitality and coffee. Nigel is a hospitality veteran from New Zealand, where he roasted and made coffees before coming to Australia and opening a bar, Safely Wolf, in Manly. Tired of working nights, Nigel moved back to day work at Corduroy Cafe in Surry Hills, before opening Brighton the Corner with Michael Coombs. Nigel also acts as Manager and Head Barista; after all, he's been hard at brewing and roasting coffee for the last twenty years – it's what he knows.

The coffee served at Brighton the Corner comes from The Little Marionette, chosen by Nigel and Michael because they like "keeping it local, and they make those little green beans taste so good". The house blend is Brighton Black Cat, a mixture of Colombia San Augustin and Kenya Rift Peaberry coffees. Michael and Nigel are also big fans of Ethiopian beans with their berry and wine flavours.

As well as espresso, Brighton the Corner offers cold drip and V60 pour over. There's even a house specialty that is one of a kind – coconut water cold drip. How exotic! Breakfast and lunch are served Tuesday to Sunday, as well as dinner on Friday nights, which is offered from a prix fixe menu that has featured such delights as seared kingfish, butifarra, cranberry beans, chives and tomato, and spiced BBQ pork shoulder, sweet potato, roast cauliflower and spinach. The four-course menu has proven extremely popular and comes highly recommended.

'...philosophy at Brighton the Corner is simple – give a lot of love and attention to the finer details.'

The philosophy at Brighton the Corner is simple – give a lot of love and attention to the finer details. The staff harbour a deep love of the coffee bean, from the crop to the cup, and relish bringing people together over a cup, morning, noon and (Friday) night.

CAMPOS COFFEE DULWICH HILL

538 MARRICKVILLE RD, DULWICH HILL · 02 9550 0705 · CAMPOSCOFFEE.COM

MACHINE: La Marzocco Linea PB and Strada
GRINDER: Mazzer Robur, Mahlkönig EK43, Mazzer Kold, Mazzer Robur E
BEANS: Campos Superior Blend, Seasonal Single Origins and Cup of Excellence
BREWING METHODS: Espresso, Cold Drip, Pour Over, Cold Brew

THE CAMPOS NAME MAY BE ANYTHING BUT NEW TO COFFEE DRINKERS AUSTRALIA WIDE, BUT ITS NEWEST SPECIALTY COFFEE BAR IN DULWICH HILL IS A STANDOUT VENUE WELL WORTH A VISIT.

The Campos Coffee brand was established in Newtown in 2002 and has since expanded across Queensland and Victoria, with its coffee being sold in a multitude of venues. Manager of Campos Dulwich Hill, Brendon King, has been working with Campos Coffee for five years and had been developing the concepts and plans for this store for two years before finally finding the right location. It's the first specialty coffee bar in the area and comes with a veteran team of baristas with the professionalism customers have come to expect from Campos.

The Dulwich Hill cafe is quickly becoming the local for many new residents as well as loyal Campos drinkers. Owner, Will Young is thrilled. He said, "Many of our original regulars from the first shop in Newtown have moved out to the Dulwich Hill area as their families have grown and they have needed more space. The originals that used to come to Newtown in 2002 with their puppies and babies are showing up to the Dulwich Hill store with their old dogs and teenagers. These customers mean the world to us and to be able to see them on an everyday basis again – well, that is very special indeed."

Campos Coffee spends 365 days a year cumulatively at origin, sourcing beans and working with producers. It spends this time ensuring the partners overseas are producing quality coffee, ethically and sustainably.

The Dulwich Hill Campos always has a single origin from the Cup of Excellence program available, as well as pour over, cold drip and cold press in bottles. The house espresso blend is Superior Blend, the company's award-winning blend it's been serving since the brand's inception in 2002. It features a toffee base with slight fruity highlights, a rich body and a sweet butterscotch finish. The Superior Blend is seasonal rather than static and a lot of effort goes into ensuring its taste profile is excellent throughout the year.

Several times a year Campos Coffee celebrates Cup of Excellence Champion Days, where customers are treated to the number one champion from the Cup of Excellence program. These days provide a rare opportunity to sample what is judged to be the best coffee in the world from a particular country, but plan ahead, because these events are popular!

> 'The originals that used to come to Newtown in 2002 with their puppies and babies are showing up… with their old dogs and teenagers.'

CAMPOS COFFEE NEWTOWN

193 MISSENDEN R, NEWTOWN · 02 9516 3361 · CAMPOSCOFFEE.COM

MACHINE: La Marzocco Linea PB and Strada
GRINDER: Mazzer Robur, Mahlkönig EK43, Mazzer Kold, Mazzer Robur E
BEANS: Campos Superior Blend, Seasonal Single Origins and Cup of Excellence
BREWING METHODS: Espresso, Cold Drip, Pour Over, Cold Brew, Cupping Sessions

HERE'S A STORY ABOUT A GUY NAMED WILL. In 1997, he was backpacking and surfing around Australia when he met a man called Andrew Gross who brewed up a specialty coffee that changed Will's life. It was sweet, flavourful, full of body and it didn't burn the inside of his mouth. Will said he had a 'coffee epiphany' on that day and dropped what he was doing to dedicate his life to sharing with others just how fantastic coffee could be. And aren't we glad he did, because this is Will Young we're talking about, president of Campos Coffee.

Will studied and read all he could about specialty coffee, worked as a barista and roaster, and then opened his first cafe in Sydney. He threw himself into it, body and soul, until in 2002 he purchased Campos Coffee in Newtown, visions and dreams became a reality and a world-class espresso bar was born.

Daniel Audy now manages the Campos Coffee flagship store in Newtown. Dan has spent time with Campos' partners in Sulawesi, learning about their coffee systems and quality control. Dan's Indonesian heritage allows him to talk directly with the farmers and translate any communications, which has helped Campos truly understand how they can best work together.

'What could be better than a not-for-profit platform that rewards small farmers for their exemplary coffee?'

Campos Coffee in Newtown always offers at least one coffee from the Cup of Excellence program. This program is extremely important to Campos. A farmer who wins this award can increase their income 20 fold. What could be better than a not-for-profit platform that rewards small farmers for their exemplary coffee? It also means Campos is able to purchase coffee that has been through both an international and a national jury and been declared one of the top for the year. Everybody wins, not least of all the Campos customers who get to enjoy the results.

You can also obtain an education on that really great cup of coffee by heading upstairs to the Cupping Room, where customers can join in on a tasting session of Campos' top single origin coffees and learn about the farms behind the coffees. The tasting sessions are run according to international standards and are a fantastic introduction into what happens to coffee through its life cycle, from growing and purchasing to roasting and cupping.

This is a respected company that works closely with its producers and demonstrates how important integrity is to them. The promises that the company made in 2002 are still carried through to this day and at the heart of it all, Campos produces ethical, sustainable and delicious coffee.

COFFEE ALCHEMY

24 ADDISON RD, MARRICKVILLE · 02 9516 1997 · COFFEEALCHEMY.COM

MACHINE: Spirit
GRINDER: Mazzer Kold E, Mazzer Major E, Anfim, BNZ Conical, Compact, Ditting, Mahlkönig EK43, Hydra, Robur E
BEANS: House Blend, Goodness Galileo
BREWING METHODS: Espresso, Pour Over, Cold Drip, The Sparkler

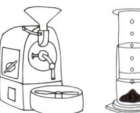   

At Coffee Alchemy in Marrickville, it's all about commitment, history, innovation and alchemy. All the blends here are named after and inspired by famous alchemists. Owner, Hazel de los Reyes, has about-as-long a history with coffee as you can get, and has made it her life's work.

Growing up amongst the coffee trees in her grandmother's big backyard, Hazel learned the art of picking the red ripe cherries, drying them on the patio, milling and roasting them. She was drinking coffee, at a very young age, and the excitement and wonder of coffee continues for Hazel – it's her way of life.

In 2004, Hazel opened Coffee Alchemy Roastery in Marrickville, and then in 2008, added the cafe, Coffee Alchemy. It's still going strong and is still 100% dedicated to specialty coffee. In fact, Coffee Alchemy doesn't sell anything else. No food, no pastries, no teas, just coffee.

All the coffee is roasted on site and sourced directly from farmers all over the world. The green coffee they purchase are the stars that shine on the cupping table. These are often only a micro lot on a given day at a farm, or a special plot of land designated to produce a specified flavour. "The farmers who work with us enable us to polish their hard work and present it to a discerning audience who treasure all the effort," said Hazel.

Manager, Sam Jessada Itthithanakorn, is always at hand, alongside members of his team, to help you choose your coffee, with six different Coffee Alchemy blends to choose from (available for purchase too). You can choose from four different single estate farms for pour over coffee. There's also cold drip coffee, made from a variety of cold drip methods and using a variety of apparatus, depending on the coffee being served that day. And there's a choice of three or four different single estates for espressos.

Then there's The Sparkler, "invented by Coffee Alchemy and since copied all around the world," said Hazel. The Sparkler has been served since Coffee Alchemy opened in 2008 and is pulled from a beer tap, it looks like Guinness, but is actually coffee they've been pulling.

All up, on any given day, there are more than 12 single estates available to buy as beans or ground to take home, or to order as an espresso, pour over, cold drip or sparkler.

The house blend, Goodness Galileo, is what Coffee Alchemy uses for milk drinks. Like all its blends, it's blended from a taste profile rather than a country-specific profile. There are a further five blends, including a blend of mountain processed decaffeinated coffee. The 'Red Tub Specials' are microlot coffees sourced from special lots produced by single farms all around the world. There are always at least five different selections for sale, roasted either for espresso or for filter.

Coffee Alchemy certainly puts the 'specialty' in specialty coffee.

> 'No food, no pastries, no teas, just coffee.'

THE COFFEE ROASTER

380 BOTANY RD, ALEXANDRIA · 02 8599 1599 · COFFEE.COM.AU

MACHINE: Wega Green Line
GRINDER: Mazzer Kold & Robur E
BEANS: House Blend
BREWING METHODS: Espresso, Pour Over, Cold Drip, Trifecta Brewed Coffee

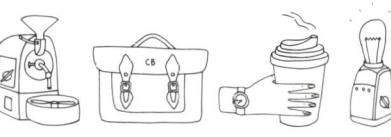

EVER WANTED TO ROAST YOUR OWN COFFEE? You could go buy a roaster and start in your garage (as so many of Australia's leading roasters did), but if you're not looking for that kind of commitment, you can head to Alexandria and check out the green coffee selection, roasting advice and revolutionary roasting technology of The Coffee Roaster all in one go.

Dan and JoAnne Fitzsimmons immigrated to Australia from Seattle in 1983. Some years later, having tired of their careers in the computer and finance industries and being coffee addicts they happily packed up their bags to travel the world and research all aspects of coffee for a year. They came back to Australia armed with first-hand experience and a better understanding of everything that goes into making a great coffee, and so, they started roasting on a 4kg air roaster in Glebe. Before long the footpath outside the terrace house was cluttered with university students on milk crates enjoying their coffee.

Today, a seriously sophisticated coffee roasting operation is taking place. You'll find tour groups passing through, local cafes perfecting their house blends, and a buzzing cafe serving breakfast and lunch alongside its freshly roasted coffee. The cafe itself offers pour over, cold drip and Trifecta brewed coffee in addition to its myriad espresso choices. Within two metres of the Piccolo Chinook coffee roaster are 36 single origins, ready to be roasted on demand.

If you're just popping in for a takeaway or a quick coffee, try the house blend, which achieved the highest score at the 2012 Sydney Royal Fine Food Show.

The Coffee Roaster sources Arabica beans from all around the world between the tropics of Cancer and Capricorn. At last count they had 86 different combinations of coffee blends and roasting recipes catalogued on their Chinook Air Roaster. Air roasting was a very conscious choice for Dan and JoAnne. On their coffee quest around the world, they met Mike Sivetz, the inventor of fluidised airbed coffee roasting. They were easily convinced that air roasting was elegantly simple, easily measured and provided "bulletproof batch to batch consistency".

They now operate a fully automated, specially designed Chinook Air Roaster, which allows roasters to produce batch after batch of consistent blends and are simple enough for visitors to learn about during a tour. Wholesale customers make up a good portion of The Coffee Roaster's clientele, returning time and again because of the product quality, roast consistency, custom blending and private label packaging.

Retail customers come in for a coffee, but they stay to witness their own coffee roasted before their very eyes, in less than 15 minutes. Just state your requirements, such as light roast for pour over, or medium city roast for espresso.

'At last count, they had 86 different combinations of coffee blends and roasting recipes...'

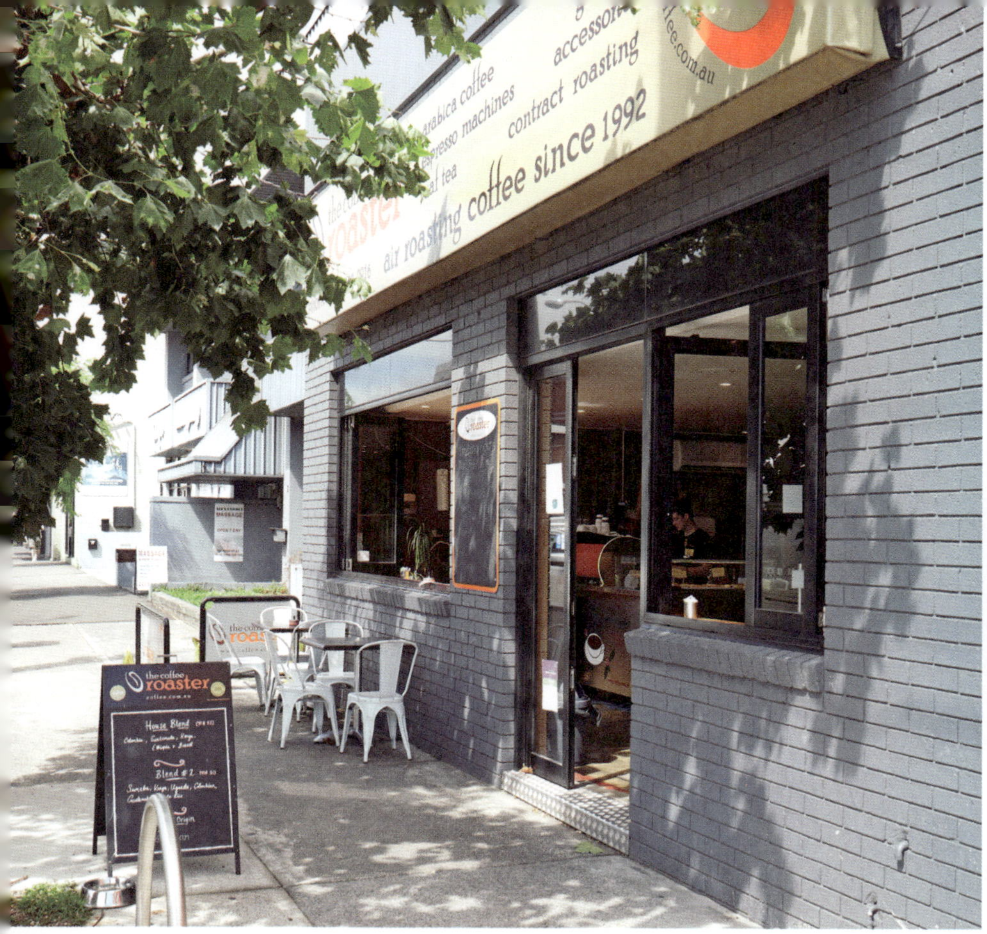
arabica coffee
contract roasting
air roasting coffee since 1992

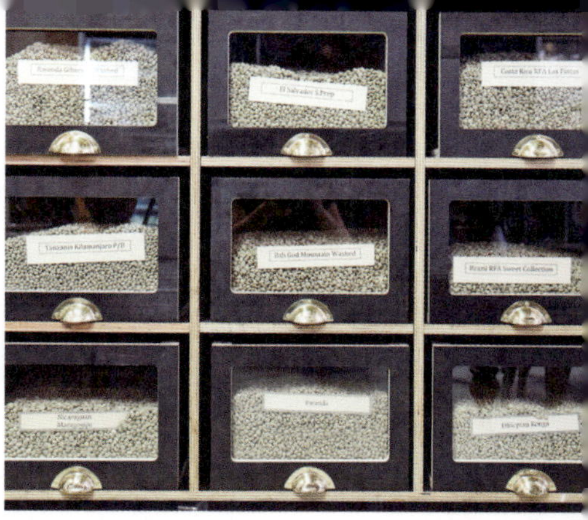

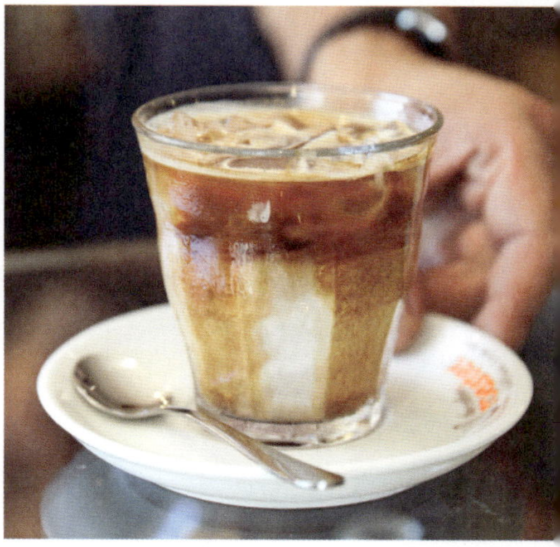

ORIGIN TRADERS
AUSTRALIA

SHB EP
GENUINE ANTIGUA
LOS VOLCANES
P02366
SYDNEY
SUPREMO
SUMATRAN

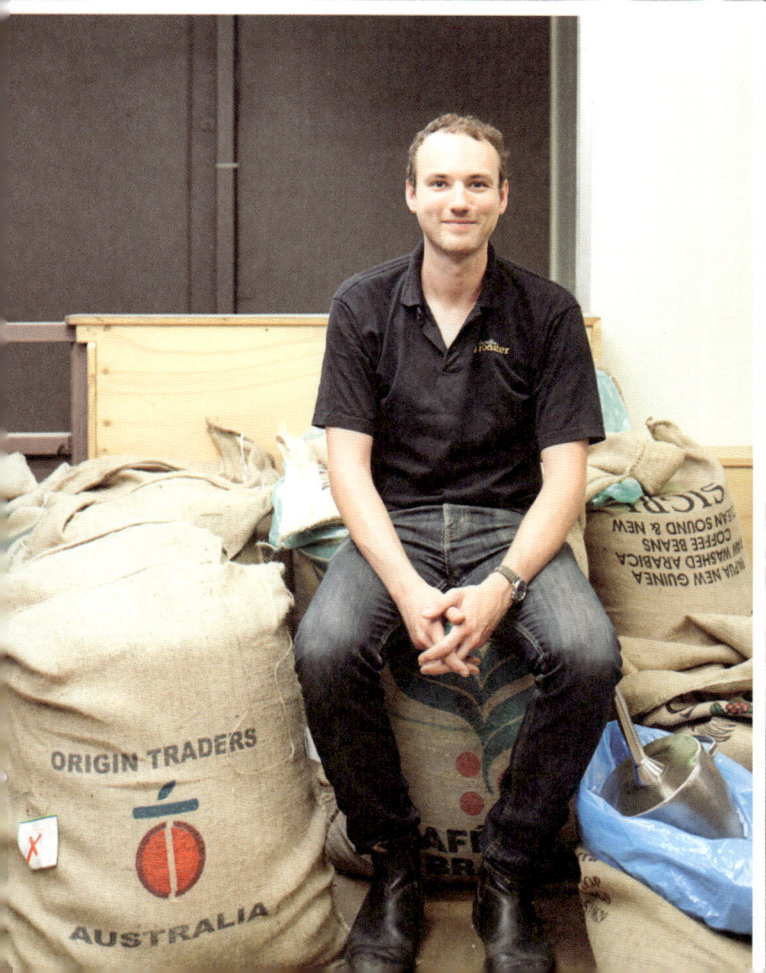

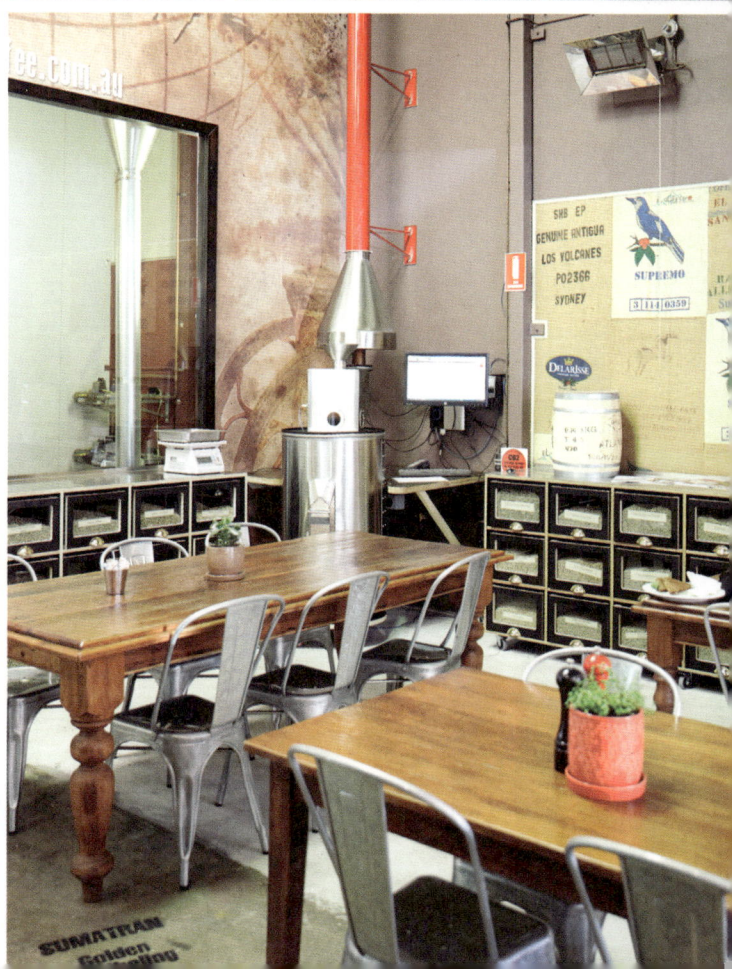

Single Origin Roasters | Botany

Life is like COFFEE its all in how YOU MAKE IT

THE COUNTER

96 AUDLEY ST, PETERSHAM · 02 9560 2949 · FACEBOOK.COM/THECOUNTER

MACHINE: La Marzocco Linea
GRINDER: Mazzer Robur E
BEANS: Coffee Alchemy
BREWING METHODS: Espresso, Cold Drip

Sydney's inner west cafe scene is alive and well, and Petersham, known to locals as 'Portugese Town', is right up there with the best of them. Just off the main drag, The Counter provides locals with expertly made coffee and inventive sweet treats as well as a comprehensive breakfast and lunch menu.

Johnny Geng has recently taken over ownership of The Counter, which was opened in 2012 by Mariella Traina, cafe owner and coffee lover for more than a decade. Johnny has taken the baton and run – experimenting with coffee preparation to extract the very best flavour from the bean. He sees this as a way to honour the hard work put in by others down the lifeline of the coffee bean – the farmers and the roasters. A perfect cup of coffee is a team effort.

To everyone at The Counter, coffee is fascinating and mysterious – every day they learn a little something new about the bean. It's a continuous learning curve. The Counter team has worked with Coffee Alchemy to create a house blend that is rich and round and enhances milk-based coffees. The flavour profile is of intense caramel, chocolate and almond tones and makes for a spectacular latte.

Coffee Alchemy sources beans from all around the globe based on the season. As a result, across the year you'll find all sorts of origins at The Counter, from Ethiopia to Indonesia and back again. Try the cold drip, too, which uses Single Estate coffee. Or try one of the staff favourites, a Yirgacheffe coffee, with its fruity, berry tones. Who are we kidding… try one of each!

The seasonal menu is complemented by a dazzling array of homemade pastries and sweets, brownies, cakes and muffins; there's just not enough time in the day to taste them all. Try the towering carrot cake or the raspberry and macadamia brownies. No, scratch that – start with the caramel slice, and a raspberry and white chocolate 'cruffin'.

> '…young hipsters, young hipster families, hipster commuters, hipster business people…'

The typical crowd at The Counter is hipsters: young hipsters, young hipster families, hipster commuters, hipster business people… you get the idea. You'll also find the local council workers and NSW transport folks here for their daily coffee – there's a friendly, community vibe with plenty of regulars.

Sit out the front and watch the world go by, or rest in the cool interior, with its exposed brick counter and subway tiled walls. With plenty of staff ready to take your order, you shouldn't have to wait too long here, even if there is a short list for a table.

CRÊPE AND COFFEE CO.

60 REGENT ST, REDFERN · 02 8065 2585 · FACEBOOK.COM/CREPE.COFFEE.CO

MACHINE: La Nouva Era - Linea Retro
GRINDER: BNZ
BEANS: Colombian Connection, Certified Organic
BREWING METHODS: Espresso

IF YOU CAN FIND YOUR WAY THROUGH THE GRAFFITI ADORNED WALLS OF REDFERN, YOU MAY JUST BE ABLE TO FIND CRÊPE AND COFFEE CO. The beach-shack inspired cafe is located just steps from the train station and has been dishing up sweet and savoury crêpes and single origin Colombian coffee since 2011.

Owner, Brad Fleming, started in the crêpe business with his Blini Bar stall at the Eveleigh Farmers' Market, building up a reputation for soft and creamy crêpes stuffed full of sweet and savoury fillings. His success led to an expansion at a permanent base nearby. He found a lifetime coffee partner in Cesaro Comestaro Vela, of Colombian Connection, who supplies the cafe with certified organic single origin beans, sourced directly from the Colombian coffee farmers.

Jordan Caibre Zordan is in charge of the coffee, turning out the full gamut of espresso-based offerings. The beans are roasted locally in Marrickville in the Colombian Connection warehouse, supplied straight from the farmers of the Tolima region of Colombia. There is a rotating list of boutique single origin beans in the grinders, all the while maintaining the distinctively smooth and caramel/chocolaty profile.

The space takes on an old world industrial meets new world chic vibe, with reclaimed timber elements covering the walls and huge French doors opening out onto the street, juxtaposed with more modern elements of raw steel, glass, large mirrors and character lighting. Lounge on the leather chesterfield sofas at the back or get up close and personal with the barista on one of the bright stools by the front. The glass panels surrounding the crêpe makers mean you can watch the masters at work. The blackboard behind the counter will let you know what's on offer, but if you're a Nutella fan, don't bother reading it.

'...dishing up sweet and savoury crêpes and single origin Colombian coffee since 2011.'

The cafe's namesake – thin French crêpes stuffed with any number of different fillings – dominates the menu. Sweet-tooths will be drooling over the classic Nutella combinations; you can pair the chocolaty-hazelnut goodness with your choice of fruits or keep it simple with lashings of the stuff. Savoury options include The French Brekkie, crispy bacon, egg and hollandaise sauce; Hook'm, shaved leg ham, cheese and sautéed mushrooms; and The Chick Club - a variation on the traditional chicken club, to name but a few.

Crêpes aren't the only food options on the menu. Stick your head in for the coffee and stay for the all-day breakfasts, including a bacon, chorizo or veg hotpot, naked eggs benedict or the classic bacon and eggs on sourdough toast. Sandwiches are also on offer for lunch, including a fancy BLAT and a gourmet chicken or gourmet salmon toastie. Those in a rush can grab something to go. And for those with a healthier outlook you really must try the popular and soul satisfying Green Smoothie.

DON CAMPOS

21 FOUNTAIN ST, ALEXANDRIA · 02 9690 0090 · CAMPOSCOFFEE.COM

MACHINE: La Marzocco Linea PB and Strada
GRINDER: Mazzer Robur Auto, Mahlkönig EK43, Mazzer Kold, Mazzer Robur E
BEANS: Campos Superior Blend, Season Single Origins and Cup of Excellence
BREWING METHODS: Espresso, Cold Drip, Pour Over, Cold Brew

THE DON IN DON CAMPOS REFERS TO THE LEADER OR BOSS. It is a term used to show respect, and in this way the Alexandria venue accurately identifies Campos Coffee as a leader of the specialty coffee industry.

Together with Will Young, the heart and soul behind Campos Coffee, Tristram Cox owns and manages Don Campos. Tristram is flying the flag high for the Campos brand, serving the Campos Superior house blend. It's 100% direct trade and is more a project in quality and consistency than a blend. It's seasonal, so the components vary from year to year, and the quality control team spends hours every day analysing the ingredients to ensure consistency is maintained even when the blend changes. As with all coffees from Campos, much time is spent at origin checking the background of every coffee to ensure it is grown ethically and sustainably.

Tristram wanted to bring a variety of coffee brewing techniques into an espresso-dominated industry. The cafe certainly still specialises in espresso, but it also features hot and cold filter styles. Pour over, cold drip, cold brew and affogatos are as important to the Don Campos team as their famous espressos. This truly is a collaboration between coffee roasters and baristas.

Situated in a converted warehouse, called 'The Fountain,' Don Campos shares tables with the Campos Rosetta Stone Bakery, which produces all the pastries and sweets sold at the Campos company stores. Combining the two in one space brings a sense of real community, while allowing each arm of the business the ability to focus completely on their main products.

As with the other Campos locations, Don Campos always serves at least one Cup of Excellence winning coffee – they also serve the overall winner several times a year. They believe, and understandably so, that it's thrilling to know that anyone, from any walk of life, can taste what was judged by an international jury to be the very best coffee of the year. This accessibility isn't present in other industries, not wine, whisky, tea or champagne!

Coffee truly means the world to Tristram, his team, and the whole Campos family. Tristram is 100% dedicated to the Campos Coffee cause; everything he does is for the customer in an attempt to ensure that they get the same amount of pleasure from coffee as he and his staff do. Everything here is served with respect and acknowledgement to the producers. Tristram has spent time at origin, which opened his eyes to the hard work and attention required to create the exemplary coffees being served at Don Campos. It really is one big, happy family.

> 'Pour over, cold drip, cold brew and affogatos are as important to the Don Campos team as their famous espressos.'

EXCELSIOR JONES

139A QUEEN ST, ASHFIELD · 02 9799 3240 · EXCELSIORJONES.COM

MACHINE: Synesso
GRINDER: Mazzer Robur E
BEANS: 5 Senses, Custom Blend
BREWING METHODS: Espresso, Batch Brew Filter

A NAME INSPIRED BY THE LATIN TERM TO GO ABOVE AND BEYOND, EXCELSIOR JONES HAS MADE ITS MARK IN THE INNER WEST, BECOMING A COMMUNITY-BASED CAFE READY TO FEED THE HOARDS OF HUNGRY LOCALS.

This quaint corner cafe is situated on a triangular block in suburban Ashfield. When the building was constructed, Queen St originally went by the name of Excelsior St and then became Jones St. Boasting a rich history, the building itself was built in 1924 and the Owners, Anthony Svilicich and James Naylor, strive to keep that history alive. The menu incorporates old local heroes, such as Angus Young from AC/DC into the design to offer customers a touch of history with their morning coffee.

Working for himself from the age of 21, Anthony developed an avid interest in the hospitality sector from a young age. His coffee journey began with a single Mobile Coffee Van that suddenly expanded into three. Feeling a need to set up shop, Anthony purchased Le Monde Cafe with his sister-in-law in 2005, which went on to win multiple awards.

It was Le Monde Cafe that brought Anthony and James together and formed the partnership they have today. James moved to Sydney in 2008 to start work at The Source Espresso Bar in Mosman. It was here that he developed a strong passion for specialty coffee and the process involved, from harvest to brew.

When choosing a coffee supplier for Excelsior Jones, it was a simple choice. "A long and productive relationship was already established with 5 Senses so enlisting their help to roast a custom house blend, as well as single origin espresso and filter roast coffees seemed natural," Anthony said.

It is that very house blend coupled with great service that brings people in from near and far. Excelsior Jones is dedicated to ensuring its custom blend achieves a rich, sweet, medium-bodied roast for its milk blend, while a single origin is on offer to perfectly showcase its black coffee too.

The extensive menu offers the essential breakfast items alongside some delicious options. Try the ricotta hotcakes or eggs benedict with streaky bacon and celery salt. If you pop in over lunch, check out the cheeseburger: grass fed Angus beef, Gruyère, tomato relish, aioli and fried spud.

In a market that is forever evolving, a partnership with a forward thinking and proactive company like 5 senses ensures a top quality product. The marriage of a great cup of coffee, along with great food ensures that at Excelsior Jones, the customers receive the best of both worlds.

> 'The menu incorporates old local heroes, such as Angus Young from AC/DC into the design...'

GRIND

SHOP 4/15 SURF RD, CRONULLA · 0403 844 533

MACHINE: La Marzocco GB/5
GRINDER: Mazzer Robur and Ditting Deli
BEANS: Own Blend
BREWING METHODS: Espresso, Pour Over, Cold Drip, Lever, Turkish

There's a fantastic coffee waiting for you a few streets back from the main drag at Cronulla, and it's well worth the trip. Grind Espresso has the feel of a trendy but grungy back lane cafe somewhere in Melbourne, but is located just one block from the beach. It's a long-standing feature of the Cronulla landscape, having opened back in 2002. Richard Calabro owns the business and his sister, Donna Rella Calabro, manages it – it's a family affair. They've been pioneers of boutique espresso in Cronulla for all these years, and are still going strong.

There's a fantastic community feel to Grind Espresso. To see that you need look no further than the large collection of photographs of dedicated customers who take photos of themselves on their travels to wild and wonderful places, with signs exclaiming 'I'd rather be at Grind'! It's a lovely touch, and testament to what an important part of the community Grind Espresso is.

You'll find all and sundry at Grind – tradies, gym junkies, seniors, swimmers, corporates, musicians, artists and surfers – a real Cronulla cross-section.

Richard grew up hanging out at his Mum's cafe, which was where his love affair with coffee started. He's a firm lover of espresso, finding joy in trying different origins and distinguishing the different tastes from each. Richard takes his fascination with coffee seriously, with a 300+ piece collection of antique coffee memorabilia and equipment, some of which lines the walls of the cafe. He loves alternative brew methods, offering cold drip, vintage lever, Turkish coffee and pour over, alongside the ever-popular espresso.

Single Origin Roasters were the first coffee company Richard felt truly understood what he wanted and needed in his signature house blend. They devised a blend he was happy with, the GRIND blend, which has changed with the times, but has always had a Colombian base, blended at different ratios with Ethiopian and Sumatran beans. Expect a big caramel base with hints of berries on the notes, and a chocolate aftertaste.

> "...testament to what an important part of the community Grind Espresso is."

Grind Espresso has been a Sydney Morning Herald 3 Cup Winner for three years in a row. As well as the house blend, you can expect to see coffee from Kenya, Uganda, Rwanda, Brazil, Bolivia, Cuba, Jamaica, Mexico and even Australia here.

All sorts of curiosities hang from the industrial ceiling, and there's a wonderful old railway sign listing the coffee offerings, instead of railway stations. The crowd spills out on to the footpath, but the service moves quickly and everyone gets their coffee hit promptly from the La Marzocco GB/5. Alongside his coffee pot collection, he's got quite the grinder collection in use too – five Mazzer Roburs and two Ditting deli grinders work hard to satisfy the masses.

Grind Espresso is open from 6am to 6pm, and offers a select menu and sweet treats. But really, everyone's there for the coffee.

GRIND INTO GEAR

111-115 PERCIVAL RD, STANMORE · 02 9560 5450 · GRINDINTOGEAR.COM.AU

MACHINE: La Marzocco
GRINDER: Mythos 1 and Mahlkönig EK43
BEANS: Pablo & Rusty's
BREWING METHODS: Espresso, Cold Drip, Batch Brew

SOUTH & WEST

SPACE, COMFORT, SERVICE AND QUALITY ARE WHAT YOU CAN EXPECT FROM GRIND INTO GEAR, WHICH OPENED NEAR STANMORE TRAIN STATION IN LATE 2014. There's a calm, casual atmosphere here, which contrasts distinctly from the rush-hour crush and impatient toe-tappers you might find elsewhere.

At Grind Into Gear you can expect friendly restaurant-style table service, top quality products and produce, and staff who thrive on making coffee drinking a true experience for each and every customer. Sit back and relax, and let the wait staff prepare your order while you get on with your important conversation!

Owner, Paul Borghetti, moved to Sydney from Brisbane with the vision of setting up his own business, and his passion for the science behind coffee made this path the clear choice. Having always worked in the hospitality industry, from bars and cafes to fine-dining establishments, Paul chose to prepare and sell the number one thing that gets him out of bed every morning: coffee. How this humble little bean stirs passion in so many of us.

Grind Into Gear sources its coffee from Pablo & Rusty's who focus on traceable, sustainable and ethically produced beans. Paul was looking for something unique and found the philosophy and approach at Pablo & Rusty's was in line with his own views.

The house blend on offer is a seasonal blend of Brazilian (Moreninha Formosa) and Panama (Don Pepe) beans. It is sweet and well balanced in milk, and Paul finds it complements Grind Into Gear's single origin offerings perfectly. Alongside the house blend, you'll find single origin espresso, filter coffee, batch brew and cold drip. Grind Into Gear also sources varieties from El Salvador, Ethiopia, Kenya and Honduras.

'...staff who thrive on making coffee drinking a true experience for each and every customer.'

As well as high quality coffee choices, Paul has harnessed his experience in fine dining restaurants and cafes to ensure there's an on-trend menu filled with produce from artisan providers. The dishes are inspired by Spanish and Mediterranean flavours and can cater to all dietary needs.

Dark wood tables and charcoal coloured walls sit calmly beneath the caged pendant lights and large floor-to-ceiling windows. Grind Into Gear is currently open Monday to Friday 7am to 5pm, and till 3pm on weekends. Keep an eye out in late 2015, when they plan to add dinner service. This brand new cafe is sure to continue blossoming into an extremely popular destination for business types, young families and Stanmore locals.

While still in its infancy, having been open only a few short months, it has already gained a dedicated following. Get here quickly, before the queue is out the door!

THE GROUNDS OF ALEXANDRIA

BUILDING 7A, 2 HUNTLY ST, ALEXANDRIA · 02 9699 2225 · GROUNDSROASTERS.COM

MACHINE: La Marzocco GS/2, Synesso Cyncra & Hydra, Steampunk Mod 2.1
GRINDER: Mahlkönig EK43, Victoria Arduino Mythos 1
BEANS: Grounds Roasters Seasonal Blend and seasonal Single Origins
BREWING METHODS: Espresso, Kalita Pour Over Filter, AeroPress, French Press, Oji Cold Drip, Steampunk

It will take you more than one visit to be able to truly appreciate everything that's going on at The Grounds of Alexandria. Located in a 1920s industrial precinct, the area has been artfully transformed into four distinct but related spaces: The Garden, The Roastery, The Potting Shed and The Atrium.

The Garden is self-explanatory; it's where the fresh produce for the cafes at The Grounds is grown. It's also a lovely, calming space for visitors, with a full time horticulturist member of staff, as well as a family of chickens. The Atrium is a gorgeous, light filled events and group bookings space, which has played host to many weddings since it opened.

The Potting Shed is a restaurant that opens for lunch and dinner, and The Roastery is just that – a roaster with an adjoining cafe. The brainchild of creative entrepreneur, Ramzey Choker, and his business partner, Jack Hanna, The Grounds of Alexandria has injected a palpable sense of excitement into the previously industrial area of Alexandria.

Jack manages the team of wholesale staff, the roasters and the baristas. He has always had a strong interest in coffee and was the youngest barista to win a world title: The World Latte Art Championships in 2007, and the 2010 Winner of Golden Bean Espresso.

The beans Jack oversees at The Grounds are selected for their unique qualities and are sourced from all around the world, including Brazil, Colombia, Ethiopia, India and Uganda. The Grounds are constantly changing the blends and rotating single origins in order to achieve the best tasting coffee possible. Jack oversees the roasting operation with a perfectionist's touch, bringing an uncompromising and unparalleled drive for quality that extends not only to the coffee experience at The Grounds but also to caffeine lovers all over the country – who order from the rapidly growing wholesale arm of the business.

The Grounds of Alexandria offers filter coffee, pour over, cold drip, AeroPress, steampunk and French press, and brew espressos on a custom rebuilt La Marzocco, circa 1980, which comes from the original Starbucks cafe in Seattle.

A visit to The Grounds of Alexandria could easily take a whole day; visitors come for brunch, wander about to say hello to the resident animals, explore the gardens and check out the wonderfully unique and hidden spaces like The Lock In, The BBQ and The Bakery. On weekends once a month, there's a market in the cafe garden where guests can buy wholesome foods and produce, listen to live music and enjoy the petting zoo – featuring the star of The Grounds, the pig Kevin Bacon!

We think The Grounds put it best themselves: "Inspired by a holistic seed-to-plate philosophy, The Grounds is a sensory feast that provides an abundance of wholesome experiences all within an inner city oasis."

'...the area has been artfully transformed into four distinct but related spaces...'

HAM HARRY & MARIO

3/17 GERRALE ST, CRONULLA · 02 8521 7219 · HAMHARRYANDMARIO.COM

MACHINE: La Marzocco Linea
GRINDER: Robur E, 3 Phase Robur, Robur Major
BEANS: Own Blend, Roasted by Bassett Espresso
BREWING METHODS: Espresso, Cold Drip, Filter, Cold Brew

PERHAPS THE BEST PERSON TO RUN A BUSINESS WITH IS YOUR BROTHER. You've grown up together, you know each other's strengths (and shortcomings), and while there may be a history of bickering and rivalry, when the chips are down, brothers pull together.

Harry and Mario Kapoulas clearly think so too, as they opened Ham Harry and Mario together in 2008, and it's still going strong. Both have worked as baristas in the past and have run local cafes and restaurants, including the Nun's Pool, Grind and Kafenio. As the name suggests, they're both equally invested in their newest venture and are a great support to one another.

Another big part of Ham's success is World Barista Champion, Paul Bassett. Harry and Mario believe Paul to be one of the most knowledgeable and skilled baristas in the world. The World Champion title seems to back that up! Paul plays a big part in the business, not only training the baristas on a monthly basis, but also by selecting and roasting the majority of the coffee sold at Ham Harry and Mario. Having their roaster so personally involved in their business means that he can give them special advice about things like the perfect dose levels, and give them an insight into what is happening at the roastery.

The cafe offers three different coffees daily. For milk-based coffees, there's a blend that Paul has hand-picked and developed specifically for Ham – the Ham Blend. He's recently redeveloped it, making sure it has enough punch to cut through milk, without being too harsh. It has flavours of dark chocolate with mixed berries, stone fruits and toffee and is made up of a Guatemalan bean from the Santa Rita Estate, a Brazilian bean from the Cambara Estate, and an Ethiopian bean from the Guji Oromia region.

For black coffees, Ham uses its black blend, an Ethiopian Sidamo coffee, using 50% washed beans and 50% natural process beans. The third coffee is a single estate, which changes weekly.

There are hints of the brothers' Greek heritage everywhere, including the food menu, but you can also see it on the coffee menu. Try a Greek Frappe for something different; or stick with what you know and choose from iced lattes, cold drip, cold brew and filter coffee.

Ham Harry and Mario was one of the first cafes in Cronulla to steer away from the main mall areas, and its corner position has become popular with the locals. The building itself was built in the 1950s, and although it went under renovation just before they moved in, it appealed to Harry and Mario because the bones of the building, including the feather red bricks, remained intact.

From Mums and bubs, to university students, to the occasional sports star, Ham Harry and Mario attract them all, for breakfast and lunch, seven days a week!

> 'As the name suggests, they're both equally invested in their newest venture and are a great support to one another.'

HANDCRAFT SPECIALTY COFFEE

67 KING ST, NEWTOWN · 02 9550 3701 · FACEBOOK.COM/HANDCRAFTCOFFEE

MACHINE: La Marzocco Strada EP
GRINDER: Mazzer Robur E and Mahlkönig EK43
BEANS: St Ali, Sensory Lab, Proud Mary, Reuben Hills
BREWING METHODS: Espresso, V60 Pour Over, AeroPress

  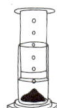 

JOHN LEE KNOWS HIS COFFEE. Evidence? Well, for a start, he's worked as a barista at places such as The Source at Mosman and Dose at Willoughby. But experience aside, all you need to do is take a look at the coffee John and his wife, Monica, have chosen to serve to see that this guy knows his stuff. If we mention names like St. Ali, Sensory Lab, Proud Mary, Reuben Hills, Market Lane and Small Batch, you'll see what we mean... the best coffee, from the best roasters in the country.

The sleek white walls and dark wood floors give Handcraft Specialty Coffee a minimalist, clean feel without being too clinical. Pendant lights hang in a line above the bar and the striking white La Marzocco Strada EP stands proudly to greet you as you come in.

Offering Newtown's biggest range of filter coffee choices, a who's who of single origins and blends from roasters around the country, and a house blend made by St Ali in Melbourne, Handcraft Specialty Coffee has taken Newtown by storm. The house blend is Orthodox and is made from Colombian San Agustin Supremo, and Brazilian Rainha Yellow Bourbon. Roasted medium to light, it is full bodied, smooth and balanced, with chocolate notes and hints of red fruit. It's delectable in milk – and with Australia's overwhelming preference for milk-based coffees, it's no wonder John and Monica selected it.

The rotating single origin offerings come to Newtown from places like Panama, Ethiopia, Honduras, Kenya, Guatemala and Colombia; John hand picks a different coffee for filter coffee and black coffees on a weekly basis. Customers can also opt for V60 or AeroPress and in the near future Handcraft Specialty Coffee plans to start offering old school French press, too. Keep an eye out - there's a focus overall on lighter roasted coffees. John said that even though they're more complicated to make, they're also more enjoyable to drink so it's worth the effort.

Handcraft Specialty Coffee is open for breakfast and lunch, Monday to Saturday and is frequented by customers of all ages, from students, coffee geeks and hipsters to Mums, work colleagues and seniors. Monica, whose childhood was spent in Brazil, heads up the kitchen. Some items on offer feature a South American twist; namely The Pastel, a savoury Brazilian fried pastry, which is served with tomato ketchup and chilli sauce.

There are North American influences too, with a ham and pickle sandwich (the pickle comes in especially from Detriot), with cheese and tomato.

One last thing – would you do us a favour? Be the first to start the ball rolling on the suspended coffee experience at Handcraft Specialty Coffee. They're keen to offer the service, but no-one's asked about it yet.

'A who's who of single origins and blends from roasters around the country...'

IN THE ANNEX

35 ROSS ST, FOREST LODGE · 02 8041 6536 · FACEBOOK.COM/INTHEANNEXCAFE

MACHINE: Keys Van Der Westin Spirit
GRINDER: Nuova Simonelli Mythos and Anfim Caiamano
BEANS: Umami Coffee Roasters and alternating single origins
BREWING METHODS: Espresso, MoccaMaster Batch Brew, V60 Pour Over, Chemex, Cold Drip

IN THE ANNEX IS THE PRODUCT OF EDRICK SANTOS' LONG AND ENLIGHTENING JOURNEY INTO THE COFFEE INDUSTRY, BUT IT'S BEEN WELL WORTH THE WAIT. This cafe is the culmination of knowledge from a decade in the hospitality industry, the ups and downs, failures and successes and the endless lessons learned along the way.

After diving in the deep end a little early and buying a cafe with his brother, Ed soon realised he needed more experience and walked away. He took his time to gain some invaluable experience through hard work and dedication at some of the best cafes in Sydney. He also travelled to the USA, New Zealand and Europe, where he experienced different brew methods and different ways to extract espresso.

After the learning came the all-important venue choice. It took almost a year for co-owner, Theo Hlorotiris (the man behind the successful Fish on Fire franchise), and Ed to transform the space from its previous life as a chemist into what is now, a relaxed, well-lived-in space. The recycled and repurposed materials are evident throughout the entire venue. The fence paling on the front counter is from a neighbour's house, the ladders on the walls come from Theo's father and the artwork featured is from local artists. It definitely creates a relaxed and homely setting to enjoy a highly sought after cup of coffee.

> 'The fence paling on the front counter is from a neighbour's house, the ladders on the walls come from Theo's father...'

The house blend is roasted by Umami Coffee Roasters and is comprised of four origins: Ethiopia, Brazil, Sumatra and India. Ed and Theo tried many variations, but the Indian Mysore gave it a dimension they couldn't predict or pass up. The Brazilian gives the body and taste you'd expect and the Sumatran cups offer something very floral, akin to bergamot.

Also on offer are alternating single origins and filter coffees from a host of different roasters, including Reuben Hills, Sample, Sensory Lab and Golden Cobra. There are even samples from around the world, like drip coffee from Sweden, and US coffee, Stumptown, Ritual, Sightglass and Heart.

In the kitchen you'll find chefs from two and three Hat restaurants and Michelin starred European venues, so you know your tastebuds are going to be pleased.

People come from all over to try out In The Annex on the weekends. During the week you'll find a strong local contingent – professionals on their way into the city, staff from the nearby hospital and Sydney uni students. There's also a good representation of local musicians that come to hang out here, too.

JOHN SMITH SPECIALTY COFFEE

1 JOHN ST, WATERLOO · 0422 855 811 · JOHNSMITHCAFE.COM

MACHINE: Synesso Hydra
GRINDER: Mazzer Roubur E and Mahlkönig EK43
BEANS: Rebel Roaster
BREWING METHODS: Espresso, Cold Drip, Pour Over, AeroPress

AN UNASSUMING NAME, MAYBE, BUT THIS CAFE HAS FIRMLY CEMENTED ITSELF AS ONE OF THE MUST-TRY CAFES FOR SYDNEY-SIDERS. Housed in an old bakery, John Smith Specialty Coffee was born in March 2014. The motivation was simple: the team had a vision of bringing together good food and great coffee under the same roof.

The heritage building has been given a breath of new life, with vibrant, colourful booths and bar-style seating facing the windows. The apparatus required for the large range of coffee offerings even line the walls - it really is a coffee-lovers' haven.

The baristas at John Smith are always striving to get the best they can in the cup and are big on educating their customers. The public can join them for public cupping sessions in the cafe – a great way to gain appreciation for your daily cup and perhaps give those in the know some hints about what origins you'd like to see served up next.

John Smith sources its coffee from its sister company, Rebel Roaster. The house blend they like to keep consistent with tasting notes of chocolate and a hint of berry, but it's in the black coffee that these boys really get to showcase their unique talent, bringing a variety of flavours to the cup. They source their guest beans from anywhere they believe has unique tasting flavours. Kenya and Ethiopia are current John Smith favourites but in the end, it always comes down to taste.

As well as espresso and milky coffees, these coffee connoisseurs happily brew up cold drip, cold brew, pour over and AeroPress coffees – unsurprisingly the cold drip is a real hit in the warm summer months.

John Smith Specialty Coffee thankfully serves breakfast and lunch all day. You can get Eggs Benedict in any self-respecting cafe, but here they serve it with pulled pork. The runny yolks combining with the tender pork and crusty sourdough makes for a meal straight from heaven. The seasonal veggie salad on the side is the perfect complement. To finish, try one of Brewtown Newtown's Brewnuts (think cronut), or a treat supplied by Little Secrets Bakehouse.

There's a real buzz here, a welcoming atmosphere from friendly staff who genuinely care that each and every customer has the best experience possible. The baristas and wait staff happily talk customers through coffee choices and are attentive and friendly. No wonder John Smith Specialty Coffee has so quickly become Waterloo's happy place.

> 'It's in the black coffee that these boys really get to showcase their unique talent, bringing a variety of flavours to the cup.'

KAIMAKI CAFE

4-9 MONTGOMERY ST, KOGARAH · 02 9553 0600 · KAIMAKICAFE.COM.AU/

MACHINE: La Marzocco
GRINDER: Mazzer
BEANS: Ducale Coffee, Monsoon
BREWING METHODS: Espresso

IT'S A WELL-KNOWN FACT THAT THE BEST BUSINESS MEETINGS HAPPEN OVER COFFEE. At Kaimaki, the cafe smack bang in Kogarah's business district, this might as well be its motto. Offering its local workers crafted coffee and fantastic fare, it's no wonder so many flock to its corner-side position.

Owner Nick has run Kaimaki for the last 14 years, ensuring locals and first-time visitors are getting a good cup of brew and a meal worth leaving the office for. After plying his trade in city cafes, he decided to venture out on his own, managing his own cafe while also taking the role of head barista. That's not to say he only has fingers in two pies – he's very hands-on and particular, meaning every product is specifically chosen for its high quality and passes by his discerning eyes before it reaches your cup or plate.

Considering his shrewd eye for quality, it's no surprise Nick has chosen Ducale Coffee's Monsoon as Kaimaki's house blend. With a pink candy stick musk and almond perfumes, the lively and complex blend features deep, dry cocoa and rich toffee flavours, with a slight orange or mandarin zest finish. Despite its heavy body, it has a very low acidity, making it perfect for milk-based drinks, bringing out sweet cocoa and malt tastes. Beans are sourced from India, where they are processed by the Monsoon Malabar method, as well as Guatemala and Nicaragua.

He chose the blend because of its full body, but recognises that it's a hard bean to work with. The processing method makes the bean somewhat unstable, meaning the baristas have to keep an eye on the grinder, adjusting settings to achieve the best possible result.

Along with the full gamut of espresso offerings, they have a rotating list of single origins from Ducale and offer cold drip. There are also plans in the future to introduce the pour over method to their menu.

While the coffee might form a large part of Kaimaki's appeal, food hasn't fallen to the wayside.

Morning visitors have a whole host of dishes to choose from, including a full range of pancakes, eggs and toasted sandwiches. Snack on Turkish toast with ricotta and honey or, if the stomach's rumbling, opt for the sweet corn fritters with prosciutto, avocado, grilled tomato and rocket, or the Superman pancakes and rolled oats, with protein, ricotta, banana, berries, yoghurt and roasted almonds.

If that's just not enough protein for you, there are over ten egg-based options to choose from, including Nick's Special, a plate of scrambled eggs, spinach, ham, tomato, mushroom, feta and avocado or a Kaimaki omelette with potato, bacon, shallots, sun dried tomato, halloumi and rocket.

The black-walled space sits just seconds from Kogarah station, meaning it's perfectly placed for a morning coffee, a long lunch or a quick meeting. Just be sure to credit Nick and his team when the deal goes through.

'...the baristas have to keep an eye on the grinder, adjusting settings to achieve the best possible result.'

Social Laneway | Redfern

THE LITTLE MARIONETTE

11 MAY ST, ST PETERS · 02 9557 6980 · THELITTLEMARIONETTE.COM

GRINDER: Mazzer Robur and Kony
BEANS: Own Blend, The Little Marionette House Blend
BREWING METHODS: Espresso, V60 Pour Over, AeroPress, Filter, Cold Brew

THE LITTLE MARIONETTE PULLS ALL THE RIGHT STRINGS TO BRING COFFEE TO LIFE: FROM EXPERT KNOWLEDGE IN AGRICULTURE AND PROCESSING TO SELECTING, ROASTING, STORING, TRAINING, SERVICE MAINTENANCE, AND EVERYTHING ELSE ALONG THE WAY. It is no wonder The Little Marionette is now the supplier of choice to countless restaurants and cafes Australia-wide.

Founder of The Little Marionette, Ed Cutcliffe, has become synonymous with quality in specialty coffee circles; here's a guy who really loves and understands coffee. Ed has been working in hospitality for more than 20 years, and roasting coffee for most of that time.

Ed's focus for The Little Marionette is spread across three key areas: quality control, customer service and producing excellent coffee. When asked what coffee means to him, Ed understandably finds it tricky to put into words. How can you quantify something that is your lifeblood, your passion?

"Every time I encounter someone along the coffee chain: farmer, operator or customer, their perception changes the way I perceive and serve coffee. When I started, I made coffee for me, and now I make coffee for the customer. Coffee is a way of life and has a lot to do with the relationships that are built around it. I believe coffee enriches these relationships."

The Little Marionette headquarters in St Peters is also a training room for wholesale customers. They also briefly open to the public, lifting the roller door for a few hours each morning to serve coffee – and only coffee. The real heart of this operation is behind the roller door and down the stairs – in the roastery.

'The real heart of this operation is behind the roller door and down the stairs – in the roastery.'

The Little Marionette team roasts crowd-pleasing blends along with carefully selected single origin beans to indulge even the most discerning of coffee nerds. Continual cupping, tasting and profiling retains the integrity of the bean.

The Little Marionette strongly favours Colombian and African beans for its blends; but their buying of green beans is based always on flavour rather than popularity. Ed's favourite region is the Huila region in Colombia – he has fond memories of the first coffees he ever bought raw and roasted.

For a coffee straight from the roller door, head down and wait amongst the artists, designers and fashion-industry types in the industrial area that houses The Little Marionette roastery.

THE LOCAL PRESS

UNIT 19/331 BALMAIN RD, LILYFIELD · 02 9818 1255 · THELOCALPRESS.COM.AU

MACHINE: La Marzocco Linea
GRINDER: Mazzer Robur E and Mahlkönig EK43
BEANS: House Blend
BREWING METHODS: Espresso, Pour Over, Batch Brew, Cold Drip

ALEX VERVERIS OPENED THE LOCAL PRESS IN LILYFIELD IN FEBRUARY 2013, AND IT QUICKLY BECAME A TRUE LOCAL HUB, WITH A FRIENDLY VIBE AND A BIG COMMUNITY FOLLOWING. Located on a corner plot near the Orange Grove Organic Market, the cafe is right across from a playground, making life easy for coffee loving Mums and Dads.

Intrigued and infatuated by the whole process of coffee from origin to cup, Alex has a strong interest in sourcing and roasting specialty coffee. Today, The Local Press roasts single origins in-house and also collaborates with Deluca Specialty Coffee Roasters and Fat Poppy Coffee. The house blend consists of three origins, with Colombian Munchique (washed) as the base, and Ethiopian Kochere (natural) and Sumatran Blue Bianca (wet hulled) coffees. The blend cuts well through milk, and gives strong nutty and chocolate notes with cocoa, raisin and hazelnut flavours.

The Local Press find themselves drawn to the bright, juicy and sweet characteristics of Ethiopian coffees and Head Barista, Arthur Pach, encourages the broad clientele to experiment with various coffee methods. Give pour over, batch brew and cold drip a try. If you're not sure what's what just ask Arthur, he has a wealth of coffee-related knowledge and is happy to share. Filter coffee is always available here, as well as a Sparkling Cascara Iced Tea, infused with vanilla bean, star anise and panela.

The food is delicious too; you'd be surprised at the wonders that are produced in such a small kitchen! All the sauces, relishes, pastes and pickles are made in-house. The menu in constantly evolving in order to showcase the effort The Local Press puts into sourcing ingredients from local farms and producers – from the cheese maker in Annandale to the bee-keeper in the Blue Mountains. All of the meats, poultry and eggs used are free range and there are great gluten free options available. Featured on the summer menu was the Breakfast Burrito with pulled pork, egg, refried beans, cheese and guacamole, and the grilled zucchini, smoked almonds, haloumi and white bean salad. Although the menu changes throughout the year you can be sure you'll be offered dishes that reflect the fresh, seasonal produce.

> '...a true local hub, with a friendly vibe and a big community following.'

The Local Press is the only cafe in the area that provides alternative brewing methods and the only cafe that works with specialty roasters and it's really not kidding with the 'local.' With the New South Wales Ambulance HQ across the street and a primary school next door, there's always a parade of Lilyfield residents popping in. Those enjoying their exercise on the gorgeous Bay Run or at nearby Callan Park drop by for some sustenance and on Saturdays you'll see bulging bags of organic produce at the feet of those on their way home from the Orange Grove Markets.

NANS PLACE

2 PORTMAN ST, ZETLAND · 02 8084 0731 · FACEBOOK.COM/NANSPLACESYDNEY

MACHINE: La Marzocco Linea
GRINDER: Mazzer Robur E
BEANS: Reubin Hills House Blend
BREWING METHODS: Espresso, Cold Drip, Filter

JODIE JOHNSON WANTED TO CREATE A CAFE WHERE THE WELCOME WAS COMFORTING, THE VIBE WARM AND FRIENDLY, AND SOMEWHERE THAT NEIGHBOURS WOULD DROP IN FOR A COFFEE AND CHAT – SOMEWHERE SORT OF LIKE YOUR NAN'S PLACE.

Jodie's beloved Nan influenced not only the name but also the menu and the general decor and vibe of the place. There's a grassy backyard with an outdoor seating area for 12, with herbs growing in the garden for use on the seasonal menu. Neighbours and locals do pop in here on a regular basis and Jodie knows the vast majority of her customers by name. Every cup of coffee is made with love and served with a smile. And it's good coffee, too.

Jodie started her coffee career at Campos, spending four years between 2008 and 2011 working with their famous blends, many single origins and Cups of Excellence. She then moved on to manage Reuben Hills in 2012 before setting up Nans Place in 2013. Reuben Hills' influence stayed with her and it's now the main supplier of coffee for Nans Place. Jodie likes that Russ from Reuben Hills has a direct relationship with the farmers who provide the beans and isn't afraid to experiment and push the boundaries of coffee.

The Nans Place house blend from Reuben Hills features Ethiopian Robot Mata, Guatemalan Rosma and Ethiopian Le Ilsa Hara and showcases sweet stone fruit, jasmine and cocoa notes. The house blend is always seasonal, so it changes every couple of months. Jodie likes to offer her loyal customers a variety, so their coffee, like their food, moves and changes with the seasons. There's also a blend from Sample Coffee, called The Pacemaker, which is made up of beans from Panama and Guatemala, with flavours of strawberry and a cocoa finish. Nans Place offers espresso, cold drip, filter and V60 and is open Tuesday to Sunday for breakfast and lunch all day. On Monday, they're spending the bingo winnings.

'Their coffee, like their food, moves and changes with the seasons.'

There's plenty of highlights on the menu, which changes with the season but retains some old favourites which Jodie wouldn't dare change. Take a breakfast favourite, Pop Johnson – signature bacon and egg roll with Jack Daniels sauce or for lunch, The Club – a roast chook, bacon, avo, cheddar and zucchini pickle sandwich served with coriander aioli, or the soft boiled eggs with soldiers. The Spring menu even featured a Vegemite and two cheese toastie and breakfast cous cous with dates, prunes, caramelised banana, orange and Pecora sheep yoghurt.

After the morning rush, you'll find the inevitable sprinkling of hipsters, as well as locals catching up with friends, mums and babies, and couples on cozy coffee dates. After all, isn't everyone welcome at Nans Place?

QUBE ON BAY ESPRESSO BAR

56 BAY ST, ULTIMO · 02 9212 0025

MACHINE: Mirge Veloce
GRINDER: Mazzer Robur E, Mazzer Robur Manual and Anfim
BEANS: Ona Coffee, The Founder
BREWING METHODS: Espresso, Cold Drip, AeroPress, V60 Pour Over, Chemex

QUBE ON BAY IS A VETERAN OF THE BROADWAY COFFEE SCENE, HAVING OPENED IN 2007. Owner and Manager, Jay Park, loves coffee for its ability to transcend culture and connect people. He didn't take the 'normal' route to owning a cafe (if there is such a thing), rather he came via the construction industry, where he was an accounting manager. His passion for coffee and great food shouted loudly and he quit his job and opened up Qube on Bay.

As a barista and cafe owner, it's of prime importance to Jay that he and his team feel connected to all parts of the coffee production process. His determination to understand and appreciate every level of the coffee journey aligns perfectly to the values and mission of his chosen supplier, Ona Coffee. Ona sources all its coffee through Project Origin, its sister company and green bean importer. Project Origin is committed to investing back into the communities it works with, raising funds for childcare services, doctors, schools, libraries, processing mills and housing. This connection with the coffee producing communities, and Ona Coffee's work empowering growers and ensuring strong outcomes in their communities, really spoke to Jay, and he proudly supplies One Coffee's product to his customers in Ultimo.

The house blend at Qube on Bay is Ona Coffee's The Founder, which is made of three origins: Supersonic, Ahuachapán and El Salvador. It is a naturally processed coffee that is picked between 1500 and 1600 metres, and is dried at 1700 metres, allowing the flavours to mature. As well as the Ona Coffee house blend, Qube on Bay also rotates guest beans from various roasters, including a guest bean of the week. The staff are more than happy to take you through what is on offer that particular week, and what philosophies the roasters work to.

On the menu you'll find some interesting options – Very Healthy is a seasonal fruit bowl with natural yoghurt, honey and Farmer Jo's muesli. Very Tasty is Bircher muesli. Very Very Healthy is crushed avocado and feta on toast with pumpkin seeds and lemon juice, while Don't Even Ask is a grilled halloumi stack with poached egg, avocado, roasted tomato and rocket. Some very filling lunch options include the Butcher's Block and the Pulled Pork Burger.

The mismatched furniture and retro decorations give the cafe a relaxed, welcoming feel, and the cold drip contraption makes a great focal point and conversation starter. There's a courtyard that makes a great sun-trap, and tables out the front for people watching. The spacious interior and courtyard mean it's a great place for families with prams, but you're more likely to see Yummy Mummies kid-less, catching up for a coffee after school drop off time.

> 'This connection with the coffee producing communities, and Ona Coffee's work empowering growers... really spoke to Jay...'

SINGLE ORIGIN ROASTERS BOTANY

28B CRANBROOK ST, BOTANY · 02 9316 9699 · SINGLEORIGINROASTERS.COM.AU

MACHINE: La Marzocco Linea PB
GRINDER: Mahlkönig EK43, Mazzer Robur E
BEANS: Reservoir
BREWING METHODS: Espresso, Cold Drip, Hario V60 Pour Over

WE CAN ALL AGREE THAT WHERE THERE'S GREAT COFFEE, THERE'S PASSIONATE, DRIVEN PEOPLE SOURCING, TASTING, TESTING, ROASTING AND SERVING IT. At Single Origin Roasters, these people just happen to be at the top of their game and at the top of the industry.

Single Origin Roasters has been impressing and delighting Surry Hills locals at its Reservoir Street address for over a decade, but 2014 saw another feather in the cap of Single O – a coffee bar located right at the doors of its roast works in Botany. Now you can drink the coffee while listening to the next batch being roasted next door (from the right spot you can even catch a glimpse inside). This coffee bar is 8-metres long and unsurprisingly the longest (albeit the narrowest) coffee bar in Botany.

Dion and Emma Cohen founded Single Origin Roasters in 2003, and now proudly supply cafes all over the country. Their Coffee Buyer and Quality Controller, Wendy De Jong, is one of those industry leaders we mentioned. Hailing from the United States, Wendy has dedicated her life to working within every level in the coffee world – from serving brews from a street cart in Seattle, to repairing grinders, to roasting coffee, to sourcing and importing it. Wendy is a judge for prestigious coffee quality competitions, including Cup of Excellence, and now leads the QC team for Single Origin Roasters.

'Try if you can, to get a seat at the far end of the bar, so that you can peek from the front of house to the business end...'

The Botany cafe serves the house blend Reservoir, the first of many blends from Single Origin Roasters, named after the street of the original cafe. It features flavours of ripe stone fruits, structured and vibrant acidity, a delicate body and a clean finish. It embodies Single O's love of bright, structured coffees and comes alive with milk.

Four single origin coffees per month are offered for black espresso and filter methods, directly sourced by Wendy. The team of baristas, led by Sean McManus, delights in offering all of the new style coffees here too – cold brew, pour over, Cascara creations and other seasonal coffee beverages. There are a few Cup of Excellence winners to try and often rare and unique coffees from all over the world.

The cafe opens Monday to Friday 6:30am until 3pm for breakfast and lunch, with the all-day menu offering everything from banana bread with espresso butter to the house specialty, the Mothership Breakfast (the roast works is nicknamed The Mothership). This signature dish changes seasonally but currently features Lamb Merguez, poached eggs, tomato salad with minted yoghurt and Za'atar on sourdough.

Try if you can, to get a seat at the far end of the bar, so that you can peek from the front of house to the business end, where all that wonderful coffee from around the world is lovingly roasted.

SOCIAL LANEWAY

SHOP 5/157-161 REDFERN ST, REDFERN · 0457 775 000 · SOCIAL-LANEWAY.COM

MACHINE: Mirage
GRINDER: Mazzer Robur E
BEANS: Own Blend, Social Laneway Espresso
BREWING METHODS: Espresso

MARINA AGUSTINA AND ROBERT IAN BONNICK ARE BUILDING THEMSELVES QUITE AN EMPIRE IN REDFERN THESE DAYS. Their fashion and events business, Social-Laneway, has blossomed to create Social-Laneway Espresso, a place for them to indulge their love of coffee.

Marina and Robert started with the important stuff – they found a house blend with a slight chocolate taste from Bespoke Coffee Traders after several cuppings and way too many late night coffee shots. They appreciate the science of coffee and are dedicated to perfecting every step, from how the bean is roasted to the way in which the milk is poured into your cup.

The blend they chose contains Ethiopian and Papua New Guinean beans. The beans are washed then soaked for up to 72 hours in fermentation tanks. This wet-process method produces intensely flavoured beans with a floral aroma and a mellow, sweet taste. The Ethiopian bean is a Yirgacheffe, the most favoured coffee grown in southern Ethiopia. It is mild, fruit-like and aromatic. The Papua New Guinea bean adds a kick to the blend with its full-bodied flavour.

The venue itself has been given a beautiful fit-out using recycled timber on the walls while plenty of books are scattered about for customers to peruse while enjoying their coffee. The food is served up on wooden boards and there's a gorgeous al fresco area, the ideal place to soak up the gorgeous Sydney weather. There's a warm vibe here, friendly and modern. Set in a laneway near the train station, there's a constant buzz coming to and from and within the cafe.

Social-Laneway Espresso is open for breakfast and lunch, seven days a week. They're even open on Thursday and Friday nights for dinner – when the espresso bar transforms into a wine bar. Be sure to stop in for what has become a firm favourite at Social-Laneway Espresso – a bowl of their own specialty spicy meatballs, matched with their Pinot Noir or Shiraz. There's also a lovely dessert selection on offer. During the day, try the berry muesli, or the All Day Breakfast, a long wooden board filled with delectable treats: soft scrambled eggs with shallots, crispy bacon, sourdough toast and fresh avocado. Lunchtime brings the generous Gourmet Pumpkin Tart with garden salad. For a sweet treat, there's a cake display to tempt you – I bet you can't go past the strawberry tart with ice cream.

'...there's a gorgeous al fresco area, the ideal place to soak up the gorgeous Sydney weather.'

While you're there, be sure to add a suspended coffee to your order. Social-Laneway participates in the Random Acts of Kindness through oneHug – which allows customers to purchase a coffee for a stranger with the hope that they will then 'pay it forward' and do something kind for someone else. It's certainly all about the love at Social-Laneway: the love of a great coffee.

SONOMA BAKING COMPANY

32-44 BIRMINGHAM ST, ALEXANDRIA · 02 9690 2060 · SONOMA.COM.AU

MACHINE: San Remo
GRINDER: Mazzer Robur
BEANS: Own Blend, Sonoma
BREWING METHODS: Espresso, Cold Drip, Cold Brew

When Andrew and Christian Connole's father decided to restore an old bake-house in Bellata, New South Wales, many deemed it wishful thinking. With not one ounce of baking experience between the father and his sons, they were embarking on a difficult journey. Fast forward a number of years and you have Sonoma Baking Company, an artisan bakery with six Sydney locations – renowned amongst food-lovers and influencers for it's authentic sourdough and pastries. In 2014, Sonoma introduced a roaster to this mix.

Andrew, the Founder, learnt his craft in the United States where he stayed with Alan Scott, an Australian who pioneered wood-fired oven building for artisan bakeries and Chad Robertson, producer of what Andrew considered to be the best sourdough he'd ever tasted.

The first loaf of what would be known as Sonoma bread was baked in 1998 and after a move to Sydney, the first wholesale loaf of sourdough bread was sold in 2001. From there, they moved to their current headquarters in Alexandria, where Andrew embarked on working with his second love, coffee. Together with Gavin Folden, Founder of Single Origin Roasters, Andrew worked to perfect a personal blend to be used in Sonoma cafes, moving the roasting process in-house in 2014 with Gavin at the helm. The result is three boutique blends, Spirit, Mind and Body, roasted in small batches and available to order or take home.

Sonoma's Spirit Blend is the cafe's house blend, a medium-full roast with flavours of dark cocoa, caramelised raisin and plum. It's ideal for non-milk based brew methods, and is made from a combination of specialty grade beans from the top 83+ percentile. They don't discriminate on region, instead choosing the best beans from each plantation in places such as Mexico, Guatemala, South America and Papua New Guinea.

The Mind Blend is a lighter roast, ideal for all brew methods. It's 100% organic, with honeycomb, nectarine and chocolate flavours. The Body Blend, a darker roast, is ideal for milk-based brew methods with a flavour profile of roasted walnut, toffee apple and apricot. When the mercury rises, cold brew is also on offer.

Coffee aside, Sonoma hasn't forgotten its bakery roots. Bread, including its famous sourdough and other baked goods, are available for sale. The breakfast menu artfully incorporates the products, including banana bread with ricotta and almond, fruit spelt toast with Sonoma jam, and baked eggs with feta and chickpea ragout. Tartines and sandwiches are also on offer for those on the go.

'With cafes in Woollahra, Alexandria, Paddington, Glebe, Waterloo and Bondi, Sonoma is at your fingertips.'

With cafes in Woollahra, Alexandria, Paddington, Glebe, Waterloo and Bondi, Sonoma is at your fingertips no matter where you live. Go for the breakfast, stay for the coffee and leave with more than just a full stomach, taking the artisan beans and bread home with you.

THREE ROSETTAS ESPRESSO BAR & CAFE

SHOP 11 / 38-50 LYONS RD, DRUMMOYNE · 02 9181 3937 · FACEBOOK.COM/THREEROSETTASESPRESSOBARCAFE

MACHINE: La Marzocco GB/5
GRINDER: Mazzer Robur, Mahlkönig EK43
BEANS: House Blend, Sensory Lab, Steadfast and various single origins
BREWING METHODS: Espresso, Cold Drip, Syphon, AeroPress, V60 Pour Over

NAMED AFTER THE THEIR THREE DAUGHTERS AND THE WELL-KNOWN LATTE ART DESIGN, THREE ROSETTAS ESPRESSO BAR & CAFE IS A POPULAR LOCAL HUB OFTEN FILLED WITH FAMILIES, FRIENDS AND LOCAL BUSINESS PEOPLE. The coffee is superb, the food is wholesome and you will quickly be forgiven if you think you have walked into someone's family home.

When it comes to talking to people, cafe owner, George Melky, is never short for words. With his roots in milk bars and corner stores, George couldn't pass an opportunity to open up his own cafe in 2010 with his wife, Lina, by his side.

"Opening this cafe is something I have spoken about for years," George said, "and I can honestly say it is the best decision we have ever made. I have always loved coffee and as a family we love venturing out and trying different cafes, so it was the perfect next step for me."

As far as the coffee goes, it is fair to say this cafe is producing some of the finest espresso in Sydney. The Three Rosettas' team works very closely with Melbourne roasters, Sensory Lab, to ensure they are at the top of their game and on track with the ever changing coffee trends. The house blend, Steadfast, is a medium bodied coffee that is complemented with milk and really comes to life when served black.

For the serious coffee lovers out there, Three Rosettas also offers a different single origin or guest blend every day. Each espresso is served with a side of sparkling water to cleanse the palate, and tasting notes to guide you through the flavours. A few of their favourites include Marvell Street, Clement, Proud Mary, Industry Beans, Seven Seeds, Market Lane and Wide Open Road.

'Each espresso is served with a side of sparkling water to cleanse the palate, and tasting notes to guide you through the flavours.'

And maybe the best part of your experience will be the knowledge passed on to you by George and the team. Whether you're purchasing beans to take home or an AeroPress for the office, you are guaranteed to have all your questions answered.

Head Barista, Alberto Fuerte, fits the mould perfectly with his rosetta tattoo on his hand and his many years of experience in the industry. Alberto prides himself on his consistency and training. With every shot of coffee weighed, you can sure bet each and every espresso has its full flavours extracted. He won't disappoint you with his mastered latte art and passion for coffee.

Extending their coffee menu beyond espresso based coffees, Three Rosettas offers a selection of filter coffees and alternative brew methods. Alberto's speciality is the AeroPress and he always manages to impress a crowd with his performance. You'll need room at the table for George and Alberto to join you and take you through the brewing method.

This cafe offers a cosy indoor dining space where images of the family's travels mark the walls, and a generous size courtyard where one can enjoy the sunshine and watch the local shoppers pass by. Locals and visitors flock for the all-day breakfast, and one can't go past the smashed av, schnitty sambo, the BLAT and the ever changing weekly specials. For a little indulgence, dive into one of the freshly baked muffins.

It is fair to say this cafe offers more than just great coffee and good food, it offers service, expertise and a place where the local community gets together and becomes part of George's family.

TOBY'S ESTATE COFFEE ROASTERS

32-36 CITY RD, CHIPPENDALE · 02 9112 1131 · TOBYSESTATE.COM.AU

MACHINE: Kees van der Westen Spirit Duette Bastone
GRINDER: Mazzer Robur, Mazzer Robur Manual and Mazzer Kony
BEANS: Toby's Estate, Woolloomooloo and weekly rotating Single Origins
BREWING METHODS: Espresso, Cold Brew, Chemex, V60 Pour Over

TOBY'S ESTATE IN CHIPPENDALE INNOVATIVELY INCORPORATES THE PLACEMENT OF A WINDOW BETWEEN THE CAFE AND THE ROASTERY. It means Toby's Estate regulars can see that the flagship roastery is actually located right behind the wall. Now the customers make a beeline for the bench seat that overlooks the roastery, so that while they sip their Toby's Estate blend or single origins, they can watch Master Roaster, Chris Bonney, hard at work with his team creating the specialty blends Toby's Estate are so famous for.

Toby Smith's coffee story is a well-known one around Sydney. He travelled to Brazil in 1998 and worked on coffee plantations, learning what he could and getting to know the farmers and the families who produced the beans. He knew that someone needed to get this coffee into the hands of coffee lovers, without it going through mass processing and big business. He came home, learned to roast in his Mum's garage, and now Toby's Estate coffee is the coffee of choice in over 600 independent cafes across Australia. You can also find it in New York, Singapore and Manila, thank you very much.

While Toby's Estate sources its beans from all over the globe, Toby is especially proud of the beans grown on his own farm, Finca Santa Teresa, in Panama. "I work very closely with the roasting team to develop a really specific profile from the beans grown on the farm, with our La Trinidad blend as the best example of what we have created from the farm," Toby explained.

The house blend, Woolloomooloo, (named after the suburb where Toby first began his coffee journey) is the most popular, with its big mouthful of body and flavour. Chris describes it as "syrupy, and round with notes of spice, earth, cocoa and caramel, with a hint of brightness to keep it lively."

In addition to the house blend and other espresso blends, Toby's Estate offers a selection of its single origins, which change daily. Included in this rotation are three Geishas from the farm in Panama, which use washed, natural and honey processing. 2013 was the first year Toby's Estate created the natural and honey Geisha, and they both won awards in the Best of Panama.

Before it was a cafe, the venue was the Kennett Ladder Company. Kennett's left a few old wooden ladders behind, and they're now hung on the walls to pay homage to the venue's history. So take a seat by the window into the world of roasting, or by the floor-to-ceiling windows filling the space with sunlight, and continue your coffee education. If you're really keen, sign up for an Espresso Class and learn the secrets of the trade from the very best!

'Take a seat by the window into the world of roasting...'

TWO CHAPS TRADING

122 CHAPEL ST, MARRICKVILLE • 02 9572 8858 • TWOCHAPS.COM.AU

MACHINE: La Marzocco Strada MP
GRINDER: Mazzer Robur and Ditting 1401
BEANS: The Blind Coffee Roaster, El Chapel
BREWING METHODS: Espresso, Pour Over, Cold Brew

BEHIND A ROLLER DOOR AND INSIDE WHAT WAS ONCE A METAL-WELDER'S WORKSHOP, TWO CHAPS BEGAN AS A SPACE FOR SPECIALTY TEA PRODUCTION AND THE LAUNCHPAD FOR THE BLIND COFFEE ROASTER. The smells of Sticky Chai being hand mixed in the back of the warehouse and the smoky aromas emitted from the chimney drew a few curious locals to the front window. Two Chaps responded to this curiosity by officially opening the cafe in early 2014 to serve their wares and begin the next project with a hand-me-down bakery trucked over from Rozelle's Pierre Labancz.

Now they've thrown open the big door entirely and have fitted out the 1960's warehouse as a funky eatery within the restored brick building. The roastery was relocated to nearby Botany as demand for more seats had to be met, although the Sticky Chai is still made on Mondays when the cafe closes for a breather.

The house blend, El Chapel, was developed for its all-round endless flavour and body, which proves a winner with any milk-based coffee. As Owner, Piero Pignatti, put it, 'It is a perfect nostalgia trip for those seeking the punchy yet articulate double ristretto of the late 2000s." The single origins coffees range from common faces on the specialty scene to some smaller, exclusive batches and there are often guest coffees from friends roasting interstate. In addition to the house blend, there is always a new single origin on offer as well as a weekly filter roast that can be had as a pour over, batch brew on the Moccamaster or as an overnight cold brew.

Head Barista, Graeme Alexander and Head Chef, Kim Douglas, lead the keen crew of coffee and food enthusiasts who produce the daily fare at Two Chaps. Everything is made from scratch and the menu is kept simple aiming purely to highlight the locally sourced produce of the week, either as a sandwich on the house baked ciabatta or as a seasonal confit served atop wild yeasted sourdough as a bruschetta. There is also a comprehensive daily pastry offering laid out in the massive glass cabinet. Two Chaps is also open two nights a week offering delicious handmade pasta and elaborate desserts conceived by Pastry Chef, Hayley Macdougall.

The folks of Marrickville sure are pleased that roller door came up to reveal the treasures within.

> 'They've thrown open the big door entirely and have fitted out the 1960's warehouse as a funky eatery...'

WICKS PARK CAFE

199 VICTORIA RD, MARRICKVILLE · 02 9518 0771 · WICKSPARK.COM.AU

MACHINE: Synesso
GRINDER: Anfim
BEANS: Double Roasters, Flight Path
BREWING METHODS: Espresso, Cold Drip

It took the discovery of the team and produce at Double Roasters to convince Jerry, the current owner, to dive back into the coffee business, taking over Wicks Park Cafe in Marrickville. After working with the mass-produced coffee of a chain, he was ready for something a lot more personal.

Formerly known as Double Roasters, Wicks Park Cafe was started by Scott Robertson, James Brown and Gary Parkes in 2011, with the intention of deepening their knowledge and understanding of coffee, developing their own blend on the way. The original plan was to roast coffee on-site and wholesale with a small cafe section for clients and walk-in customers to sample its products.

The cafe side of the business grew exponentially, selling 160 kilograms of coffee per week from the premises. In 2013 the roastery was separated from the cafe before the boys decided to let go of the cafe and focus on the coffee bean business. This is where current owner, Jerry, came in, bringing six years' hospitality experience to the table. He's followed the mantra 'if it's not broken, don't fix it,' keeping the same menu and Double Roasters' coffee.

The interior of Wicks Park Cafe also hasn't changed, retaining the warehouse feel, with exposed steel beams, high ceilings, natural timber furniture and the iconic diagram of a roaster on the wall. If a drawing isn't enough, there's also a vintage roaster in the corner, giving customers an inside glance into the process.

The house blend, provided by the boys at Double Roasters just down the road, is looked after by Head Barista, Yama Kim. Named Flight Path, it features beans from Brazil, Colombia and Costa Rica, combining to produce a rich and smooth consistency with notes of dark chocolate, hazelnuts and brown sugar. It binds beautifully with milk, a result of its balanced flavours. It's so named after the low-flying aircraft from the nearby airport. If it really takes your fancy, there are beans available to take home too. Coffee adventurers can also try the single origin on offer, iced coffee, cold drip and the cafe's unique double tonic: a combination of espresso, tonic and lemon.

Manager, Michael Stewart, has more than 10 years of hospitality experience and is an important and essential member of the team. His profound sense of what a great cafe should be shapes the culture and guarantees customer satisfaction.

Wicks Park is a one-stop shop and the food meets the same standard as its caffeinated companion. Try layered bircher muesli with apples, dates and toasted macadamias or corn and zucchini fritters with avocado salsa, jalapeño crème fraiche and a poached egg. Lunch options include a roast pork belly sandwich with apple and mint relish or a kale salad with dates, toasted almonds, cherry tomato, goats' cheese and fattoush bread.

> 'Wicks Park is a one-stop shop and the food meets the same standard as its caffeinated companion.'

John Smith Cafe | Waterloo

Byron Bay Coffee Company | Byron Bay

REGIONAL NEW SOUTH WALES

REGIONAL NEW SOUTH WALES

1. B-Side Espresso — 423
2. Barefoot Brew Room — 424
3. Bayleaf Cafe — 427
4. Bills Beans East Orange — 428
5. Byron Bay Coffee Company — 431
6. Cafe Cappello — 432
7. Cassiopeia — 435
8. Delano Specialty Coffee — 436
9. Fat Goose Cafe (The) — 441
10. Glass Onion Society (The) — 442
11. Good Brother Espresso Shop — 445
12. Good Eddy — 446
13. Republic of Coffee — 449
14. Social Grounds — 450
15. Suspension Espresso — 453
16. Uprising — 454

Suspension Espresso, Islington

REGIONAL BARISTAS

BILLS BEANS EAST — Erick Holborrow

I HAVE MY COFFEE…
Long and black.

IF I WASN'T A BARISTA I WOULD BE…
A stripper.

WHEN I'M NOT MAKING COFFEE I AM…
Taking my dogs for a run and hanging in my veggie patch.

CASSIOPEIA — Meghan Smith

I HAVE MY COFFEE…
Black and fruity.

IF I WASN'T A BARISTA I WOULD BE…
Living in Leh, India.

WHEN I'M NOT MAKING COFFEE I AM…
Studying interior design and learning to sew.

CAFE CAPPELLO — Tony Pilati

I HAVE MY COFFEE…
Cafe Corretto.

IF I WASN'T A BARISTA I WOULD BE…
Lost.

WHEN I'M NOT MAKING COFFEE I AM…
Fishing or playing on the family fig farm.

DELANO SPECIALTY COFFEE — David Mason

I HAVE MY COFFEE…
For breakfast, lunch and dinner.

WHEN I'M NOT MAKING COFFEE I AM…
When I'm not making coffee I am: playing gigs and recording music.

GIVE ME A QUOTE…
'Please alter my pants as fashion dictates.' – Jasper

REGIONAL BARISTAS

THE GLASS ONION SOCIETY — Ben Wright

I HAVE MY COFFEE…
with milk in the am, black after lunch.

WHEN I'M NOT MAKING COFFEE I AM…
Playing bass guitar with Tropical Zombie and Pepa Knight.

FORGET COFFEE, MY FAVOURITE PLACE TO EAT OUT IN SYDNEY IS…
Eathouse Diner, Redfern.

GOOD EDDY — Toby Howell

I HAVE MY COFFEE…
To keep the mood swings away.

IF I WASN'T A BARISTA, I'D BE…
A tennis umpire.

GIVE ME A QUOTE…
You're only as good as your last mugacino.

SOCIAL GROUNDS — Andrew 'Bourkey' Bourke

I HAVE MY COFFEE…
Black and White.

IF I WASN'T A BARISTA, I'D BE…
Roaster/sloth.

WHEN I'M NOT MAKING COFFEE, I AM…
Golfing/talking about coffee.

Bayleaf Cafe | Byron Bay

Good things happen over coffee

B-SIDE ESPRESSO

CORNER SMART & PEARSON ST, CHARLESTOWN · 02 4023 1811 · FACEBOOK.COM/BSIDEESPRESSO

MACHINE: La Marzocco Linea
GRINDER: Anfim Super Barista and Anfim Super Caimano
BEANS: DC Coffee, B-Side Blend
BREWING METHODS: Espresso, Cold Drip

   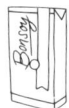

EVERY SO OFTEN YOU HEAR ABOUT A CAFE'S SPECIALTY BLEND being named after the cafe it was developed for. But how often to you hear of the cafe being named after the coffee? Jordan Bale opened B-Side Espresso in 2014, but before he did he went looking for the right house espresso blend to serve. He knew someone from Melbourne-based roaster Ducale Coffee, and promised to humour his friend by trying the coffee. Jordan enjoyed it so much he named his cafe after one of their blends!

B-Side Espresso sits on a corner in what has become the 'second CBD' of Newcastle. When looking for a home for his new cafe, Jordan chose a location that was growing rapidly but that so far lacked a good quality, intimate cafe.

Hospitality is nothing new to Jordan's family – they've been running pubs all over New South Wales since the 60s. This may be the first coffee shop in the family but the old school tradition of good service and a laid back, welcoming atmosphere has well and truly rubbed off on Jordan.

Ducale Coffee (DC) supplies all of B-Side Espresso's coffee, obviously including its B-Side Blend. Made up of Panama Mamacarta, Guatemala San Antonio and Brazil Sitio Pinheirinho, B-Side has low acidity, brown sugar, apple and pepper fragrances and flavours of cacao, raw sugar and nectarine.

The name not only represents the coffee and, as a result, the cafe, but also signifies DC's connection to its social initiative 'dc Tunes', which started in 2012. It is all about celebrating music and supporting new talent by giving local independent and unsigned musicians opportunities to perform at live music venues. Part of the profits from the B-Side Blend go towards paying for bands to feature in the dc Tunes gig list. It's a project that DC coffee, and Jordan are very passionate about.

B-Side Espresso is open for breakfast and lunch. Although it has a limited space for cooking it still manages to serve up a mean selection of closed toasties, bruschetta style open toasties and salads. In winter you'll find plenty of warming dishes coming out of the slow cooker (think pulled-beef burritos, hearty stews and Cuban sandwiches).

Situated next to one of the largest shopping centres in New South Wales, B-Side Espresso is one of the only independent coffee shops in their region. Its laid-back style and superior coffee has meant instant success, and a lot of grateful locals.

> 'The old school tradition of good service and a laid back, welcoming atmosphere has well and truly rubbed off on Jordan.'

BAREFOOT BREW ROOM

1A LAWSON LN, BYRON BAY · 0430 316 066 · BAREFOOTROASTERS.COM.AU

MACHINE: Victoria Arduino Black Eagle
GRINDER: Mythos 1 Grinders and Ditting Bag
BEANS: Barefoot Roasters
BREWING METHODS: Espresso, Cold Drip, AeroPress

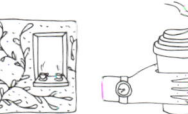   

Ask a local in Byron Bay where you can get a really good coffee, and they'll probably lead you off the main drag and down an alley way. Don't fear…they're taking you to the Barefoot Brew Room in Lawson Lane, a hole-in-the-wall espresso bar operated by the team from Barefoot Roasters.

Owner, Rodney Contejohn, who comes to the coffee world with 20+ years in hospitality, ably leads that team. He began roasting coffee as a trainee roaster at Di Bella Roasting Warehouse and since branching out on his own, he has enjoyed great success, including multiple awards. Roasting coffee started as a hobby for Rodney, who spent his time creating blends that he personally enjoyed. He now roasts coffee sourced from Cofi-Com, and has found that the blends he creates are a hit with his customers, too.

His house blend is Blend II – the aptly named second blend he created once the espresso bar was opened. It features beans from Costa Rica, Colombia and Sumatra which are roasted in a 1982 vintage Probat as a medium to dark roast. There are flavours of dark cocoa, hazelnut and hints of grapefruit. Blend II was recognised in the Golden Bean awards in 2013; Rodney was amongst the top 10 roasters that year, too.

As well as his popular blends, Rodney also offers single origins from a variety of countries as well as Byron Blue Estate Australian coffee, sourced directly from a (very) local coffee farmer.

Co-owner, Dawn Beaumont, spends some of her time in digital marketing, but relishes her 'other' life, as a barista working on the Barefoot Brew Room's iconic Victoria Arduino Black Eagle machine. Dawn and Rodney also serve up cold drip, AeroPress and drip pot for those wanting to side step the ever-popular flat white or cappuccino.

The crowd here is made up of locals who work in the area and have been visiting the Barefoot Brew Room since it opened, often toting their own cups and mugs. There's the expected influx of tourists over summer too, of course.

There's a range of breakfast and lunch nibbles available – toasted bagels, fresh baked brownies, and a selection of banana breads, that sort of thing. Could there be any better start to the day than a thick slice of banana bread and an espresso?

Try the Dark Star blend, a dark espresso roast with a rich body. You'll taste sweet caramel first, followed by hints of apricot and a bright, spicy black-pepper finish.

And the best thing about popping in for your morning coffee is that you can buy a bag of one of Barefoot's fantastic blends or single origins to get you through the rest of the day.

'…a hole-in-the-wall espresso bar operated by the team from Barefoot Roasters.'

BAYLEAF CAFE

2 MARVELL ST, BYRON BAY · 02 6685 8900 · FACEBOOK.COM/BAYLEAFCOFFEE

MACHINE: Synesso Hydra
GRINDER: Mazzer Robur E and EK
BEANS: Marvell St Coffee Roasters, Daily Grind
BREWING METHODS: Espresso, AeroPress, V60 Pour Over, Cold Drip, Mocchamaster

BAYLEAF CAFE IN BYRON BAY LIKES TO KEEP IT LOCAL – ITS COFFEE SUPPLIER IS THE PREVIOUS OWNER OF THE CAFE, MARVELL STREET ROASTERS, WHO ACTUALLY RUNS ITS ROASTERY NEARBY.

Nikki Muling and Dan Readman took over Bayleaf Cafe in 2013, and have recently renovated the venue. They're still serving the same coffee, though – they might have a riot on their hands if they tried to change it. Nikki came to Bayleaf Cafe having managed cafes in Melbourne and worked in specialist coffee at Padre Coffee. She comes from a family of baristas – her three brothers were all baristas, and they've all worked together at some point. Nikki, Dan and their baristas spend a lot of time with Marvell Street Roasters cupping coffee, then in turn go back to Bayleaf Cafe and train up the front of house staff.

Byron Bay locals have come to love and respect the Marvell Street coffee, which changes weekly but always retains the best quality available. Each week, Marvell Street advises Nikki and Dan as to what the standouts are and they choose a selection of single origin espresso and filters for the week. They try to mix it up a bit; keeping those they think are incredible for the entire month.

The ever-changing house blend is always a mix of two beans, at a ratio of whatever works best. Currently it's a combination of Colombian El Paraiso and Ethiopian Kolowa, roasted just enough to achieve full development, whilst maintaining balance of flavour, body, sweetness and acidity. It's beautifully sweet, with or without milk, and also stands out in Bayleaf Cafe's Vietnamese Iced Coffee. Occasionally you'll see Rwandan coffee, from the rugged northwest town of Musasa, or Colombian micro-lot coffees farmed by Daniel Sanchez and his family. There's AeroPress, V60, batch brew and cold drip here, as well as iced coffee served with coffee-infused ice cubes.

'Head Chef, Adam Hill, in turn designs food specials to match the coffee flavour profile.'

There's nothing quite like Bayleaf Cafe anywhere else in Byron. Its 'whole food' philosophy extends not only through the food menu, but to the coffee too – the fact that it has a seasonal blend is really important to Bayleaf. Head Barista, Riki 'Bobby' Eketone, and his wingman, Keisuke, 'The Master' Masuda, create monthly coffee specials to keep things really interesting. Head Chef, Adam Hill, in turn designs food specials to match the coffee flavour profile. It's a truly 'holistic' approach.

As you'd expect in Byron, the clientele is an eclectic mix of artists, musicians and travellers of all ages. On the side of the building is an ever-changing artist wall: Bayleaf Cafe's way of supporting local and international street artists. The artwork changes every three months, and as of the beginning of 2015, the whole year is booked out already.

BILLS BEANS EAST ORANGE

148 MCLACHLAN ST, ORANGE EAST · 02 6361 1611 · BILLSBEANSEAST.COM

MACHINE: Wega
GRINDER: Mazzer
BEANS: Own Blend
BREWING METHODS: Espresso

LOCATED IN AN OLD BUTCHER'S SHOP, ON THE CORNER OF TREE-LINED MCLACHLAN STREET, LIES A TRUE LOCAL CAFE. Bills Beans East Orange has been a community hub, a daily stopover and a local meeting place for Orange locals for more than eight years now. It is one of those places where the barista knows everyone's name and their coffee order and where customers come in with a story to share. It is where the local community thrives.

Ricky Carver and Carlie Beer both come from a background in hospitality and two years ago they bought this cafe and made it their own. Ricky has experience as a chef and a manager and Carlie as a front of house manager. Together they have created a place where Orange locals love to come for their daily espresso fix.

Bills Beans East Orange, it will come as no surprise, serves Bills Beans, which are roasted locally in Orange, just round the corner in Kite Street. Bills Beans is unique amongst Australian roasters in that it roasts at 860 metres above sea level, in a cooler, dryer environment. This allows them to use less gas pressure in their roasting, creating a fuller roast profile and allowing the natural flavours to come to the forefront of their blends.

The house blend at Bills Beans East Orange is a chocolaty, smooth blend, with a slight citrus tone at the end, which cuts through milk and has a good zing for an espresso. It's made up of a Costa Rican Bandola honey-processed microlot, a Colombian Supremo washed processed, a Brazilian Yellow Bourbon natural processed and an Ethiopian Kembata. Bills Beans source directly from the farmers throughout South America, Africa and Asia. The coffee is available for sale as take-home packs too.

Coffee is the focus here, but of course there are quick, fresh lunches available too. It really depends on what they've decided to whip up, but if you're lucky, the pulled pork, Asian slaw, caramelised onion and cheddar roll will be on offer when you're visiting. Or perhaps they'll be serving their sweet corn and haloumi fritters with Trunkey bacon, roast tomato and rocket. Either way, there'll be a delicious muffin of the day that will be perfect alongside the house blend, or a guest single origin.

In the dark depths of the early morning, through the large window by the counter, you'll spy Head Barista, Erick Holborrow, behind the Wega machine getting ready for the day. On weekends, he's ready for the onslaught of lycra-clad men and women on their regular cycling circuit that stop in at their regular coffee spot. The dappled sunlight from the large, leafy trees and the welcoming, homely atmosphere means people gather here and sit for hours. It really is Orange's public living room.

'...a daily stopover and a local meeting place for Orange locals for more than eight years now.'

BYRON BAY COFFEE COMPANY

169 BROKEN HEAD RD, NEWRYBAR · 02 6687 1043 · BYRONBAYCOFFEECO.COM.AU

MACHINE: Wega, Orchestrale and La Marzocco
GRINDER: Mazzer Super Jolly
BEANS: House Blends
BREWING METHODS: Espresso

IN THE HILLS BEHIND BYRON BAY, WITH VIEWS OVER MACADAMIA PLANTATIONS AND RAINFOREST, LIES A FAMILY OWNED AND OPERATED ROASTERY JUST FIVE MINUTES FROM THE BEACH.

Annie and Franco Ivancich's boutique roastery, Byron Bay Coffee Company, celebrated its 25th anniversary in 2014 – and they're still passionate about the evolving coffee industry. Annie and Franco left Sydney with their children in 1989 and settled onto 12 acres in Newrybar, which they transformed into a coffee plantation. Franco took care of the farming, blending and roasting with Annie selling the beans at the local markets and establishing the sales and administration side of things. Twenty-five years on, they are still operating as a family business and now source only premium beans from all around the world.

The Byron Bay Coffee Company supplies cafes Australia wide, as well as internationally.. It produces four espresso blends, four plunger blends and a Mexican Mountain Water decaf for both espresso and plunger. The company also created a line of chocolate-coated coffee beans, drinking chocolates and chocolate coated macadamias. All of the products can be ordered from the website and delivered to your door.

Franco has over twenty years experience roasting coffee and believes the key to good roasting is to enjoy what you do. He is quite the perfectionist and is continually running trials, adjusting temperature and airflows and searching for the roast profiles that will bring the optimum flavours out of the beans. He chooses to blend coffee so that different single origins complement and enhance each other, creating well balanced and full bodied flavours. The result is a unique tasting cup that is vibrant, rich and complex, and the critics agree, with more than 120 coffee awards to their name since 1999.

Franco and Annie source their beans from the coffee distributor Cofi-com. The beans come from all over the world, depending on availability and quality. At any one time they may be roasting beans from Indonesia, Guatemala, Costa Rica, Mexico, Honduras, Kenya, Ethiopia and Tanzania. Establishing good relationships with cafes, providing ongoing support and barista training is also key to how the business operates.

Coffee is one of the most traded commodities of our times and to Byron Bay Coffee Company that means it is particularly important to use environmentally and ethically sustainable practices where possible. Annie and Franco feel strongly about providing certified organic and Rainforest Alliance certified coffee to their customers. Clients are supplied with BioPak takeaway cups and branded KeepCups. Currently the company also supports Rainforest Rescue and Sea Shepherd.

The team at Byron Bay Coffee Company share a passion for all things coffee. Every step, from sourcing quality beans to the final cup of coffee is exciting to them. You can taste this passion in every cup.

> 'The team at Byron Bay Coffee Company share a passion for all things coffee.'

CAFE CAPPELLO

24 CARRINGTON ST, LISMORE · 02 6622 5969 · FACEBOOK.COM/CAFECAPPELLO

MACHINE: La Marzocco
GRINDER: Mazzer Swift
BEANS: Marco Vianei
BREWING METHODS: Espresso, Cold Drip

Every year the city of Lismore celebrates the infamous Lismore Lantern Parade, an annual community arts festival which celebrates the Winter Solstice, the longest night of the year. On the night of the Lantern Parade in 2012 Lismore had more than one reason to celebrate – it was also the day Café Cappello opened; an auspicious day for this Lismore local, or what?

Tony Pilati, owner and co-manager of Café Cappello, was already well known around town. He's owned and run businesses in Lismore for over 30 years. From fruit shops to restaurants to pubs, Tony is a Lismore entrepreneur of no small repute. His Italian culture, and in particular, the cuisine of his ancestors' home in the Veneto region of Northern Italy, was the driving force behind the dream of Café Cappello. And it goes without saying that Italians know a good coffee when they meet one, and Tony was determined to offer the very best in the cups, as well as on the plates.

Tony manages the business with his partner, Tamaya Rose. Theirs is a story of love blossoming over coffee. Tony and Tamaya were baristas in rival restaurants when they first met and fell in love. Today they have come together to serve Espresso Botero coffee from their very own café. Tony acts as Head Barista, and in fact, the house blend was created specifically for Tony, with the plan that he would be the face of the blend.

'...it goes without saying that Italians know a good coffee when they meet one...'

The house blend, Marco Vianei, is a medium roast made up of seven South American beans. It yields a deeply nutty coffee with a creamy mouth feel. Marco transfers beautifully in milk, and has all the elements of a stunning signature coffee. Café Cappello serves Marco Vianei for their espresso-based coffees, and serves single origins for their cold drip. Being an Italian café, they also serve Caffe corretto, an Italian drink consisting of a shot of espresso served with a small amount of liquor; try grappa, Sambuca or brandy. In Italian, 'corretto' means 'correct' – sounds like the correct way to drink coffee to us! Naturally, there's also affogatos on offer, as well as iced coffee with gelato. The perfect combination of all things Italian!

Café Cappello is open for breakfast, lunch and afternoon coffee and cake, and you're going to want to stay in for a meal. Tony said his customers "truly do come in for the coffee then stay for the Italian food journey and culture right here in Lismore." Tony's mamma, Betty, cooks the main traditional dishes, specialising in the home-style traditional Northern Italian cuisine. The signature dish of the restaurant is prepared by Tony and Betty twice a week – Fresh Gnocchi with Sugo Di Casa or creamy Gorgonzola. Try also the Porcini Risotto, with porcini mushrooms from the Alps.

Café Cappello has a true family atmosphere, loads of regular customers, and excellent coffee, right in the heart of the Lismore CBD.

CASSIOPEIA

79 LURLINE ST, KATOOMBA · 02 4782 9299 · CASSIOPEIA.COM.AU

MACHINE: La Marzocco GB/5
GRINDER: Mazzer Robur E
BEANS: Cassiopeia House Blend
BREWING METHODS: Espresso, Batch Brew, V60 Pour Over

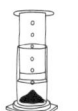 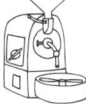  

Zac Suito certainly has a lot of courage, drive and determination, and Katoomba locals are grateful. Zac, having just left school (and with an after school job in a coffee shop), decided he'd like to run his own cafe. So, in 2006, he opened Pink Papaya in Springwood. It's now called Cassiopeia, the same as his Katoomba store, which he opened a few years later at the tender age of 25. But it's not 'just' a cafe, it's a roastery too, where Zac and Managers, Meg and Lachlan, source and roast specialty coffees from around the world, and serve them up to their very dedicated regulars.

Coffee is a lifelong learning experience for Zac; it wasn't until he opened his first cafe that he really fell in love with coffee and wanted to learn as much as he could, from sourcing and roasting to cupping, processing and harvesting – the whole lot. Zac buys his coffee seasonally, and only in the amounts they need, to ensure the green coffees stay fresh. He is very dedicated to pricing transparency and pays well above the Fair Trade price for his coffee.

Cassiopeia Coffee, the Katoomba branch, is set back from the main street, in what some would consider an out-of-the-way location that misses a lot of tourist foot traffic. But it hasn't mattered; anyone who loves a good coffee knows where to find Cassiopeia, and can enjoy their cup without the hustle and bustle of the main street, and with gorgeous natural light, particularly on winter mornings.

Stu Smith is Cassiopeia Coffee's head roaster and works with green beans sourced through Silo Coffee. Cassiopeia Coffee also has a direct relationship with Elida Estate in Panama, where Zac has spent time with the owner and where he discovered an exciting new coffee crop. He's been serving it for the past three years and truly loves it; his customers do too.

Stu roasts most of the coffee to a light roast, in order to properly showcase all the intricacies of the bean as well as the time and effort the producers have put in. The house blend is made up of coffees from Colombia, Costa Rica and Ethiopia; you'll also see other beans from Central America and Kenya here, as well as some delicious Burundi and Rwanda flavours coming in 2015.

Zac simply loves showcasing the single origins they buy in small lots from all over the world; they're generally juicy, sweet and floral. The opportunity to show someone how different 'real' coffee can be for the first time is enough to keep Zac going for a whole career! The different flavours unique to each origin, the way the flavours are enhanced when roasted well – no wonder this young man couldn't wait to open his cafes! And The Blue Mountains are all the better for it…

> '…opportunity to show someone how different 'real' coffee can be for the first time.'

DELANO SPECIALTY COFFEE

85 MONTAGUE ST, NORTH WOLLONGONG · 02 4254 1423 · DELANOCOFFEE.COM.AU

MACHINE: La Marzocco Linea PB
GRINDER: Robur and Ditting
BEANS: Single Origin Roasters, Reuben Hills, Seven Seeds, Dukes
BREWING METHODS: Pour Over, Cold Drip, Siphon

A PSYCHOLOGIST, A BRAND STRATEGIST AND A MARKETING EXPERT WALKED INTO A CAFE… No actually, they opened a cafe, and the results are no joke! In fact, the three partners not only opened a cafe, but a specialty coffee roastery, too – the only one in the Illawarra. And the name? That came about right at the start, when one of the founders was on holiday in Florida, sitting outside his hotel, enjoying the sand, surf and sun. He decided in that moment he wanted to start a specialty coffee company. And the hotel he was sitting at? The Delano Hotel in Miami.

If you haven't guessed already, Delano Specialty Coffee is a real passion project; led by the sort of passion that makes grown men leave behind their lucrative professional careers to roast coffee. That passion carries on right through the entire Delano team; Manager, David Ryan, also left a high flying career, because he liked to be around people and coffee more than he liked being around money and economics.

Head Roaster, Drew Corbin, and Head Barista, David Mason, lead a team of coffee professionals who are ready, willing and able to give advice to their customers. The staff are happy to talk you through the coffee choices, all of which are roasted on-site and delivered fresh.

Delano Specialty Coffee offers rotating seasonally focused single origins as well as their own blends. Peek through the window into the roastery and see them being created right before your eyes. The house blend was specially developed for the cafe and is roasted to have a high acidity that cuts through milk nicely, while retaining sweetness and complexity.

Delano Specialty Coffee is located in an industrial area of Wollongong, without any real passing foot traffic. That doesn't stop a steady stream of coffee lovers following their GPS' though, and as a result, the clientele is made up of tradies and blue collar workers from the area, as well as students and coffee aficionados who find the short drive well worth it. There's breakfast and lunch on offer as well, Monday to Friday.

Try the cold drip or the V60 for something a bit different, secure in the knowledge that every coffee you drink at Delano Specialty Coffee is made from specialty grade coffee, has been sourced from ethical and sustainable origins, and then roasted in season and served fresh. Take a bag home with you, too – we recommend the Seasonal Organic Blend, with its flavours of malt, caramel and cocoa.

Delano source their coffee from all over the world – from Ethiopia, Tanzania and Kenya in Africa, to Brazil, Colombia and Guatemala in the Americas, to Indonesia and Papua New Guinea closer to home. The staff have a lot of stories about the origins of their beans and stories from their own travels – perhaps they'll spin you some yarns if you ask.

'Peek through the window into the roastery and see them being created right before your eyes.'

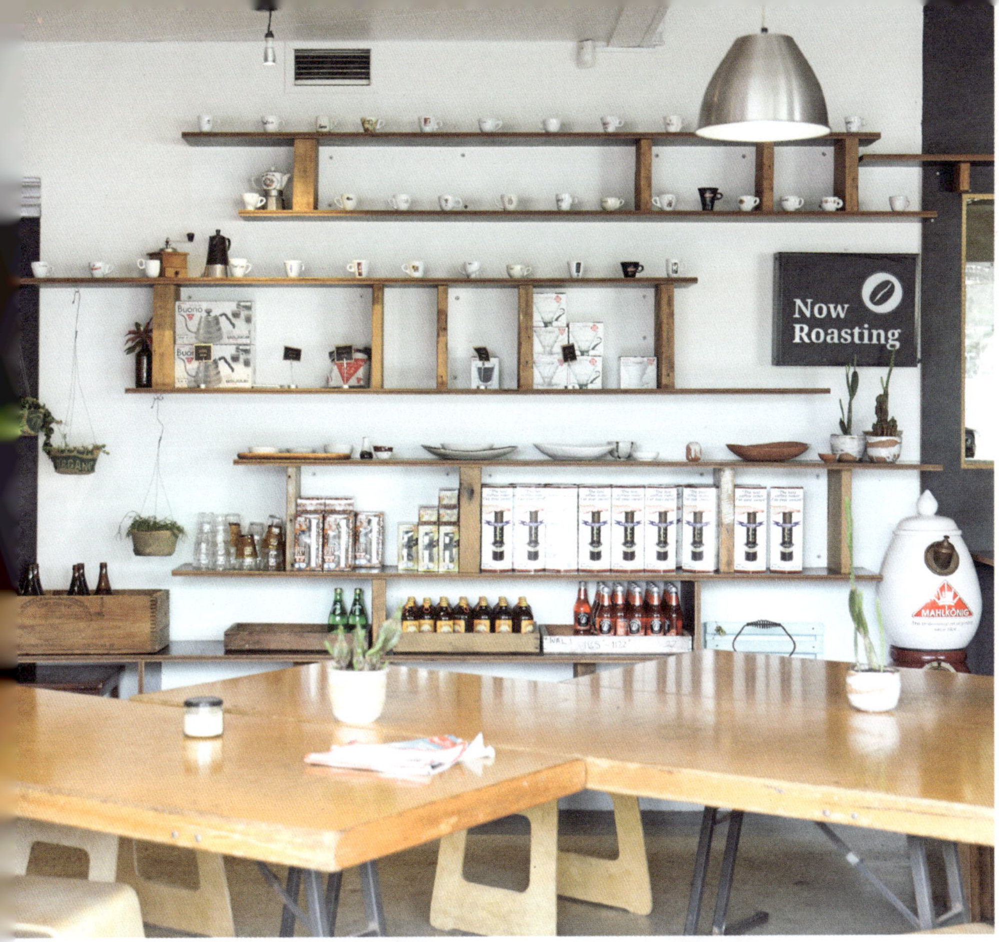
Now
Roasting
MAHLKÖNIG

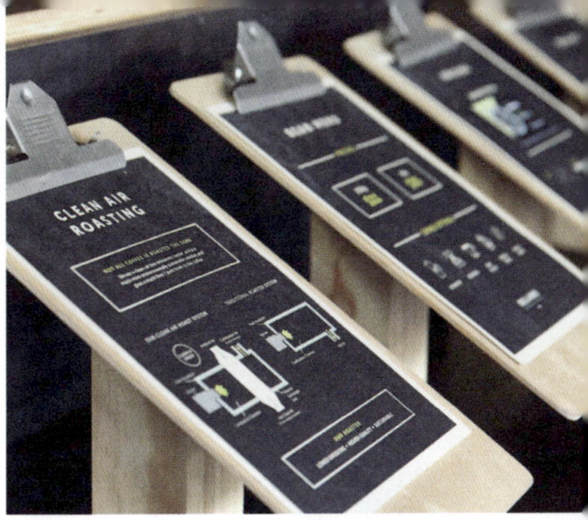
CLEAN AIR
ROASTING

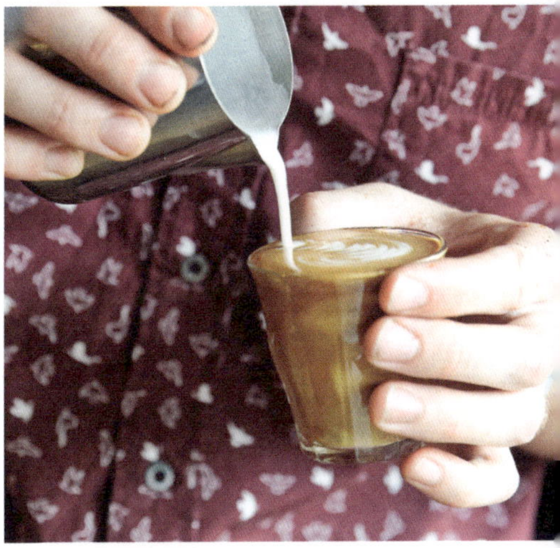

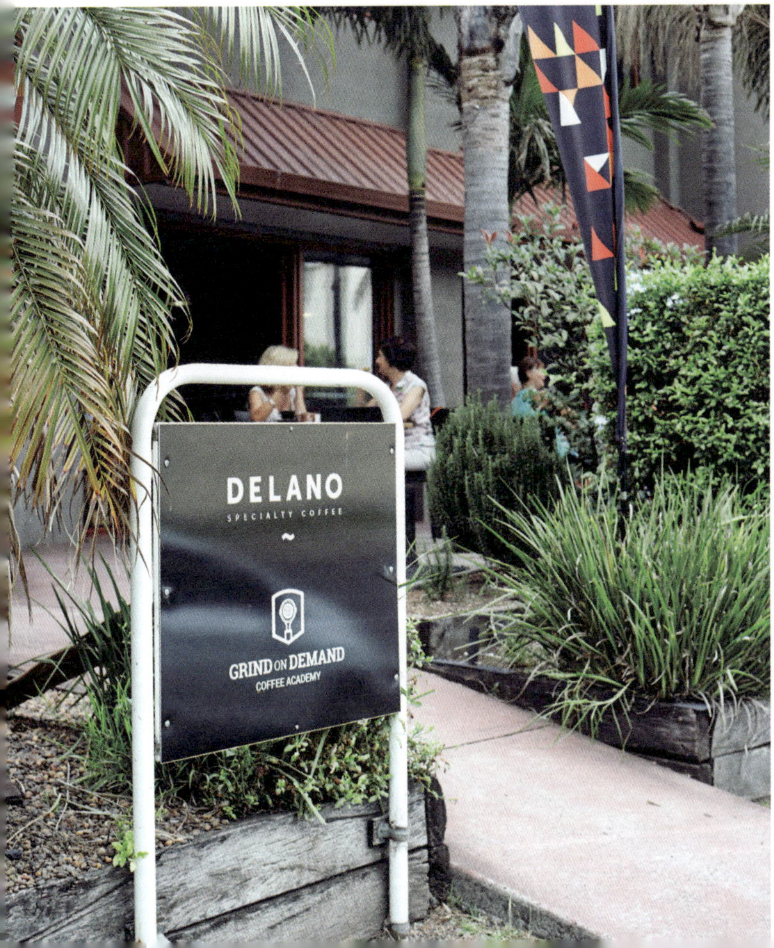
DELANO
SPECIALTY COFFEE
GRIND ON DEMAND
COFFEE ACADEMY

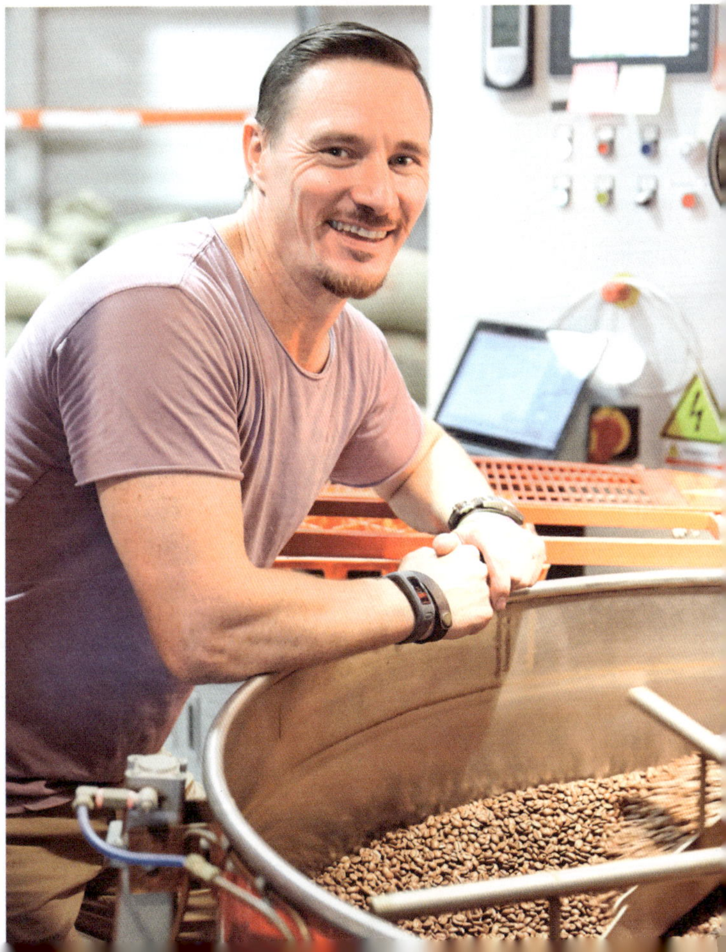

May your COFFEE be strong and your MONDAY be short

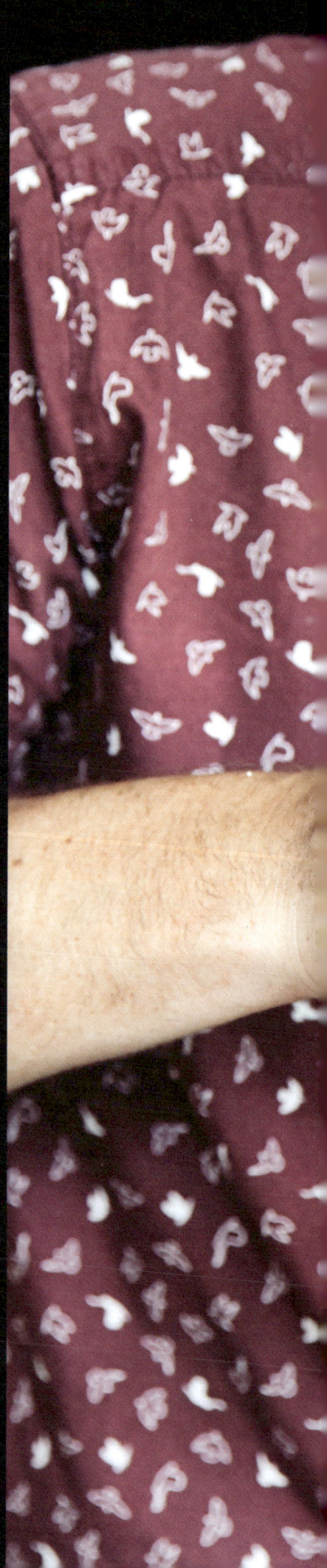

Delano Specialty Coffee | North Wollongong

THE FAT GOOSE CAFE

SHOP 3, KILLCARE RD, HARDY'S BAY · 02 4360 1888 · THEFATGOOSE.COM.AU

MACHINE: Simonelli
GRINDER: Mazzer Automatic
BEANS: Fat Goose Specialty Coffee
BREWING METHODS: Espresso

PICTURE THIS: THE SPARKLING BLUE WATERS OF HARDY'S BAY, PALM TREES AND TROPICAL PLANTS LINING THE STREETS, A SHORT DRIVE THROUGH BUSHLAND TO AN UNSPOILED BEACH, AND A SMALL COMMUNITY ENJOYING THE VERY BEST OF LIFE ON THE AUSTRALIAN EAST COAST. This pretty much sums up the Killcare and Hardy's Bay region on the New South Wales central coast, and makes the perfect backdrop for The Fat Goose Cafe, located just a stone's throw from the water.

Sarah Doak Stride and Mike Stride, originally from New Zealand and England respectively and moved their family to Killcare in 2008 and opened The Fat Goose Cafe. It quickly became a local favourite and a must-visit destination for the many seasonal holidaymakers who visit the area.

Part cafe, part bakery and deli, The Fat Goose Cafe caters for breakfast and lunch diners, coffee enthusiasts, takeaway customers and those looking for something special to go with their meal at home. The deli does a roaring trade, selling Australian and international cheeses, deli meats and gourmet sauces and accompaniments, while the patisserie offers freshly made bread, pastries, pies and quiches.

The Fat Goose Cafe sources its much loved coffee from Fat Poppy Specialty Coffee; Sarah and Mike were looking for a well-rounded flavour profile that could respond well to both black and milk coffee, and Fat Poppy delivered the goods.

'...caters for breakfast and lunch diners, coffee enthusiasts, takeaway customers...'

The roasting method, on custom designed equipment, allows them to achieve a consistent and high quality product.

The house blend is made up of three origins. There is a 100% Heirloom natural processed bean from Ethiopia, a Bourbon natural processed bean from Brazil, and a Canephora fully washed bean from India. The result is a blend that is full bodied, has low acidity and is smooth and rich. As well as its house blend, The Fat Goose Cafe also offers a decaf blend.

The cafe boasts an extensive menu for breakfast and lunch, featuring items from the patisserie and deli as well as other concoctions from the kitchen. Try the Bakers Brekky: fennel rosti served with roasted mushroom, smashed avocado, roasted tomato, fresh rocket and a soft poached egg. Or for lunch, the Life Raft Burger, grilled beef patty with sweet pepper pesto, lettuce, beetroot, caramelised onion and tomato on a homemade bread roll.

Being so close to the water you might prefer the Sensational Squid, shallow fried salt and pepper squid with cous cous and rocket salad and Fat Goose Moroccan chilli lime dressing.

The cafe, set down from the road and surrounded by greenery, welcomes families with kids, is pram and wheelchair friendly and will happily supply the little ones with pens and paper to keep them occupied. All you need to do is relax and enjoy your gourmet pie and Fat Poppy coffee.

THE GLASS ONION SOCIETY

1/308 THE ENTRANCE RD, LONG JETTY · 02 4326 1650 · THEGLASSONIONSOCIETY.COM

MACHINE: ECM Michelangelo, built in Milan
GRINDER: Azkoyen Q9
BEANS: Own Blend
BREWING METHODS: Espresso, Cold Drip

REGIONAL NSW

NOT MANY CAFES CAN SAY THEY'VE SINGLE-HANDEDLY BEEN INSTRUMENTAL IN THE REVITALISATION OF THEIR LOCAL AREA, BUT THE GLASS ONION SOCIETY IS ONE OF THE FEW THAT CAN. Situated in the heart of Long Jetty, in an area that had previously been written off, The Glass Onion Society has seen a cultural rebirth going on right outside its doors.

For the first time, the central coast region has a hub for the counter-culture, a place where like-minded individuals meet and eat, a place for the artists, the thinkers, the poets, the musicians, and everyone else who is flocking to this brand new, trendy district. Many attribute the transformation of the suburb and its upward growth solely to The Glass Onion Society, and they're happy to take that mantle and hold it proudly aloft.

Ana Koutoulas and Ben Wright are the brains and the personalities behind this exciting coffee venture; they took a leap of faith and have been rewarded for their courage. As well as creating the cafe they also have an art gallery space where they feature young local artists and host live music events. It's a true social hub for Long Jetty, and is full of buzz.

The coffee house blend was especially created for The Glass Onion Society. Espressology roasts it for Ana and Ben, using Brazilian, Indian and Ethiopian Djimma coffees. It's full bodied, has low acidity and is smooth and rich, with chocolate and sweet caramel praline notes. The Glass Onion Society call it "a classic Napoli style blend with a new world zest!" The Ethiopian natural process Djimma contributes the unique natural fermented fruit character, while the Indian washed coffee binds the whole blend together with a rich cocoa aftertaste.

The Glass Onion Society house blend is cellared in a climate-controlled environment prior to delivery, which results in a denser, more stable crema and a smoother tasting espresso than other boutique coffees. What a journey our coffee goes on…

'…seen a cultural rebirth going on right outside its doors.'

The Glass Onion Society also has a rotating single origin grinder, serving different origins on a weekly basis. Chances are you'll find one of Ben and Ana's favourite Ethiopian, Guatemalan or Kenyan single origins waiting for you. If it's available, try the Kenya Kamuya: a fragrant coffee displaying tropical fruits, honey sweetness, lime acidity and green apple. Or for a deeper, richer cup try the Brazil Progresso Estate, with its brown sugar, cocoa and floral aroma and notes of walnut and honey.

Manager, Matt Richardson, welcomes in a very diverse crowd for breakfast and lunch Tuesday to Sunday. He's a bonafide coffee addict. Aren't we all, though? The menu is separated into dishes for Herbivores and dishes for Carnivores. Vegetarians and vegans are well catered for - their only issue is going to be making a selection.

GOOD BROTHER ESPRESSO SHOP

40 KING ST, NEWCASTLE · 02 4023 3158 · FACEBOOK.COM/GOODBROTHERESPRESSOSHOP

MACHINE: Faema
GRINDER: Mazzer
BEANS: Suspension Coffee
BREWING METHODS: Espresso

GOOD BROTHER ESPRESSO SHOP IS A FUNKY CAFE WITH AN INDUSTRIAL FEEL, BRINGING QUALITY ESPRESSO AND GREAT VIBES TO THE NEWCASTLE CAFE SCENE. Good Brother Espresso Shop is the second cafe for Christopher Johnston and Stephanie Whitehead, who also own Suspension Espresso in Islington. They're still serving Suspension Coffee, from husband and wife team, Mishka and Rachael Golski, in Sydney, but this time in Newcastle's east end, by the sea.

The area has really come alive in the last few years, and Good Brother Espresso Shop sees a regular parade of Mums and bubs, professionals on their way to work, students and beach goers, and of course the local regulars. Chris and Steph count many of the customers amongst their friends, and the vibe here shows it – relaxed, welcoming and friendly. Steph loves the culture of coffee in Australia; it's as much about people interacting and being part of their community as it is the actual drink in the cup.

While Good Brother Espresso Shop has its own personality and its own unique feel, it serves up the same excellent coffee that Chris and Steph's Islington customers love: Suspension Espresso. "We use different blends all the time to keep things interesting, but Kongi Gold, which grows wild in Papua New Guinea is our base bean. Someone once gave a batch to Mishka as they couldn't get the profile right. Mishka worked to create a good profile for the bean, and eventually turned it into one of our best – robust, smooth and earthy," Stephanie said. The coffee is small batch roasted for Good Brother Espresso Shop, and alongside the Kongi Gold, they also serve whatever else Mishka likes to roast, the trust in Mishka's talent is solid, and rightly so.

With blends from a name like Suspension Coffee, it's only fitting that Good Brother Espresso Shop has a healthy suspended coffee tradition. Thanks to their generous customers, Chris and Steph are able to pass on coffees to those unable to afford it.

The venue is hard to miss on King Street; the vibrant terracotta façade opens up into a funky space with an industrial vibe. The exposed brick wall and long communal table give it an open, airy feel, and on nice days (with which Newcastle is rather spoiled) customers relax out the front on wooden beach chairs. A large window faces the street, with stools pulled up to the bench table; long bench seating lines the brick wall, too. There's plenty of room for a catch up with friends.

The food is good, solid fare, with breakfast rolls, toasties, wraps and sandwiches, and muesli with natural yoghurt and khoshaf (Middle Eastern dried fruits in rosewater). There's also a daily specials menu available for breakfast and lunch, and plenty of baked treats. Everything's available to have in or take away. Lucky Newcastle!

> '...it's as much about people interacting and being part of their community as it is the actual drink in the cup.'

GOOD EDDY

187 LORDS PL, ORANGE · 02 6361 7379 · GOODEDDY.COM.AU

MACHINE: La Marzocco Linea PB
GRINDER: Victoria Arduino Methos One Clima Pro, Mahlkönig EK43
BEANS: Seven Seeds Seasonal House Blend
BREWING METHODS: Espresso, AeroPress, V60 Pour Over, Wilfa Svat, Cold Drip

THE CITY OF ORANGE HAS A FLOURISHING FOOD AND WINE CULTURE, EMBRACING A LARGE NUMBER OF CAFES AND RESTAURANTS. Standing apart from the rest comes Good Eddy, a cafe that serves up great coffee that shows respect to the entire coffee making process, from bean to cup.

Good Eddy has found a home within this long-standing 1930s building, previously used as a printing works and renovated to fit this modern cafe, whilst maintaining its original charm. This contemporary cafe has a large wooden sign outside its door marked COFFEE so there's no question as to what they specialise in. A retail space is attached, which also doubles as an exhibition space. Brewing gear is on sale, along with retail beans, beautiful blooms and other little goodies.

Owners, Toby and Maddy Howell, have worked in cafes for their entire careers, fuelling their passion for Specialty Coffee. Toby worked as a roaster at Seven Seeds, and as a Barista at Melbourne's iconic cafes, Brother Buba Budan and St Ali. Maddy managed a number of leading cafes, most recently Deadman Espresso. Good Eddy is a culmination of experience in the industry and a passion for great coffee. You can be sure that respect has been shown to every link in the process here, from growing the crops through to brewing and serving excellent coffee.

Both manage the cafe while Toby doubles as Head Barista.

"We use a number of brew methods, rotating guest coffee roasters, reverse osmosis water filtration systems, great milkshakes for all ages, delicious sweet treats, all set in a tranquil contemporary space with friendly staff," he said. Good Eddy also explores a variety of guest roasters, changing weekly, allowing Toby to explore a number of fresh crop coffees from Australia's best boutique roasters.

With a love for all coffee, Toby and Maddy don't like to limit themselves to certain countries, regions or flavor profiles – they much prefer to base their choices on the product. Some boutique roasters that you can expect to see include Rueben Hills, Small Batch, Proud Mary and Brigade Espresso.

Seven Seeds firmly holds the title of the house blend. Toby's history with the company was formed around a fondness of the product and the company's ethics. Roasting with Seven Seeds for many years, he gained a respect for how they source and roast their coffee beans.

As Orange offers up something for everyone, it brings in a diverse clientele and culture that has been embraced by the Good Eddy staff. You can find a hipster sitting down next to an old farmer having a chat. You can find families, friends, corporates and tourists alike. It is the kind of cafe that brings all kinds of people together with a common love for coffee.

'...a diverse clientele and culture that has been embraced by the Good Eddy staff.'

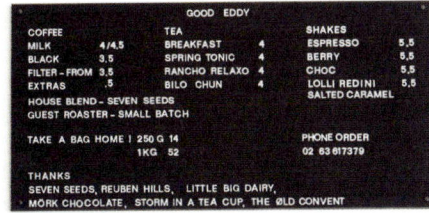

REPUBLIC OF COFFEE

98 MAGELLAN STREET, LISMORE · 02 6622 6134 · REPUBLICOFCOFFEE.NET

MACHINE: Dalla Corte DC Pro
GRINDER: Anfim S450
BEANS: Own Blend
BREWING METHODS: Espresso, Cold Brew, Bunn Trifecta

  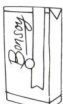 

NICK AND EVE MULLER OPENED REPUBLIC OF COFFEE ON MAGELLAN STREET, LISMORE, IN 2011. Nick had worked as a barista for a decade and starting learning to roast coffee himself about five years ago. Coming from positions at renowned Toby's Estate and with Mark Bullivant at Independent Coffee Professionals, Nick knew that in his own cafe, he wanted to focus solely on providing fantastic coffee. So, there's no kitchen here, no breakfast and lunch menus to discuss – just excellent coffee, which you can guarantee has been selected, roasted and blended with the utmost care and attention, with no distraction.

Nick appreciates that his customers' time is precious, so he's all about producing a fantastic cup of coffee quickly and efficiently so his takeaway customers can get on with their day. You can sit in too, of course, if you have the time. Nick works on a specialist Dalla Corte DC PRO machine, which has four independent boilers. Nick said, "We can control the temperature of water passing through the coffee to within one tenth of a degree. Our grinder also has electronic dosing set to within 100th of a second, so the amount of coffee is strictly controlled. We can make very precise adjustments to the process which makes a huge difference to the extraction of flavour." Republic of Coffee purchases green beans from H.A. Bennetts and roasts them themselves. The house blend changes depending on what is available and what Nick and Eve think their customers will enjoy the most. They're motivated by the passion and complexity involved in the whole process, of growing, roasting and brewing coffee. It's all about the customer service here – providing the Lismore locals with something they'll love, something that might challenge them, something they'll keep coming back for, day after day, and they do!

> 'Nick knew that in his own cafe, he wanted to focus solely on providing fantastic coffee.'

Currently, the house blend is made up of coffees from Colombia, Guatemala, Costa Rica, East Timor and Ethiopia. All the coffees are wet processed and some of them are also certified organic or part of the Rainforest Alliance program. This seems like a sentence is missing before - what / which is their best seller by far? It's also no surprise that Republic of Coffee does a roaring retail trade, selling its coffee to the public, as well as to cafes, mostly those in the Northern rivers area. Republic of Coffee also offers accredited barista training courses.

Open from 6.30am (for the morning rush) until 2pm, Monday to Friday, Republic of Coffee sees a lot of local professionals as well as a wider cross-section of Lismore locals. It offers AeroPress and cold brew, as well as the more unusual Bunn Trifecta. There's graffiti on the walls, and the bustling Magellan Street just past the palm trees out the front. It's the place to be for a no-fuss, top quality, timely coffee.

SOCIAL GROUNDS

SHOP 1, 151 GORDON ST, PORT MACQUARIE · 0423 240 635

MACHINE: La Marzocco MP Strada
GRINDER: Mazzer Robur
BEANS: Story Coffee
BREWING METHODS: Espresso, Organic Cold Brew

  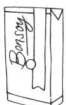

BEST MATES, ANDREW "BOURKEY" BOURKE AND CHRIS "TRUEY" BRADTKE, ARE THE BRAWN AND BRAINS BEHIND SOCIAL GROUNDS, THE CAFE JUST A FEW STREETS BACK FROM THE MAIN TOWN OF PORT MACQUARIE.

Andrew and Chris have been mates for more than 10 years, living and working together in that time. Prior to opening Social Grounds, Chris cut his teeth in some of the UK's best fine dining restaurants and specialty bars before moving back to Sydney to work at The Winery in Surry Hills, developing his knowledge and passion for the industry. Andrew had been travelling with his partner for the past four years, alternating between snow seasons down south and going tropical across South East Asia. He continued to work as a barista during his travels and in that time developed a true passion for the coffee industry.

Two weeks after receiving the keys to the premises, Social Grounds opened to the masses. The dark walls and dramatic chandeliers of the interior give way to a spacious and sunny, all-weather deck offering natural lighting, beautiful greenery and a backdrop of amazing graffiti artwork. If that's not open-air enough, benches in the back garden are perfect to perch on with a cup of brew.

Coffee was always the boys' main focus. Labelling themselves as obsessed, they are in charge of the brew, while Emma Nagel, Andrew's partner, and Olivia Clarke take care of the business. Beans come courtesy of Story Store, a Gold Coast-based distributor that roasts its beans in a top-secret location in Sydney. Andrew discovered the blend while working on the coast and deemed it the best in Australia. After meeting with Dean Hyland, co-owner of Story Store, a beautiful partnership was formed.

The blend features beans from Ethiopia, Kenya, Java and Sumatra, resulting in a medium balanced blend with soft aromas of spicy dried fruits and notes of chocolate and caramel. It's been designed to slice through the milk and hit you with a bold, sweet kick. Single origins are rotated every few weeks for the discerning black drinkers. When a hot day calls for cold coffee, the boys deliver with a cold brew, made on-site.

Along with the house-made baked goods, Social Grounds offers a simple, yet effective, breakfast and lunch menu. Start with free-range eggs on sourdough and add your choice of sides, or opt for a beetroot and cauliflower burger with kale and hand-cut chips. Its specials live up to the promise, with past plates including French toast with mashed banana and homemade caramel on organic sourdough, and fragrant spiced duck leg salad with grilled pears, potato, walnut and rocket.

'When a hot day calls for cold coffee, the boys deliver with a cold brew, made on-site.'

SUSPENSION ESPRESSO

3 BEAUMONT ST, ISLINGTON · 02 4962 2717 · SUSPENSIONESPRESSO.COM.AU

MACHINE: La Marzocco Linea
GRINDER: Mazzer
BEANS: Suspension Coffee
BREWING METHODS: Espresso

THE OWNERS OF SUSPENSION ESPRESSO SEE THE CAFE AS MORE OF A COMMUNITY HUB THAN A BUSINESS. Based in the vibrant area on the wrong side of the tracks of Islington, Suspension Espresso "is not necessarily the most hip or slick operation around, but it is full of heart," said owners, Christopher Johnston and Stephanie Whitehead. They're both lovers of the community side of coffee – the way it brings people together, to chat, create, debrief, and develop relationships. It's a real love story.

Islington is a true melting pot of different groups and is home to a very creative community. The Suspension Coffee clientele is made up of everyone from "barefoot bohemians to brain surgeons and all in between," said Chris. They're a generous bunch, too – the suspended coffee tradition is alive and well here, thanks to the kind folks of Newcastle. A true community spirit abounds.

Suspension Espresso started as a roasting house. It was first roasted in the cafe itself, and is still roasted by Mishka and Rachael Golski, who started the roastery together. They now roast in Sydney but retain strong links back to the cafe where it all started. Suspension Espresso changes its blend daily, and its coffee offerings are totally dependent on what Mishka and Rachael have discovered or felt like roasting on any particular day.

The staff are skilled in pouring different blends and single origins, and are well versed on the broad variety of coffees that come from the ever-inventive Mishka. There's a range of fifteen or so origins that are used over time, just to keep it interesting.

There's no fancy syphon coffee or other brewing methods here, just straight up espresso, made with love. There's no Head Barista, either – the whole is greater than the sum of its parts here, and everyone contributes to serving up great espresso with a smile.

There's seating out the front in the shade of the awning, but most prefer to kick back in the shady courtyard, where there's plenty of space to relax and indulge in your favourite brew. The fit-out is eclectic and retro without feeling too kitschy.

There are comfy couches, cool coffee tables with mismatched chairs and lovely wood flooring. The long floorboards lead you from the front door right out the back into the shady courtyard, where you'll find locals relaxing with the newspaper over a hearty, healthy breakfast such as saffron poached pear muesli.

If you love your Suspension espresso (which you will), you'll have to take a bag or three home with you; they're available for purchase in the cafe. Some say grungy, some say retro, some say trendy; all say well worth it.

> 'Islington is a true melting pot of different groups and is home to a very creative community.'

UPRISING

21/25 DOWNIE ST, MARYVILLE · 02 4962 5669 · BAKEDUPRISING.COM.AU

MACHINE: Victoria Arduino
BEANS: Pablo & Rusty's, Seven Seeds
BREWING METHODS: Espresso

What started as a home-based wholesale cake business and accompanying blog, has grown into Uprising, a thriving warehouse bakery and kitchen, tucked away in the back streets of sleepy Maryville in Newcastle's northern suburbs.

Owner, Alice Lees, first got a taste of the hospitality world in Canberra at Tosolini's Manuka while studying silversmithing. She then moved back to Newcastle where she waitressed at Three Bean while working part time as a teacher and commuting to Sydney. Alice started selling cakes back to Three Bean in 2010, documenting her progress online. Other local cafes soon jumped on the bandwagon, triggering Alice to hold a weekly stall at the Newcastle Farmers Market. In December 2013 she went all in and created a permanent shop front in a light-filled warehouse that wouldn't look out of place in the back streets of Surry Hills.

Combining her design history and expertise in baked goods; Alice created a white-walled, concrete-floor space with an open-plan kitchen giving the public full access to the baking process. The simply designed space means the daily products and weekly floral arrangements take centre stage while also keeping the industrial heritage of the warehouse in tact.

Luke Marshall is the man in charge of keeping coffee front and centre in the Uprising experience. He said, "Coffee is a lifestyle, it occupies a big part of mine and everyone's day. It's a really big responsibility knowing you can make or break someone's day when you hand them their coffee in the morning and we take our role within the bakery extremely seriously."

Beans are sourced from Melbourne roasters Seven Seeds and Proud Mary's, as well as Sydney-based Pablo & Rusty's. Luke and his team love the Melbourne-style lighter roasts for their unbeatable flavour and balance. Currently in the grinders is a Seven Seeds blend, Golden Gate. Made up of fully washed Ethiopian and Colombian beans, it makes for a super rich and sweet coffee, perfect black or with milk. A unique blend from Pablo & Rusty's is also on offer, featuring three El Salvadorian beans naturally processed and blended together. The complexity of the blend means rich fruit notes shine through, even when served with milk.

If a freshly baked berry brioche or sourdough doesn't tickle your fancy, try a coffee-inspired treat. Uprising has been experimenting with bringing coffee into the kitchen, incorporating it into cakes, syrups and soaked sponges to make its popular coffee lamington. They have recently been experimenting with coffee nougat and a cracked coffee-topped caramel, so keep your eye out for these delicious confectionery.

'...a thriving warehouse bakery and kitchen, tucked away in the back streets...'

Social Grounds | Port Macquarie

THE ORIGINS OF COFFEE

We have travelled the world in search of the best beans – from Indonesia and Papua New Guinea to Colombia, Brazil and Costa Rica… and as far as Ethiopia, Kenya and Uganda.

We have had the joy of meeting the growers at origin to learn about all that goes into producing their crops. This bunch of passionate farmers has followed a desire for developing the best crops they can – organic, rainforest, certified or not – in order to give us our daily cup of coffee.

For a quick refresher on the various coffee processing methods from crop to cup, head to page 12 and equip yourself with all of the basic terminology.

To travel back to the origin of the bean is where every good coffee book should begin. Here we hope to discover the source of true Geisha, still growing in the wild lands of the African bush.

Travelling to Ethiopia in early 2015 to seek out the best beans for his customers, Sasa Sestic, World Barista Champion 2015, went on a journey to discover the original bean and hoped to find the Geisha. Here is his story…

After changing four planes and travelling for 38 hours from Canberra to Addis Abbaba we finally managed to get to Ethiopia. I felt as thought my travel agent was angry with me and bought me the longest possible flight. Well either that or it really is just a really long way from Australia to Ethiopia.

Anyway, this long journey did not stop me from having a super quick shower in the hotel before heading straight into my first cupping session. It was here that I tasted around 40 cups and found a few highlights from Beloya, Konga and Aricha cooperatives. All three coffees were clean and naturally processed with very distinct flavours.

I visited Beloya a few years ago and the soil is a really special colour: purple and full of different minerals. The Beloya was an interesting cup with a really nice white grape acidity, strawberries, a hint of floral and a medium to full body. As this coffee cooled it became sweeter and a lot creamier.

Konga had typical notes of dark cherries, vanilla and a hint of blackcurrant; perfect for blends that bring nice fruity notes. Konga is not as clean as the other two coffees, but it is definitely a full body coffee.

The coffee that really made my day was Aricha. It had distinct apricots, blueberries, and sparkling citric acidity, medium to full body and was super sweet. As it cooled down it tasted more like apricot nectar. It's a really versatile cup, which I believe can suit filter, espresso and also milk-based coffees.

After a 12-hour drive we made it to Sidamo, Yirgacheffe. The first stop was the Ethiopian Commodity Exchange (ECX) warehouse in Sidamo. Here all of the washing stations within Sidamo bring their coffee, wrapped in parchment. Random bags of coffee are checked for moisture and a maximum of 13% is allowed. Samples for green bean evaluation and roasting are also taken. Coffee is then graded by Q graders and finally sold in ECX.

Local exporters would have to buy approximately 15 lots of the same grade coffee to make up one container that is ready for export. It is no surprise that when buyers purchase a container of coffee from ECX; there is lot of inconsistency in flavour notes. Unfortunately trading coffee this way makes it impossible to achieve traceability and it is also really hard to have consistent tasting coffee.

Luckily for Project Origin, I managed to find a way to escape ECX and buy coffee direct from the washing and milling stations. It is a rare find to come across a producer that one can buy directly from in Ethiopia but I even managed to buy directly from small producers in the Yirgacheffe Kochere Worka region. The farm is owned by Geligelu Edemi and it has 11 hectares of heirloom trees that are approximately 15 years old. The farm is sitting at 2050m above sea level. There are more than 20 members of the family and they all pick and dry their coffee. All coffee is dried on their own African beds also at 2000m.

Coffee in Kochere has a really nice tropical sweetness with notes of apricots, honey sweetness, lime acidity and a hint of strawberry. They even have their own storage where they keep all of their coffee. This year ECX told them they can no longer sell directly to customers but they have approximately 90 bags of amazing coffee that will be mixed with so many other lots and sold as Yirgacheffee natural grade one if it goes to the ECX.

ETHIOPIA

with Ona Coffee

However using some connections... We will hopefully be able to buy their lots directly this year. This business for the family would mean that they will be able to complete their storage and improve their house for the entire family. For us at Project Origin it would be an amazing success to be able to buy 100% traceable coffee every year and also continue working with the Edemi Family to provide us with a consistent flavour profile.

On this same trip we also visited a lot of different washing and drying stations in the Yirgacheffe and Sidamo regions. These washing stations buy coffee from farms within an approximate 10km radius; and then carry on the next steps in processing. Most mills will have the same techniques to process washed and natural coffees.

With washed process coffee, a higher premium is awarded for red cherries. After this, coffee is pulped using traditional disk pulpers. Separation of light and dense beans is done through their traditional gravity system. The coffee is then fermented in concrete pools for two to three days in clean spring water. Once there is no more mucilage, coffee is rinsed several times in concrete channels and taken to another pool for another day of soaking. This traditional way of processing really helps to highlight clarity in flavour and acidity in washed Ethiopian coffees.

On our first day in Yirgacheffe, we visited a washing and drying station in the Dumerso area. This station sits at 1750m and they specialise in preparing high quality natural process coffee. Their attention to detail starts from the fact that they pick cherries from within a small, selected area. The coffee is sun dried on African beds for approximately 20 days. The days get extremely hot so the cherries are covered during the day so they don't dry too quickly.

Coffee is spread very thin and for the first three days it is not moved at all, this is to ensure they do not damage the cherry. After three days coffee is moved several times a day to ensure even drying but also so that slightly under and over ripe cherries are removed.

I really enjoyed visiting Aricha, Konga and Cheleletku but the most unique experience was in one of the stations at Kochere. Upon arriving I was greeted by a really passionate manager who started giving me samples of their coffees for me to cup and offer feedback. This inspired me as these people are growing one of the best coffees in the world but still they want to make their coffee better. In the following days I cupped over 20 different lots from Kochere and all of them scored 86 points or more. This was a huge score considering coffees are really fresh and did not have time to rest.

As the manager was explaining how they dry natural process coffees in African beds I spotted these beautiful, long and thin coffee cherries, together with other common, smaller cherries. These big, bold cherries can only be found in one particular area and only a few growers have these coffee trees. No one has ever asked for this coffee to be separated so they never realised the potential of what this can taste like as a single varietal. To me, tasting these coffee cherries reminded me of tasting Papaya.

As a result of my inquisition, we separated approximately 500g for me to taste and if we get some really exciting flavours they are happy to prepare a 30-bag lot and prepare this coffee exclusively for us.

After a few exciting days in Yirgacheffe we headed back to Addis to have several more cupping sessions. The most exciting day for me was driving to the Kafe region, to visit a farm we work with near Bita town.

BITA BONGA

with Ona Coffee

ON THIS SAME TRIP TO ETHIOPIA I RETURNED TO BITA BONGA, TO A FARM I DISCOVERED 18 MONTHS PRIOR. Mahabb Mustefa owns an 800 hectare farm in Bita Bonga, which was established in 2009 and sits at 1950m.

Here, coffee trees are planted in the deep forest together with a few wild coffee trees. This is the most sustainable practice to run a farm. There are three varietals at the farm 71010, 71012 and 71014. All three varietals are sectioned and separated.

On the farm they also employ a full time ergonomist. Both the ergonomist and manager of the farm are extremely knowledgeable about growing and cultivating great quality coffee. Approximately 400 people work on the farm, and during harvesting season, up to 700. They have basic facilities for workers including a childcare centre, and the local primary school is only 2km away. This year, they are also building a mill for washed process coffees.

One of the most exciting projects they are doing is giving seeds to local people who have land capable of growing coffee, with the idea of forming an alliance with small farmers. This will also assist people in the area to have a secure source of income.

When I taste Bita Bonga back in Australia, I can often identify distinct Jasmine notes. As this farm is located in the Gesha region, I thought there would be a high chance to find the geisha varietal. This varietal was originally discovered in this region in the 1930s. One of the reasons for my visit was to hunt geisha trees or forest coffee, collect seeds and then send them to have a DNA analysis.

After another 12 hours in the car we finally arrived at the farm. We immediately went to search for wild coffee trees. As we were heading into the forest, I looked up and saw a very tall, skinny tree with long, thin leaves, very similar to Geisha trees in Panama. The manager explained that this was a hybrid from the Djima research centre called 71014, and not a Geisha.

As we were driving I realised that I would not be able to take any seed samples as harvest had finished approximately three weeks prior. This was really disappointing! Even from the African drying bed I could see the big varietal mixed together with other 71010 and 71012 varietals, which are a lot smaller and rounder.

Although we could not do our analysis, we did find some wild coffee trees deep in the forest in the Gesha region. The shape of the tree was completely different to any other coffee tree I have seen. They have been completely untouched and have not ever been cupped as a single varietal. The pickers at Bonga would pick these wild coffee trees and just mix it in with the other varietals.

Unfortunately, it looks like I will have to come back in the middle of next harvest in order to complete my geisha varietal hunt. I spent the rest of my time working with management from Bonga to improve their picking, drying and also storing systems in order for us to have even better coffee next year.

Our last visit in Djima was the Ethiopian Institute Of Agricultural Research centre. To organise a visit was not easy but somehow we managed to get there. This institution was founded in 1967 and they specialise in researching coffee plants. I was hoping I could find some answers about geisha here.

They have developed 37 new varietals that are completely resistant to coffee bora and taste better with higher yields (in their opinion). Some of these varietals are used in Bita Bonga, which seem to be performing at that farm very well. At the research centre they have over 183 hectares of land where they have planted more than 300 different varietals, including wild forest varietals, and geisha (hmmm, well, they said it was geisha).

In their opinion, geisha is very small plant that is grown only on low altitudes, below 1500m, and the tiny seed is round like bourbon. In fact, this coffee does not have any characteristics of geisha. It tasted like chocolate and had an apple-like acidity with brown sugar sweetness; a solid 83 points coffee. This made me think that they are not on the right track with geishas, and when I asked a few more questions they were starting to get uncomfortable, so our visit was a lot shorter than what I was hoping.

At least I learnt that they do not have geisha in their lab.

So on my last day before I was heading back to Canberra, I organised another tasting session to select some more lots and to taste some coffees from some mills, as well as some privately owned farms that I visited in the Yirgacheffe region. In this session we cupped some really distinct flavour profiles.

One coffee really stood out on the table; we all scored it at 91 points or more. This coffee had mango sweetness, a creamy mouth feel, floral, earl grey, strawberry and cherry aftertaste with distinct red fruit aroma. Local cuppers were also pleasantly surprised with the flavour profile of this coffee. We all wanted to find out what it was.

Finally the head cupper from the lab told me, "This is your coffee Sasa!" I was confused by what he meant. He said, "This is your long bean that you separated in Yirgacheffe on the private estate farm." I could not stop smiling…

This coffee I picked had come from an African bed while it was still drying and I had separated only the large, bold beans with a certain colour. Even more pleasing was that this coffee had not had any rest, which means in a few months it will score at least three to four points more.

Adrenalin started pumping through my blood when the producer told me that they will take all the dried coffee cherries on the African bed and hand select only the bold beans with the specific colour that I requested. Next year we will be able to organise this preparation a lot easier and also in larger quantities.

I will be sending these seeds to Denver for further lab testing so that we can discover the DNA of the seeds. I still have hope that we will rediscover Geisha or maybe even another new varietal.

I could not hope for a better result from this coffee hunting trip in Ethiopia and I cannot wait for our customers to taste the coffees I selected.

When you think of Panama, you no doubt conjure images of white sandy beaches, tropical jungles and the world's most famous canal. However, there's more than meets the eye…

Panama is the southern-most country of Central America, located on a narrow peninsula that connects it to South America. The landform was shaped by thousands of years of volcanic activity that created steep mountains and the continental divide. It is in these areas that the right climatic conditions combine with high altitude to form an area that is perfect for growing high quality coffee.

The capital is Panama City, without doubt the most cosmopolitan centre in Central America. The city is a thriving hub of economic activity and rivals any of the great cities in the developing world, be it Beijing, Buenos Aries or Nairobi. With the Panama Canal came international investment and influence from the USA and the rest of the world. As a result Panama City became the Central American hub for banking, international trade and finance. Its skyline is something to behold too. For a city of only 450,000 people, the extent of shimmering glass high-rises is astonishing and makes for beautiful viewing by night.

To the north of Panama lies the Caribbean Sea and to the south the Pacific Ocean, and both coastlines offer the kind of picturesque scenery you would expect to see in a travel documentary. You can find beautiful archipelagos surrounded by crystal clear blue-green water, bordered by white sand beaches and covered in tropical jungle. The area is teeming with several marine national parks that are in place to protect the ecosystems so it's a perfect place for di¬ving and snorkelling.

In the centre of the country running the length east to west is a beautiful mist covered mountain range called the Cordillera Central. Throughout these steep mountains and rolling hills are the spectacular highland rainforests that hold Panama's most biodiverse ecosystems. To the east in Darien the rainforests remain in pristine condition, virtually unchanged for thousands of years. Native inhabitants, the Embera and Wounaan, maintain their traditional practices and customs that have been passed down through the generations. To the west where it is more accessible and temperate, is where we find the majority of the country's coffee plantations.

Panama is the largest coffee exporter in the local area, though coffee production serves as a relatively small portion of that. Since 1985 there has been a steady reduction in the quantity of coffee produced, dropping by more than 60%. The silver lining is that in recent years the quality of green bean exports has been increasing, providing the local farmers with a higher price for the product they produce.

FINCA SANTA TERESA

with Toby's Estate

FINCA SANTA TERESA IS A HIGH ALTITUDE COFFEE PLANTATION LOCATED IN THE CHIQUIRI PROVINCE OF PANAMA, RENOWNED FOR PRODUCING HIGH QUALITY COFFEE FOR THE SPECIALTY MARKET. Not so long ago the plantation was in dire straits; a vicious cycle of declining yields and inadequate investment left the farm in a state of disrepair.

The lack of herbicides allowed a fungal infection to take hold, causing the plants to lose their leaves and reduce their yields. So perilous was the situation that the previous owner considered replanting the farm with tea before finally deciding to put it on the market for sale.

After some thorough research and a few visits Toby Smith decided to purchase Finca Santa Teresa. Since then, with the appropriate investment, the farm has flourished and Toby's first harvest was a bumper crop. The biggest attraction for Toby was that the coffee was being produced on the 100 hectare farm and that there are three varieties of coffee growing.

Caturra is the predominant species taking up the majority of the farm. It grows well at high altitude and is a versatile variety, producing a good cup for both espresso and filter coffee with great acidity and body.

The farm also produces Catuai on a small 10-hecatre plot of land. Such are the vagaries of farming coffee that this variety will only grow on a certain aspect and hillside of the farm.

The jewel in the crown of Finca Santa Teresa is the rare and exciting Geisha. Ten years ago a Panamanian coffee family entered some Geisha into a coffee competition; it scored incredibly well and got the industry talking. It's a variety of coffee that has a big presence in the cup, with an abundance of fruit, herbs, aromatics and complexity that aren't present in other varieties.

Geisha is extremely difficult to grow and provides only small yields compared to other varieties. But it fetches a high price on the market and luckily for Toby, Finca Santa Teresa is the perfect environment for growing Geisha, which is thriving in this high altitude plantation.

Finca Santa Teresa is a high altitude farm situated on a landform created by volcanic activity, and as a result the terrain is very steep. This means that picking is done by hand and the farm enlists the help of locals to pick the coffee.

During the picking season the farm swells to 150 employees from the surrounding hills, who work from 8am to 5pm picking particular patches of ripe cherries. Each section of the plantation will be picked three times. Once picked, more beans will ripen and the trees can be picked again. During this period pickers may relocate and in order to accommodate the influx of children, Finca Santa Teresa provides a school for the younger children and a bus to the local school for the older children. This ensures the children aren't working in the fields, and helps to provide greater education.

Once the coffee is picked it is loaded into the truck and taken to the main farm to be processed. In order to ensure a premium quality coffee it must undergo processing immediately.

There are three ways the coffee is processed. Natural processing consists of taking the entire cherry picked from the tree and placing it on raised drying beds in the sun. It takes longer to dry this way and requires regular turning to stop any fermentation. The result is a rich full bodied coffee with raisin dry fruit flavours, spice, depth and character.

The most common form of processing is a washed coffee where the outer skin is pulped by a machine. It then sits in water tanks overnight allowing the enzymes to break down the mucilage around the bean. The seed is then cleaned and dried either in the oven or in the open. The result is a clean and fresh tasting cup that is perfect for espresso or filtering.

The third method is relatively new. The outer skin is taken but the mucilage is left; the coffee is then dried in raised sun beds. This is referred to as honey coffee with a sweet rich flavour coming through when roasted.

Jose Raul is a local boy from a nearby town who manages the farm for Toby. Jose is married with a six-year-old son and he and his family live together on the farm. His wife works full time at Finca Santa Teresa as a cook, providing meals for the children at the school, the same school that is funded by and located on the farm. His son attends the school during the day, but at every opportunity will tail his father at work, be it helping or hindering the men loading 100kg coffee bags into the truck. Wherever Jose is, his son won't be far behind.

A day in Jose's life is everything you would expect from a Panamanian coffee farmer. He is up at six, rounding up the troops to be ferried to the plantation for picking to commence at 8am. During the day he spends his time in the processing plant organising orders, quality testing the coffee and fixing any problems that might arise. At 5pm during picking season he picks up the workers and the coffee they have picked. In peak season this is when the work begins. The freshly picked coffee must be processed immediately to optimise its quality. This process will generally take until 9pm but often stretches late into the night. Jose said he doesn't mind, it's all part of the job.

INDONESIA IS A DIVERSE, UNIQUE and intriguing country that gives even the most experienced traveller a sense of wonder and awe.

SPREAD OVER 17,508 ISLANDS AND THREE TIME ZONES, THE WORLD'S LARGEST ARCHIPELAGO OFFERS A BREADTH OF EXPERIENCE UNAVAILABLE ELSEWHERE. Located on the edge of four tectonic plates, the complex tectonics create a dynamic geological environment; this has been responsible for the formation of thousands of Islands. The nature of the wide ranging geography makes Indonesia an incredibly diverse country. It includes over 150 volcanoes, whimsical tropical islands, rugged mountain ranges and dense tropical rainforest.

240 million people live throughout the 6,000 populated islands of Indonesia, with the majority inhabiting the island of Java that contains the capital Jakarta. A country heavily populated and widely dispersed, it has developed diversity in culture, customs, animals and food, making Indonesia more like 100 small countries packed into one.

Of the thousands of Indonesian islands only some have the conditions necessary for growing coffee. Sulawesi has become famous for the great coffee that it is producing. Located between Borneo and the Malukuk Islands, Sulawesi is the fourth largest island in Indonesia and the 13 largest in the world. It is immediately recognisable by its unique shape, and it is made up of four separate peninsulas, connected by a rugged mountainous interior. Sulawesi is thought to have been part of the land bridge used when modern humans spread from Africa through Indonesia to Australia up to 45,000 years ago. The earliest inhabitants lived in hunter gatherer societies, utilising stone as their technology for tool making.

Throughout the years of human occupation, a complex society developed with unique cultural practices. The primary area of Arabica coffee production is in the rugged mountain ranges of the southern peninsular. The central highlands, around Toraja, have become internationally recognised for producing unique and delicious coffee. The diurnal temperature variation is thought to be one of the key reasons for the great taste of the coffee. The temperature varies greatly from day to night, helping the cherry ripen slowly and improve the sugar content.

In Indonesia coffee processing is done differently. They use a system of wet hulling, which is quite different from the rest of the world. The differences in processing helps to create the unique flavour profile of Sulawesian coffee. The majority of the coffee is produced by small land owners, who farm individual plots, only a small portion being produced by large estates. Sulawesi is a land rich in culture and history. Stunning to witness, it is a place that has retained much of its uniqueness and character as it comes to terms with the challenges of the modern world.

To ensure a delicious cup of coffee, attention to detail is paramount throughout every step in the supply chain. Everyone involved, from the coffee picker to the farmer to the barista has the opportunity to affect the end result. Each actor has an obligation to pay respect to the hard work of the previous custodian, by doing their job well and maintaining quality. Quality coffee starts at the farm.

When the cherry is picked, the bean holds its entire flavour potential, and from there, attention to every detail is required to produce a great cup of coffee. This thinking drives the Campos philosophy. Campos believes in producing the best quality coffee possible, but it wants to do so while simultaneously having a positive impact on the local community and ensuring everyone is respected and rewarded throughout the supply chain.

In 2009 Will Young, the founder of Campos Coffee as it exists today, had an epiphany he calls his 'realisation day.'

SULAWESI

with Campos Coffee

When he stopped to think about how he wanted to move forward as a business, he realised that there was a gap in the company's approach to coffee. They paid so much attention to everyone they interacted with on a daily basis – the barista, wholesaler, customer and all their employees. But the problem was he had never considered the entire process, before the coffee even hit the shore in Australia. The logical decision to ensure this ongoing respect was to go back to the beginning of the chain.

Will had never seriously considered the most vital component, the people growing the coffee. Suddenly Will realised that the farmers were part of the Campos family and they needed to be afforded the same respect, recognition and appreciation as the rest of the team. He decided right there and then, that he wanted to meet every producer who supplied Campos with coffee. And so Will started booking plane tickets around the world.

Coincidentally, in 2010, Sydney University lecturer, Jeff Nielsen, was conducting a research project about improvements in coffee quality and the standards of living in the Indonesian village of Benteng Alla Utara. He first visited Benteng Alla in 2003 and began working with the town chief, Patolla, in 2008, as part of his Livelihoods of Smallholder Coffee Farmers in Eastern Indonesia research.

Will was introduced to Jeff who invited him to get involved in the project. It was a perfect fit for the first trip to origin. Jeff wanted Will to meet with the town's Chief, Patola, in his home, deep in the mountains of Northern Sulawesi. There was an immediate connection between Will and Patola. It is amazing how people who lead such different lives can connect through a common set of core values. Both men wanted to form a mutually beneficial relationship; they wanted to help Patola improve the quality of the coffee and they wanted the financial reward to be shared with the people who need it most – the farmers and the local community.

From that day, Will made a commitment that he would buy all the specialty coffee that Patola could provide. This gives the farmers at Benteng Alla the confidence that they can continue to produce higher quality coffee, knowing that they will receive a financial reward. Importantly there was no exclusivity in their deal. If Patola could receive a higher price elsewhere then that was welcomed. While Will would be disappointed to miss out, he was happy that the community was receiving a greater financial reward.

Since 2010 the relationship has continued to grow. Each year Campos sends a team to meet with Patola to discuss the upcoming harvest and negotiate the price. Each season the price has risen with the assumption of an improvement in quality. Receiving a unique and delicious coffee that is not available elsewhere has been Campos' reward for their commitment. The quality has increased to the point that it is now available as a single origin coffee of the month. On the most recent visit, Will presented Patola with a bag of roasted coffee that had a picture of Patola's house, his name, and the name of the town on the label. This is a point of pride for Patola and all of the farmers in the cooperative, to see their town on a label that is sold on the other side of the world.

The purpose of forming these relationships is to create a business environment that is mutually beneficial. Patola has the comfort of knowing that all the specialty coffee he can produce will be purchased at a price that rewards him for quality, to people with whom he shares common values. He also has the comfort of knowing exactly where the coffee is sent and how it is used. There's a level of transparency that's uncommon in the coffee industry.

BENTENG ALLA UTARA

with Campos Coffee

For Campos, they know that they can work with Patola, providing him with feedback on his coffee and creating a level of communication that assists with the ongoing process of improving the quality of the coffee. They can also be sure that they have a consistent supply of great coffee with a clear conscience, knowing that their sourcing decisions are making a positive impact on people's lives.

Deep in the rugged mountain ranges of Southern Sulawesi, lies the coffee growing region of Toraja. Steep mountains, wild rivers and tropical rainforests dominate this remote part of Sulawesi and engulf the small town of Benteng Alla.

This typical Sulawesi Central Highland village has a population of around 2000 people. The standard of living is relatively low, with the majority of the income coming from agricultural production. Despite this, there is a striking sense of community. One does not just inhabit the town inhabitants become a part of the whole.

When it rains in Sulawesi, it pours, which means little work can be done in the fields. Instead of isolating themselves at home and watching television, like many western communities, in Benteng Alla it's seen as an opportunity to gather together. They laugh, chat and play games, strengthening social bonds and enjoying each other's company. There is something special about a mother and child playing card games on the front porch, laughing with delight as cards are thrown to the ground, while the rain tumbles down around them.

Every morning at 5am the first prayer of the day begins over a loud and distorted PA, the local Mosque calls people to prayer. One after another, each mosque follows suit until the last chant is far in the distance. From 7am, the school children wander down the road. There are no buses or carpools here. The children walk hand in hand, three and four abreast, wave after wave of children, giggling their way to school. No detentions for uniforms here – each child is dressed immaculately in red and white for the local primary school. A sense of pride is taken in the uniform, a symbol of their aspirations in life.

The people of Benteng Alla live a largely agricultural existence. They grow chilli, cabbage, sweet potatoes and various other vegetables, for their own consumption and for local markets. While not destitute, life is not easy; running water and plumbing are a luxury, with a warm shower nowhere to be seen. The largest cash crop in the area is Arabica coffee as the climate and altitude ensure that the area is capable of producing seriously good coffee. The key is to make sure that the farmers share in the wealth.

The chief of the town and head of the coffee cooperative is Patola, a man, small in stature but large in heart. He values family and community above all else and wishes to improve the lives of those around him. He is a man of great modesty, and though young he is respected in the community and he takes the responsibility with pride, remaining humble in his approach and gentle with exchanges. Patola is a man of the town, he inherited the land on which he lives from his ancestors, and works the land in much the same way. He farms the land by choice.

As a younger man, he left the town to pursue an education in agriculture in the regional centre of Makassar. After some time away, the community convinced him to return to help improve the lives of others. When he returned he saw that the coffee farmers were producing good coffee, but not sharing in the wealth. He saw their lives were not improving. Patola

returned, ready to devote his life to coffee and determined to improve the situation of the community he loves.

He met Jeff Nielsen and they started to work together to improve the quality of the village's coffee and to increase the standard of living for the farmers. They used a cooperative model where the farmers work together for the benefit of the greater good, but they aren't locked in to a contract and can choose to sell their coffee elsewhere at any time.

As it stands at the moment, there are 36 happy members and with each harvest the numbers are growing. The cooperative helps the farmers in three key areas. Firstly the members work together: each day the entire membership of the cooperative works on an individual farm. Be it pruning, fertilising or picking ripe cherry, they work together to share the load – creating something greater than the sum of their parts.

Secondly the cooperative provides education to the farmer. A lot of coffee farming is done based on tradition; farming practices are passed down through the generations, never questioned, or altered. They do things simply because that is how they have always been done. The cooperative is educating farmers about new farming practices and techniques. New farming practices give the farmers an opportunity to improve the quality and quantity of their yield, with minimum additional cost.

Thirdly, and possibly most importantly, the co-op provides a central location for coffee processing. Previously farmers would pick the cherries each day and, to minimise work, they would leave those cherries sitting until they were ready to process, up to five days later. In this time the cherry ferments and the quality of the coffee is immediately tainted. The cooperative offers the farmers the service of collecting and processing the cherry for them.

Because they are now processing the specialty coffee way: picking only the red cherry and applying stricter monitoring and labeling of each lot, the quality of the coffee has increased. Better quality coffee obtains a higher price and that reward is shared with the farmers. Some would think it an easy sell – less work for more money. Unfortunately human beings are creatures of habit and even the best laid plans take time to implement.

The farmers were initially sceptical of the cooperative model and weren't willing to change their practices, however Patola likes a challenge and, over time, with the right communication, he has been able to start to change minds. The repeat visits from Campos Coffee increases the perceived stature of the program too. In the first year, their specialty coffee produced less than 1 tonne. Fortunately, each year the capacity has grown, and this year they are expecting to produce 15 tonnes of specialty coffee.

With an increase in quantity has come a steady increase in the quality. As Patola and the cooperative learn more about processing and improve their techniques, the quality of the coffee improves. As the farmers witness the benefits, they buy into the theory of only picking the ripe red cherry, and the quality continues to improve.

The result is that they are producing higher quality coffee and they are being rewarded financially from this improvement. In the co-op system the wealth is shared, so these changes see improvements in all farmers' standards of living.

With direct help from Campos Coffee, Patola and the cooperative are starting to improve people's lives, but this is of course an ongoing journey.

Brewtown Newtown | Newtown

INDEX

SYMBOLS

22 grams	257–262
67 Union St Deli	171

A

AeroPress	88
Air Roasting	56–59
Alexandria	
Coffee Roaster, The	360
Don Campos	369
Grounds of Alexandria, The	377
Sonoma Baking Company	403
Allpress Espresso	339
Ampersand Cafe & Bookstore	258
Annandale	347
Anvil Coffee Co Kirribilli	172
Artarmon	221
Artificer Specialty Coffee Bar and Roastery	261
Ashfield	370
Australian Specialty Coffee Association	106
Avalon	229

B

Bakke, Kent	42
Balmain	340
Bambi, Piero	41
Barefoot Brew Room	424
Barefoot Coffee Traders	175
Baristas	52
City Side	114–115
East Side	250–255
Regional	418–419
South & West of the City	330–335
Baron, The	176
Bay Coffee	179
Bayleaf Cafe	427
Bean Drinking	180
Belaroma Coffee Centre	183
Bellagio Cafe	262
Bertoni Casalinga	340
Bills Beans East Orange	428
Black Groodle, The	343
Black Market Roasters	344
Black Toast	347
Bondi Beach	
Sensory Lab	312
Shop and Wine Bar, The	315
Bondi Junction	299

Bonsoy	76–79
Book Kitchen, The	265
Botanica Garden Cafe	184
Botany	
Black Market Roasters	344
Single Origin Roasters Botany	399
Bread & Butter	187
Bread & Stone	348
Brew Collective	119
Brewtown Newtown	351
Brighton the Corner	352
Brito, Marcio	65
Brooklyn Hide	266
B-Side Espresso	423
Bunker, The	269
Butcher's Block, The	188
Byron Bay	
Barefoot Brew Room	424
Bayleaf Cafe	427
Byron Bay Coffee Company	431

C

Cabrito Coffee Traders	120
Cafe Cappello	432
Cafe Con Leche	270
Café Hernandez	273
Cafe Tramezzini	123
Cairns, Lachie	71–74
Campos Coffee Dulwich Hill	355
Campos Coffee Newtown	356
Cassiopeia	435
Castle Hill	176
Charlestown	423
Chatswood	
Elbow Room Espresso	197
Steam Engine	233
Chemex	91
Chinook Coffee Roasting Systems	56–59
Chippendale	407
Church Point	241
Circular Quay	127
Coffee Alchemy	359
Coffee Roaster, The	360
Coffee Taster Flavours Wheel	16
Coffee Tea & Me	274
Cold Drip	92
Colombian Connection	48–51
Cook & Archies	277

INDEX

Corduroy Cafe	281
Counter, The	365
Cremorne	187
Crêpe and Coffee Co.	366
Cronulla	
Bread & Stone	348
Grind	373
Ham Harry & Mario	378
Crows Nest	180

D

Dachshund Coffee	191
Darlinghurst	
Bunker, The	269
Edition Coffee Roasters	286
Latteria	294
Royal Darlinghurst, The	308
Salvador Espresso Bar	154
Stop Valve Espresso	316
DaVinci Gourmet	84–85
DC Specialty Coffee	71–74
Delano Specialty Coffee	436
Devon Cafe	282
Di Bella Coffee Roasting Warehouse	285
Don Campos	369
Dose Espresso	192
Double Bay	289
Drummoyne	404
Dulwich Hill	355

E

East of the City	245–325
22 grams	257–262
Ampersand Cafe & Book store	258
Artificer Specialty Coffee Bar and Roastery	261
Bellagio Cafe	262
Book Kitchen, The	265
Brooklyn Hide	266
Bunker, The	269
Cafe Con Leche	270
Café Hernandez	273
Coffee Tea & Me	274
Cook & Archies	277
Corduroy Cafe	281
Devon Cafe	282
Di Bella Coffee Roasting Warehouse	285
Edition Coffee Roasters	286
Filosofy	289
Flat White Cafe	290
Joe Black	293
Latteria	294
Nelson Road Tuckshop	299
Orto Trading Co	300
Reformatory Caffeine Lab, The	303
Room 10	304
Rose Bay Diner	307
Royal Darlinghurst, The	308
Sample Coffee Pro Shop	311
Sensory Lab	312
Shop and Wine Bar, The	315
Single Origin Roasters Surry Hills	319
Sly Espresso	320
Stop Valve Espresso	316
Uliveto	323
Ed Cutcliffe	60–63
Edition Coffee Roasters	286
Elbow Room Espresso	197
Encasa Deli	124
Espresso	95
Ethiopia	461–469
Excelsior Jones	370
Exporting the Beans	13

F

Fat Goose Cafe, The	441
Fika Swedish Kitchen	198
Filosofy	289
Fitzsimmons, Dan	56–59
Flat White Cafe	290
Flavours Wheel	16
Forest Lodge	382
Forsyth, Abagail	75
Foundry Fiftythree	201
French Press	96
Future of Coffee, The	22–25

G

Glass Onion Society, The	442
Glenhaven	238
Good Brother Espresso Shop	445
Good Eddy	446
Grading and Sorting	13
Grind	373
Grinders Coffee	55
Grinding the Beans	13
Grind into Gear	374

INDEX

Ground Control Cafe — 127
Grounds of Alexandria, The — 377
Gumption by Coffee Alchemy — 128
Gusto On The Beach — 202

H

Ham Harry & Mario — 378
Handcraft Specialty Coffee — 381
Harvesting — 12, 13
Hiron, Craig — 68
History of Coffee — 20
Home Grown Coffee Machine — 68
Hornsby — 234
Hunters Hill — 191

I

Incinerator Willoughby, The — 205
In The Annex — 382
Islington — 453

J

Jim, The — 131
Joe Black — 293
John Smith Specialty Coffee — 385

K

Kaimaki Cafe — 386
Katoomba — 432
KeepCup — 75
Killcare — 441
Kingswood Coffee — 132
Kirribilli — 172
Klink Handmade Espresso — 135

L

La Marzocco — 41
Lane Cove — 209
Latteria — 294
Lilyfield — 392
Lismore
   Cafe Cappello — 432
   Republic of Coffee — 449
Little Guy, The — 68
Little, Jibbi — 83
Little Marionette, The — 60–63, 391
Livelo Espresso & Kitchen — 138
Local Press, The — 392
Long Jetty — 442

M

Macnamara, Shae — 55
Manly
   Barefoot Coffee Traders — 175
   Fika Swedish Kitchen — 198
   Foundry Fiftythree — 201
   Market Lane Cafe — 206
   Shop Next Door — 222
   Showbox Coffee Brewers — 226
Manly Vale — 183
Marcelle — 141
Market Lane Cafe — 206
Marlowe's Way — 142
Marrickville
   Coffee Alchemy — 359
   Two Chaps Trading — 408
   Wicks Park Cafe — 411
Maryville — 454
McMahons Point — 171
Mecca Coffee — 145
Methods to Make Coffee — 87
Metropole — 146
Milk Connection, The — 76–79
Milsons Point — 213
Mona Vale — 237
Mosman
   Penny Royal — 210
   Source Espresso Bar, The — 230

N

Nans Place — 395
Nelson Road Tuckshop — 299
Neutral Bay — 179
Newcastle — 445
Newport — 225
Newtown
   Brewtown Newtown — 351
   Campos Coffee Newtown — 356
   Handcraft Specialty Coffee — 381
noOk urban fresh bar — 149
Northbridge — 217
North of the city
   67 Union St Deli — 171
   Anvil Coffee Co Kirribilli — 172
   Barefoot Coffee Traders — 175
   Baron, The — 176
   Bay Coffee — 179
   Bean Drinking — 180

INDEX

Belaroma Coffee Centre	183
Botanica Garden Cafe	184
Bread & Butter	187
Butcher's Block, The	188
Dachshund Coffee	191
Dose Espresso	192
Elbow Room Espresso	197
Fika Swedish Kitchen	198
Foundry Fiftythree	201
Gusto On The Beach	202
Incinerator Willoughby, The	205
Pablo & Rusty's Lane Cove	209
Penny Royal	210
Ricky's Cafe Under The Bridge	213
Roots Espresso, The	218
Salvage Specialty Coffee	221
Shop Next Door	222
Shotlab Espresso	225
Showbox Coffee Brewers	226
Smalltown	229
Source Espresso Bar, The	230
Steam Engine	233
SteamTank	234
Three Doors Down	237
Tuckshop, The	238
Waterfront Store and Cafe	241
NSW Latte Art Champion	83

O

Opera Bar Cafe	150
Orange	
Bills Beans East Orange	428
Good Eddy	446
Origins of Coffee, The	459
Orto Trading Co	300

P

Pablo & Rusty's	37
Pablo & Rusty's 161	153
Pablo & Rusty's Lane Cove	209
Paddington	258
Panama	471–475
Penny Royal	210
Petersham	
Brighton the Corner	352
Counter, The	365
Planting	13
Port Macquarie	450
Potts Point	
Café Hernandez	273
Coffee Tea & Me	274
Marcelle	141
Uliveto	323
Prana Chai	80

Q

Qube On Bay Espresso Bar	396

R

Randwick	257–262
Redfern	366
Reformatory Caffeine Lab, The	303
Regional	
B-Side Espresso	423
Barefoot Brew Room	424
Bayleaf Cafe	427
Bills Beans East Orange	428
Byron Bay Coffee Company	431
Cafe Cappello	432
Cassiopeia	435
Delano Specialty Coffee	436
Fat Goose Cafe, The	441
Glass Onion Society, The	442
Good Brother Espresso Shop	445
Good Eddy	446
Republic of Coffee	449
Social Grounds	450
Suspension Espresso	453
Uprising	454
Republic of Coffee	449
Ricky's Cafe Under The Bridge	213
Ritual Coffee Traders	217
Roasting the Coffee	13
Room 10	304
Roots Espresso, The	218
Rose Bay Diner	307
Royal Darlinghurst, The	308

S

Salvador Coffee	65
Salvador Espresso Bar	154
Salvage Specialty Coffee	221
Sample Coffee Pro Shop	311
Sensory Lab	312
Sestic, Sesa	52
Setting Up a Micro Roastery	65–68

INDEX

Shop and Wine Bar, The	315
Shop Next Door	222
Shotlab Espresso	225
Showbox Coffee Brewers	226
Single Origin Roasters	48–51
Single Origin Roasters Botany	399
Single Origin Roasters Surry Hills	319
Sly Espresso	320
Smalltown	229
Social Grounds	450
Social Laneway	400
Sonoma Baking Company	403
Source Espresso Bar, The	230
South Curl Curl	202
South & West of the City	
Allpress Espresso	339
Bertoni Casalinga	340
Black Groodle, The	343
Black Market Roasters	344
Black Toast	347
Bread & Stone	348
Brewtown Newtown	351
Brighton the Corner	352
Campos Coffee Dulwich Hill	355
Campos Coffee Newtown	356
Coffee Alchemy	359
Coffee Roaster, The	360
Counter, The	365
Crêpe and Coffee Co.	366
Don Campos	369
Excelsior Jones	370
Grind	373
Grind into Gear	374
Grounds of Alexandria, The	377
Ham Harry & Mario	378
Handcraft Specialty Coffee	381
In The Annex	382
John Smith Specialty Coffee	385
Kaimaki Cafe	386
Little Marionette, The	391
Local Press, The	392
Nans Place	395
Qube On Bay Espresso Bar	396
Single Origin Roasters Botany	399
Social Laneway	400
Sonoma Baking Company	403
Three Rosettas Espresso Bar & Cafe	404
Toby's Estate Coffee Roasters	407
Two Chaps Trading	408
Wicks Park Cafe	411
Soy Latte	79
Stanmore	374
Steam Engine	233
SteamTank	234
Stewart, Rob	71–74
Stop Valve Espresso	316
Stovetop	100
St Peters	
Little Marionette, The	391
Sample Coffee Pro Shop	311
Sulawesi	479–485
Surry Hills	
Artificer Specialty Coffee Bar and Roastery	261
Book Kitchen, The	265
Brooklyn Hide	266
Cafe Con Leche	270
Cook & Archies	277
Corduroy Cafe	281
Devon Cafe	282
Di Bella Coffee Roasting Warehouse	285
Joe Black	293
Orto Trading Co	300
Reformatory Caffeine Lab, The	303
Single Origin Roasters Surry Hills	319
Sly Espresso	320
Suspension Espresso	453
Sydney CBD	111–157
Brew Collective	119
Cabrito Coffee Traders	120
Cafe Tramezzini	123
Encasa Deli	124
Ground Control Cafe	127
Gumption by Coffee Alchemy	128
Jim, The	131
Kingswood Coffee	132
Klink Handmade Espresso	135
Livelo Espresso & Kitchen	138
Marcelle	141
Marlowe's Way	142
Mecca Coffee	145
Metropole	146
noOk urban fresh bar	149
Opera Bar Cafe	150
Pablo & Rusty's 161	153
Salvador Cafe	154
Syphon	103

INDEX

T

Three Doors Down	237
Three Rosettas Espresso Bar & Cafe	404
Toby's Estate Coffee Roasters	407
Tuckshop, The	238
Two Chaps Trading	408

U

Uliveto	323
Ultimo	
Black Groodle, The	343
Qube On Bay Espresso Bar	396
Uprising	454

V

V60 Pour Over	104
Vela, Cesar	48–51
Venue Categories	108

W

Wahroonga	188
Waterfront Store and Cafe	241
Waterloo	385
Waverly	262
Waverton	184
What is Specialty Coffee?	11
Where Does Coffee Come From?	46–47
Who Drinks What?	34
Wicks Park Cafe	411
Williams, Brent	106
Willoughby	
Dose Espresso	192
Incinerator Willoughby, The	205
Wollongong, North	436
Woollahra	290
World Barista Champion 2015	52
World of Coffee, The	42–45
Wright, Saxon	37–40

Z

Zetland	
Allpress Espresso	339
Nans Place	395

ABOUT THE PUBLISHERS

L-R: Daniele, Jonette & Kaitlyn

Like all great ideas, Smudge Publishing was once just a dream. Conjured up by our fearless Editor-in-Chief, Jonette George and her two daughters, Daniele and Katie Wilton, the mission was simple, to create beautiful books that celebrate and showcase the abundance of produce, wine and culinary talent in Australia.

Now 6 years on with a staff of 14 team members as well as a wide network of freelance writers, Smudge Publishing is a collective of passionate individuals who strive to constantly unearth the best of the best in all things foodie.

With 16 titles already published, including the award winning Flavours of Melbourne which received a bronze medal for Best International Travel Guidebook at the International Publishers Awards as well as being named Best Culinary Travel Cookbook in Australia by the Gourmand World Cook Book Awards, Smudge Publishing is now expanding the Flavours Series to more great cities and destinations in Australia. This includes the recently published Flavours of Sydney and Flavours of Urban Sydney and the soon to be published Flavours of Queensland and Flavours of South Australia.

Smudge titles are available nationwide at Dymocks and Berkelouw Books as well as hundreds of independent booksellers. They are also through most of the venues featured within their pages and on our own online bookstore.

Not ones to dream small, 2015 will see the team moving beyond Australia borders to produce Flavours of Bali & Beyond and Flavours of New York as well as launching an online magazine, Smudge Eats, which will include an online directory of the best places to eat and drink in Australia and beyond.

Smudge Books are distributed in all good bookstores Nationwide.

We distribute through Woodslane and Brumby Sunstate.

smudgepub.com.au

Eat drink Laugh Love

Reformatory Caffeine Lab | Surry Hills

ABOUT THE ILLUSTRATORS

BIANCA TAYLOR-ANDREWS

Bianca Taylor-Andrews is a freelance designer specialising in design, illustration and lettering. She finds the big blue (ocean), delicious coffee and eccentric conversation to be the perfect mix of inspirations to keep her work fresh and focused.

After completing her bachelor of Digital Media through the Queensland College of Art, Bianca has stepped back into analogue practices for the bulk of her workload. She is the human persona of the quote 'don't trust a designer with clean hands', more often than not spotted with ink splattered up to her elbows.

behance.net/biancataylorandrews

ALEXIS WINTER

Alexis Winter is a freelance designer, specialising in illustration. With a Masters of Communication Design, her love of word-play coupled with her zest for narrative inspire her to design things across all different mediums, with a particular penchant for publications and illustration.

alexiswinter.com

MORE SMUDGE TITLES

Available from major booksellers throughout Australia, from participants in our books and smudge-eats.com

Flavours of Sydney

You haven't seen Sydney in this light before! This stunning, pictorial registry of the who's who in food and wine – where to go, what to eat and what to cook at home using the chefs' signature recipes! Visit this vibrant city's smorgasbord of venues, serving a multi-cultural array of meals from around the globe. Some chefs specialise, some infuse, some blend, and yet others simply create a whole new style. You have to take you hat off to them – our chefs are creating wonders!

Flavours of Urban Sydney

A journey through the city's suburbs, enjoy the multi-cultural influence on the city's food culture. Find out where to go, what to eat and even what to cook at home using the chefs' signature recipes! Work your way through the book by visiting one venue at a time… ask the chef at each restaurant to sign your book on their page, and collect them like stamps in a passport. Prepare at home the chefs' array of signature recipes that will give you the real flavours of this robust and playful city, Sydney.

Flavours of Melbourne

Flavours of Melbourne has won three international awards for excellence, as well as prestigious reviews from all over the nation. The success of this bible about the best restaurants, cafes and bars in Melbourne's CBD, inclusive of signature recipes from the city's best chefs, makes this stunning, coffee table book the best culinary travel book in Australia this year. Beautiful photography joins editorial that puts you in the armchair and gives you the tools to unlock the secrets of the world's most livable city.

Flavours of Urban Melbourne

Exploring the full extent of this wonderful city, the authors have produced this wonderful ode to multicultural fusion. East meets west, meets north, and meets south in this stunning, pictorial guide to urban Melbourne. A fusion of cultures blend together, as well as flourish side-by-side, as we are given recipes from the best urban chefs. It is hard to put a finger on the pulse, but the authors of this book have managed to put the pieces together to showcase the suburbs of this wonderful city.

The Specialty Coffee Book, Victoria

It is often a challenge to forgo the norm of "just the usual thanks", and explore the unchartered territory of coffee's vast offerings. An informative insight into the realm of coffee, The Specialty Coffee Book Victoria is a detailed guide for the coffee curious, giving its readers a behind the machine look into what goes into your daily caffeine fix and the industry in pursuit of that perfect cup.

The Burger Book Victoria

Armed with a spatula in one hand and great ingredients in the other, Victorian burger chefs are serving up their pride and joy night after night to the growing hordes of burger lovers across the state. The authors have searched through pub and parlour, trekked from cafe to corner store, roamed from restaurant to bar, to compile this book about the best burgers Victoria has to offer. This books provides mouth-watering pages of signature burgers. You need only provide big eyes and an empty stomach.

Coffee Encounters, Adventures To Origin

Welcome to the world of coffee – from crop to cup. The journey begins at origin, and the authors have spared no hardship to get to the coffee pickers and farmers to discover their story. Enjoy the journey through Latin America and Indonesia, following the humble coffee bean's journey and the passion that has gone into producing, selecting, transporting, roasting and extracting the best flavours, to enrich your appreciation of your daily cup of coffee. Learn to love your coffee for all the right reasons.

Produce to Platter: Victoria's High Country

Through the eyes of locals who are dedicated to making the best regional food and wine, you will discover new taste sensations that have been foraged from wineries, restaurants, farm gates and more in this arm-chair journey through the Victorian High Country. Discover this vast, historic territory of hilly grasslands, bubbling estuaries and snowy alps. The stories, photography and recipes will entice you to visit and take home the delights of these six regions encapsulated in Produce to Platter, Victoria's High Country.

Copyright © Smudge Publishing

Reprint April 2015 by Smudge Publishing

smudgepub.com.au

All rights reserved. No part of this publication may be reproduced, stored in a retrieval system or transmitted in any form by any means, electronic, mechanical, photocopying, recorded or otherwise, without the prior written permission of the publishers and copyright holders.

National Library of Australia

Cataloguing in Publication Data

All images Copyright © Smudge Publishing except the following; page 22, 24, 25 by Ric Warren, page 40 and 43 by Sven Hoffman, courtesy La Marzocco; page 430 by Jonatan & Sebastian Lundmark; pages 53, 463, 464, 467, 468-469 by Jeff Hann, courtesy Jeraff.

Who Drinks What? Statistics taken from Cafe Pulse survey 2013.

The Specialty Coffee Book – New South Wales

Includes Index

ISBN 978-0992-318352

Printed by 1010 Printing International Limited

Smudge Culinary Travel Publishers